The Organization Pyra

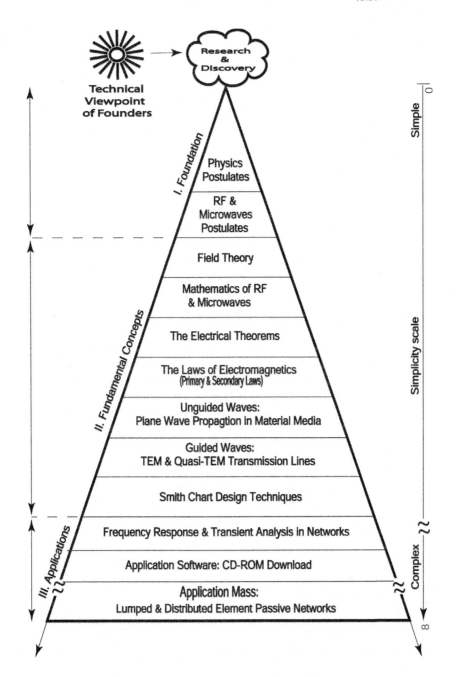

Research & Discovery

Technical Viewpoint of Founders

Simple — 0

I. Foundation

Physics Postulates

RF & Microwaves Postulates

Field Theory

Mathematics of RF & Microwaves

The Electrical Theorems

The Laws of Electromagnetics
(Primary & Secondary Laws)

Unguided Waves:
Plane Wave Propagtion in Material Media

Guided Waves:
TEM & Quasi-TEM Transmission Lines

Smith Chart Design Techniques

Frequency Response & Transient Analysis in Networks

Application Software: CD-ROM Download

Application Mass:
Lumped & Distributed Element Passive Networks

II. Fundamental Concepts

III. Applications

Simplicity scale

Complex — ∞

The Complete Smith Chart (ZY)

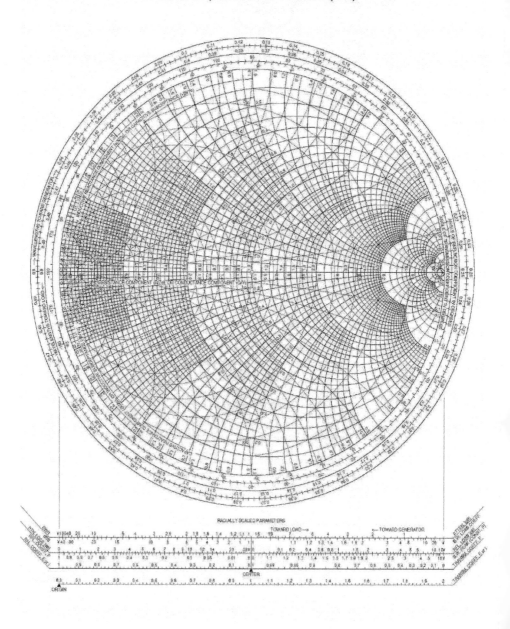

RADIALLY SCALED PARAMETERS

Electronic Waves
&
Transmission Line
Circuit Design

Your Illustrated Guide to
Wave Engineering

Matthew M. Radmanesh, Ph.D.
Professor of Electrical
& Computer Engineering,
California State University,
Northridge

authorHOUSE

1663 LIBERTY DRIVE, SUITE 200
BLOOMINGTON, INDIANA 47403
(800) 839-8640
www.authorhouse.com

AuthorHouse™
1663 Liberty Drive
Bloomington, IN 47403
www.authorhouse.com
Phone: 1-800-839-8640

First published by AuthorHouse   04/05/2011

ISBN: 978-1-4389-6862-9 (sc)
ISBN: 978-1-4389-6863-6 (hc)

Library of Congress Control Number: 2011903605

Printed in the United States of America

Electronic Waves & Transmission Line Circuit Design

Matthew M. Radmanesh, Ph.D.

Why This Book?

Our modern technical world utilizes electronic waves of all types, shapes and frequencies amongst which, radio waves, lasers, infra-red beams, sunlight, microwaves are just a few examples.

This book breaks apart this fascinating subject into its component parts and presents a clear view of the subject of Electromagnetic (EM) waves in an understandable fashion and explores many new aspects of this remarkable subject.

Moreover, this book not only provides the scientific foundation of our modern transmission lines in simple terms, but also explores a myriad of applications and design techniques leading to a plethora of application mass.

This book simplifies the subject of electromagnetic waves, particularly the high frequency RF and Microwaves arena, making it accessible to professional engineers and modern educators by bringing the fundamentals to the forefront, thus ushering in a new era of incredible development for mankind!

For more information please visit:

www.KRCbooks.com

THE FRONT COVER IMAGE

The Andromeda Galaxy is a spiral galaxy approximately 2.5 million light-years away in the constellation Andromeda. It is often referred to as the Great Andromeda Nebula in older texts. Andromeda is the nearest spiral galaxy to the Milky Way, and is visible from Earth as a faint smudge on a moonless night. It gets its name from the area of the sky in which it appears, the Andromeda constellation, which was named after the mythological princess Andromeda. Andromeda is the largest galaxy of the Local Group, which consists of the Andromeda Galaxy, the Milky Way Galaxy, the Triangulum Galaxy, and about 30 other smaller galaxies. Although the largest, Andromeda may not be the most massive, as recent findings suggest that the Milky Way contains more dark matter and may be the most massive in the grouping. The observations by the Spitzer Space Telescope revealed that the Andromeda Galaxy contains one trillion (10^{12}) stars, about triple of the number of stars in our own galaxy, estimated to be around 200-400 billion.

Contents

PART II   PROPAGATION OF WAVES 141

Chapter 5   RF & MICROWAVES BASICS   143

Chapter 6 PLANE WAVES IN MATERIAL MEDIA 169

Chapter 7   TRANSMISSION LINE FUNDAMENTALS   203

Chapter 10 LOSSY TRANSMISSION LINES 265

Chapter 11   LUMPED ELEMENTS ON THE SMITH CHART 289

Chapter 12 DISTRIBUTED ELEMENTS ON THE SMITH CHART 303

Chapter 13 FREQUENCY RESPONSE OF PASSIVE NETWORKS   339

PART III   CIRCUIT DESIGN ESSENTIALS 359

Chapter 14 LUMPED MATCHING NETWORK DESIGN 361

Chapter 15   DISTRIBUTED MATCHING NETWORK DESIGN 385

Dedicated to
the Best of Mankind,
Which Has Made Us the Proud Emperor of Earth
and
Has Held the Worst of Mankind at Bay!

Preface

The initial motivation was to bring the basics to the forefront and orient the reader in such a way that he or she can think with these fundamentals correctly. This eventually led to writing and preparing the current textbook.

In preparing this book, the emphasis was shifted from rigorous and sophisticated mathematical solutions of Maxwell's equations and instead has been aptly placed on RF and microwave circuit analysis and design principles using simple concepts while emphasizing the basics all the way.

It is a book written primarily for the RF/microwave engineering students at the senior and graduate level standing. This book will surely serve also the technical inventors in the microwave industry who are looking for inspirations and new ideas to imbue them with enough understanding to finalize and materialize their thoughts into reality.

This book is intended to be used in a 2-semester course in RF and microwave electronics engineering for senior-level or graduate students and should serve as an excellent reference guide for the practicing RF and microwave engineer in the field as well.

The current work starts from very general postulates, considerations and laws and, chapter by chapter, narrows the focus to very specific concepts and applications, culminating in the design of various RF and microwave circuits. The book, divided into three parts and 17 chapters, develops and presents these chapters progressively in a systematic approach as depicted in the organization pyramid on the front page of the book as follows:

Part I- The Fundamentals

Chapters 1–4 form the foundation of RF and microwave engineering and lay the groundwork for future chapters.

Part II- Propagation of Waves

Chapters 5–13 present the basics of RF and Microwaves, wave propagation, Smith Chart and its applications using lumped or distributed elements.

Part III- Circuit Design Essentials

Chapters 14-17 deal with the analysis and basic considerations in passive circuits, design of matching circuits and transient response to pulsed signals.

A list of symbols used in each chapter and a series of problems are included at the end of each chapter to help the reader gain a fuller understanding of the presented materials. The book ends with a glossary of technical terms and several important appendixes. These appendixes cover physical constants and other important data needed in the analysis or design process.

The Importance of Work

This book has some unique strengths which make it different from prior literature and an attractive reference for the reader.

1.   The presentation of a series of scientific postulates and axioms at the start of the book lays the foundation for any of the engineering sciences and is unique to this book compared with similar RF and Microwave texts.

2.   The presentation of classical laws and principles of electricity and magnetism, all inter-related, conceptually and graphically.

3.   There is a shift of emphasis from rigorous mathematical solutions of Maxwell's equations, and instead has been aptly placed on simple yet fundamental concepts that underlie these equations. This shift of emphasis will promote a deeper

understanding of the electronics, particularly at RF/Microwave frequencies.

4.   New technical terms are precisely defined as they are first introduced, thereby keeping the subject matter in focus and preventing misunderstanding, and finally the abundant use of graphical illustrations and diagrams brings a great deal of clarity and conceptual understanding, enabling difficult concepts to be understood with ease.

A comprehensive glossary of technical terms provided at the end is a great aid in understanding RF and Microwaves and makes this book invaluable for anyone aspiring to master this field of study. The appendix section provides information on many physical constants, mathematical identities, and generally known laws and makes them sufficiently accessible for easy reference.

The Author's Goals

The author intends to bring forth a deeper awareness of how the waves particularly RF and microwaves travel in transmission lines and how a basic knowledge of the subject can lead to a plethora of applications.

The technical reader will be invited to examine a series of basic materials that will enable him/her to understand this powerful far better than ever before. He/she will be exposed to materials of considerable significance, which surely would open up the gates of knowledge along with a wider horizon of understanding.

Any communications in the way of a healthy criticism and/or correction are welcome. Moreover, the author considers it one of the most rewarding things to have others grasp the materials in all of their simplicity and increase their own potential survival in this universe and help others to achieve their goals. In the process, this helps make Man take control of his own destiny, without being shackled by the chains of higher authority or superstition.

Therefore, in order to improve the quality of this work, the author would like to have all comments or suggestions be sent directly to:

Dr. Matthew M. Radmanesh
18111 Nordhoff Street,
Department of Electrical and Computer Engineering,
California State University, Northridge, California 91330.
Or email to: **matt@csun.edu**

You can also check out these related websites for more information:
www.KRCbooks.com
www.csun.edu/~matt

Matthew M. Radmanesh, Ph.D.

Acknowledgements

The author would like to express deep gratitude to L. Ron Hubbard, the first scientist who was able to expand the concept of sciences, particularly electricity and waves, beyond the realm of pure mathematics into mechanics of life, and align it well with humanities. This is truly a monumental achievement, which was accomplished for the first time on earth.

The author would also like to thank many of his professional colleagues, particularly Dr. S. K. Ramesh (Dean of Engineering, CSUN), Dr. Asad Madni, Dr. Charles Alexander (Dean, Cleveland State University), Dr. Ali Amini (ECE Dept. Chair), Dr. I. Hashimoto, Dr. S. Rengarajan, Dr. Nagwa Bekir, Dr. Tim Fox, dear friends at CSUN, Philip Arnold (Agilent), a good friend, Dr. George Haddad & Dr. C. M. Chu (University of Michigan,), the early mentors in Michigan, Dr. M. Torfeh and Dr. B. Salajekeh (Kettering University, Flint, MI), very old friends. Their support and collegiality through the years are definitely appreciated.

Finally, the author's deep gratitude belongs to his kind wife, Jane Marie, and his lovely son, William, for making life enjoyable during this intense project and to his parents, Mary and the late Dr. G. H. Radmanesh, for their true love and unconditional support.

Matthew M. Radmanesh, Ph.D.
Dept. of Electrical and Computer Engineering,
California State University, Northridge,
February 2011

What Sets This Book Apart

What sets this book apart is the clarity of presentation of concepts and the approach taken in bringing about simple solutions to complex problems.

Here is a book where, for the first time, we have undertaken the task of breaking the subject of RF and microwaves into its many components, by discussing and analyzing each subcomponent separately and then putting it all together at the end of the process to form a whole new functional unit.

This book lays the trail map of how to design any passive microwave circuit using lumped or distributed elements. The list of circuit applications is endless. Prominent amongst them are filter circuits, resonant circuits, transmission line circuits, so on and so forth.

The approach taken in this book is by starting at the postulate level and then narrowing it down to more specific topics chapter by chapter. This is unparalled in all modern textbooks and promises to bring on a new era of novel designs and applications in the microwave world!

This book is the road map of circuit design for both low and high frequency signals and through the use of numerous examples presents detailed and yet powerful analysis techniques that anyone can learn!

PART I

THE
FUNDAMENTALS

CHAPTER 1

The Postulates of RF and Microwaves

1.1 INTRODUCTION

There are very basic concepts that underlie all education in electrical or electronics engineering. Knowing these basic concepts enables one to have a much deeper grasp of the more sophisticated concepts and prevents great amount of confusion and discouragement in studying this subject.

The science of electrical engineering sits squarely on the premises of the science of physics and its fundamental postulates. The science of physics deals with the fundamental building blocks of the whole physical universe, which has been discovered to be composed of matter and energy in constant interaction with each other through a medium called linear space. This constant interaction leads to another factor, i.e., time.

These components will be specifically defined so that the reader may gain familiarity and understand their nature and properties. For example, take a transistor operating in a circuit. This transistor has a mass (semiconductor materials, metal, etc. used in its fabrication) and handles electrical energy (current, voltage, etc.). Furthermore, it is presupposed that it occupies a certain space in which the device exists and also has time built into it due to the interaction of various energy forms with its matter from its inception until now.

To proceed further in our study of electronics we have to have specific definitions of the building blocks of the science of physics, i.e., energy and matter.

1.2 UNDERSTANDING POSTULATES

We need to define the term "postulate" at this stage of our work, because it will be used over and over throughout this book. By *"Postulate"* we mean, *"**An assumption or assertion set forth and assumed to be true unconditionally and for all times without requiring proof, especially as a basis for reasoning or future scientific development**."*

Of course, if postulates are chosen as close as possible to the truth of the situation at hand, then they can be used as a basis for reasoning and, more importantly, as a solid foundation for a workable science.

On the other hand, totally arbitrary postulates can be formed, without any basis in truth or reality of the situation. Adoption of such arbitrary postulates would bring about a field of study, which is totally void of any valid truth or natural laws and would be a constantly shifting subject. The subject would be randomly workable and have a lot of false data.

As an example, one may consider the field of art where the critic, the artist, the reviewer, and the public each have introduced their own arbitrary postulates to create a totally unworkable subject without the discovery of any natural laws. Based on this observation, the following conclusion can be drawn:

In any given subject, the number of arbitrary postulates made in that subject, which have no basis in fact or truth, inversely determine the workability of that subject. Moreover, the lesser the number of arbitrary postulates and the closer they are to truth, the more workable that subject becomes.

Thus we can see that in any given subject, the number of arbitrary postulates made in a subject, which have no basis in fact or truth, inversely determine the workability of that subject. Moreover, the lesser the number of arbitrary postulates and the closer they are to truth, the more workable that subject becomes.

Physics and engineering have become two dominant fields in our highly technical society. There are a series of exact postulates, which have led to the current high degree of workability and successful application techniques and sophisticated technology.

The main postulates that have been discovered by observations of the physical universe can be summarized as:

1) *Existence of energy in many forms such as thermal, optical, electrical, magnetic, audio, electromagnetic, etc.*

2) *Existence of matter in gas, fluid, plasma, and solid forms.*

3) *Conservation of all forms of energy to hold valid at all times.*

4) *Conservation of any form of matter under all conditions and at all times (primarily used in classical physics).*

5) *Existence of a viewpoint to act as a reference point for all subsequent measurements. This postulate is implicit in physics.*

6) *Existence of a linear space in which to place matter and energy. This is another postulate implicit in physics.*

8) *Existence of a constant rate of motion or constant rate of change of particle's position in space. This postulate instantly leads to a linear time base, which is also implicit in physics and can be considered to be the seventh postulate. Such a constant and linear time base is currently supplied by the earth's spin around itself and rotation around the sun. It should be noted that this choice of time measurement is completely arbitrary but very convenient since the concept of time has existed from the beginning of man's civilization on earth.*

Time, in general, is an abstract consideration, which can be measured by any constant motion or oscillation and does not necessarily have to be in terms of seconds, minutes, hours, days, years, or even closely associated with the earth's movement in space. The fact that we take the notion of time for granted and measure it exclusively in terms of the above units is an insidious act of disregard for its more general concept and deeper connotations, of which more later.

In the above discussion, postulate #5 (viewpoint) is the most senior of the seven postulates, followed by postulate #6 (space), #1 (energy), #2 (matter), #3 (conservation of energy), #4 (conservation of matter) and #8 (time) in importance. However, the order of presentation of these postulates is, of course, to conform to the current state of physics texts, which make no mention of #5 and #6 as the senior postulates.

However, the presented sequence of postulates is universally accepted as valid in the scientific community and most scientists take it for granted. This can be considered to be a major oversight and shortcoming in the extant physical sciences.

1.3 THE MAIN POSTULATES

We can see that the physical universe, at first glance, appears to be built upon four *primary postulates* of:

   a) **Space,**
   b) **Energy,**
   c) **Matter, and**
   d) **Time.**

However, upon further examination of these four postulates we can see that the third and the fourth postulates have a common denominator, which allows us to further reduce the four primary postulates to only three. The new and reduced set of three postulates essential to the creation of the physical universe, are called the original postulates, which are but irreducible!

The three *original postulates* can be summarized as:

   I. **Space**
   II. **Energy (or Force)**

III. Change

Combining postulates (II) and (III), we can actually obtain the third and the fourth primary postulates discussed earlier (i.e., matter and time). For example, if we "change" the created space, in which certain energy particles exist, in such a way that the volume is reduced, then the energy particles become more condensed and thus we get "matter" (the third primary postulate).

On the other hand, if we "change" the position of a matter particle or an energy form in space, we get "time" as the fourth primary postulate. Upon these four primary postulates, which furnish the necessary building blocks of postulates for the creation of any universe or physical science, the microscopic and macroscopic universes are founded as shown in Figure 1.1.

Therefore, we can see that we only need three original postulates to create the entire physical universe—from an atom to a galaxy and beyond. The three original postulates bring a considerable simplification of the primary postulates and display a higher level of truth than one can ever obtain from a detailed examination of the components of the physical universe as done in the science of physics.

Of course, one should be reminded that once these three postulates, on a microscopic and macroscopic level, were implemented and put into effect on an automatic level of operation, the ensuing complexities of great magnitude, which was brought forth as a result may have well been outside the scope and grasp of the original postulates and may actually have been totally unforeseen to this day.

It is interesting to note that from pure observation, one can see that the third original postulate (change) has actually been put on automatic in the physical universe. We can take earth as an example. We can see that our planet revolves around the sun at a predetermined rate of 66,000 miles per hour while spinning around itself at a fantastic speed of about 1000 miles per hour—all done on an automatic, unthinking, and involuntary manner, causing an automatic time stream called mechanical time.

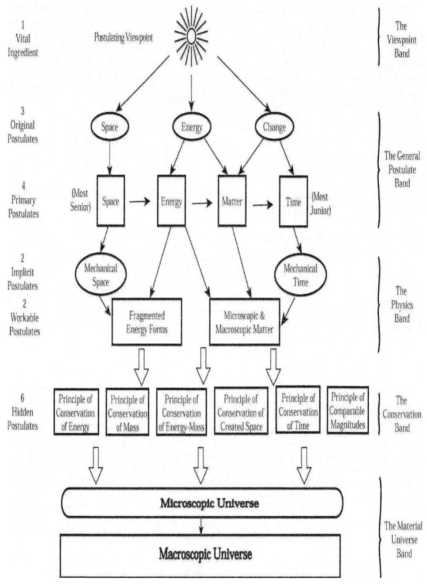

FIGURE 1.1 The construction of the physical universe (the macroscopic and microscopic universes) from the original and primary postulates.

1.4 THE FOUNDATION OF ELECTRICITY

From the viewpoint of considerations, any extant science (including electricity) has a foundation upon which it is built. This is very similar to a building structure where its footing and foundation is of essential importance, since it supports the weight of all the upper floors and its contents. The foundation of electricity consists of two parts:

a) The fundamental postulates
b) Natural laws

Upon this solid foundation rests all theoretical research, extrapolations and design methodologies, application mass and all future explorations, inventions and discoveries. The natural laws are discovered by observation and study but nevertheless have a lot in common with the fundamental postulates of electricity.

It can be observed that the fundamental postulates of electricity forms the bedrock upon which all natural laws rest. This means that the postulates and the discovered natural laws together, form the foundation of electricity. It is an important concept, which is omitted in the majority of scientific texts. All the remaining considerations such as scientific conclusions, technical data, design methods, rules, etc. and the entire application mass of the subject rests on top of the foundation. Figure 1.2 shows the pyramid of knowledge in a workable science such as electricity.

There were a series of monumental discoveries over approximately a period of three hundred years, spanning form from 1600 to 1894. This period of time in Man's history, an unparalleled period of intense scientific developments, started with the discovery of electric charge (by William Gilbert) and culminated in the discovery of electronic waves directly related to and as a result of "electric charge" and its motion, by James Maxwell and Heinrich Hertz.

These were a series of breathtaking discoveries, which put man, as a species, a head and shoulder above the rest of the creatures of this forlorn planet and shaped our current highly sophisticated and fast-paced society!

A very brief introduction of these discoveries is quite appropo if we plan to grasp the foundation of this subject and achieve a mastery of this mazing subject.

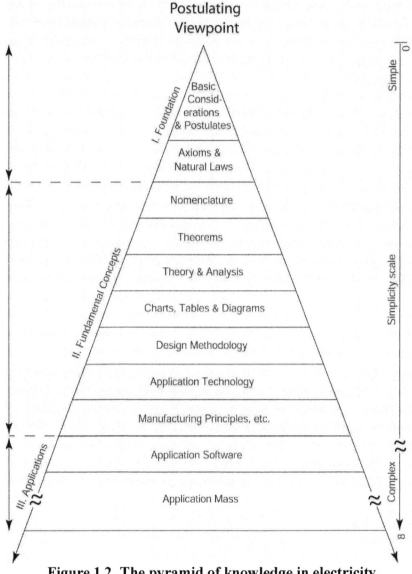

Figure 1.2 The pyramid of knowledge in electricity.

1.5 THE FUNDAMENTAL POSTULATES OF PHYSICS

It is of interest to briefly introduce the postulates behind the science of physics so that we have a better understanding of electricity since its laws are uniformly derivable from physics.

1. *Postulate #1: Existence of energy, on a classical and/or quantum level.*

2. *Postulate #2: Existence of matter particles.*

3. *Postulate #3: Principle of conservation of energy to be held valid under all circumstances and for all times.*

The above three postulates presuppose the existence of a continuous and linear space, in which all the energy and matter particles can be placed. Thus, a primary postulate should be added to the list, that is: *Postulate #4: Existence of a continuous and linear space.*

The above four postulates in action (i.e. particles in motion relative to one another in a linear space) instantly gives birth to a new phenomenon: time. Thus, a secondary and fifth postulate can also be added to the list:

Postulate #5: Existence of a continuous and linear index of motion commonly known as time.

To compare and measure all other motions relative to one another, a linear time reference is needed. Such a linear time reference is best furnished by having a number of particles, which are moving relative to one another at a definite and fixed rate of motion.

For example, rotation of the planets and their associated moons in the solar system (e.g. earth and its moon) around the sun at a regular and constant rate of motion establishes the necessary time standard against which all other motions can be measured.

1.6 THE SCIENCE OF ELECTRICITY

The science of electricity subdivides itself into two main areas: a) Static electricity, and b) Kinetic electricity. These two main subdivision of electricity further subdivide into many subtopics and ramifications, which bring about a panoramic view of the whole field of study known as "electricity" as shown in Figure 1.3.

Furthermore, electricity as actually shown in this book, is derived from six monumental discoveries and no more. All of the known laws, working principles and equations of electricity, magnetism, electromagnetism, wave propagation, etc., can all be derived from these six powerful discoveries. Moreover, most of the supplemental discoveries can be derived from these monumental discoveries

This means that to understand the essence of any subject, one needs to discover and understand the relevant principles and postulates and then work out all of the derivations and ramifications of the basic principles to achieve a full knowledge of that subject.

Once the basic principles of a subject have been discovered and the subject has been thoroughly codified and understood, the most complex situations can be dissected and solved with relative ease.

Figure 1.4 shows how the discovered principles in the field of electricity form the apex of the pyramid of knowledge in electricity.

Moreover, Figure 1.4 also shows the emergence of six distinct fields of study, i.e.,
- *Electrostatics,*
- *Electrokinetics,*
- *Magnetostatics,*
- *Electrodynamics,*
- *Electromagnetics and*
- *Electronic Waves*

FIGURE 1.3 The two main subdivisions of electricity and its many subtopics and fields of study.

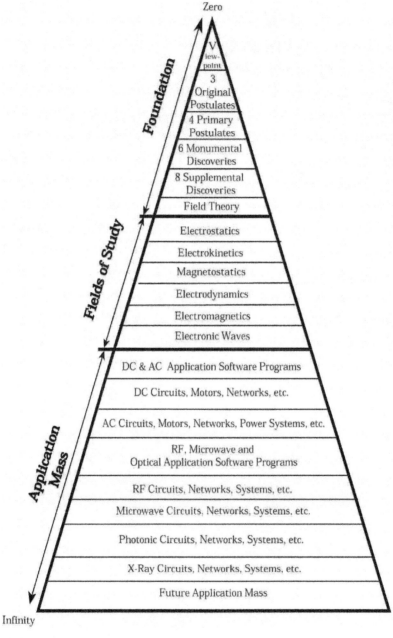

FIGURE 1.4 The pyramid of knowledge in electricity and the six distinct fields of study.

Using any of these fields of study, one can develop a plethora of application mass, which will benefit man in many ways for all future generations to come. The entire application mass thus generated in all of these fields of study will accompany this precisely formulated and codified mental triumph called "electricty!"

Electricity as briefly discussed above is merely a subset of a much larger arena, namely, the physical universe. The physical universe, itself, could be categorized as a "total-effect" or "action-reaction" type universe. However, it is the life force imbuing the physical universe, with the consequence of using electricity in so many applications in daily routine (from mental recordings and digital computations to tele-communications and image/data transmission) that has made the subject of electricity such an exciting field of study with unlimited capability.

1.7 THE POSTULATES OF LOW FREQUENCY (LF) ELECTRICITY

Having discovered electricity in terms of the six monumental and the eight supplemental discoveries, we are now ready to state the two classes of postulates of **Low Frequency** electricity: **a) Main LF postulates, and b) Auxiliary LF postulates.**

1.7.1 The Main LF Postulates

There are five main LF postulates that form the most fundamental aspects of electricity. These are:

MAIN LF POSTULATE #1: Let there be electric charges existing in opposite characteristics, or more precisely in a dual pair form (i.e., positive and negative charges).

MAIN LF POSTULATE #2: Let there exist electric field emanating from the positive charges and terminating on the negative charges. The electric field is capable of exerting a force on a nearby charge.

MAIN LF POSTULATE #3: Let there be an electromotive force (emf) required to cause a charge to move in a closed path of travel, i.e., creating a current. In other words, let the source or cause of a circulating current be the emf, which is the electric pressure. This causes a current to flow from a higher potential to a lower one.

MAIN LF POSTULATE #4: Let there be a magnetic field circulating an E-field, which lies in the path of a moving charge (i.e., a current), whose direction is given by the right-hand rule.

The magnetic field is capable of exerting a force on other magnetic poles. This postulate establishes the link between the electric and magnetic fields and indicates the fact that these two coexist as dual fields for any time-varying signal.

MAIN LF POSTULATE #5: Let there exist a force from the magnetic field on the electric field (or on the moving electric charges) and vice versa, let there exist a force from the electric field on the magnetic field, thus forming dual forces.

These five main postulates state the most distilled concepts about electricity, from which we can derive all of the major laws of electricity, magnetism, electromagnetism and electromagnetic optics. For example, **Coulomb's law and electric Gauss's law** can be derived from the LF postulates #1 and #2; **Biot-Savart law, Ampere's law,** and **magnetic Coulomb's law** are derivable from the LF postulate #4; **Lorentz force law** and **Faraday's law of induction** are byproducts of the LF postulate #5,.

1.7.2 The Auxiliary LF Postulates

There are also several auxiliary postulates that are not as basic but help to understand electricity better:

AUXILIARY LF POSTULATE #1: Let the electric field contain potential electric energy and the magnetic field contain magnetic potential energy (a dual pair), which are capable of conversion into kinetic energy in each case. Electric energy and the magnetic energy can also be converted into each other.

AUXILIARY LF POSTULATE #2: Let there exist linear electrical and magnetic materials. This postulate leads to constitutive relations and several important proportionality constants such as permittivity (ε), permeability (μ), conductivity (σ), resistivity (ρ), resistance (R), conductance (G), reluctance ($\mathfrak{R}$), capacitance (C), inductance (L), etc.

AUXILIARY LF POSTULATE #3: Let electric charge be conserved, which causes electric current to be also conserved.

AUXILIARY LF POSTULATE #4: Let there be no magnetic charge or source, which makes magnetic flux never to emanate from or to terminate at any point in space (unlike electric field) but always circulate and thus be conserved. This postulate makes a magnetic pole not a true source of magnetic field, but an apparent one.

AUXILIARY LF POSTULATE #5: Let electric field be a path-independent field (also called a conservative field), thus causing voltage to be conserved.
Auxiliary postulates #3, #4, and #5 are the result of a higher postulate, i.e.,

AUXILIARY LF POSTULATE #6: Let electric energy and its dual, magnetic energy, each be conserved as separate entities.
NOTE: Auxiliary LF postulate #6 is a subset of a much bigger postulate, i.e., The principle of conservation of energy.

From these six auxiliary LF postulates, some of the important laws of electricity can be derived. For example, all of the **energy storage equations** can be derived from the auxiliary postulate #1; **Ohm's law and generalized Ohm's law** are derivable from the auxiliary postulate #2; **electric Kirchhoff's current and voltage laws (EKCL and EKVL)** can be derived from auxiliary postulates #3, #5 and #6; **magnetic Kirchhoff's laws (MKCL and MKVL), and magnetic Gauss's law** can all be derived from auxiliary postulates # 4 and #6.

1.8 HIGH FREQUENCY (HF) POSTULATES OF ELECTRICITY

At high frequencies electrical enrgy behaves in a wave-like manner composed of E- and H-fields and is given by five main HF postulates as follows:

MAIN HF POSTULATE #1: Let there be oscillating electric charges, acting as the source of propagating waves.

MAIN HF POSTULATE #2: Energy at high frequencies exists in the form of waves. The waves propagate as a coexisting package of electric and magnetic fields, which transfer energy between two points in space by propagating at the speed of light in free space.

MAIN HF POSTULATE #3: A changing magnetic field (H-field) causes an electric field (E-field), and vice versa, an oscillating electric field causes an H-field. These two fields are normal to each other in free space, and coexist simultaneously regardless of any material medium.

MAIN HF POSTULATE #4: The direction of wave propagation in free space is perpendicular to the plane containing the E and the H-field and is exactly established by the cross product of E into H (i.e., ExH).

MAIN HF POSTULATE #5: All waves and their behavior in any medium or transmission structure (e.g. waveguide, etc.) are governed by the four Maxwell's equations. This postulate applies to any and all EM waves at any frequency (e.g., RF, Microwave, optical, X-Ray, etc.) only on a classical level and becomes null on a quantum level.

1.9 WAVES ON A TRANSMISSION LINE (TEM MODE)

The analysis of any uniform two-conductor transmission line using the Maxwell's equations reveals one unique mode called the "Transverse Electromagnetic mode" or TEM for short, which has no cutoff frequency, i.e., it propagates from DC to any microwave frequency. In this mode the electric fields are perpendicular to the magnetic fields everywhere in a plane transverse to the direction of propagation along the length of the line.

Therefore, when we mention a "transmission line", it is commonly understood to be any system of two-conductors suitable for conducting TEM-mode electromagnetic waves efficiently between source and load. Common examples of TEM-mode transmissions lines are telephone lines, power lines, coaxial lines, parallel plate lines, etc.

At lower frequencies the length of the line is much smaller than the signal wavelength and thus the transmission line can be treated as a "lumped element" with almost zero loss and no time delay for signal propagation between two points.

However, at high RF/microwave frequencies the length of the line is comparable to the signal wavelength and the time delay of propagation (and the corresponding signal phase shift) can no longer be ignored.

Under these conditions, the "distributed circuit model" is used to analyze a transmission line. Such a model provides the governing differential equations for voltage and current waves propagating along a transmission line without a need to resort to Maxwell's equations to solve for the electromagnetic field quantities.

1.10 THE POSTULATES OF TRANSMISSION LINES
The postulates regarding transmission lines can be briefly stated as:

Postulate #1- THE UNIFORMITY POSTULATE: A uniform transmission line consists of two straight parallel conductors.

The term "uniform" means that the materials, dimensions and cross sectional geometry of the line immersed in a dielectric remain constant throughout the length of the line.

This postulate does not require that the two conductors be of the same shape or identical cross-sectional area. The two conductors may be of any material, with completely dissimilar cross sections as long as they remain parallel and uniform throughout the length of the line.

Therefore, in addition to the simple example of two-parallel wire of circular cross-section, we may conceive of many other forms of structures, such as coaxial line, shielded-pair line, image line, stripline, etc. This postulate encompasses transmission lines with more than two parallel conductors, as long as they are interconnected in such a way as to present only two terminals at the points of connection to the source and the load.

This postulate has a uniformity assumption built into it, which could get violated in a twist or bend and thus create effects not explainable by the theory evolved around and based on this postulate. However, this would still be valid if the rate of bend (θ) does not exceed about one degree (i.e. $\theta \leq 1°$), in a length of line (ℓ) comparable to the separation of the two lines (d); that is to say if $\ell \approx d$, then we can still apply the uniformity postulate. For example if the separation of the two lines is 1 cm, then we can still use this postulate for bends (i.e. deviations from the straight line) which is less than one degree per centimeter.

Furthermore, this postulate could also get violated by any discontinuity in a line, which interrupts the uniformity of the line such as the termination points to the source or load, or the point of connection to another line that differs physically in some respect. The discontinuity at any point on the line creates effects which are usually confined to within a few separation distances (d) on either side of the conductor and therefore, on a larger scale of length, could be ignored.

Postulate #2- THE LONGITUDINAL CURRENT POSTULATE: The currents in the line conductors flow only in the direction of the length of the line.

This is a basic premise of electric circuit theory, which is mostly taken for granted by the engineers. However, such a postulate precludes the existence of currents which are perpendicular (transverse plane) to the direction of propagation along the length of the wire. These perpendicular currents, known as "transverse currents," which are circulating on the conductor's surface and not in the dielectric medium between the two conductors. The transverse currents lead to "waveguide modes" of propagation, which are discussed later in this chapter.

Postulate #3- THE OPPOSITE CURRENT POSTULATE: At any point on the transmission line, the instantaneous total current in one conductor is equal but opposite to the current in the other conductor.

This postulate allows the instantaneous currents to be of different value at different points on the line but the same magnitude if opposite, at each point in each conductor. Such a postulate at first glance appears to violate the Kirchhoff's current law (KCL), however, within this postulate is embedded the possibility of having transverse currents which exist in the dielectric between the conductors. The provision for such transverse currents is explored further in postulate #5.

Postulate #4- THE VOLTAGE POSTULATE: At any point on the transmission line, there is a unique value of the potential difference between the two lines, which is the line integral of the electric field along any path traveling from one line to the other.

This postulate asserts that the electric field existing between the two conductors is conservative, i.e., the work done in moving a particle from one conductor to the other is path independent.

Postulate #5- THE CIRCUIT COEFFICIENT POSTULATE: The electrical behavior of a transmission line is completely described by four electric circuit coefficients, whose values per unit length are constant everywhere on the line.

Each infinitesimal length of the transmission line can be modeled by a total of four electric circuit coefficients, two series (R, L) and two shunt (G, C) as shown in Figure 1.5. These circuit coefficients are:

R=Resistance per unit length
L=Inductance per unit length
C=Capacitance per unit length
G= Conductance per unit length

This postulate clearly states that the values of the four distributed circuit coefficients (R, L, C and G) are truly constants and solely are determined by the materials, dimensions and geometry of the conductor lines and not a function of time, current or voltage. In other words, this postulate sets up the stage to analyze a linear passive network.

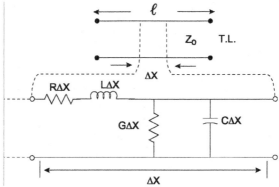

FIGURE 1.5   An infinitesimal portion of a transmission line (TL).

The existence of the distributed parameter "L" allows the storage of magnetic field, whereas the existence of "C" allows the existence of electric charge storage per unit length of the line.

Similarly, the existence of the distributed parameter "R" allows power loss as the current flows along the line whereas the existence of "G" allows power loss in the medium between the conductors due to the current flow between the conductors as a result of the existence of the potential difference.

Postulate #5 clearly integrates postulates #3 and #4 into a tangible package, which lends itself for further mathematical analysis. This postulate allows current to be different at two points along the line due to existence of G and C, which makes the current between the conductors to consist of conduction current (G), a leakage current, and displacement current (C) due to time rate of change in voltage. It also makes the voltage at two points along the line to be different due to existence of (L) and (R), which allow a voltage drop along the line. The transverse voltage between the lines can be expressed in terms of the electric field existing between the two lines.

1.11 TE AND TM MODES
A complete analysis of any transmission line can be made by starting with Maxwell's equations and then by using the boundary conditions imposed by the line conductors, we obtain the solution to the problem. Such an analysis would reveal:

a) *The TEM mode*, and
b) *The waveguide modes* (mentioned briefly in postulate #2).

The waveguide modes fall into two categories commonly known as:

1. *TE (Transverse Electric) mode, having a magnetic field along the length of the line*, and

2. *TM (Transverse Magnetic) mode, having an electric field along the length of the line*.

For each transmission line configuration, there are an **infinite** number of TE and TM modes, each with its own specific patterns of electric and magnetic fields. However, there is only one TEM mode, with a **unique** pattern of electric and magnetic fields, having a zero-cutoff frequency.

TE and TM modes, in any particular transmission line, each has a minimum frequency called the **cutoff frequency**, below which it would not propagate. This cutoff frequency can be calculated exactly for each separate mode based on the material and geometry of the line. If the separation of the conductor lines are less than a few inches, then the cutoff frequency is in the order of tens of GHz and thus waves would not propagate if the line is operated from DC to cutoff frequency.

When the transmission line is operated at microwave or millimeter-wave frequencies above the cutoff, the presence of these modes will result in excessive line losses and signal distortion. Therefore, care must be taken to avoid the occurrence of such modes.

Even though the TE and TM modes are not used for the two-conductor transmission lines (existing at frequencies above the cutoff), however, they are the basis of operation for the single-conductor transmission systems, in the form of hollow metal pipes, called waveguides (circular or rectangular). The analysis of such modes in waveguides is relegated to more advanced textbooks.

1.12 ENGINEERING PHILOSOPHY OF ANALYSIS

In this introductory chapter, it is essential for us to introduce some basic concepts which will be used often in solving engineering problems.

There are several methods of thinking used commonly in scientific studies amongst which the following are prominent:

A. Approximation Methodology
1. First-order of approximation
2. Nth-order of approximation

B. Linearization Methodology
1. Matrix technique
2. Extrapolation technique
3. Interpolation technique

These two methodologies are used to obtain simple solutions to very complex problems encountered in the scientific arena. These methodologies could also be used to obtain a higher level of knowledge from basic information about something or any given set of data already established as facts.

Using these two methodologies, one can start *predicting the future before it arrives* and can have actually a head start in the preparation process of dealing with inevitable outcomes, good or bad! One begins rapidly to acquire quite a bit of answers and knowledge to the puzzles and enigmas that life hands one on a daily basis.

One's knowingness and one's reaction time as well as one's health and preparedness in the combat zone called life goes up substantially; proportionately to the degree one has learned and mastered the fundamentals upon which life is based and has married them into his own personal life successfully!

1.12.1 Approximation Methodology

The English dictionary defines approximation as: *"coming near or close enough to the exact answer."* In other words, *approximation* is a method of obtaining an estimate that is nearly correct, i.e., finding simple answers that are correct within a range of tolerance.

Example 1.1

In mathematics, we know the following infinite series (called **Binomial Series**):

$$(1+x)^n = 1+nx+[n(n-1)/2]x^2 + [n(n-1)(n-2)/6]x^3 + \ldots + x^n + \ldots$$

where "n" can be any value. If "n" is a positive integer (i.e., n=1,2,3,...) then the binomial series converges and becomes the **Binomial Formula** with only n+1 terms, and all terms after x^n disappear.

Let us say that we want to find the approximate answers to:
$y=1/(1+x)^{1/2}$, where $x \ll 1$

As a **first-order of approximation**, we take the first two terms in the above identity and obtain:

$$y=(1+x)^{-1/2} \approx 1-0.5\,x$$

This answer is accurate as long as x is very small.

As a **second-order of approximation**, we take the first three terms in the above identity and obtain:
$$y=(1+x)^{-1/2} \approx 1-0.5\,x + 0.375x^2$$

This answer is more accurate but more complicated than the first – order case. This process of approximation can be continued up to the

Nth level **(Nth-order of approximation)** by taking the first N+1 terms and obtain consecutively more accurate answers than the previous stage.

Note: *Since we are dealing with an infinite series, this approximation can be continued infinite number of times at which time we get the most accurate answer at the expense of enormous complexity!*

Example 1.2

Another example is in optics, where we can approximate a spherical wave by a paraboloidal wave at distances far away from the source. The approximate form is simpler, easier to work with and can be obtained as:

$$U(R)=(A/R)e^{-jkR} \quad \text{(A Spherical Wave)}$$

Using binomial series first-order of approximation, we obtain:
$$R=(x^2+y^2+z^2)^{1/2} = z[1+ (x^2+y^2)/z^2]^{1/2} \approx z[1+ 0.5(x^2+y^2)/ z^2]$$
Where for large "z" (i.e. z>>1), and for points (x,y) close to the z-axis we can write:
$$(x^2+y^2)/ z^2 << 1$$

Therefore, the equation for a spherical wave can be written as:
$$U(R) =(A/R)e^{-jkR} \approx (A/z)e^{-jkz[1+ 0.5(x2+y2)/ z2]} = (A/z)e^{-jkz} \; e^{-jk0.5(x2+y2)/z}$$
$$\text{(A Paraboloidal Wave)}$$

Thus we can see that a spherical wave can be approximated and simplified by a paraboloidal wave which is a plane wave (Ae^{-jkz}) which is modulated by a phase term ($e^{-jk\,(x2+y2)/2z}$) at large distances. The phase factor bends the plane wave's wavefronts (plane waves) into paraboloidal surfaces (Note: the equation of a paraboloidal surface is given by $[(x^2+y^2)/z$ =constant]. This approximation is known as **Fresnel approximation** in the optics community.

Point of Interest

Since the sensitivity of phase to errors is greater than the errors in the magnitude, a more accurate value of "R" is used in the phase part. In other words, we have used two types of approximation as follows:

$R \approx z$ *(for magnitude part)*

$R \approx z[1 + 0.5(x^2 + y^2)/z^2]$ *(for phase part)*

1.12.2 Linearization Methodology

In this method we develop linear mathematical models of nonlinear systems under certain conditions and therefore simplify the analysis process greatly by using the simpler linear models.

a. Matrix Technique

The concept of linearization is based upon the concept of linearity, meaning that any *effect is exactly proportional to its cause*. That is to say, the **"effect" or output** can be described as a linear function of the **"cause" or input**.

There could be several *effects or outputs* but they all can be precisely defined in terms of linear equations wherein the *causes or input variables* appear only in the first power.

As a general example, if we have two effects or outputs (y_1 and y_2) and two causes or inputs (x_1, x_2), then we can write:

$y_1 = Ax_1 + Bx_2$ $\qquad\qquad$ (1.1)

$y_2 = Cx_1 + Dx_2$ $\qquad\qquad$ (1.2)

A, B, C, and D are called the proportionality constants.

Example 1.3 (Electronics)

In the field of electronics, a nonlinear two-terminal device such as a diode can be linearized under small signal conditions to obtain:

$v_d = r_d\, i_d$ (diode)

Where r_d is the inverse of the slope of the diode characteristic curve at the Q-point:

$r_d = 1/g_m = (\partial i_d / \partial v_d)^{-1}$

For a three terminal device such as transistor, the process of linearization under small signal condition is the same and we obtain a popular linear model commonly referred to as hybrid-pi model as follows:

Input or cause (i_b)

Output or effect (i_c, v_{be})

$v_{be}=r_\pi\, i_b$

$i_c= g_m\, v_{be} =\beta i_b$

We will now consider another example at high frequencies, which is used in microwave circuit design, particularly transistor amplifier design.

Example 1.4 (Microwaves)

In the field of microwaves, we have incident voltage waves as causes or inputs and reflected or transmitted voltage waves as effects or outputs. For example, for a two terminal circuit we can write the outputs or effects (v_1^-, v_2^-) as a function of the inputs or causes (v_1^+, v_2^+) in terms of scattering parameters (or S-parameters) as follows:

$$V_1^- = S_{11}V_1^+ + S_{12}V_2^+$$
$$V_2^- = S_{21}V_1^+ + S_{22}V_2^+$$

Or, in matrix form we can write:

$$\begin{bmatrix} V_1^- \\ V_2^- \end{bmatrix} = \begin{bmatrix} S_{11} & S_{12} \\ S_{21} & S_{22} \end{bmatrix} \cdot \begin{bmatrix} V_1^+ \\ V_2^+ \end{bmatrix}$$

Or,

$$[V^-]=[S][V^+]$$

Where,

$$[V^-]=\begin{bmatrix} V_1^- \\ V_2^- \end{bmatrix},$$

$$[V^+]=\begin{bmatrix} V_1^+ \\ V_2^+ \end{bmatrix}$$

and,

$$[\mathbf{S}] = \begin{bmatrix} \mathbf{S}_{11} & \mathbf{S}_{12} \\ \mathbf{S}_{21} & \mathbf{S}_{22} \end{bmatrix}$$

The matrix **[S]** whose elements are S_{11}, S_{12}, S_{21}, and S_{22} is known as the **Scattering** matrix. It completely characterizes the microwave circuit in a linearized fashion.

Let us now consider the field of optics as a final example. We can linearize any device, process or operation and turn it into a matrix as shown below.

Example 1.5 (Optics)
In the field of optics, we have incident rays of light as causes or inputs and reflected or transmitted rays as effects or outputs.

For example, an optical system consiting of optical components placed between two transverse planes located at z_1 and z_2 (referred to as the input and outout planes), we can completely characterize it by its effect (at plane z_1) on incoming rays of arbitrary position and direction (y_1, θ_1). The system will bend the incoming rays of light to the position (y_2) and direction (θ_2) at the output plane $(z2)$ such that:

$Y_2 = \mathbf{A}\, y_1 + \mathbf{B}\theta_1$
$\theta_2 = \mathbf{C}y_1 + \mathbf{D}\theta_1$

Or, in matrix form we can write:

$$\begin{bmatrix} y_2 \\ \theta_2 \end{bmatrix} = \begin{bmatrix} \mathbf{A} & \mathbf{B} \\ \mathbf{C} & \mathbf{D} \end{bmatrix} \cdot \begin{bmatrix} Y_1 \\ \theta_1 \end{bmatrix}$$

and,

$$[\mathbf{M}] = \begin{bmatrix} \mathbf{A} & \mathbf{B} \\ \mathbf{C} & \mathbf{D} \end{bmatrix}$$

The matrix **[M]** whose elements are A, B, C, and D is known as the **Ray-Transfer Matrix**. It completely characterizes the optical system in a linearized fashion.

---

b. Extrapolation

The English dictionary defines *"extrapolation"* as: *"to estimate a value (beyond the known range) on the basis of certain variables within the known range, from which the estimated value is assumed to follow."*

Using this technique we can arrive at answers and results by hypothesizing consequences based on known facts, observations or conclusions. For example, we constantly extrapolate that sun will shine tomorrow based on the observations of the past. This extrapolation about natural repeatable events has provided us with a certain level of predictability which we may take for granted.

However, in the scientific arena this is a common occurrence and we use it to predict the future events based on the extrapolation that the probability equations provide based on the volatility of the variables. For example in the gunnery and artillery, the trajectory of a missile and its point of landing (unknown data) can be precisely extrapolated from the angle of the gun and the initial or muzzle velocity of the missile (known facts).

c. Interpolation
The English dictionary defines *"interpolation"* as: *"to estimate a value (missing in the known range) on the basis of certain variables within the known range, from which the estimated value is assumed to follow."* Such an estimation is usually done by taking a weighted average of known values at the neighboring points and using them to arrive at an estimate of the missing value.

For example, if the value of a function between two points (x=1 and x=2) is known as 10 and 20, respectively, and a value between these two points (x=1.5) is desired, then one has to take an average of the two neighboring points and arrive at an estimate of 15, barring any abnormality at this point.

1.13 SUMMARY AND CONCLUSIONS
The rediscovery of these postulates is an important milestone in understanding the pillars holding up the powerful subject of electricity and further points to the fact that these can get lost in time

if no one brings them to the forefront in education. Their neglect would cause an interesting state of affairs, where they have to be discovered all over again (accidentally or not) just like Gilbert, Coulomb, Volta, Oersted, Ampere, Faraday, Maxwell and Hertz did over a period of three hundred years[†].

[†]**NOTE**: *It is interesting to note that the discovery of kinetic electricity by Galvani and Volta as well as the link between magnetism and electricity (by Oersted) were totally accidental and yet they were the most significant parts of the puzzle of electricity; and were it not for these bright and inquisitive minds we might still be living in the dark ages of ignorance about the physical universe and our own whereabouts on many levels such as our immediate physical surroundings, composition of matter, other galaxies, mental phenomena, and so on ad infinitum.*

Figure 1.6 shows how the monumental as well as the supplemental discoveries led to the uncovering of the LF postulates. The discovery process is a process of traveling in the reverse direction of the pyramid of knowledge; it is from the base to the apex in the hope of uncovering the postulates, which have been lost sight of in the progression of time.

Therefore, knowing these LF and HF postulates as well as the associated auxiliary postulates in its complete purity, enables one to soar to new heights of understanding of this vital field of study, where one can master any one of the subfields of study in the subject of electricity (such as RF electronics, Microwaves, electro-optics, microelectronics, etc.) and thus become a successful professional in a short period of time.

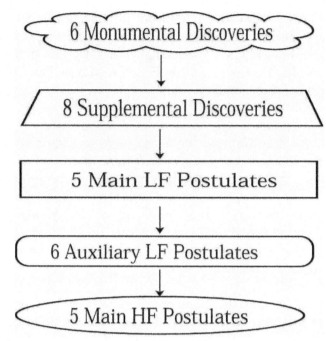

FIGURE 1.6 The discovery process leading to the uncovering of the postulates of electricity.

In retrospect, knowing the materials presented in this and the previous Chapters, would have enabled one to predict the field of electricity far in advance of its actual discovery, and in fact would have enabled one to derive all of its postulates and natural laws from the primary postulates and the main principles discussed so far.

For example, using the dichotomy principle one can derive the existence of positive and negative charges (LF postulate #1). Utilizing the action of charge in space (primary postulate #1), one can develop the concept of electric field (LF postulate #2). Using the duality principle and the electric field concept, leads to the magnetic field as the dual of the electric field (LF postulate #4). Existence of energy (primary postulate #2) leads to force (LF postulate #5), etc.

Moreover, since the postulates of electricity are subordinate to those of physics or the physical universe, therefore its knowledge as vital as it may be to man's survival, is junior in importance to the basic concepts of existence aspresented in the beginning parts of this chapter.

CHAPTER-1 PROBLEMS
1.1 What is the importance of a postulate?
1.2 Describe what are the main postulates?
1.3 Describe what is meant by a scientific postulate?
1.4 What are the main postulates of LF electricity? Explain.
1.5 What are the auxiliary postulates of LF electricity? Explain.
1.6 What are a postulate's byproducts? Explain.
1.7 What are the main postulates of HF electricity? Explain.
1.8 What are the auxiliary postulates of HF electricity? Explain.
1.9 What are the postulates of transmission line? Explain.
1.10 Describe what are the TE and TM modes?
1.11 Describe what is meant by the engineering philosophy of analysis?
1.12 Describe what is the foundation of electricity?
1.13 What are the fundamental postulates of physics?
1.14 What does the science of electricity consist of?
1.15 What is the approximation methodology and give an example?
1.16 What is the linearization methodology? give an example.
1.17 Describe what is the first discovery of electricity?
1.18 How could electricity have been developed in retrospect? Explain.
1.21 What are the subdivisions of the approximation methodology?
1.22 What are the subdivisions of the linearization methodology?

FIGURE 2.0 Michael Faraday
(1791-1867), English Scientist.

CHAPTER 2

The Discovery of Force Fields

2.1 THE CONCEPT OF FIELDS

The monumental discovery of major principles about the nature and behavior of electricity and magnetism and their combination helped to establish it, as a vital and powerful subject, on solid grounds. The cornerstone of modern electromagnetic concepts and laws is based upon the postulation of field theory which needs further amplification and elucidation at this point.

2.2 THE POSTULATION OF FIELD THEORY

The modern field theory is the most pervasive postulate that creates a foundation bedrock upon which we can build all of the other postulates in electromagnetics. It is used to describe directly or indirectly the behavior of all electrical or magnetic phenomena. Therefore, let us define it at this point:

FIELD THEORY (also called the FIELD-OF-FORCE THEORY) : *A theory in which the basic quantities are fields; It is the concept that within the space in the vicinity of a particle there exists a field containing energy and momentum and this field interacts with neighboring particles and their fields.*

Let us define the concept of field precisely at this point:
DEFINITION-FIELD: *a) A spatial distribution of a quantity, which may or may not be a function of time, b) An entity which acts as an intermediary agent in interactions between particles, which is distributed over a region of space, and whose properties are a function of space and time in general; examples include electric field, magnetic field, gravitational field, sound field, etc.*

Definition (a) includes scalar (one-valued) fields and vector (three-valued) fields, whereas using the definition (b), we can see that the concept of "field" implies that there is an applied force (magnitude and direction) at each point in space, and thus we are dealing perforce with a vector quantity, distributed in a region, whose magnitude and direction varies in space and time.

There is also a short-hand definition for "field" given by:
A SHORT-HAND DEFINITION -FIELD: *Cause (or action) at a distance.*

By definition (b), we can see that a **force field (or simply field)** *is an invisible entity, distributed over a region of space, whose properties at each point can be expressed in terms of a magnitude and a direction.*

In general, when dealing with the concept of fields we need to consider the concept of scalars and vectors, defined as:

DEFINITION-SCALAR: *Is any quantity, which has a magnitude but no direction, i.e., a one-component quantity.*

DEFINITION-VECTOR: *Is any quantity, which has a direction as well as a magnitude, i.e., a three-component quantity.*

In this work we will primarily employ the definition (b) as the main launching point for many of the new concepts and phenomena.

The discovery of fields was an important milestone principle that helped to explain the mechanism by which electricity interacted with matter. The discovered principle was clearly the work of a pragmatic genius, named Michael faraday, who through observation and mental foresight was able to discover the nature of energy and how its distribution in space was an important concept in the evolution of electricity and magnetism toward its final make-up and governing equations.

Faraday observed that energy, such as electricity or magnetism, do not act or apply force on matter directly (see Figure 2.1). This monumental discovery was about energy acting on matter via an intermediary agent called "field". Thus the concept of field theory was born.

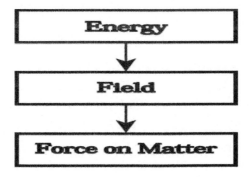

FIGURE 2.1   Definition of "field" and its connection to "force".

Field-of-force theory was such an impelling and all-inclusive concept that within a few years of its publication, led to the theoretical discovery of the electromagnetic waves by Maxwell.

In this chapter we will discuss how the Newtonian concepts of force were deficient and had to be supplanted by the more factual concept of field of force theory. This chapter lays the groundwork for understanding all future discussion and analysis of electromagnetic waves particularly Radio Frequency (RF), Microwaves and light-waves.

Knowing the exact definition of "field" along with the reasons why the field-of-force theory is needed, we are well equipped to make a foray into the subject of electronic waves without loss of focus.

2.3 The Newtonian Theory

The science of Ampere's era was dominated by the theories of motion and gravitation evolved by the English philosopher and mathematician by the name of Sir Isaac Newton (1642-1727).

Newton's mechanics were based on the view that all matter is composed of elementary, changeless particles of matter (also called point masses), which have the power to act on each other directly, through empty space. A general body is composed of many point masses and can be represented by a center of mass or center of inertia, which we define as:

DEFINITION-CENTER OF MASS (OR CENTER OF INERTIA): *Is a theoretical point of a material body which moves as though the body's total mass existed at that point with all external forces applied at that point.*

Newton's law of gravitation stated that the attractive forces between two bodies, was proportional to their product of their masses and inversely to the square of the distance between them. According to this theory, the attractive forces acted instantly and in a straight line through the center-to-center of masses (see Figure 2.2).

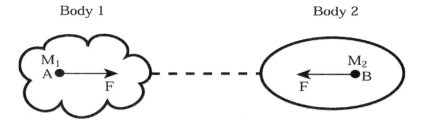

A = Center of mass for M_1

B = Center of mass for M_2

FIGURE 2.2   Newton's law of gravitation.

Followers of the Newtonian theory were led to expect that the law of gravitation would apply to other forces such as those of electricity and magnetism. When Coulomb's work demonstrated that electrostatic forces between point charges and magnetic forces between point poles was the product of their intensity and inversely proportional to the square of their separation, it appeared that laws of electricity fitted exactly into the Newtonian framework.

Like the Newtonian theory of gravitation, Ampere's theory of electric currents was also one of instantaneous, direct-action at a distance. Ampere hypothesized that electricity consisted of small charged particles (which later was discovered to be electrons). The motion of these charged particles created electric currents.

The electromagnetic forces between two infinitesimal current elements were proportional to the product of the magnitude of the two currents and inversely to the square of their separation.

Of course, the measurement of interacting electromagnetic forces between current elements (as current sources) could not be done individually, but only in the aggregate which was by working with real currents in closed circuits. Various forms of circuits were in fact what constituted the experiments by which Ampere developed his electrodynamics circuital laws. Considering infinitesimal current elements collectively (acting like Newtonian point masses), Ampere was somehow able to show loosely that electromagnetic forces, fitted into the Newtonian model described earlier.

2.4 THE NEWTONIAN MISCONCEPTIONS

The Newtonian explanation of electromagnetism had several flaws and deficiencies and thus was not able to explain the observed phenomena fully. The points of discrepancy could be summed up as:

a) *The electromagnetic forces had a direction with a right angle relationship between the current and the resulting magnetism. This fact introduced the possibility of rotation. This was in contradiction with the Newtonian concept of forces acting in a straight line (or direct-action forces).*

b) *The electromagnetic forces implied the possibility of a time factor, which was directly associated with the distance between the source location and the receipt point.*

These new observations could not be explained by Newtonian theory and thus a search for a new theory to include these phenomena had begun.

2.5 A REVOLUTIONARY DISCOVERY

The most anti-Newtonian theory was postulated by one of Ampere's contemporary by the name of Michael Faraday (1791-1867). He rejected the idea of "instant straight line action at a distance" theory and introduced a revolutionary concept of "field of force" theory.

Faraday pictured the force-field by lines of force which connected the point of emanation to the point of termination.

The monumental discovery by Faraday *was the Realization of Force Fields.* The force field concept explained that in general, any physical process was determined by field lines which had a magnitude and direction (i.e. a vector) at each point in space.

Ampere's Newtonian theory of electro-magnetism was no longer accepted as a natural explanation of electromagnetic forces and once

James Clark Maxwell put this concept into a mathematical format, the field of force theory became the dominant theory in the scientific community.

The important point to note here is that Faraday's concept not only presented a comprehensive view of electricity but also shaped all future developments in the electromagnetic arena and made the subject fully aligned with the observed phenomena about electricity.

2.6 THE UNIVERSAL NATURE OF FORCE

In 1832, Faraday presented his vision of the physical universe, where all world forces such as electrical, magnetic, gravitational, chemical, nuclear and others were various forms of a fundamental force. He considered that all natural forces were essentially identical in their origin and could be converted from one form to another.

In a series of experiments, he actually showed that he could get the same chemical and magnetic effects regardless of the source of electricity. He developed the relation between electricity and magnetism and the propagation of their effects.

Faraday had a philosophical approach to his work and believed in the "unity of physical phenomena", in particular, he considered that matter, electricity and light were of the same origin.

Faraday's philosophical considerations about matter, electricity, and light conform to the modern discoveries, since we know today that these are all derived from "energy", each having progressively a higher frequency with a corresponding decreasing wavelength.

His metaphysical probing into the ultimate reality of force and matter were to have a great impact on the future development of electromagnetism. Faraday saw iron filings arrange themselves in a pattern when he sprinkled them on paper held over the poles of a magnet. Faraday conceived that the *patterns were the representation of the real lines of an underlying invisible field of force existing in space.*

He envisioned that a basal field of force (such as one exhibited by magnetism) accounted for the substance and operation of all nature. His vision was based on the oldest and yet continuing quest in the philosophy of science-- the **Basal Unity in Nature** i.e. *all forces or energy sources come from a common source and therefore are convertible into one another (see Figure 2.3).*

Faraday viewed static charge and magnetism acting via a field of force occupying the whole space, which progressed continuously from force point to force point. He believed the attractions and repulsions of static electricity and magnetism was due to fields between force center, which caused physical deformation, deflection or strain (change in length).

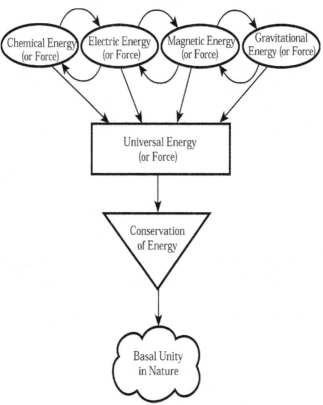

FIGURE 2.3 The basal unity in nature.

Physical substance itself could be considered to be a convergence or focus of force fields. Thus Faraday's force Field theory abolished the distinction between matter and energy, since it was later discovered that matter is a condensed form of energy.

Thus we can conclude that all physical entities are derived from energy. Using this new understanding of matter and energy, Faraday rejected instantaneous action at-a-distance central force theory of Newton.

He advocated the more modern concept of force transference impelled through space as time progressed; each element impacting on a contiguous neighboring element.

His theory provided for *curved progression* of attractive or repulsive forces (rather than straight line as proposed by Newton), since they involve forces of tension and compression.

2.7 LINES OF FORCE

One of the most pervasive supports for the Faraday's field of force theory was the conception of lines of force. These lines of force were not merely a pictorial representation of an idea, but actually what comprised the "field of forces". Force fields are represented by means of "lines of flux" or "lines of force".

The lines of force concept would be most vividly seen in the action between two magnetic poles. The lines streamed out from magnetic sources and filled the surrounding space around the poles. The intensity of the field was graphically represented by the space between lines. Thus as the intensity decreased with distance, the spacing between lines increased (see Figure 2.4).

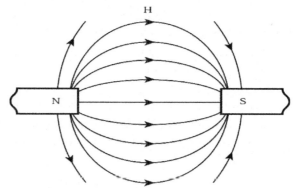

FIGURE 2.4 Magnetic lines of force.

Faraday considered the lines of force (particularly lines of magnetic force) as lines shown with an arrow, which pointed toward the direction of the field, whereas the closeness of the lines (i.e., space between lines) represented the intensity of the field in a given region.

Therefore, we can define "Line of Force" as follows:

DEFINITION-LINE OF FORCE (ALSO KNOWN AS FLUX LINE OR LINE OF FLUX): *Is an imaginary line in a field of force (such as electric field, etc.), whose tangent at any point provides the direction of the field at that point; The lines are spaced so that the number of lines through a unit area perpendicular to the field represents the intensity of the field (See Figure 2.5).*

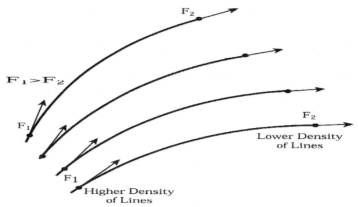

FIGURE 2.5 Lines of Force.

By definition, electric lines of force emanate from positive charge and terminate on negative charge. Similarly, magnetic lines of force emanate from the north pole of a magnet and terminate on its south pole.

Lines of force concept was an unorthodox scientific concept at the time since it flew in the face of all conventional Newtonian physics. The "lines of force" concept as lines of force traversing all space came about due to Faraday's pragmatic experience with electricity and magnetism, which differed from the mathematicians view of the same phenomena as centers of forces (i.e. localized forces, which are not distributed in space) acting at a distance.

The fifth monumental discovery is based upon the works of Michael Faraday, who laid the groundwork and paved the way for the era of electronic waves to be ushered in shortly thereafter. In the next section we will examine several types of force fields.

2.7.1 Types of Force Fields

The concept of force fields, as put forth by Faraday, proposes the theory of **"non-physical conduction of electricity."** It proposes that to conduct electricity from one point to another, one does not need to have a physical contact (such as wires, conductors, etc.), so long as invisible fields exist.

This concept fundamentally revolutionized the way scientists of the time regarded electricity (which was electric transmission through the use of wires), and made electricity leap the boundaries of the physical materials into the unlimited free space.

There are many types of force fields. Wherever we have a form of energy, perforce, we will have a field associated with that form of energy. For example, bodies with a mass exert gravitational forces on each other, thus there is a gravitational field distribution in the space occupied by these bodies; or in a region where there is a noticeable sound volume, we will have a sound field distribution in that space, so on and so forth.

Examples of important force fields pertaining to our subject of discussion, embrace two major heading: a) Electric field, and b) Magnetic field. Understanding these two types of fields, with their exact definitions, are vital in the grasp of any future concepts presented in this subject. From these two basic types of fields, we derive four basic vector quantities described as:

a) Electric field intensity, **E** (also called electric field strength, electric field vector or electric vector),

b) Electric displacement vector, **D** (also called electric flux density),

c) Magnetic field intensity, **H** (also called magnetic field strength, magnetic intensity, magnetic field, magnetic force and magnetizing force),

d) Magnetic Displacement Vector, **B** (also called Magnetic Induction, Magnetic Flux Density)

e) Electromagnetic Fields (**E** and **H** in combination).

These two basic types of fields are used throughout the electrical and electronics industry as fundamental concepts, which need to be mastered at an early stage of one's education in the subject. To this end we define them precisely at this point:

DEFINITION-ELECTRIC FIELD: *Is the electric energy existing in the space surrounding an electric charge or a charged body, which acts as an intermediary agent in interactions between the charge and other charges.*

a) Electric Field Intensity, E (also called electric field strength, electric field vector or electric vector): *is the electric force per unit test charge caused by the electric energy existing in the space surrounding an electric charge or a charged body.*

b) Electric Displacement Vector, D (also called electric flux density): *is a quantitative measure of electric field in a material* *medium and is proportional to the electric field intensity in isotropic media.*

DEFINITION-MAGNETIC FIELD: *Is the magnetic energy existing in the space surrounding a magnetic pole or a magnetized body, which acts as an intermediary agent in interactions between the magnet (or the magnetized body) and other magnets.*

c) Magnetic Field Intensity, H (also called magnetic field strength, magnetic intensity, magnetic field, magnetic force and magnetizing force): *is the magnetic force per unit test pole caused by the magnetic energy existing in the space surrounding a magnetic pole or a magnetized body.*

d) Magnetic Displacement Vector, B (also called Magnetic Induction, Magnetic Flux Density): *is a quantitative measure of magnetic field in a material medium and is proportional to the magnetic field intensity for isotropic media.*

e) Electromagnetic Fields (E and H in Combination): *Electromagnetic fields are a combination of time-varying electric and magnetic fields simultaneously coexisting and intertwined into a whole package, which is essential to the mechanism of wave propagation.*

It is interesting to note that as long as the fields remain static and unchanging in time, we have a total separation of the two fields (i.e., electric and magnetic) as specified in (a) and (b) above.

However, the moment, we introduce any type of temporal (time) change into the magnitude or direction of these two fields (i.e., dynamic fields), they instantly become dual companion of each other and remain inseparable as long as the fields remain time-variant.

By definition, electric lines of force emanate from positive charges and terminate on negative charges. Similarly, magnetic lines of force emanate from the north pole of a magnet and terminate on the South Pole.

Using lines of force theory, Faraday was able to theorize well in advance of its time, the future of electromagnetics as being able to radiate out into space. He considered radiation to be a category of vibrations along the lines of force. In 1846, Faraday published his findings in a paper entitled "Thoughts on Ray Vibrations", where he foretold the future of electromagnetics as being able to radiate out into space.

What Faraday had predicted at this early stage, still needed years of theoretical development to come. Moreover, his prediction of wave propagation needed rigorous experimental proof before it could be used effectively in the scientific community.

Nevertheless, Faraday through close examination of the five discovered principles and the way they had unfolded so far took a very intelligent look into the future and saw where the science of electromagnetism was heading toward. This was in no small measure a guess or a speculation, rather an unemotional and cold look at the existing facts and formulated truth that had gathered up to that time.

There was not enough evidence theoretically or experimentally for the existence of EM waves. Yet with the prediction of wave propagation, which took place years before Maxwell's mathematical modeling or his discovery of the displacement current, Faraday showed his pragmatic mind and his utter genius in understanding this unfolding jigsaw puzzle well before its final resolution by Hertz in 1890s.

2.7.2 Polarization

Before we discuss the concept of polarization, we need to define it:
DEFINITION-POLARIZATION: *Is the direction of vibration of the electric field (or the displacement vector) of a wave, which is constant (linear polarization) or varies in some definite way (circular or elliptical polarization).*

Therefore the electric field of an electromagnetic wave can have either a) Linear polarization, b) Circular polarization (right-hand), c) Circular polarization (left-hand), or d) Elliptical polarization, but not all simultaneously!

2.8 CONSERVATION OF CHARGE

Static electricity had been the subject of investigation for over two centuries. Friction machines generated sparks and Leyden Jars were used to store them. Various materials were tested in order to find their ability in holding or transmitting electricity. The concept of conductors and dielectrics were being finalized.

The sum of knowledge of Man about electricity could be summarized in terms of the following developments:

a) The original theory of electricity was that it was made up of two fluids.

b) This theory was later replaced by Franklin's one fluid proposal. In his proposal, Franklin explained that electricity obtained through friction was simply an act of "separation."

c) The act of separation of charge left one object with an excess charge (called positive charge) and a deficiency of charge (called negative charge).

d) Coulomb demonstrated that force between point charges at rest was proportional to the magnitude of charges and inversely to the square of separation.

Applying the lines of force theory to the field of electrostatics, Faraday finished off Coulomb's work in 1835. His findings modernized the previous knowledge of electrostatics and created its current perspective that we study today.

He concluded that the creation of a single charge was impossible since every positive charge's line of force must terminate on a negative charge, which meant that charges could only be separated and not created.

Figure 2.6 shows the lines of force for two dissimilar charges as well as two similar charges, where the direction of arrow in the lines of force indicates the direction *"a unit positive test charge"* would move if placed in that electric field.

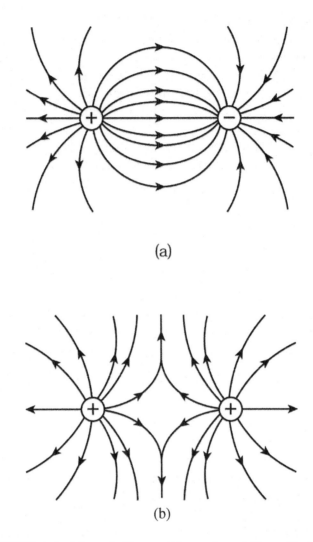

(a)

(b)

FIGURE 2.6 Electric lines of force for a) Two dissimilar charges, and b) Two similar charges.

He established that there was no "absolute charge" existing as a single entity. His line of force theory required that there be field lines emanating from the positive charges and terminating on the negative charges. Thus the creation of separate charges was impossible.

In other words, every charge must be matched up by an equal and opposite charge existing nearby: *The opposite charges were only the different ends of the lines of force*.

This led to a very important conclusion and a major principle of electrical engineering, aptly named "conservation of charge", which is defined as:

THE PRINCIPLE OF CONSERVATION OF CHARGE: *This principle states that in any closed system existing in the physical universe, charge can neither be created nor destroyed but only separated and thus is conserved.*

Since charge is a form of energy, we can see that this principle can be considered to be a subset of principle of "conservation of energy". It has been uniformly adopted as a basic postulate in classical physics and electrical engineering and is widely accepted without any proof.

2.9 MATHEMATICS OF FORCE FIELDS

Since Faraday was not a professed mathematician, he described most of his discoveries in natural and non-technical language. James Clerk Maxwell was a strong supporter of the force field theory and made it the keystone of his electromagnetic theory which he presented as a technical paper to the Cambridge philosophical society in 1865. In this technical paper entitled "on Faraday's lines of force" Maxwell was the first to put Faraday's concept of lines of force into a mathematical format.

A few years later, Maxwell had developed the Faraday's idea of vibratory radiation along the lines of force and presented it as the electromagnetic theory of light. This was not only a revolutionary advance in physics but also made the phenomena of light and optics a subdivision of electromagnetics.

2.10 APPLICATIONS OF FORCE FIELDS

The Discovery of Force Fields, is fundamental to many fields of study and today many subjects such as fluid dynamics, astrophysics, etc. utilize the concept of fields in the body of their work. However, when it comes to electricity, all of the governing laws and equations have been re-cast in the form of fields and as a result a tremendous amount of simplification has been achieved when it comes to explaining many of the existing phenomena or describing the internal operation of an electrical device.

The following series of applications is a brief sample of the myriad of applications possible, all based on this major discovery. However, the important thing to remember here while reading these application samples is that they show how the basic fundamental concepts can be used to obtain application mass. Simple or complex, all application mass in this section have the same common denominator: Force Fields.

2.10.1 The First Electromagnetic Transformer

Faraday invented the first electromagnetic transformer (also known as the Faraday's ring) and produced the first electromagnetic induction as shown in Figure 2.7.

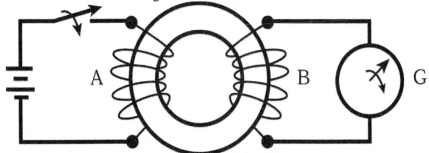

FIGURE 2.7   The first electromagnetic transformer.

When winding (A) was energized by the battery, the galvanometer needle connected to winding (B), spun around several times. The needle would soon come to rest and become indifferent to the steady current. The needle responded similarly but in a reversed fashion when the battery was disconnected. The rise and fall of magnetism in the iron core of the ring, with the making and breaking of the current to winding (A), induced current in winding (B) as indicated by the galvanometer (G). It gradually became clear that change of magnetism was essential for induction.

Repeating this and other similar experiments, Faraday soon came to the realization that he had finally discovered the key to induction. **The key to induction was "CHANGE"; The change of the magnetic field strength in the core.** *This is clearly an example of original postulate #3 in action.*

Therefore, Faraday had demonstrated that electricity could be produced from magnetism—utilizing the principle of induction!

2.10.2 The Mystery of Arago's Disk

In 1824 in France, Francois Jean Arago (1786-1853) had mystified the scientific community by his apparatus as shown in Figure 2.8.

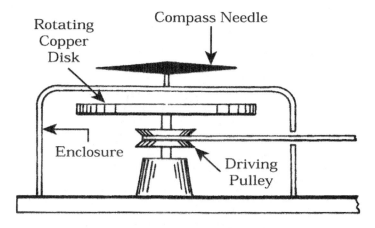

FIGURE 2.8   Arago's disk

By some unexplained force, the compass needle would spin around whenever the enclosed copper disk was rotated by the diving pulley. Many scientists had labored at various explanations for this strange action, but it was Faraday who finally resolved the mystery.

Faraday's discovery of electromagnetic induction revealed that rotation of the compass needle was the result of interaction between the magnetic needle and the disk. The magnetic needle induced a current in the moving disk, which in turn set up a magnetic field. This induced magnetic field (caused by the induced current in the disk) would now interact with the magnetic needle and thus causing it to spin.

2.10.3 The Earth's Ionosphere

The earth's ionosphere, composed of plasma, starts at roughly 80 km above the earth's surface. This plasma is formed from air molecules that are excited by ultraviolet radiation from the sun. It has been found that for frequencies lower than 9 MHz, the ionosphere will reflect electromagnetic radiation. At frequencies above 9 MHz, the ionosphere allows electromagnetic radiation to pass through with very little reflection.

At the lower frequencies, the result is a standing wave in the air below the ionosphere and an exponential decline in the electric field strength with increasing depth Into the Ionosphere (see Figure 2.9).

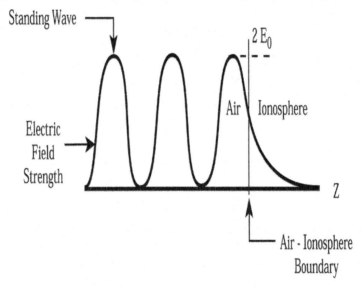

FIGURE 2.9   The earth's ionosphere

WAVEGUIDE PROPERTIES
Because of the reflective properties of both the earth and the ionosphere at lower frequencies, they effectively form a parallel plate waveguide (see Figure 2.10). The earth's-ionosphere waveguide allows transmission of signals around the world.

However, higher frequency signals, such as TV, pass through the ionosphere without being reflected. This is why you must normally be within line of sight of a station's TV transmitter in order to receive that particular station well. This example is furtehr nalyzed in Chapter 4.

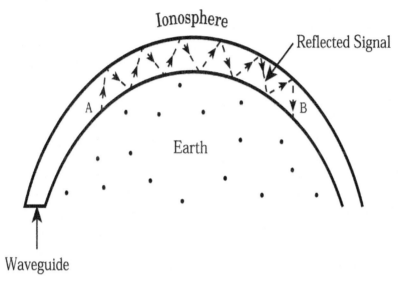

FIGURE 2.10   The earth's ionosphere and its waveguide property.

2.10.4 Antenna Orientation

The orientation of the electric field in a broadcasted signal determines the best antenna configuration to receive the signal. For the sake of this application we can consider the following cases:

AM RADIO:

AM radio signals are broadcast with their electric field perpendicular to the ground. Thus, the receiving antenna is best oriented perpendicular to the ground to detect the radio signal. An example of this type of antenna is a typical straight car antenna.

FM RADIO:

FM radio signals are circularly polarized. Because of this, any antenna orientation is effective as long as the antenna is facing a direction perpendicular to the velocity of the wave,

TELEVISION:

TV signals are broadcasted with their E-field parallel to the ground, therefore TV antennas are most effective if their wires are oriented parallel to the ground. The two cases of AM and TV antennas are shown in Figure 2.11.

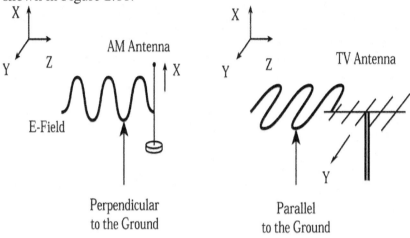

(Ground is the Y - Z Plane)

FIGURE 2.11 Antenna orientations for a) AM radio, and b) TV.

2.10.5 Doubled Communication Using Polarization

Because of the popularity of satellite use, the frequency bands for satellites are crowded, In order to increase the amount of information that can be transmitted in a given band, satellite systems transmit two distinct signals polarized 90° apart. By using such orthogonal polarization, the satellite can transmit twice the amount of information in a given bandwidth with no interference between signals (see Figure 2.12).

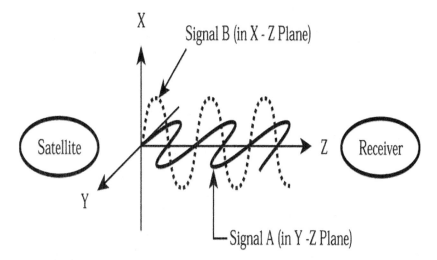

FIGURE 2.12   Transmission of two signals polarized 90° apart.

2.10.6 Grating Reflector

When the incoming electromagnetic wave is linearly polarized, reflection can be accomplished with parallel wires instead of a plate as in satellite TV dish antennas.

OPERATION:

Reflection of a signal with a grating is possible because when a polarized wave strikes a surface, there is only surface current flowing in the direction of the polarization of the electric field. Thus, if the incident wave is polarized with its E-field in the y-axis, a grating of wires in the y-direction would effectively reflect this signal (see Figure 2.13). Waves with x- or z-directed E-fields will pass through the grating, without being reflected.

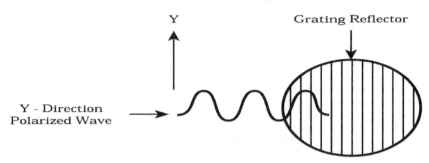

FIGURE 2.13 A grating reflector.

In order for the grating to be effective, the spacing of the grates must be much smaller than the wavelength of the incident wave.

CONCLUSION: *Grating reflectors are very useful because they are lighter, cheaper, and with less wind-resistance than solid reflecting plates.*

2.10.7 Frequency Meter

A frequency meter is used to determine the frequency of an unknown electromagnetic wave.

OPERATION:
A frequency meter uses the fact that a conducting metal cavity of the right length will cause an electromagnetic wave inside the cavity to become a standing wave, which really means that a resonance will occur (see Figure 2.14).

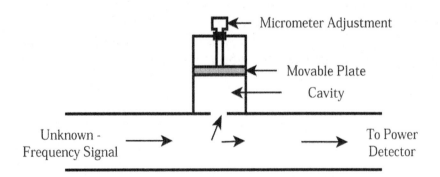

FIGURE 2.14 A frequency meter.

In a frequency meter a cavity is coupled to a waveguide through a small opening. A micrometer adjusts the length of the cavity by moving its free end to cause resonance. A probe at the end of the waveguide senses the power of the unknown frequency signal.

To find the signal frequency, the micrometer is adjusted until the detector registers a decrease in power. This decrease indicates that the signal is resonant in the cavity and it is drawing power to maintain this resonance. The micrometer reading is then compared to a chart to determine the signal frequency.

CONCLUSION: *The resonant-cavity method is a relatively simple way to determine the frequency of an unknown electromagnetic wave.*

2.10.8 Wavelength Measurement
The measurement of the wavelength of an electromagnetic wave is an important capability in any modern measurement equipment.
OPERATION:
The wavelength of the electromagnetic wave is measured by sending the signal in a special coaxial cable. This cable has one end shorted together by a conducting annular ring (see Figure 2.15).

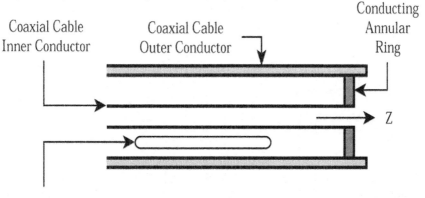

FIGURE 2.15 Wavelength measurement setup in a coaxial cable.

The result is that a standing wave is produced along the coaxial cable. If a lengthwise slit is made in the cable, a probe can be inserted that will measure the power of standing wave. As the probe is moved along the cable, a standing wave pattern will be registered. The wavelength of the unknown electromagnetic wave will be twice the wavelength of the standing wave. The standing wave is measured using the probe and will have a reading as a result of the combination of two waves: a) Incident wave, and b) Reflected wave.

Analysis:

The Incident, reflected and standing waves are given as follows:

a) Incident wave:

$$\overline{E}_i = \hat{r}\frac{V_o}{r}e^{-jkz} \tag{2.1}$$

$$\overline{H}_i = \hat{\phi}\frac{V_o}{\eta r}e^{-jkz} \tag{2.2}$$

where η is the intrinsic impedance of the medium, given by:

$\eta = \sqrt{\mu/\varepsilon}$

b) Reflected wave:

$$\overline{E}_r = -\hat{r}\frac{V_o}{r}e^{jkz} \tag{2.3}$$

$$\overline{H}_r = \hat{\phi}\frac{V_o}{\eta r}e^{jkz} \tag{2.4}$$

c) The resultant standing wave is given by:

$$\overline{E} = \hat{r}\frac{-j2V_o}{r}\sin(kz) \tag{2.5}$$

$$\overline{H} = \hat{\phi}\frac{2V_o}{\eta r}\cos(kz) \tag{2.6}$$

Summary:

From this analysis, we can see that the resultant standing waves for both electric and magnetic fields are oscillating signals, and are no longer propagating, but have a definite location.

2.11 CONCLUSIONS

As discussed in this chapter, we can see that the subject of fields is a fascinating subject and since its advent by Faraday, it has been able to lift the subject of electricity to a whole new level and make many of today's advances possible.

The subject of fields, even though primarily proposed by Faraday for electricity and magnetism, has actually spread out to other subjects (such as Gravity, Fluid Dynamics, etc.), and thus has made the respective scientists, able to inject and integrate the concept of fields into their respective subjects, all to make them more practical and closer to truth. It has even spread to such distant fields as spiritualism and mental phenomena, where research has shown that there is an electric field surrounding the human body which can be influenced by the spirit or mind.

So overall the concept of fields, as delineated in this chapter, has revolutionized many subjects and has had a great impact on the way we think about the forces we experience in the physical universe.

POINT OF INTEREST: *Faraday's name lives forever in the vast range of investigations and the effects he discovered. Even though he did not formulate the laws mathematically himself (that was done by Maxwell and others) yet his genius shines through all of his brilliant work, particularly his field of force theory depicted by the lines of force concept.*

His name was immortalized by the First International Electrical Congress in 1881 by naming the electrical unit of capacitor as "Farad".

Chapter 2 Problems

2.1 What is the definition of field?
2.2 Why is the Newtonian theory deficient in the field of electricity? What are the shortcomings of this theory with regard to electricity?
2.3 What was the Newtonian misconception?
2.4 What is the fifth monumental discovery?
2.5 What is meant by the universal nature of force?
2.6 What are lines of force?

2.7 What is the principle of conservation of charge and what led to its development?

2.8 What was Faraday's prediction well in advance of its discovery?

2.9 Give a few examples of force fields.

2.10 What is a transformer? Explain its theory of operation.

2.11 What is an electromagnetic motor? Draw a diagram and show how it works.

2.12 What is Arago's disk? How does it work and what is the main operating principle here?

2.13 How does Earth's ionosphere interact with radio frequency signals?

2.14 What is antenna orientation and how does it affect signal reception?

2.15 How can we double the communication capacity by using polarization?

2.16 What is a grating reflector and how does it work?

2.17 What is a frequency meter and what can it be used for?

2.18 How is the wavelength of a signal measured? Explain.

2.19 Why the concept of fields has revolutionized many areas of study?

2.20 What is meant by basal unity in nature?

CHAPTER 3

The Mathematics of RF and Microwaves

3.1 INTRODUCTION

In this chapter, we will lay the groundwork for basic mathematical concepts including phasors, basic circuit elements, Ohm's law, Kirchhoff's voltage and current laws, basic network theorems and the decibel scale. The main purpose of presenting these concepts is to aid the reader in better comprehension of the ensuing materials and enhance the analysis and design of electronic circuits, which will be the main focus of this work.

3.2 THE PHASOR CONCEPT

The following conditions should be present before the phasor concept can be used effectively:

a.   *The circuit or system under consideration is linear,*
b.   *All independent sources are sinusoidal,*
c.   *Only the steady state response is desired.*

Having met the above three strict conditions, then phasors can be employed with considerable ease in the analysis or design process of any circuit. With the help of Euler's identity (which relates the polar representation of a complex number to its rectangular representation), we can write:

$$e^{\pm j\theta} = \cos\theta \pm j\sin\theta, \tag{3.1}$$

where $j=\sqrt{-1}$ is a unity imaginary number.

We will see shortly that the existence of a phasor is based on the concept of a mathematical transform from one domain to another, which is a change in the mathematical description of a physical variable in order to facilitate computation (see Figure 3.1).

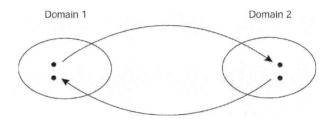

Domain 1   Domain 2

Figure 3.1 Transformation from domain to domain 2.

3.3 PHASOR TRANSFORM

Consider a sinusoidal waveform of a voltage, current or an electromagnetic (EM) wave given by:

$$x(t) = A_m \cos(\omega t + \varphi) \tag{3.2}$$

Using Euler's identity, $x(t)$ can be written as:

$$x(t) = \text{Re}[A_m e^{j\varphi} e^{j\omega t}] \tag{3.3}$$

The coefficient, $A_m e^{j\varphi}$, of the exponential term ($e^{j\omega t}$) is a complex number that carries the amplitude and phase angle of the given sinusoidal function. This complex number is defined to be the phasor representation [or the phasor transform (A)]of the given sinusoidal waveform:

$$A = A_m \cdot e^{j\varphi} \tag{3.4}$$

Thus a phasor transforms the sinusoidal waveform from the time domain to the complex number domain (or to the frequency domain even though we have suppressed the exponential frequency factor $e^{j\omega t}$) as shown in Figure 3.2.

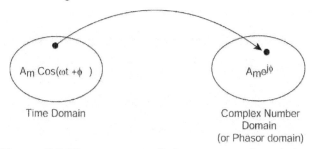

Figure 3.2 The concept of phasor transformation.

DEFINITION - PHASOR: *A phasor is a result of a mathematical transformation of a sinusoidal waveform (voltage, current, or EM wave) from the time domain into the complex number domain (or frequency domain) whereby the magnitude and phase angle information of the sinusoid is retained.*

Note: *The value of ω cannot be deduced from a phasor quantity since it carries only the amplitude and the phase information while the frequency information is suppressed.*

3.4 INVERSE PHASOR TRANSFORM

The reverse operation which is going from the phasor transform: $A=A_m.e^{j\varphi}$ to the time domain is called the inverse phasor transform. It is obtained by multiplying the phasor by $e^{j\omega t}$ and taking its real part, i.e.,

$$\text{Phasor } A \Rightarrow \mathbf{Re}[A\,e^{j\omega t}] = \mathbf{Re}\,[A_m e^{j\varphi}\,e^{j\omega t}]$$

$$= A_m \cos(\omega t + \varphi) = x(t) \qquad (3.5)$$

This is shown in Figure 3.3.

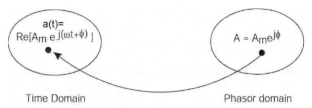

Figure 3.3 Inverse Phasor transform.

3.5 REASONS FOR USING PHASORS

The reasons for using phasors can be summarized in terms of the following facts:

Reason #1. The algebraic sum of any number of sinusoids of the same angular frequency (ω) and any number of their derivatives of any order is also a sinusoid of the same angular frequency (ω).

This fact suggests that we can treat sinusoids by algebraic methods where with the use of phasors this operation is greatly facilitated. This is simply due to the fact that the problem of finding the amplitude and phase angle of the steady state sinusoidal response is reduced to the problem of algebra of complex numbers.

Reason #2. Knowledge of a phasor (representing a sinusoid), determines the amplitude and the phase but not the frequency. When performing phasor calculations, it is important to keep in mind the frequency of operation (ω).

Reason #3. Summing sinusoids (voltages, currents, etc.) of the same frequency is very common in circuit theory and EM wave analysis. Therefore, use of phasor transform is very useful in this regard by considering the following:

Let $X_i(t) = a_i \cos(\omega t + \varphi_i)$, $i = 1, \ldots \ldots , n$
Then the sum of "n" sinusoids, $X(t)$, can be written in time domain as:
$$X(t) = X_1(t) + X_2(t) + \ldots \ldots \ldots \ldots \ldots + X_n(t) \qquad (3.6)$$

The phasor transform of the sum sinusoid, A, can be written as:
$$A = A_1 + A_2 + \ldots \ldots \ldots \ldots \ldots \ldots \ldots + A_n \qquad (3.7)$$
Where $A_i = a_i \, e^{j\varphi_i}$ ($i = 1, \ldots \ldots n$) is the corresponding phasor for each individual sinusoid $X_i(t)$. From (3.6) and (3.7) we can write:
$$X(t) \Rightarrow A$$

Therefore as shown above, the phasor representation of the sinusoidal sum is the sum of the phasors of the individual terms. Knowing the sum phasor (A) one can find the total sinusoid [$X(t)$] in the time domain and vice versa. Example 3.1 below further illustrates this point:

Reason #4. Differentiating a time domain sinusoid $(dX(t)/dt)$ amounts to the multiplication of the corresponding phasor (A) by $j\omega$ as shown below:

$$dX(t)/dt=d[Re(A_m e^{j\omega t+\varphi})]/dt=Re\ [d(A_x e^{j\omega t})/dt]=Re[A_x\ j\omega\ e^{j\omega t}]$$

$$(3.8)$$

Where $A_x=A_m e^{j\varphi}$ is the phasor for $X(t)$.
Therefore:

$$dX(t)/dt \Rightarrow j\omega A_x \tag{3.9}$$

Reason #5. Integrating a sinusoid in time domain corresponds to dividing the phasor by $j\omega$ with the use of (3.9) as follows:

$$Y(t)=\int X(t)dt +Y_0$$
$$\Rightarrow X(t)= dY(t)/dt \Rightarrow A_x= j\omega A_Y \tag{3.10}$$
Therefore:
$$A_Y=(1/\ j\omega)A_x \tag{3.11}$$

Where A_x and A_Y are the phasors for $X(t)$ and $Y(t)$, respectively.

EXAMPLE 3.1
Determine the total sinusoidal function, X(t), when it is given by:
$$X(t)=20\ cos(10t-30°)+40cos(10t+60°)$$
Solution:
$$A=20e^{-j30°}+40e^{j60°}=20(cos30°-jsin30°)+40(cos60°+jsin60°)$$
$$A=38.3+j24.6=44.8e^{j33°}$$
Once the sum phasor (A) is known, the corresponding sum sinusoid in the time domain [X(t)] can easily be found by the inverse transform:
$$X(t)=Re[Aej^{10t}]=44.8cos(10t+33°)$$

3.6 THE GENERALIZED OHM'S LAW
When dealing with linear circuits under the influence of time harmonic signals under the steady-state condition, Ohm's law is modified to include the storage elements (L, C). The result is called the generalized Ohm's law, which is useful in the phasor domain defined as follows:

Generalized Ohm's Law-*The phasor voltage drop (V) across any lumped linear element is equal to the element's impedance (Z) multiplied by the phasor current (I) through the element, i.e.*

V= Z.I $\qquad\qquad$ (3.12)

Where in general **Z= R +j(ωL-1/ωC)**.

PROPERTY NAME	TIME DOMAIN	FREQUENCY DOMAIN
Voltage	v(t)	V(ω)
Current	i(t)	I(ω)
Capacitor	i(t)=C dv(t)/dt	I=jωCV
Inductor	v(t)=L di(t)/dt	V=jωLI
Ohm's law	v(t)=Ri(t)	V=RI
Generalized Ohm's Law	$v(t)= Ri + 1/C\int_0^t idt + Ldi/dt$	V(ω)=Z(ω)I(ω), Z=R+j(ωL-1/ωC)
KCL	$\sum_{n=1}^{N} i_n(t) = 0$	$\sum_{n=1}^{N} I_n(\omega) = 0$
KVL	$\sum_{m=1}^{M} v_m(t) = 0$	$\sum_{m=1}^{M} V_m(\omega) = 0$

Table 3.1 Summary of time and frequency domain relationships.

3.7 FUNDAMENTAL CIRCUIT THEOREMS

There are several fundamental circuit theorems that need to be considered in order to simplify circuit analysis and design. These are Thevenin's, Norton's, and Superposition theorems.

By definition, theorems are mathematical statements of identity, which can be proven rigorously. Therefore the use of these theorems facilitates the solution to circuit problems by presenting an equivalent statement of the truth, which is simpler and more workable.

Since all of these theorems apply only to linear networks, it behooves us well to define this term at the outset of this section.

DEFINITION-A LINEAR NETWORK: *Is defined to be a network in which the parameters of resistance, inductance and capacitance of the lumped elements are constant with respect to current or voltage, and in which the voltage or current sources are independent of or directly proportional to other voltages and currents or their derivatives, in the network.*

Furthermore, we need to note that all of these theorems allow calculation of the performance of a network from only its terminal properties without ever being concerned about what happens inside the network.

With this preamble we are ready to embark upon the description of the three main theorems:

3.7.1 Thevenin's Theorem

This theorem is also known as Helmholtz's theorem. Consider Figure 3.4 where the current (I_L) in the load (Z_L) are desired to be determined.

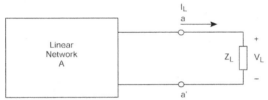

FIGURE 3.4 Linear network connected to a load.

Thevenin's theorem states that:

At any given frequency, the current (I_L) that will flow through a load impedance (Z_L) when connected to any two terminals of a linear network is equal to the open-circuit voltage (V_{oc} or V_T), with the load (Z_L) removed, and divided by the sum of the load impedance and the impedance (Z_T) obtained by looking back from the open terminals into the network with all independent sources reduced to zero (i.e. replacing each independent source by its internal impedance) as shown in Figure 3.5.

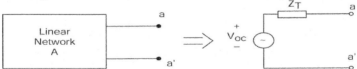

FIGURE 3.5 A linear network's equivalent circuit.

This valuable theorem in solving network problems allows calculation of the performance of a network (or device) from its terminal properties only. Thus according to this theorem, the linear network [A] simplifies into the following circuit as shown in Figure 3.6.

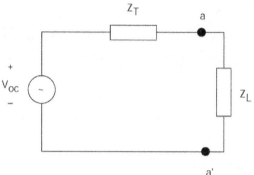

FIGURE 3.6 Thevenin's equivalent circuit.

Connecting the load back to the Thevenin's equivalent, the current through the load can easily be found to be:

$$I_L = \frac{V_{OC}}{Z_T + Z_L} \tag{3.13}$$

3.7.2 Norton's Theorem

Norton's theorem is the dual of Thevenin's theorem and states that:

The voltage across a load element (Z_L) that is connected to the two terminals of a linear network is equal to the short-circuit current (I_{sc}) between these terminals in the absence of the load element divided by the sum of the load admittance(Y_L) and the admittance (Y_T) of the network when looking back into these terminals while setting all independent sources to zero (as shown in Figures 3.8 and 3.9).

By observation: $Y_T = \dfrac{1}{Z_T}$

NOTE: *Norton's theorem results from a more general principle, i.e., the duality principle that is based on the duality theorem discussed next.*

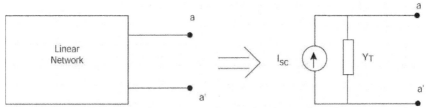

FIGURE 3.8 Norton's equivalent circuit.

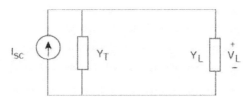

FIGURE 3.9 Norton's equivalent circuit connected to a load.

3.7.3 Duality Theorem

Duality Theorem *states that when a theorem (or statement) is true, it will remain true if each quantity and operation is replaced by its dual quantity and operation. In circuit theory, The dual quantities are "voltage and current", "impedance and admittance" and the dual operations are "series and parallel" and "meshes and nodes."*

Using the duality principle and the fact that a Thevenin's equivalent and its corresponding Norton's equivalent are representing the same network, the terminal voltages for Norton's and Thevenin's theorem must be the same; Thus we obtain:

$$V_T = Z_T . I_{sc} \qquad\qquad (3.14)$$

In actuality we can observe that the duality principle is based upon a much more fundamental truth, which in essence states that for every datum or concept, there must be another one of comparable magnitude. In other words a datum can not exist all by itself (i.e., an absolute), as stated by the non-absoluteness axiom.

For example, for positive charge there is negative charge, for KVL there is KCL, for Thevenin's Theorem there is Norton's Theorem, etc. A summary of dual quantities in electrical engineering is presented in table 3.2.

Quantity or Operation	*Dual Quantity or Operation*
Electron	Hole
Current	Voltage
KCL	KVL
Node	Mesh
Inductor	Capacitor
Parallel elements	Series elements
Current source	Voltage source
Norton's Theorem	Thevenin's Theorem

Table 3.2 Dual quantities in electric circuits.

In a broader arena of electromagnetics, we can see that numerous quantities, laws, and theorems in the field of electricity have duals in magnetism. These are briefly listed in table 3.3.

Quantity, Law or Theorem	*Dual Quantity, Law or Theorem*
Electric charge	Magnetic pole
Electric Field	Magnetic Field
Electrostatics	Magnetostatics
Permittivity	Permeability
Electric current	Magnetic flux
Electromotive force (emf)	Magnetomotive force (mmf)
Resistance	Reluctance
Scalar Potential Function	Vector potential function
Electric Ohm's law	Magnetic Ohm's law
Electric Kirchhoff's law	Magnetic Kirchhoff's law
Electric Coulomb's law	Magnetic Coulomb's law
Scalar Poisson's Eq.	Vector Poisson's Eq.
Electric gauss's law	Magnetic gauss's law
Faraday's law	Ampere's law

Table 3.3 Dual laws and theorems in electricity.

EXAMPLE 3.2

Given the following circuit (as shown in Figure 3.10):

a) Find the voltage across the load (Z_L) using Norton's theorem,
b) Find the Thevinin's equivalent

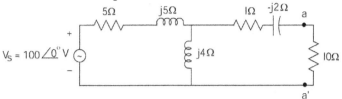

Figure 3.10 Circuit for example 3.2.

Solution:

a) To find the load voltage and the Norton's equivalent, we do the following steps:

STEP 1. Disconnect the load and find $Y_T=1/Z_T$ by shorting the voltage source.

let:

$Z_1=5+j5$, $Z_2=j4$, $Z_3=1-j2$.

Thus Z_T is given by:

$Z_T=Z_3+(Z_1||Z_2)=(93+j34)/53=1.85+j0.64 \ \Omega$

STEP 2. We now find I_{sc} by shorting the terminal a-a' as shown in Figure 3.11:

$I=V_s/(Z_1+Z_2||Z_3)$

$I_{sc}=[(Z_2/(Z_2+Z_3)] \ I =20.5 + j3.24$ A

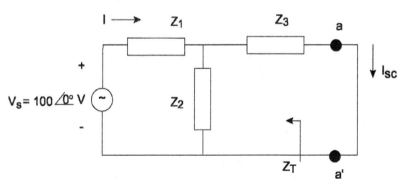

FIGURE 3.11 Circuit for step 2 of solution.

STEP 3. The Norton equivalent is as shown in Figure 3.12. The current through the load is found by using current division rule:

$$I_L = I_{SC} \frac{Z_T}{Z_T + Z_L}$$

I_L= (1.85+j0.64)x(20.5+j3.24)/(11.85+j0.64)=3.28∠26° A

V_L=10 I_L= 32.8∠26° V

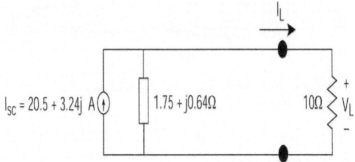

FIGURE 3.12 Circuit for step 3 of solution.

STEP 4. Using the Duality principle, we obtain:

V_{OC}=$Z_T I_{SC}$ = (1.85+j0.64)(20.5+j3.24)= 1.86 ∠20° x 20.85 ∠9°
=38.6 ∠29°

The Thevenin's Equivalent is shown in Figure 3.13.

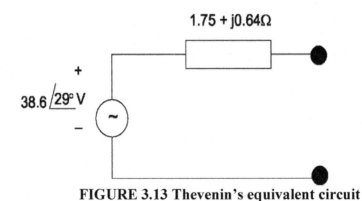

FIGURE 3.13 Thevenin's equivalent circuit

EXAMPLE 3.3
Given the circuit shown in Figure 3.14, find its corresponding dual.

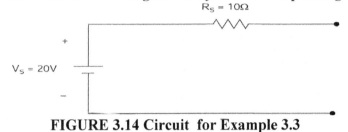

FIGURE 3.14 Circuit for Example 3.3

Solution:
We know that the dual quantities are:
Voltage ↔ current
Series ↔ parallel

Thus the voltage source is transformed into a current source (I_p) connected in parallel with a resistor R_p as shown 3.15.

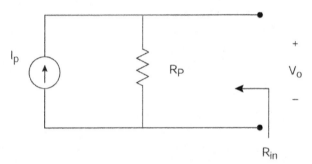

FIGURE 3.15 The corresponding dual circuit.

In order to have equivalent performance, the output voltage (V_o) must be equal to $V_s=20V$ and the input impedance equal to $R_s=10\ \Omega$.

Thus we have:
$R_p=R_s=10$
$V_s=I_p R_p=20 \Rightarrow I_p=2$ A
The final circuit is shown in Figure 3.16.

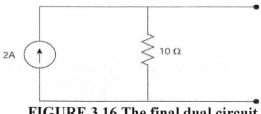

FIGURE 3.16 The final dual circuit.

3.7.4 The Superposition Theorem

Superposition applies to a situation where multiple causes (or independent sources) create one combined response at the output. With the help of this theorem, one can take apart this complicated response into its smaller components, which are easy to calculate.

This theorem states that:
In a linear network, the voltage or current in any element resulting from several sources acting together is the sum of the voltages or currents resulting from each source acting alone, while all other independent sources are set to zero, i.e.:

$$f(v_1+v_2+\ldots\ldots\ldots+v_n) = f(v_1)+f(v_2)+\ldots\ldots\ldots+f(v_n) \quad (3.15)$$

EXAMPLE 3.4
Find the current (I) in the 6Ω resistor as shown in Figure 3.17.

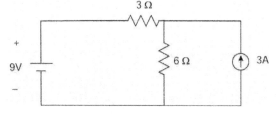

FIGURE 3.17 Circuit for Example 3.4.

Solution:
STEP 1. First set the current source to zero as shown in Figure 3.18.
$I_1=9/9=1$ A

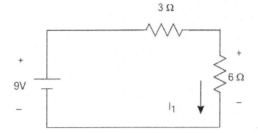

FIGURE 3.18 Circuit for step 1.

STEP 2. Set the voltage source to zero as shown in Figure 3.19.
$I_2=3\times3/9=1$ A

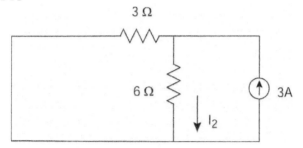

FIGURE 3.19 Circuit for step 2.

STEP 3. Thus the total current (I) is given by:
$I=I_1+I_2=2$ A

NOTE: *All of these three theorems apply equally to time domain as well as the phasor domain (problems and solutions), as long as the network remains linear.*

3.7.5 Miller's Theorem

As will be seen in the next chapter, at higher frequencies there are transistor circuits where a passive element (usually a capacitor) bridges the output to the input by appearing in the feedback path. Such a feedback complicates the circuit analysis at such high frequencies as shown in Figure 3.20.

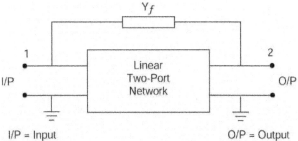

I/P = Input   O/P = Output
FIGURE 3.20 A linear two-port network with feedback.

There is a circuit theorem that replaces such a bridging element (Y_f) with two grounded elements. This replacement greatly simplifies circuit analysis, but more importantly it shows the effect of the bridging parasitic elements on the frequency response of a circuit at high frequencies.

Consider a linear two-port network (as shown in Figure 3.20) where the feedback (or the bridging) element with admittance (Y_f) is connected from the output to the input. The overall voltage gain ($v_0/v_i=K$) is expected to be known already through independent means.

With this assumption in mind, **Miller's Theorem** states that:
The feedback element can be equivalently replaced by two admittances, Y_i and Y_o, as follows:

a. Y_i between input node (1) and ground having a value of
$Y_i = Y_f(1-K)$ (3.16)

b. Y_o between output node (2) and ground with a value of

$$Y_o = Y_f\left(1-\frac{1}{K}\right)$$ (3.17)

The equivalent circuit is shown in Figure 3.21.

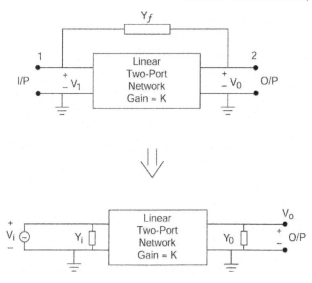

FIGURE 3.21 Miller's Theorem.

This theorem, in essence, shows the affect of the deterioration of the effective input impedance caused by the presence of a feedback from the output port to the input port of a linear network.

POINTS OF CAUTION:
1. *Miller's theorem assumes that the voltage gain (K) can be determined by independent means beforehand.*

2. *The Miller's equivalent circuit (see Figure 3.21) is valid as long as none of the conditions that existed in the original network (when K was determined) are changed. Therefore Miller's theorem can only be used in the input impedance calculations of the network when the voltage gain is known. This means that this theorem cannot be used to calculate the output impedance since doing so requires that the input source be eliminated and be replaced with a source at the output terminals. Such an action would change the value of K in general, thus making the Miller's equivalent circuit invalid.*

EXAMPLE 3.5
A broadband amplifier has an input impedance of $R_{in}=100\ k\Omega$ at low frequencies. Calculate the total input impedance at a higher

frequency of f=1 MHz. The feedback capacitor' value is C=1 pF and the overall gain is measured to be:
K= -100 at f=1 MHz (see Figure 3.22).

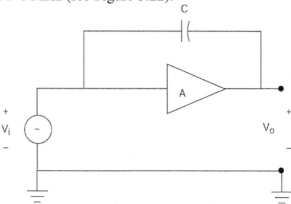

FIGURE 3.22 The amplifier circuit.

Solution:
The miller's equivalent circuit is shown in Figure 3.23 where:
$C_i=[1-(-100)]C=101$ pF
$C_o=(1-(-1/100)]C=1.01$ pF

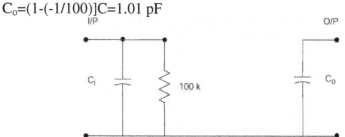

FIGURE 3.23 Miller's equivalent circuit for Example 3.5.

This indicates that the feedback capacitor appearing at the input is multiplied more than 100 times (known as Miller's effect) with a reactance of :
$jX_C=1/(j2\pi x10^6x101x10^{-12})= -j1.58$ KΩ
Therefore the overall input impedance is substantially reduced from its original value since:
$Z_{in} = 100k||-j1.58= 0.025-j1.55$ KΩ
This substantial reduction in the input impedance is equivalent to "shorting out the input" which leads to tremendous deterioration of the high frequency performance of the amplifier.

3.8 RELATIONSHIP OF CIRCUIT THEOREMS TO CIRCUIT LAWS

A summary of all of the four theorems discussed so far is depicted in Figure 3.24 which shows that by applying KCL, KVL and generalized Ohm's law we can analyze a circuit and predict its behavior under different signal conditions.

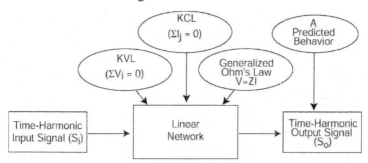

FIGURE 3.24 Low frequency circuit analysis.

For a linear network, we can first simplify the circuit and obtain an equivalent circuit by applying one or more of the above four theorems (i.e. Thevenin's, Norton's, superposition or Miller's theorems) and then proceed to use KCL, KVL and generalized Ohm's law to obtain the desired output signal as shown in Figure 3.25.

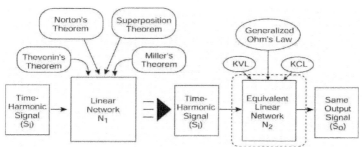

FIGURE 3.25 Relationship of theorems to actual circuit analysis.

CHAPTER-3 PROBLEMS

3.1) Define a phasor and describe what its applications are?

3.2) What are the reasons for using phasors? Describe each reason.

3.3) Determine the phasors that represent the following real-valued time functions:
   a) $A(t)=10\cos(2t+30°)+5\sin2t$
   b) $B(t)=\sin(3t-90°)+10\sin(3t+45°)$
   c) $C(t)=\cos(t)+\cos(t+30°)-\cos(t+60°)$

3.4) Find the steady state voltage, v(t), represented by the phasor:
   a) $V=10\angle-140°$ volts
   b) $V=80+j75$ volts

3.5) Express the following summations into one single sinusoid,(i.e. $a\cos\omega t$):
   a) $A(t)=2\cos(6t+120°)+4\sin(6t-60°)$
   b) $B(t)=5\cos8t+10\sin(8t+45°)$
   c) $C(t)=2\cos(2t+60°)-4\sin2t+d/dt(2\sin2t)$

3.6) A current in an element is $2\cos100t$. Find the steady state voltage v(t) across the element if the element is:
   a) A resistor: $R=20\Omega$
   b) An inductor: $L=20$ mH
   c) A capacitor: $C=20$ mF

3.7) Find the input impedance and admittance at terminals a-b. For the circuit shown in Figure P3.7 where $\omega=100$ rad/s.

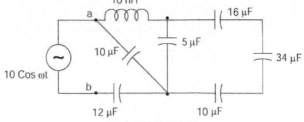

FIGURE P3.7.

3.8) Find the steady-State voltage(v) when $Is=20\cos\omega t$, $\omega=1000$ rad/s for the circuit shown in Figure P3.8.

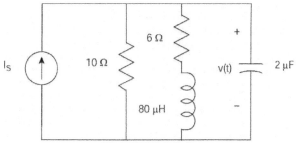

FIGURE P3.8.

3.9) Find the steady-state current, i(t), when $V_S=10\cos 3t$ Volt for the circuit shown in Figure P3.9.

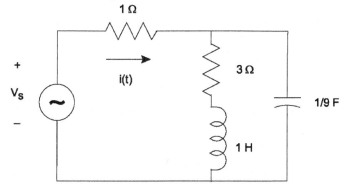

FIGURE P3.9.

3.10) In the circuit shown below, determine the voltage across the inductor, $V_L(t)$, when $V_{S1}=20\cos\omega t$, $V_{S2}=30\cos(\omega t-90°)$ and $\omega=1000$ rad/s.

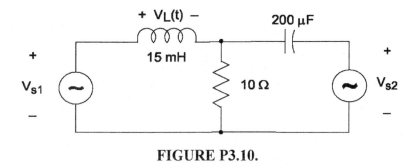

FIGURE P3.10.

3.11) Find the current through the load ($Z_L=8-j4$ Ω) in which $I_1=V_{OC}/10$, where V_{OC} is the voltage across the output terminals(ab)for a disconnected load (see Figure P3.11). Determine I_L using a) the Thevenin's theorem b) the Norton's theorem.

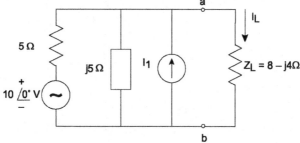

FIGURE P3.11.

3.12) Using superposition theorem determine i(t) in the circuit shown in Figure P3.12 when $V_S(t)=10\cos10t$.

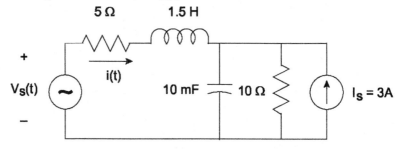

FIGURE P3.12.

3.13) Calculate the power ratios for the following decibel values:

a)5
b)25
c)50
d)75

3.14) The input signal to a three-stage system is -35dBm. The first stage has a gain of 28 dB, the second stage has a loss of 3 dB and the third stage has a gain of 7 dB. What is the power output at each stage in milliWatt?

3.15) Find the rms value of the voltage (v) for:

a) v=2 - 4cos2t V
b) v=3sinπt+2cosπt V
c) v =2cos2t +4cos(2t+π/4)+12sin2t V

3.16) Find the instantaneous power, the average power and the complex power for the circuit shown in Figure P3.16 ($V_S=10Cos2\pi x10^9t$ Volts).

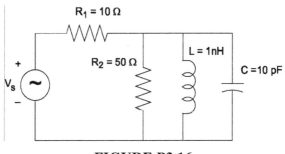

FIGURE P3.16

CHAPTER 4

The Laws of Electromagnetics

4.1 INTRODUCTION

In this chapter we will lay the groundwork for basic mathematical concepts including phasors, basic circuit elements, Ohm's law, Kirchhoff's voltage and current laws, basic network theorems and the decibel scale. The main purpose of presenting these concepts is to aid the reader in better comprehension of the ensuing materials and enhance the analysis and design of electronic circuits, which will be the main focus of this work.

4.2 THE FIELD OF ELECTRONICS

Electronics is a subset of science of physics and needs to be defined at this juncture:

DEFINITION-ELECTRONICS: *is the field of science and engineering concerned with the behavior of electrons (or lack thereof) in devices and the utilization of such devices.*

With this definition in mind we can see that electronics is, in essence, a field of science that deals with the study, control and conduction (through different media e.g. semiconductors, conductors, insulators, gases, vacuum, etc.) of electricity which is electrical energy in the form of electrons.

Knowing this definition and the above preamble on the basics of the physical universe, we need to know what the essential facts of the subject of electronics are in order to understand and deal with it correctly.

One needs to be thoroughly familiar with several fundamental concepts of the subject of electronics before one has gone very far in this field of study. These can be briefly summarized as follows:

A. Fundamental Concept #1- Electric charge: The basic building block of electrical energy is electric charge (in motion or not).

B. Fundamental Concept #2- Byproducts of charge: Dealing with electric charge, one needs to be familiarized thoroughly with all of its different phenomena, byproducts and ramifications that it creates. These different aspects of existence of charge could be summed up as:

Byproducts of charge (e.g., electrons, protons, etc.)
  1. Byproduct #1: generation of forces and fields
      1a. Electric force
          Electric field
      1b. Electric current
          Magnetic force
          Magnetic field

  2. Byproduct #2: Performing work
      2a. Work
      2b. Voltage or electrical potential difference- Defined as Work per unit charge.
      2c. Power- Defined as work per unit time.

  3. Byproduct #3: Transfer of electrical energy
      3a.   RF Waves
      3b.   Optical Waves
      3c.   Cosmic Rays (e.g. Gamma Rays, X-Rays, etc.)

C. Fundamental Concept #3- Electrical energy: The field of Electronics deals with electrical energy that is either:

a. *In the form of charge, which is either flowing (current) or is being stored (voltage)in various devices, transmission lines, elements, etc.,* or,

b. *In the form of one of the byproducts of charge, such as electric field, magnetic field, electromagnetic waves, etc.*

All of the electrical and/or magnetic laws on a classical level of observation deal with the flow or storage effect of charge or its byproducts under idealized conditions. This is a sweepingly general statement that applies to all known natural laws in the field of electrical engineering. Thus to sum, our primary target in this text is the study of electrical energy flow (or lack thereof) through a region of space created by a device, a transmission line, an element, etc.

D. Fundamental Concept #4- Mathematical models: The use of exact mathematics to describe various forms of electric energy and its related laws and equivalent theorems greatly simplifies the analysis of idealized problems and assists the engineering design process.

The utilization of exact mathematical models (under ideal conditions) to describe processes and flows in this finite, non-ideal and imprecise physical universe, can only be justified by noting that the mathematical answers obtained should never be interpreted as the exact numerical values that one is going to encounter in measurements in the real world but only the best approximation that one is hoping for.

These concepts exist regardless of the type or form or the degree of sophistication of mathematics involved. The building blocks of any subject are the "fundamental concepts," with mathematics serving only as an aid in expressing various concepts, problems and solutions in shorthand notation. Therefore this book is written in such a way that concepts are the primary focus, with the mathematics only as a servomechanism (or an aid or crutch) in arriving at or expressing the final answer in short-hand notation.

The concept of charge leads to all other phenomena and fields of study as shown in Figure 4.1. From this diagram several concepts need to be expanded in further depth since they are essential to the understanding of the whole field of electronics.

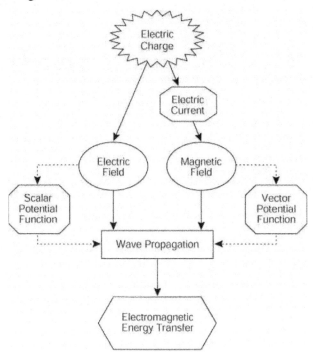

FIGURE 4.1 Diagram showing the electric charge as the cause of all electric and magnetic Phenomena.

4.3 THE GOVERNING LAWS OF ELECTRICAL ENGINEERING

There are certain laws that the electrical energy follows. To discover these laws, great minds have been at work for centuries. Therefore these laws represent the cumulative knowledge of mankind about electricity, electric charge flow and magnetism and should not be regard lightly.

One point of interest should be brought forth at this time and that is these laws have been cast into a mathematical format to ease their communication, simplification and manipulation, and by themselves they represent a theoretical and an ideal yardstick—an absolute!

Since absolutes are unobtainable, one should only expect an approximate correlation between the actual measurements and the ideal answers that these laws provide.

Some of the most important laws, which are needed greatly in comprehending electrical engineering, are presented in a chart form as shown in Figure 4.2.

From this chart we can see that the primary principles and laws of electronics in the order of importance are as follows:

I. Principle of Conservation of Energy

II. Primary laws : Maxwell's Equations
    a. Ampere's law
    b. Faraday's law
    c. Electric Gauss's law
    d. Magnetic Gauss's law

III. Secondary laws and equations:
    a. Scalar Poisson's and Laplace's equations
    b. Vector Poisson's equation
    c. General wave equations
    d. Transmission line and waveguide equations.
    e. Helmholtz's equations
    f. Electric and magnetic Coulomb's laws
    g. Electric and magnetic Ohm's laws
    h. Electric and magnetic Kirchhoff's laws

Even though these laws will be discussed throughout this book on a "need to know" basis, a certain amount of familiarity are assumed to exist in the reader's mind, which would facilitate the comprehension of this book to a greater degree.

Before we discuss these laws and equations in the next several sections, it is imperative that we understand the basic underlying assumption that is being held in common back of any area of study. That commonality, of course, is the principle of conservation of energy which deserves to be precisely defined at this early stage with all of its main features and frailties fully delineated.

4.4 PRINCIPLE OF CONSERVATION OF ENERGY

This principle is one of the most fundamental axioms in all of sciences, which needs special attention and must be considered and defined precisely at this point:

Principle of conservation of energy (excluding all metaphysical sources and causes of energy): *This fundamental law simply states that any form of energy in the physical universe, can neither be created nor destroyed but only converted into another form of energy.*

In simple terms, we can say that in the physical universe "energy comes from somewhere and goes somewhere"; which means that in order to have energy, in a particular form and for a certain task, one needs to use another form of energy (or matter) and convert it into the desired form first and then use it to perform the required task.

For example to light up a room by means of a flashlight, we need optical energy. To obtain this form of energy (i.e., optical), we use electrical energy. Now, to obtain electrical energy, we need to use a battery to convert chemical energy into electrical energy which then can be used in a flashlight to produce light.

Thus any form of energy in the physical universe can only be obtained from the conversion of another source into the desired form of energy. This law could also be called the Principle of "immortality of energy." All of the laws of electricity have this principle in common as shown in Figure 4.2.

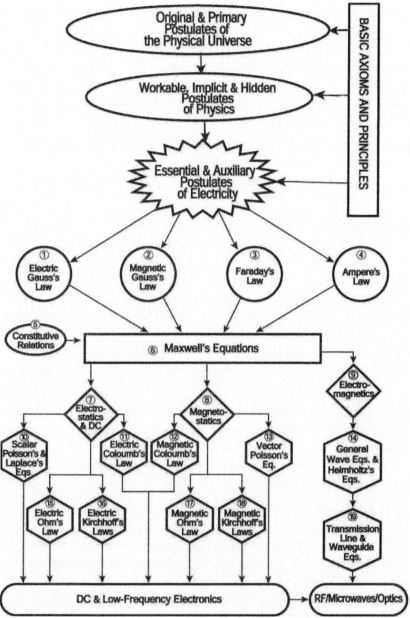

FIGURE 4.2 All Fundamental principles and laws of electricity and its magnetic dual.

There is another closely related principle and that is the principle of **"conservation of matter"** which follows the principle of conservation of energy through the Einstein's relation: $E=mc^2$. This relation states that mass is equivalent to energy through a proportionality constant of $"c^2."$ The law of conservation of mass can be seen to be a corollary to the law of conservation of energy, since matter is a condensed form of energy.

OBSERVATION: *It is interesting to observe that the any and all physical laws are built on the principle of conservation of energy and all express the fact that one form of energy is equivalent to another form of it.*

For example let us examine ohm's law (V=RI). This law simply states that voltage (V) across a resistor (as one form of energy, i.e., potential energy) is equivalent to current (I) as another form energy (kinetic energy), through a proportionality factor called resistance (R). Another example is the Faraday's law. Through simple observation of this law, we can conclude that it is merely stating a basic energy conversion fact, i.e., electrical energy in the form of electric field (E) equals another in the form of magnetic energy (H), through the use of spatial and time operators.

Of course, this approach may be to some extent an oversimplification of the physical laws, however, it is helpful in that it increases their comprehension as a whole and creates a more comfortable frame of mind toward them, where one is no longer overwhelmed by either their theoretical description or their mathematical complexity.

POINT OF CAUTION: *The principle of conservation of energy is a basic postulate that has been uniformly adopted as an underlying fundamental for all physical sciences practiced today. However, it should be noted that the principle of conservation of energy applies only to an existing form of energy and can predict its future form or magnitude. It makes no determination or prediction about the origin of energy, its initial source or how it comes about in the first place. It only discusses what happens to it once it exists in the physical universe. In this regard, this fact could be a limiting factor and a major shortcoming, built into all of our extant physical sciences.*

4.5 PRIMARY LAWS: THE MAXWELL'S EQUATIONS

Maxwell's equations are a series of four advanced classical equations developed by James Clerk Maxwell between 1864 and 1873, which describe the behavior of electromagnetic fields and waves in all practical situations. They relate the vector quantities for electric and magnetic fields as well as electric charges existing (at any point or in a volume), and set forth stringent requirements, which the fields must satisfy.

From these equations, Maxwell predicted the existence of electromagnetic waves whose later discovery made radio possible.
Maxwell showed that where a varying electric field exists, it is accompanied by a varying magnetic field induced at right angles, and vice versa, and the two form an electromagnetic field that could propagate as a transverse wave. He calculated that in a vacuum, the speed of the wave was given by $1/\sqrt{(\varepsilon_0\mu_0)}$, where ε_0 and μ_0 are the permittivity and permeability of vacuum, respectively. The calculated value for this speed was in remarkable agreement with the measured speed of light, and thus he concluded that light is propagated as an electromagnetic wave.

4.5.1 Primary Law #1: Ampere's Law

AMPERE'S LAW – *Current flowing in a wire generates a magnetic flux that encircles the wire in a clockwise direction when the current is moving away from the observer. Mathematically, we can write:*

Differential Form: $\nabla \times \overline{H} = \overline{J} + \dfrac{\partial \overline{D}}{\partial t}$,   (4.1a)

Integral form: $\displaystyle\oint_C \overline{H} \cdot \overline{d\ell} = I + \int_s \dfrac{\partial \overline{D}}{\partial t} \cdot \overline{dS}$ (4.1b)

Where H, D, J and I are "the magnetic field intensity vector," "Electric filed displacement vector," "the current density vector," and "the total current" respectively.

Note: CURL OPERATION ($\nabla \times$F or CurlF)

Curl is an operation on a vector field (F), which creates another vector whose magnitude measures the maximum net circulation per unit area of the vector field at any given point and has a direction perpendicular to the area, as the area size tends toward zero. The cause of the curl of a vector field is a vortex source. For example electric current is the vortex source for magnetic field.

4.5.2 Primary Law #2: Faraday's Law

FARADAY'S LAW – *When a changing magnetic field exists, such as when a magnetic field cuts a conductor or when a conductor cuts a magnetic field, then a circulating electric field is created in such a way as to oppose the original cause (i.e., the magnetic field). Mathematically, we can write:*

Differential Form: $\nabla \times \overline{\mathbf{E}} = \dfrac{-\partial \overline{\mathbf{B}}}{\partial \mathbf{t}}$,   (4.2a)

Integral form: $\oint_C \overline{\mathbf{E}} \cdot \overline{\mathbf{d\ell}} = -\int_S \dfrac{\partial \overline{\mathbf{B}}}{\partial \mathbf{t}} \cdot \overline{\mathbf{dS}} = -\dfrac{\mathbf{d\Phi}}{\mathbf{dt}}$ (4.2b)

Where B, E are "the magnetic flux density vector," and "the Electric filed intensity vector," respectively. B and E are related to D and H (in a homogeneous and linear material) through the constituve relations given by:

$\overline{\mathbf{D}} = \varepsilon \overline{\mathbf{E}},$

$\overline{\mathbf{B}} = \mu \overline{\mathbf{H}}$

Where ε and μ are the permittivity and permeability constants of the dielectric material surrounding the fields, respectively.

The symbol Φ is "the total magnetic flux" and is given by:

$$\Phi = \int_S \overline{B} \cdot \overline{dS}$$

Symbols C and S are the closed path of travel and the corresponding surface for the integration process, respectively.

Note: *The existence of the electric field can cause an electrical current to flow through a conductor if a closed path is provided over which the current can circulate.*

4.5.3 Primary Law #3: Gauss's Law (Electric)

We can define this law as:

GAUSS'S LAW (ELECTRIC) – *The summation of the normal component of the electrical displacement vector over any closed surface is equal to the electric charge within the surface, which in essence means that the source of the electric flux lines is the electric charge. Mathematically, we can write:*

Differential Form: $\nabla \cdot \overline{D} = \rho$,   (4.3a)

Integral form: $\oint_S \overline{D} \cdot \overline{dS} = \int_V \rho dv = Q$ (4.3b)

Where *ρ and Q are the volume charge density and the total charge enclosed within a volume (v) enclosed by surface (s), respectively.*

ALTERNATE DEFINITION: *Electric Gauss's law states that the total electric field (E) emanating from any closed hypothetical surface [called a Gaussian surface (S)] equals the net amount of electrostatic localized charge (Q) enclosed by the surface divided by permittivity (ε), i.e.,*

$$\varepsilon \oint_S \overline{E} \cdot \overline{dS} = Q$$ (4.4)

Where ε is the permittivity constant of the dielectric material surrounding the charge.

Or, if the charge is distributed in a region of space with a volume charge distribution density of $\rho(x,y,z)$, then we can write:

$$\varepsilon \oint_S \overline{E} \cdot \overline{dS} = \int_V \rho(x,y,z)dV$$ (4.5)

Where V is the volume created by the closed Gaussian surface (S).

NOTE: Coulomb's law of interaction (preceding Gauss's law historically) expresses an inverse square relationship between point electrostatic charges but can be deduced as a special case of Gauss's law.

Note: DIVERGENCE OPERATION ($\nabla \cdot$F or **DivF**)

Divergence (of a vector field, F) is a scalar, which represents the net outflux per unit volume at any given point in a vector field, as the volume size shrinks to zero [symbolized by divF). The cause of the divergence of a vector field is called a flow source. For example, positive electric charge is the flow source for the electric field and creates a net outflux of E-field per unit volume at any given point.

4.5.4 Primary Law #4: Gauss's Law (Magnetic)

GAUSS'S LAW (MAGNETIC) - *The summation of the normal component of the magnetic flux density vector over any closed surface is equal to zero, which in essence means that the magnetic flux lines have no source or origin.*

Differential Form: $\nabla \cdot \overline{B} = 0$,   (4.6)

Integral form: $\oint_S \overline{B} \cdot \overline{dS} = 0$ (4.7)

ALTERNATE DEFINITION: *Magnetic Gauss's law states that the net magnetic flux (Φ) through any closed Gaussian surface (S) is always zero.*

It expresses the fact that "isolated" or "free" magnetic poles have not been found, which is to say that the lines of magnetic flux have no beginning or end, i.e.,

$$\Phi = \oint_S \overline{B} \cdot \overline{dS} = 0$$ (4.8)

where $\overline{B}$ is the Magnetic flux density vector.

NOTE: GRADIENT OPERATION (∇f or Gradf)

Gradient (of a scalar function) is a vector, which lies in the direction of maximum rate of increase of the function at any given point and therefore is normal to the constant-value surfaces. Mathematically, it is a vector obtained from a real function f(x,y,z), whose components are the partial derivatives of f(x,y,z), given in the Cartesian coordinate system as:

$Gradf=(\partial f/\partial x, \partial f/\partial y, \partial f/\partial z),$ (4.9a)

Or,

$$\nabla f = \frac{\partial f}{\partial x}\hat{x}+\frac{\partial f}{\partial y}\hat{y}+\frac{\partial f}{\partial z}\hat{z} \qquad (4.9b)$$

In other coordinate systems (e.g. cylindrical or spherical), the mathematical expression as given in equation 4.9, would change accordingly.

4.6 SECONDARY LAWS AND EQUATIONS

There are secondary laws and equations which can be summarized as follows:

    a. Electric and magnetic Coulomb's laws
    b. Electric and magnetic Ohm's laws
    c. Electric and magnetic Kirchhoff's laws
    d. Scalar Poisson's and Laplace's equations
    e. Vector Poisson's equation
    f. General wave equations
    g. Transmission line and waveguide equations.
    h. Helmholtz's equations

These are described in the next several sections.

4.7 SUBFIELDS OF ELECTRICITY

Using Maxwell equations, we can observe that the field of electrical engineering can be roughly subdivided into three distinct fields of study:

a. Electrostatics & DC,
b. Magnetostatics, and
c. Electromagnetics.

These three areas are shown in Figure, 2.14 and are briefly described below.

4.8 ELECTROSTATICS & DC

The field of electrostatics is a subset of the Maxwell's equations. To be specific, we define this field as:

DEFINITION – DC (DIRECT CURRENT): *A constant current, which always flows in one direction.*

DEFINITION- ELECTROSTATICS: *is that branch of electricity concerned with electrical charges at rest and their corresponding byproducts and effects such as electric fields, potential function, etc. Such a stationary distribution of charge produces a static electric field. An example of such a case would be the fields associated with a fully charged capacitor at steady state.*

POINT OF CAUTION: *It should be noted that such an assumption of stationary distribution of charge is only possible at a classical level of observation (i.e., macroscopic or large-scale level relative to atomic dimensions) and can never be used at the quantum level of observation, where every charged particle is in constant motion due to presence of several factors, such as thermal energy, Coulombic forces, potential energy distribution in the material, etc.*

In this field of study we find many of the commonly used laws which are referred to in many popular texts. The Maxwell's Equations simplify into:

$$\nabla \times \overline{E} = 0$$
$$\nabla \cdot \overline{D} = \rho$$
$$\overline{E} = -\nabla V \quad\quad (4.9c)$$
$$\overline{F} = q\overline{E}$$

where V is the scalar potential function.

For application purposes, these set of four equations would lead to several important concepts and laws as follows:

4.8.1 Electric Coulomb's Law

Electric Coulomb's Law states that the electric forces of two electrified point charges (Q_1 and Q_2), being either repulsion or attractive forces, are proportional directly to the magnitudes of the charges and inversely to the square of the distance (d) between the two, that is,

$$\overline{F} = (\frac{Q_1 Q_2}{4\pi\varepsilon R_{12}^2})\hat{a}_{R12} \quad\quad (4.10a)$$

Or, in terms of differential field quantity (dE) caused by a differential charge (dQ), we can write Electric Coulomb's Law as:

$$\overline{dE} = (\frac{dQ}{4\pi\varepsilon R^2})\hat{a}_R \qquad\qquad (4.10b)$$

Where $\varepsilon = \varepsilon_0\varepsilon_r$ is the permittivity, ε_r the relative permittivity (also known as relative dielectric constant or simply dielectric constant) and ε_0 is the permittivity of free space given by:

$$\varepsilon_0 = 8.854 \times 10^{-12} \, F/m \approx (1/36\pi) \times 10^{-9} \, F/m. \qquad (4.10c)$$

Coulomb noted the similarity of his discoveries to that of Newton's law of gravitation involving also an inverse square-of-distance, and action at a distance type of force.

NOTE: This law has embedded within it the "Newton's law of action and reaction" (also called Newton's law of interaction). In simple terms, it means that if there is a force of magnitude (F) exerted on charged body (A) due to charged body (B) (called the action force), then there is an equal and opposite force (-F) on the charged body (B) due to the charged body (A) (called the reaction force).

Furthermore, Newton's law of action and reaction establishes the " two-way communication nature" of the physical universe, which says that there is always a mutual effect on two bodies of comparable size and it can never occur on one charged body unilaterally!

4.8.2 Electric Force

The electric force on a charged particle of charge (Q) immersed in an electric field (E) can be found using Coulomb's law and is given by:

$$\overline{F} = Q\overline{E} \qquad\qquad (4.11)$$

4.8.3 Electric KCL

EKCL is based on the law of conservation of charge and states the following:

ELECTRIC KIRCHHOFF'S CURRENT LAW (EKCL): *In any lumped-element network and at each instant of time, the algebraic sum of the currents at each node must be equal to zero, i.e.,*

$$\sum_{n=1}^{N} I_n(t) = 0 \tag{4.12}$$

Where N is the total number of branches connected to any given node and $I_n(t)$ is the current in the nth branch. as shown in Figure 4.3.

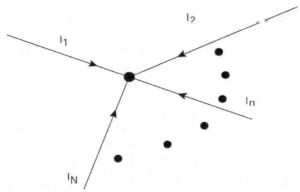

FIGURE 4.3 A node with N branches and N currents.

NOTE: *EKCL assumes that radiation effects at each node are negligible, i.e., EKCL is only valid and can primarily be applied to lumped elements operating at DC or lower frequencies, where radiation effects are negligible. Moreover, EKCL imposes a linear constraint on the branch currents and is valid for both time and frequency domains.*

There are several assumptions that are built into this law as follows:

Assumption #1. KCL assumes that the frequencies of interest are low enough such that there is no radiation at any of the nodes.

Assumption #2. KCL imposes a linear constraint on the branch currents

Assumption #3. KCL is valid both in time and phasor domain.

4.8.4 Electric KVL

ELECTRIC KIRCHHOFF'S CURRENT LAW (EKVL): *In any lumped-element network and at each instant of time, the algebraic sum of the branch voltages around a closed loop must be equal to zero, that is,*

$$\sum_{m=1}^{M} V_m(t) = 0 \tag{4.13}$$

Where M is the total number of branches($M=M_1+M_2$) in the loop and $V_m(t)$ is the branch voltage in the mth branch.

We can write this equation more explicitly as:

$$\sum_{k=1}^{M_1} emf_k = \sum_{i=1}^{M_2} V_i \tag{4.14}$$

Where emf_k is the voltage of the kth source (e.g. a battery) and V_i is the voltage drop across the ith element in the loop, as shown in Figure 4.4.

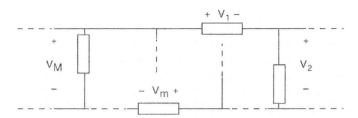

FIGURE 4.4 A loop with M branches.

KVL is based on the following Assumptions:

Assumption #1. KVL assumes that all electric fields involved are "conservative fields," i.e., the work done on a particle in moving it from one point to another depends only on the particle's initial and final positions and not on its path of travel.

Assumption #2. KVL imposes a linear constraint between branch voltages of a loop.

Assumption #3. KVL as expressed in (4.13) is valid for both time and phasor (frequency) domain.

Both of Kirchhoff's current and voltage laws apply to any and all **lumped network,** i.e., it does not matter whether the circuit elements are linear, nonlinear, passive, or active, as long as they are lumped.   In other words, KCL and KVL are independent of the nature of the elements.

4.8.5 Electric Ohm's Law

OHM'S LAW: *The current value is the algebraic sum of all electromotive forces in the circuit divided by the total resistance, i.e.,*

$I = \Sigma(emf)/\Sigma(R)$ (4.15a)

Or if we designate " $\Sigma(emf)$" by "V", and $\Sigma(R)$ by R, we can write:

$V = RI$ (4.15b)

Equation (4.15) represents the "integral form" of the Ohm's law.

NOTE 1: *In the Equation 4.14 above, Electromotive Force "emf" supplied by the battery, is the cause of the circulating current, and R (resistance) is given by:*

$$R = \frac{\ell}{\sigma A}$$ (4.15c)

Where σ, ℓ and A are the conductivity, length and the cross sectional area of the material, respectively.

NOTE 2: *Ohm's law, as represented by Equation (4.15), applies to the macroscopic world where the lengths involved are noticeably large. However, on a microscopic scale the Ohm's law at each point in a material under the influence of an electric field (E), can be written as:*

$J = \sigma E$ (4.16a)

Where J is the current density given by:

$J = I/A$ (4.16b)

and A is the cross sectional area of the material. Equation (4.16a) represents the point form of Ohm's law on a microscopic scale.

NOTE 3: *The integral form of Ohm's law can be derived from the point form for a material of length (ℓ) and constant cross sectional* *area (A) under the influence of a uniform electric field (E), as follows:*

$$J = \sigma E \quad \Rightarrow I/A = \sigma(V/\ell) \qquad (4.17a)$$

yielding:

$$V = (\sigma \ \ell/A)I = RI \qquad (4.17b)$$

4.8.6 Scalar Poisson's Equation

Scalar Poisson's equation, which describes Potential function's behavior in a region filled by a charge distribution, is given by:

$$\nabla^2 V = -\frac{\rho}{\varepsilon} \qquad (4.18a)$$

When the region under consideration is free of any charged particles (such as free space), then Equation (4.18a) is called the Laplace's equation and is given by:

$$\nabla^2 V = 0 \qquad (4.18b)$$

4.8.7 Energy Storage in Electric Fields

Electric energy stored: $W_E = \dfrac{1}{2}\displaystyle\int_v \rho V dv = \dfrac{1}{2}\int_v \overline{D}\cdot\overline{E}dv = \dfrac{1}{2}\int_v \varepsilon|\overline{E}|^2 \ dv$ (4.19)

Where v is the volume in which the fields are nonzero, ρ is the volume charge density, D and E are two vector quantities representing different forms of electrical energy.

4.8.8 Electrostatics & DC Examples

A few solved examples may serve to further elucidate some of these laws in actual practice .

EXAMPLE 4.1: The Lightning Rod

The lightning rod, with its use pioneered and advocated by Benjamin Franklin, provides a practical example of electrostatic charge principles and the laws of electrostatic fields.

OPERATION:

The reason lightning strikes a lightning rod (as opposed to another part of a building) is due to the way the rod concentrates electric charge. The increased charge concentration at the tip of a lightning rod produces a strong electric field, which aids in the breakdown of the dielectric (air). The breakdown of air causes a rapid discharge (of the opposing charge in the cloud) to the ground.

The following analysis will help Illustrate why a lightning rod works. This is not a model for a lightning rod, but is a simple concept of the field-concentrating effect of connecting two charged conducting spheres (A,B) of different radii (a,b). In actuality, the tip of the lightning rod would take the place of the smaller sphere and the building plus earth would take the place of the larger sphere (see Figure 4.5).

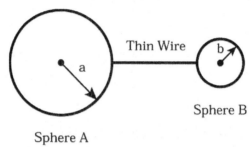

FIGURE 4.5   Two charged conducting spheres connected by a thin wire.

ASSUMPTIONS:
1) Spheres A and B (a>b) are both perfect conductors with uniform charge distributions.
2) The wire has no charge because it is very thin,

ANALYSIS:
Through some mathematical work we can derive the electric fields and find the ratio of the electric fields at the surface of the two spheres can be found as:

$E_a=q/[4\pi\varepsilon a(a+b)]$

$E_b=q/[4\pi\varepsilon b(a+b)]$

Thus we have:

$E_b/E_a=a/b$

Since a>b $\Rightarrow E_b>E_a$

To illustrate these results, let a=1000 m, b=1 m and q=10 C, then we have:

E_a=8.98x10^4 V/m

E_b=8.98x10^7 V/m

Therefore,

E_b/E_a=1000

CONCLUSION:

As can be seen, the effect of attaching a small sphere is to intensify the electric field by the ratio of the radii of the two spheres. Note that in this analysis, the electric field strength at the large sphere is below E_{bn} for air (breakdown E-field for air is equal to E_{bn}=3x10^6 V/m), while the electric field strength at the small sphere is above E_{bn} for air, thus breaking down the air and allowing it to conduct electricity. This means that lightning will discharge through the rod (by breaking down the air) rather than conducting through the building.

EXAMPLE 4.2: The Van de Graaff Generator

Another application of electrostatics is the Van de Graaff generator, invented by Robert Van de Graaff (1901-1967), which can be described as follow.

OPERATION:

The insulator belt, made of silk or rubber, passes near a charge source of several kilovolts, which sprays positive charges on the belt. The belt is moved by two pulleys. As the charges are carried into a metal dome, a metal brush takes up these charges.

The governing principle behind the operation of the Van de Graaff generator is the fact that charges cannot exist inside a hollow, perfectly-conducting sphere (see corollary 5b of the fifth supplemental discovery). The dome of the generator approximates a hollow conducting sphere and consequently, any charge that is brought inside the dome migrates to the outside. As the charge is being built up, the voltage also rises proportionately. The limit for the voltage built-up is the breakdown of air under the intense E-field (see Figure 4.6).

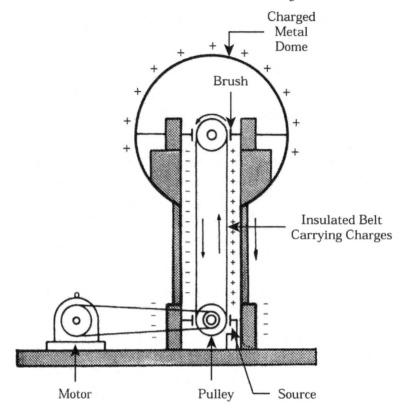

FIGURE 4.6 The Van de Graaff Generator

Such high voltage generators are used in nuclear physics to accelerate charged particles to high speeds, which can be used for example to generate neutrons by collisions with atoms. Generation of neutrons is especially useful in drilling for oil explorations. If the drill is surrounded by salt water, the generated neutrons will be absorbed quickly, whereas their rate of absorption is reduced if the drill is surrounded by oil. This phenomenon will show on the detection instruments, which would indicate whether the drill is in an oil-bearing or in a water-bearing zone.

ANALYSIS:
The following analysis will provide a sample calculation of how to deal with Van de Graaff type of generators.

Step 1: Considering the dome radius to be (a=0.1 m), we shall calculate the needed charge to cause a breakdown in the air surrounding the dome (breakdown E-field for air is equal to $E_{bn}=3 \times 10^6$ V/m): The E-field at the surface of the dome is given by:
$E=Q/4\pi\varepsilon a^2$

If we set the E field equal to the breakdown field, we obtain the required stored charge on the surface of the dome:
$Q=4\pi\varepsilon a^2 E_{bn}=4\pi(8.85 \times 10^{-12})(0.1)^2(3 \times 10^6)=3.34 \times 10^{-6}$ C

Step 2: If we now assume that charge is being deposited on the dome at a rate of 8×10^{-9} C per second (i.e., the current charging the dome is $I_o=8\mu A$), then the time required to fully charge the dome is given by:
$I_o=Q/\Delta T \Rightarrow \Delta T=Q/I_o$
which gives:
$\Delta T=3.34 \times 10^{-6}$ C/$8 \times 10^{-9}=417.2$ S=6 min., 57.2 Sec.

Step 3: Next, we shall calculate the voltage at the surface of the dome relative to ground:
$V_o=Q/4\pi\varepsilon a=3.34 \times 10^{-6}/4\pi(8.85 \times 10^{-12})(0.1)=300,010$ V

Step 4: If now the dome is suddenly discharged to the ground in 100 micro-seconds to a nearby ground wire, the average discharge current can be calculated to be:
$I_o'= Q/T_d=3.34 \times 10^{-6}/100 \times 10^{-6}=33.4$ mA.

From this calculation we can see that the dome of the Van de Graff generator is equivalent to a hollow, perfectly conducting sphere, which can be charged just like a capacitor. If enough charge is put on the surface of the sphere, breakdown of the surrounding air will occur with a consequent discharge of the dome.

EXAMPLE 4.3: Electrostatic Separation
Electrostatic separation is one of many applications that utilizes the discovered principles of electrostatic forces. Electrostatic separation is used in industry to sort material that is composed of two types of granules. An example of this type of sorting is the electrostatic

separation of phosphate and quartz, which are found together in raw ores as described below.

OPERATION:

The granules to be separated fall from a hopper onto a vibrating table, where they rub together and become charged by the friction of rubbing against each other. After this initial process, they fall off the table between two charged electric plates, which attract the granules and thus alter their trajectories. The quartz granules with a positive charge are attracted by the negative plate, and the phosphate granules with a negative charge are attracted by the positive plate. The deflected granules fall into two separate collecting bins (see Figure 4.7).

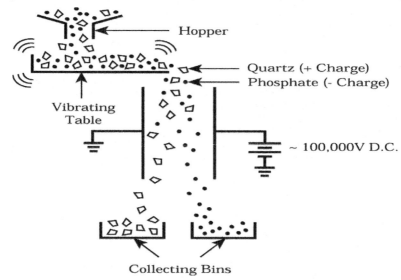

ELECTROSTATIC
SEPARATOR

FIGURE 4.7   Electrostatic separator.

ANALYSIS:

To calculate the forces on the granules and their deflection, we will assume that the charged plates are 0.6 m apart and 0.8 m from top to bottom. The vibrating table produces 1×10^{-5} C of charge per kilogram of ore.

From Electrostatic force equation we have:
F=qE,
Where
E=V/d=100,000/0.6=166.667 kV/m

Thus we have:
$F=1 \times 10^{-5} \times 166,667=1.667$ N/kg

To find the deflection of the ore, we must find how long the ore will be exposed to the plates. The ore is falling in the earth's gravitational field ($g=9.8$ m/s^2):
$g=dv_g/dt=d^2x/dt^2 \Rightarrow x=gt^2/2$

Thus the exposure time to the deflection forces is calculated to be:
$t = \sqrt{2x/g} = \sqrt{2x0.8/9.8} = 0.404$ s

Thus the deflection can be calculated to be:
$F=m(dv_d/dt)=m(d^2x_d/dt^2)$

Integrating this equation with respect to "t", we obtain:
$\Rightarrow x_d=Ft^2/2m$
Let m=1 kg. Then we have:
$x_d=1.667 \times (0.404)^2/2=13.6$ cm

Conclusion:
The distance that the granules are deflected is proportional to the top-to-bottom length of the electric plates and the voltage between the plates.

EXAMPLE 4.4: Condenser Microphone
The condenser microphone, a part of most tape recorders and portable stereos, is an application of electro-quasi static fields which is analyzed below.

OPERATION:
 The condenser microphone operates as a microphone because sound waves strike the flexible top of the condenser (also known as a capacitor) and cause it to vibrate. This flexible top is usually a

polyester film coated with a thin layer of highly conductive metal. A voltage is applied between the flexible outer plate and the inner one, causing them to be charged. The vibration due to the sound waves brings the flexible plate closer to, and farther from, the inner plate. This change of distance varies the capacitance of the condenser and produces a current (see Figure 4.8).

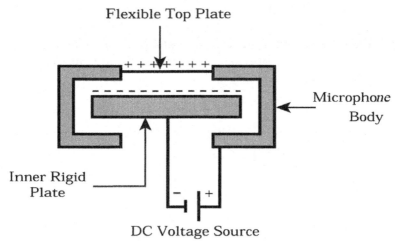

FIGURE 4.8 A condenser microphone.

ANALYSIS:
The charge on a capacitor is given by:
Q=CV

The current in a capacitor can be obtained as:
I=dQ/dt=d(CV)/dt=CdV/dt+VdC/dt

Since the applied voltage is DC, we can write:
dV/dt=0

Thus we have:
I=VdC/dt
Where C=εA/x and "x" is the distance between the two plates of the capacitor. Therefore, we can write:
I=εAV[d(1/x)/dt]=(-εAV/x²)dx/dt

Since capacitance (C) is proportional to the sound intensity or the vibration of the plates (dx/dt), the result is a current signal that varies in proportion to the sound that strikes the microphone.

The condenser microphone is a simple, widely-used device and since the vibrations of sound are of relatively low frequency (quasi-static fields), therefore we can conclude that it operates on the principles of electro-quasi static fields.

4.9 MAGNETOSTATICS

The second subset of Maxwell's Equations is the field of Magnetostatics defined as:

DEFINITION-MAGNETOSTATICS: *The study of magnets and magnetic fields that are neither moving nor changing directions. Such a field could be produced by a stationary magnetic pole or by a DC current flowing in a stationary conductor.*

The main laws governing this field of study can be briefly summarized as:

$$\nabla \times \overline{H} = \overline{J}$$
$$\nabla \cdot \overline{B} = 0$$
$$\overline{B} = \nabla \times \overline{A}$$
$$\overline{F} = Q(\overline{v} \times \overline{B})$$

$$(4.20a)$$

Where $\overline{F}$ is the Lorentz Force, which can also be written as (for a current carrying conductor):

$$\overline{F} = I\overline{dl} \times \overline{B} \qquad (4.20b)$$

For application purposes, these four equations would lead to several concepts and laws as follows:

4.9.1 Magnetic Coulomb's Law

Magnetic Coulomb's Law *states that the magnetic forces of two magnetic poles (M), repulsive or attractive, are proportional to the* *magnitude of the poles and inversely to the square of the distance between the two:*

$$\bar{F} = (\frac{M_1 M_2}{4\pi u R_{12}^2}) \hat{a}_{R_{12}}$$ (4.21)

Where $\mu = \mu_0 \mu_r$ is the permeability, μ_r the relative permeability, and μ_o is the permeability of free space ($\mu_o = 1.25 \times 10^{-6}$ H/m).

4.9.2 Magnetic KCL

MAGNETIC KIRCHHOFF'S CURRENT LAW (MKCL): *In any magnetic network and at each instant of time, the algebraic sum of the magnetic flux at each node must be equal to zero, that is,*

$$\sum_{i=1}^{N} \Phi_i(t) = 0$$ (4.22a)

Where N is the total number of branches connected to any given node and $\Phi_i(t)$ is the magnetic flux in the ith branch.

4.9.3 Magnetic KVL

MAGNETIC KIRCHHOFF'S VOLTAGE LAW (MKVL): *In any magnetic network and at each instant of time, the algebraic sum of the magnetic voltages around a closed loop (F_i is the magnetic voltage drop across the ith element in the loop) must be equal to zero, that is,*

$$\sum_{i=1}^{M} F_i = 0$$ (4.22b)

Where M is the total number of branches in the loop and F_i is the branch magnetic voltage in the ith branch.

We can write this equation more explicitly as: $\sum_{k=1}^{m_1} \mathbf{mmf}_k = \sum_{i=1}^{m_2} \mathbf{H}_i \ell_i$

Where mmf_k is the magnetomotive force of the kth N-turn coil (i.e., $\text{mmf}_k = NI_k$) in the magnetic loop, and $M = M_1 + M_2$ *is the total number of branches in the loop, respectively.*

NOTE: *Similar to the electric voltage, the magnetic voltage F in a magnetic circuit is given by:*

$$F_{21} = -\int_1^2 \overline{H} \cdot \overline{d\ell} \approx \Delta(H_i \ell_i) \tag{4.23a}$$

$$[cf., \ V_{21} = -\int_1^2 \overline{E} \cdot \overline{d\ell} \approx \Delta(E_i \ell_i) \ ]$$

Therefore Equation (4.22) can be written as:

$$\sum_{k=1}^{M_1} mmf_k = \sum_{i=1}^{M_2} \Delta(H_i \ell_i) \tag{4.23b}$$

4.9.4 Magnetic Ohm's Law

THE MAGNETIC DUAL OF THE SECOND SUPPLEMENTAL DISCOVERY: *There is a linear relationship between the flux lines of the magnetic field and the Magnetomotive force (mmf).*

Considering the electric Ohm's law, we can see that the magnetic flux (Φ) and magnetic applied voltage (F) are analogous to current (I) and (V) in an electric circuit, respectively; whereas magnetic reluctance ($\Re$) is analogous to electrical resistance (R). Thus the magnetic Ohm's law can be stated as:

MAGNETIC OHM'S LAW: *The magnetic flux (Φ) is the algebraic sum of all magnetomotive forces (mmfs) in the circuit divided by the total reluctance ($\Re$), i.e.,*

$\Phi = \Sigma(mmf) / \Sigma(\Re)$ (4.24a)
Or, if we designate " $\Sigma(mmf)$" by "F_{tot}", and $\Sigma(\Re)$ by $\Re_{tot}$, we can write:
$F_{tot} = \Re_{tot} \Phi$ (4.24b)

NOTE: *In the above equation, Magnetomotive Force "mmf" being the dual of Electromotive Force (emf), is the cause of magnetic flux circulation and is given by:*
mmf=NI (4.25)
where N is the number of turns in a coil and I is the current in the coil. The reluctance ($\Re$) is the dual of electrical resistance and is given by:
$\Re = \ell /\mu A$ (4.26a)

where μ, ℓ and A are the permeability, length and the cross sectional area of the magnetic material.

4.9.5 Vector Poisson's Equation

Vector Poisson's equation (Magnetic Potential function caused by a current distribution) is given by:

$$\nabla^2 \overline{A} = -\mu \overline{J}$$

(4.26b)

4.9.6 Biot-Savart Law

The Biot-Savart Law, considered by some to be the Coulomb's Law of Magnetostatics, is expressed in terms of field vector quantity (*H*). The differential magnetic field strength (dH), at point (P) a distance (R) due to one of the differential current elements (Idℓ) is given by:

$$d\overline{H} = \frac{Id\overline{\ell} \times \hat{R}}{4\pi R^2}$$

(4.27)

Equation (4.27) expresses two main facts about a current-produced magnetic field:

   a) The magnetic field magnitude varies inversely with the distance squared, and

   b) The magnetic field has a direction perpendicular to both the current element (Idℓ) and $\hat{R}$, where $\hat{R}$ is the unit vector pointing from the current element to the point "P", i.e.,

$$\hat{R} = \frac{\overline{R}}{|R|}$$

(4.28)

4.9.7 Magnetic Force on Charge

LORENTZ FORCE EQUATION: A charged particle in motion in a magnetic field (B) experiences a force at right angles to its velocity vector, with a magnitude proportional to the charge value, the velocity ($\overline{v}$), and the magnetic flux density, given by:

$$\overline{F} = Q\overline{v} \times \overline{B}$$

(4.29)

4.9.8 Magnetic Force on Current

MODIFIED LORENTZ FORCE EQUATION: If instead of a single moving charge (as in B.13), there is a current-carrying wire (I) of length (L), then the magnetic force on the wire is given by:

$$\overline{F} = \int_L I d\overline{\ell} \times \overline{B} \qquad (4.30)$$

The above laws can be derived from Maxwell's Equations with relative ease and are relegated to more basic texts for a more detailed coverage.

4.9.9 Energy Storage in Magnetic Fields

Magnetic Energy Stored: $W_H = \dfrac{1}{2}\int_v \overline{B} \cdot \overline{H} dv = \dfrac{1}{2}\int_v \mu |\overline{H}|^2 \, dv \quad (4.31)$

Where v is the volume in which the fields are nonzero, ρ is the volume charge density, D and E are two forms of electric field, and B and H are two forms of magnetic fields.

4.9.10 Magnetostatics Examples

A few solved examples may serve to further elucidate some of these laws in actual practice .

EXAMPLE 4.5: The Magneplane
The magneplane is a high-speed transportation vehicle that flies above a conducting track. It is a practical way of transporting people more quickly and cheaply than electrified trains. This type of trains are also called magnetic levitation (or Mag-Lev for short) trains as discussed below.

OPERATION:
The magneplane operates on the principle of magnetic levitation and magnetic force.   There are two parts to the operation of the magneplane: levitation and propulsion.
Magnetic levitation allows the magneplane to travel 30 cm. above its conducting track.   The magneplane's levitation is caused by the repulsion of two opposing magnetic fields.   Inside the vehicle there is a super-conducting coil, parallel to the track, carrying a large

current. This current produces an image current in the conducting track that is the same wave shape, but opposite in direction. The fields produced by these two current-carrying loops oppose each other and produce a repulsion force, which levitates the vehicle.

The magnetic propulsion is provided due to the same principle that moves a synchronous motor. The "vehicle and its coils" take the place of the rotor of the synchronous motor whereas the "track with specially laid coils" take the place of the stator. When three-phase current is fed into the track coils, a moving magnetic field is formed which interacts with the field from the vehicle's coil and propels the vehicle (see Figure 4.9).

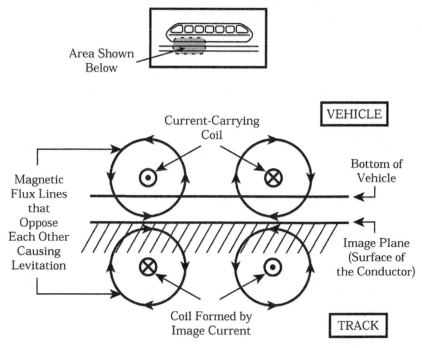

FIGURE 4.9   The Magneplane.

ANALYSIS:
The magnetic levitation force is:
$F = 2\mu_o I_v I_i \ell / \pi d$

Where I_v, I_i are the vehicle coil current and image current, "ℓ" and "d" are the length of a coil side and distance between the vehicle and image coils, respectively.

EXAMPLE 4.6

What is the levitation force on a vehicle with a coil $\ell=1$ m, $I_v=I_i=2x10^5$ A and a distance of 0.25 above the track?

Solution:
The distance "d" is twice the distance above track, i.e.,
d=2x0.25=0.5 m
Thus the force is given by:
$F=2(4\pi x10^{-7})x(2x10^5)x1/\pi(0.5)= 6.4x10^4$ N
From this example we can see that the enormous current (I_v=200,000 A) would require a superconducting coil.

EXAMPLE 4.7: **The Rail Gun**
The rail gun has several advantages over conventional guns. Rail guns have the ability to give projectiles higher velocities than conventional guns. In addition, rail guns are silent and more accurate than conventional guns. These advantages make them attractive as weapons or as accelerators of fuel pellets in thermonuclear reactions as described below.

OPERATION:
A rail gun operates on the magnetic expansion force found in any current-carrying loop. As seen in Figure L.6, the parallel rails represent the "barrel" of the gun. The projectile is in contact with both rails and completes the loop. Large amounts of current are put through the loop and the result is acceleration of the projectile, since the movement of the projectile is equivalent to expanding the loop. After being accelerated by the magnetic force, the projectile leaves the "barrel" at a high velocity (see Figure 4.10).

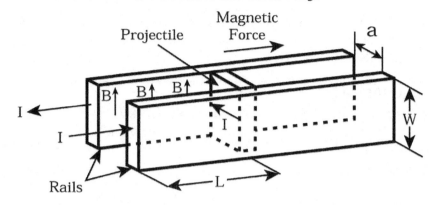

FIGURE 4.10   The rail gun.

ANALYSIS:

The magnetic field strength (H) for parallel rails (or parallel plates) of width (w) carrying a current (I), is equal to the surface current density and can be written as:

$H = I/w$

The total flux between the rails (with cross sectional area A) is given by:

$\varphi = BA = \mu HA = \mu Ia\ell/w$

The inductance of the rail gun (L) is given by:

$L = \varphi/I = \mu a\ell/w$

The magnetic energy stored (U) is accomplished through work (W') being done on the rail gun and is given by:

$U = W' = LI^2/2$

The magnetic force (F_m) is related to the work done (W') by:

$W' = \int F_m \cdot d\ell$

Thus F_m can be found as:

$F_m = dW'/d\ell$

Or,

$F_m = 1/2(I^2 dL/d\ell) = I^2 \mu a/2w$

EXAMPLE 4.8
Given a=0.1 m, w=0.3 m and I=3x10⁵ A, calculate:
*   a) The force on the end plate (i.e., projectile).*
*   b) The speed of the projectile (m=3 g) upon exit from the end*
*   of the gun if the gun barrel has a length of (x=3 m).*

Solution:
a) The force of the projectile is given by:

$F_m = I^2 \mu_o a/2w = (3 \times 10502(4\pi \times 10^{-7})(0.1)/2 \times 0.3 = 1.9 \times 10^4$ N

b) From elementary physics, we can write:

$F_m = md^2x/dt^2 \Rightarrow d^2x/dt^2 = F_m/m = 1.9 \times 10^4/0.003 = 6.33 \times 10^6$ m/s

b.) Upon integration, we have:

$x = (6.33 \times 10^6 \, t^2)/2 \Rightarrow t^2 = x/(3.167 \times 10^6) \Rightarrow t = 0.973 \times 10^{-3}$ s

$v = x/t = 6164$ m/s

CONCLUSION:
The rail gun can accelerate small projectiles to very high speeds. However, because of its enormous current requirements (300,000 A), super-conducting materials must be used in the circuit to make it practical. Superconducting materials are now being developed that work at higher temperatures, thus, making rail guns more feasible.

4.9.11 Interaction Of Kinetic Electricity With Matter
When electricity is put into motion by means of an EMF source connected by wires and conductors such that it forms a closed loop, then it interacts with matter particles in its vicinity by applying a force on them. This force causes matter particles to move in a certain and yet predictable manner which could be used in many applications. The following examples will illustrate this point further.

EXAMPLE 4.9: Isotope Separation
Magnetic isotope separation is used to separate atoms that have the same atomic number but different atomic weights (e.g., Uranium

235 and Uranium 238). These isotopes cannot be separated by traditional chemical means as discussed and anayzed below.

OPERATION:

The atoms to be separated are vaporized and then ionized. Once ionized, the atoms are passed through slits in a parallel-plate region, where the parallel plates are charged by a high voltage DC source. The resulting electric field accelerates the ions, giving them a high velocity as they enter a region of strong magnetic field. Magnetic forces act on the ions, causing them to move in a semicircle, Heavier Isotopes will have larger radii, allowing them to be collected separately from the lighter isotopes (see Figure 4.11).

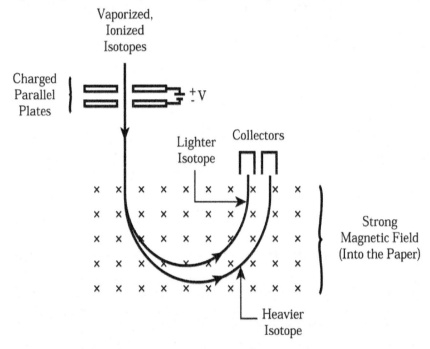

FIGURE 4.11   Isotope separation.

ANALYSIS:

From the setup shown we can see that this is an energy conversion process, where the ions gain kinetic energy (i.e., speed up to a velocity, v) due to the potential energy resident in the voltage of the charged plates. The radius (R) of the semicircles due to the ion

having a mass (m) with charge (q) moving with speed (v) in a magnetic field (B), can be calculated to be:
R=mv/qB

Thus we have:
$R_{235}/R_{238}=(m_{235}v_{235}/m_{238}v_{238})$

Moreover, since the kinetic energies ($KE=mv^2/2$) for the two types of isotope are equal (because different isotopes have the same charge value, thus the same force is applied to them by the high voltage field), we can write:
$m_{235}/m_{238}=(v_{238}/v_{235})^2$

Thus we can write:
$R_{235}/R_{238}=(m_{235}/m_{238})^{1/2} =(235/238)^{1/2}=0.9937$

CONCLUSION:
As illustrated in the above analysis, the radii of the two isotope particles are different. The ratio 0.9937 is used to calculate the position of the two collectors that receive the separated particles.

EXAMPLE 4.10: Cyclotron
Cyclotrons are used to produce high-energy charged particles for use in other experiments.

OPERATION:
Two D-shaped copper electrodes are placed between magnets. Low energy charged particles are injected into the center of the gap between the electrodes, where they are accelerated from side to side by a strong electric field. The electric field is repeatedly reversed at a frequency ($f_c = qB/2\pi m$, called the cyclotron frequency) that is dependent on the particle characteristics and the magnetic field strength.

The magnetic field causes the particles to move in a circular path. The particles are accelerated to higher speeds and ever-widening circles. After many revolutions the ions exit as high-energy, high-velocity particles (see Figure 4.12).

Derivation of the cyclotron frequency:

To derive the cyclotron frequency, we consider a particle of mass (m) and charge (q) moving with a velocity (v) in the +x direction in a uniform magnetic field (B), which is pointing in the –z direction. Using Lorentz force equation we obtain:

$$\overline{F} = q\overline{v} \times \overline{B} = qv\,\hat{x} \times B(-\hat{z}) = qvB\,\hat{y}$$

Because F is always perpendicular to v, a circular motion occurs. To maintain the circular motion, force (F) must be equal to centrifugal force (F'=mv^2/R, where R is the radius of the circle of motion). Thus we can write:

$$qvB = mv^2/R \quad \Rightarrow R = mv/qB$$

The angular frequency (in rad/s) is given by:

$\omega_c = v/R = qB/m$, and

$f_c = \omega_c/2\pi = qB/2\pi m$

It is interesting to note that the cyclotron frequency is independent of the velocity(v). This means that if we inject several identical charged particles of different velocities and masses, they will move in different circles (faster particles in larger circles) but with the same frequency.

Furthermore, since F is always perpendicular to the velocity (v) and thus the direction of motion, therefore W=∫ F.dℓ=0, i.e. the magnetic field, even though may change the direction of motion of the particle, however, the particle's speed remains the same, thus it never does any work to the charged particle

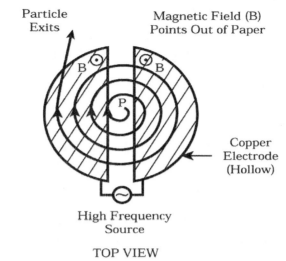

Particle
Exits

Magnetic Field (B)
Points Out of Paper

B

B

P

Copper
Electrode
(Hollow)

High Frequency
Source

TOP VIEW

South Pole

B

P

Electrode

North Pole

Particles
Injected Here

SIDE VIEW

FIGURE 4.12 A cyclotron.

ANALYSIS:

The kinetic energy of a charged particle with mass (m) and charge (q) and speed (v) traveling in a circular path is given by:

$KE=mv^2/2$

Where $v=\omega_c R$, with $\omega_c =2\pi f_c$ and $f_c =qB/2\pi m$. Thus we have:

$KE=m(\omega_c R)^2/2=(RqB)^2/2m$

CONCLUSION:

To accelerate a given charged particle to higher energy, the cyclotron must either be made bigger (increase R) or a stronger magnetic field B must be applied.

The following example will illustrate this point further.

EXAMPLE 4.11

Consider a Deuterium particle of mass $(m=3.34x10^{-27}$ kg) and charge $(q=1.6x10^{-19}$ C), which is accelerated in a cyclotron of radius R=1 m and magnetic field B=2 Wb/m². Calculate the following:

  a) The frequency of the alternating source
  b) The energy of a Deuterium exiting the cyclotron

Solution:

a) $f=f_c=qB/2\pi m=(1.5x10^{-19}x2)/(2\pi x3.34x10^{-27})=15.2$ MHz

b) The exiting isotope has a kinetic energy given by:

$KE=m(\omega_c R)^2/2$

Using this equation we obtain:

$KE= (3.34x10^{-27}x2\pi x15.2x10^6x1)^2/2=1.53x10^{-11}$ J=95.8 MeV

4.10 ELECTROMAGNETICS & WAVES

As the frequency of the signals in a circuit, component or system is increased beyond DC, the field of electricity and magnetism gradually becomes interwoven and can no longer be separated into two separate fields of electricity and magnetism.

As a result of this phenomenon, a new field of study was born into existence to encompass this much wider sphere of activity. The beginning of this extremely vital field was finally put forth on solid ground by James clerk Maxwell in his celebrated Maxwell's Equations (1864-1873). We now define this field as:

DEFINITION-ELECTROMAGNETICS: *The study of charges in motion resulting in electric and magnetic fields which are inter-dependent and inter-related, where electric phenomenon can not exist by itself without magnetic effects and vice versa. Examples of such a case*

are light emission from the sun and stars, Thunderstorms and lightning, radio and television waves, power lines, radar, etc.

This is quite contrary to the previous two fields of study where electric and magnetic phenomenon can exist completely separate from the other. It can be shown with relative ease that "Electromagnetics" is a field of study which includes both fields of electrostatics and magnetostatics.

Due to the exact nature of its formulation and precise nomenclature employed to describe its various concepts, it has created a world of enormous possibilities and a myriad of present and potential applications. It could easily be said that the field of electromagnetics put man on the moon and opened up the solar system to mankind's present and future space explorations, and will enable us someday to conquer the whole galaxy!

The field of electromagnetics has several subdivisions such as electrodynamics, physical optics, etc. However, one of the vital subdivisions of this exciting field is "electromagnetic wave propagation" which has tremendous applications in the field of RF and microwaves. The governing equations concerning the field of electromagnetic wave propagation can be written as:

$$\nabla \times \overline{E} = -\frac{\partial \overline{B}}{\partial t}$$

$$\nabla \times \overline{H} = \frac{\partial \overline{D}}{\partial t} + \overline{J} \qquad (4.32a)$$

$$\nabla \cdot \overline{D} = \rho$$

$$\nabla \cdot \overline{B} = 0$$

Under steady-state sinusoidal time dependence, the Maxwell's Equations become:

$$\nabla \times \overline{E} = -j\omega\mu\overline{H}$$
$$\nabla \times \overline{H} = j\omega\varepsilon\overline{E} + \overline{J}$$
$$\nabla \cdot \overline{D} = \rho \qquad\qquad (4.32b)$$
$$\nabla \cdot \overline{B} = 0$$

where

$$\overline{J} = \sigma\overline{E}$$
$$\overline{D} = \varepsilon\overline{E}$$
$$\overline{B} = \mu\overline{H}$$

$$(4.32c)$$

where ω and σ are the angular frequency and the conductivity of the medium under consideration and $j=\sqrt{-1}$.

This field of study can be roughly divided into three subdivisions, with each being more general than the next one:

4.10.1 General Wave Equations

Dealing with general time-varying fields, the General Wave Equation can be derived from the Maxwell's Equations in a lossless medium (σ=0) and is given by:

$$\nabla^2 \overline{E} - \mu\varepsilon \frac{\partial^2 \overline{E}}{\partial t^2} = 0$$

$$(4.33a)$$

$$\nabla^2 \overline{H} - \mu\varepsilon \frac{\partial^2 \overline{H}}{\partial t^2} = 0$$

General Wave Equations in a lossy medium ($\sigma \neq 0$) can be written as:

$$\nabla^2 \overline{E} - \mu\varepsilon \frac{\partial^2 \overline{E}}{\partial t^2} - \mu\sigma \frac{\partial \overline{E}}{\partial t} = 0$$

$$(4.33b)$$

$$\nabla^2 \overline{H} - \mu\varepsilon \frac{\partial^2 \overline{H}}{\partial t^2} = 0$$

4.10.2 Helmholtz's Equations

Dealing with time-harmonic fields and waves (i.e., fields that vary sinusoidally), the General Wave Equation can be simplified and is given by the Helmholtz's Equation for two cases:

A. Homogeneous Vector Equation:

$$\nabla^2 \overline{E} + k^2 \overline{E} = 0, \qquad\qquad (4.34a)$$

$$\nabla^2 \overline{H} + k^2 \overline{H} = 0 \qquad\qquad (4.34b)$$

B1. Inhomogeneous Scalar Equation:

$$\nabla^2 V + k^2 V = -\frac{\rho}{\varepsilon} \qquad\qquad (4.35)$$

B2. Inhomogeneous Vector Equation:

$$\nabla^2 \overline{A} + k^2 \overline{A} = -\mu \overline{J} \qquad\qquad (4.36)$$

Lorentz Condition relates A to V:

$$\nabla \cdot \overline{A} = -j\omega\mu\varepsilon V \qquad\qquad (4.37)$$

Wave Number (K) is given by:

1. Non-Conducting Media:

$$k = \omega\sqrt{\mu\varepsilon} = \omega/v_P = 2\pi/\lambda \qquad\qquad (4.38a)$$

where V_P is the phase velocity given by:
$V_P = 1/\sqrt{\mu\varepsilon}$

2. Conducting Media:

$$k = \omega\sqrt{\mu_o\varepsilon}, \quad \varepsilon = \varepsilon_o(1 - j\frac{\sigma}{\omega\varepsilon_o}) \qquad (4.38b)$$

Please note that ε for a conducting media is no longer a real number but becomes a complex number.

4.10.3 Waves on a Transmission Line

Dealing with time-harmonic waves on a transmission lines, the General Wave Equation becomes:

TEM waves- $E_z=0$, $H_z=0$
I. Field Equations

$$\nabla_t^2 \overline{E}_t + (k^2 - \beta^2)\overline{E}_t = 0 \qquad\qquad (4.39a)$$

$$\nabla_t^2 \phi = 0$$

$$\overline{E} = -\nabla_t \phi e^{\mp jkz} \qquad\qquad (4.39b)$$

$$\overline{H} = \pm\frac{1}{\eta}\hat{z}\times\overline{E} \qquad\qquad (4.39c)$$

where

$$\eta = \sqrt{\frac{\mu}{\varepsilon}}$$

$$\beta = k = \omega\sqrt{\mu\varepsilon} = \omega/v_P = 2\pi/\lambda$$

II. Current and Voltage Equations

Sinusoidal current and voltage waves caused by TEM field waves are given by:

$$\frac{d^2 V(x)}{dx^2} - \gamma^2 V(x) = 0 \qquad\qquad (4.40a)$$

$$\frac{d^2 I(x)}{dx^2} - \gamma^2 I(x) = 0 \qquad\qquad (4.40b)$$

Where

$$I(x) = (\frac{-1}{R + j\omega L})\frac{dV(x)}{dx},$$

$$\gamma = \sqrt{(R + j\omega L)(G + j\omega C)} = \alpha + j\beta \qquad\qquad (4.40c)$$

III. Lossless Transmission Lines (R, G=0)

Transmission line Equations for this lossless case further simplify into:

$$\frac{d^2V(x)}{dx^2} + \beta^2 V(x) = 0,$$

$$\frac{d^2I(x)}{dx^2} + \beta^2 I(x) = 0,$$

$$I(x) = (\frac{-1}{j\omega L})\frac{dV(x)}{dx}$$

$$\beta = \omega\sqrt{LC}$$

4.10.4 Waves in a Waveguide

Waves in a waveguide divide into two classes:

I. TE waves: $E_z=0$, $H_z\neq0$

$$(\nabla_t^2 - \beta^2)(\overline{H}_t + \overline{H}_z) = 0 \qquad\qquad (4.41a)$$

II. TM waves: $E_z\neq0$, $H_z=0$

$$(\nabla_t^2 - \beta^2)(\overline{E}_t + \overline{E}_z) = 0 \qquad\qquad (4.41b)$$

Where

$$\nabla = \nabla_t - j\beta\hat{z}$$
$$\nabla^2 = \nabla_t^2 - \beta^2$$
$$\overline{E} = \overline{E}_t + \overline{E}_z$$
$$\overline{H} = \overline{H}_t + \overline{H}_z \qquad\qquad (4.41c)$$

For further details and an in-depth derivation of these equations, the reader may consult other basic texts in this field.

4.10.5 Power and the Poynting Vector

The instantaneous rate of energy flow per unit area at any point in space is measured by the Poynting vector:

$$\overline{P}(t) = \overline{E}(t)\times\overline{H}(t) \qquad\qquad (4.41d)$$

The Poynting vector gives the direction of energy flow in real time due to its vector nature. However, if we wish to find the time average value of $(\overline{P})$, then we need to use the phasor form of E and H as follows:

$$\mathbf{P_{av}} = 1/2[\mathbf{Re}(\overline{\mathbf{E}} \times \overline{\mathbf{H}}^*)] \qquad\qquad (4.41e)$$

Where (H*) designates the complex conjugate of H.

NOTE: *The equation for the average power of electromagnetic waves is very similar to the average power equation for electric circuits given by:*
$P_{av}=1/2Re(VI^*)$
Where V and I are the phasors for current and voltage in the circuit. Furthermore, from this equation we can see that E is analogous to V and H to I, thus wave theory merges neatly with circuit theory.

4.10.6 Electromagnetics & Waves Examples

A few solved examples may serve to further elucidate some of these laws in actual practice . Microwave applications are quite prevalent in our society today, specially as our information infrastructure advances toward high frequency continuously. The following is a brief sample of applications in this field.

EXAMPLE 4.12: **Radio Communication Between Submarines**
Communication with a fleet of submarines that are underwater is an important capability. Without it, submarines must surface to transmit and receive information and commands. Radio communication from submarine to submarine and submarine to base is very difficult because seawater highly attenuates electromagnetic waves as analyzed further below.

ANALYSIS:
The relative permittivity (ε_r) of seawater is roughly 81. The conductivity of seawater (σ) is about 4 mho/meter. To find the attenuation of electromagnetic waves in water, we use the wave number ($jk=\alpha+j\beta$).

The attenuation constant (α), is given by:
$\alpha=\{\omega\sqrt{(\mu_0\varepsilon)}\}[1+(\sigma/\omega\varepsilon)^2]^{1/4} \sin[0.5\tan^{-1}(\sigma/\omega\varepsilon)]$

At very high frequencies (i.e., $\sigma/\omega\varepsilon<<1$), we can write:
$\alpha \approx 0.5\sigma\sqrt{(\mu_0/\varepsilon)}=83.7$ N/m=728 dB/m

Since signal power is halved every 3 dB, therefore 728 dB/m (containing approximately 250 times 3 dB per meter), corresponds to 3 dB in 4 mm. Because the signal power is reduced in half every 4 millimeter of wave propagation, we have very high attenuation in this case.

To reduce this attenuation, the transmission frequencies must be kept low. For a 1 kHz signal, the attenuation is α = .126 N/m =1.1 dB/m. Thus, a signal transmitted at 1 kHz will be attenuated 110 dB in only 100 m. Attenuation must be reduced to keep transmission power requirements reasonable, Therefore, transmission frequencies of 50 Hz and below are used, However, at these rates, transmitting a single word can take hours.

EXAMPLE 4.13 Microwave Ovens
Microwave ovens are extremely popular for thawing, cooking, and reheating foods in homes and restaurants. The ability of microwaves to penetrate and begin heating the inside as well as the outside of a material has made microwave ovens very useful. Also, because of the properties of microwaves, some materials such as polystyrene absorb virtually none of the microwave energy and thus remain cool.

OPERATION:
A microwave oven converts normal household power into radiation at a microwave frequency (2.45 GHz). This radiation is directed into the food, which acts as a lossy medium. Because the loss tangent of most foods is high, part of the power of the radiation is lost to the food as the radiation passes through the food. This power is transformed into heat energy, which warms the food.

EXAMPLE 4.14
What is the penetration depth of a bottom round steak at f=2.45 GHz?

Solution:
The permittivity and conductivity of steak is given by:
$\varepsilon = 40\varepsilon_o$,
$\sigma/\omega\varepsilon = 0.3$

At 3 GHz, we find the complex propagation constant (γ) for the EM fields to be:

$\gamma = j\omega[\sqrt{(\mu\epsilon)}][1-j\sigma/\omega\epsilon]^{1/2} = 59 + j402$ rad/m

We know that $\gamma = \alpha + j\beta$, and amplitude of the E-field decreases by a factor of $e^{-\alpha x}$ as the waves propagate in the x direction. Therefore, the depth of penetration (δ) for the E-field, where the E-field magnitude is reduced to 37% of its original magnitude, is given by:

$\delta = 1/\alpha = 1/59 = 1.70$ cm.

Since the penetration depth (δ') for the power is half of the (δ) for the electric field, that is,

$\delta' = \delta/2 = 0.85$ cm

Therefore, the power heating the steak at 0.85 cm below its surface is 37% of the power at its surface.

EXAMPLE 4.15 Microstrip Lines

Microstrip lines are employed commonly in microwave integrated circuits (MICs) since they are easily integrated in a planar geometry of Microwave Integrated Circuits (MICs) and have superiority over other types of transmission lines particularly those used in lower frequency Integrated Circuits (ICs) as discussed below.

OPERATION:

The microstrip line is essentially a parallel plate waveguide with a dielectric as a separating material (see Figure 4.13). As long as the width of the microstrip line is much larger than the separating thickness, the dominant fields in the microstrip line will be quasi-TEM waves.

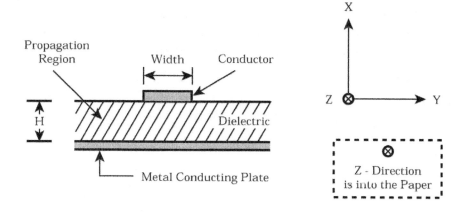

FIGURE 4.13   A microstrip line.

ANALYSIS:

If the propagation is taken in the positive z-direction, the solutions for the field equations for the microstrip line are shown to be:

$E_x = E_o e^{-jkz}$

$H_y = H_o e^{-jkz}$

The surface currents and charges for the upper and lower strips are given by:

Location	Surface Current	Surface Charge
Upper Strip	$J_S = -\hat{z}\dfrac{E_o}{\eta}e^{-jkz}$	$\rho_S = -\varepsilon E_o e^{-jkz}$
Lower strip	$J_S = \hat{z}\dfrac{E_o}{\eta}e^{-jkz}$	$\rho_S = \varepsilon E_o e^{-jkz}$

Where $\eta = \sqrt{(\mu/\varepsilon)}$ is the intrinsic impedance of the medium.

4.11 THE GENERALIZED OHM'S LAW

we will now revisit the generalized Ohm's law (see Chapter 3), as it is an important concept and thus needs to be grasped in its entirety .

THE GENERALIZED OHM'S LAW: *Under steady state conditions and or time–harmonic signals, the applied voltage in a circuit consisting of a resistor (R) in series with a capacitor (C) and an inductor (L), can be written as:*
$$V=Z.I, \qquad\qquad\qquad (4.42a)$$

Where,
$$Z=R+j(\omega L-1/\omega C), \quad \omega=2\pi f \qquad\qquad (4.42b)$$
V and I are voltage and current phasors, respectively; ω is the
Where,
$$Z=R+j(\omega L-1/\omega C), \quad \omega=2\pi f \qquad\qquad (4.42c)$$
V and I are voltage and current phasors, respectively; ω is the frequency of operation and Z is a complex number called the "impedance" of the circuit.

The concept of impedance is similar to resistance, except that it is no longer a constant real value, but a complex number whose value is variable and depends on the frequency of operation (f).

In general, the impedance (Z), being a complex number, has a real part (called resistance, R) and an imaginary part (called reactance, X), given by:
$$Z=R+jX \qquad\qquad\qquad (4.43)$$

The principal sources of reactance (X) are twofolds:
1. Reactance due to changing magnetic field and associated magnetic flux in the coils. This is associated with the magnetic inductance (L) of the circuit and its coils ($jX_L=j\omega L$), and
2. Reactance due to changing electrical fields in the capacitors. This is associated with the electrical capacitance (C) in the circuit ($jX_C=1/j\omega C$).

Note: *From The fourth supplemental discovery we know that: "All current-carrying electrical wires exhibit self induction when the* *current is changed in magnitude or direction. The self induction impedes the current flow and thus causes a voltage drop."*

From this principle an important relationship can be derived by noting that the magnetic flux (Φ) is proportional to the current:

$$N\Phi = Li(t) \tag{4.44a}$$

where L is the coefficient of self-induction, and N is the number of turns.

Differentiating both sides we obtain the induced voltage (V) as:

$$v(t) = dN\Phi/dt \tag{4.44b}$$

Or,

$$v(t) = Ldi/dt \tag{4.44c}$$

The induced voltage (V) opposes the original applied emf and thus appears as a voltage drop in the circuit. Thus if we have time-harmonic signals [$v(t)=V\cos\omega t$; $i(t)=I\cos\omega t$] applied to the circuit, then we can write:

$$v(t) = L\,d(I\cos\omega t)/dt \tag{4.44d}$$

In phasor form, Equation (4.44d) becomes:

$$V = j\omega LI$$

Or,

$$Z_L = j\omega L$$

Similarly, the current through a capacitor [$i(t)$] is proportional to the rate of change of voltage across it [$i(t)$], i.e.,

$$i(t) = Cdv/dt \tag{4.45a}$$

Thus if we have time-harmonic signals [$v(t)=V\cos\omega t$; $i(t)=I\cos\omega t$] applied to the circuit, then we can write:

$$i(t) = L\,d(V\cos\omega t)/dt \tag{4.45b}$$

In phasor form, Equation (4.45b) becomes:

$$I = j\omega CV \tag{4.45c}$$

Or,

$$Z_C = 1/j\omega C = -j/\omega C \tag{4.45d}$$

CHAPTER-4 PROBLEMS

4.1) What are meant by the governing laws of Electrical Engineering?

4.2) What is the Principle of Conservation of Energy?

4.3) What are the Primary Laws? Describe each conceptually and mathematically.

4.4) Describe what is meant by the Secondary Laws and equations?

4.5) What are the Subfields of Electricity?

4.6) What is meant by a) "**ELECTROSTATICS,** b) DC? Give an example for each.

4.7) What is the single fundamental upon which the whole field of electronics is built? Define it.

4.8) What is **ELECTRIC COULOMB'S LAW**? Give an example.

4.9) Describe what is meant by ELECTRIC FORCE?

4.10) What is meant by ELECTRIC KCL and KVL conceptually and mathematically? Give an example for each.

4.11) What is meant by Electric Ohm's Law? Give an example.

4.12) Describe Scalar Poisson's Equation and its potential applications?

4.13) Describe what is meant by Energy Storage in Electric Fields?

4.14) Provide two modern examples each for a) Electrostatics, and b) DC? Describe the principles of operation in each example.

4.15) What is Magnetostatics? Describe its potential applications.

4.16) Describe what is meant by Magnetic Coulomb's Law?

4.17) Describe what is meant by Magnetic KCL and KVL? Give an example for each.

4.18) Describe what is meant by Magnetic Ohm's Law?

4.19) Describe Vector Poisson's Equation and its potential applications?

4.20) Describe Biot-Savart Law and give an example.

4.21) What is meant by Magnetic Force on a) Charge and b) current? What are the force equations?

4.22) Describe what is meant by Energy Storage in Magnetic Fields?

4.23) Provide two modern examples of Magnetostatics Examples. Describe the principles of operation in each case.

4.24) Describe what is meant by Interaction of Kinetic Electricity with Matter?

4.25) What is the definition of a) Electromagnetics, and b) Waves?

4.26) What is the General Wave Equation?

4.27) What are the Helmholtz's Equations?

4.28) Describe what type of waves and how they propagate on a TEM transmission line? What are the governing equations? Describe.

4.29) What types of Waves exist in a Waveguide? What are the governing equations? Describe.

4.30) Describe what is meant by electromagnetic Power and the Poynting vector? What are the equations?

4.31) Provide two modern examples of Waves. Describe each.

4.32) Describe what is meant by The Generalized Ohm's Law? Give an example.

4.40) Derive Ohm's law from Maxwell's equation.

4.41) Derive KVL and KCL from Maxwell's equation.

4.42) Derive coulomb's law from Maxwell's equation.

4.43) Write an essay describing which one of Maxwell's equation is used in the operation of a generator? Explain by diagram(s).

4.44) Write down two examples for each subfield of electricity that you have observed in your surroundings. Briefly describe each.

4.45) What are the assumptions built into KVL and KCL?

4.46) Describe how a rail gun and a Van de graaff generator work?

4.47) What are the principles of operation and equations for:
a) A lightning rod,
b) A magneplane,
c) A cyclotron and isotope separation,
d) A Microwave oven,
e) The wavelength measurement technique,
f) The radio communication technique under water,
g) Electrostatic separation and a condenser microphone.

4.48) How does the earth's ionosphere help to transmit waves, and what is plasma frequency?

4.49) Describe wave propagation in a microstrip line? Write equations for the E- and H-fields and describe their meaning.

4.50) Describe how polarization is embedded in every EM wave?

PART II

PROPAGATION OF WAVES

CHAPTER 5

RF and Microwaves Basics

5.1 INTRODUCTION

This chapter lays the foundation for understanding higher frequency wave phenomena and compartments the task of active circuit design RF/MW frequencies into specific concept blocks. The concept blocks create a gradient approach to understanding and designing RF/MW circuits and represent specific realms of knowledge that need to be mastered in order to become an accomplished designer.

Before we proceed into analysis and description of these types of waves we need to consider why RF/Microwaves as a subject have become so important as to be placed at the forefront of our modern technology; and furthermore, we need to expand our minds to the many possibilities that these signals can provide for peaceful practices by exploring various commercial applications useful to mankind.

5.2 A SHORT HISTORY OF RF & MICROWAVES

Circa 1864-1873, James Clark Maxwell integrated the entire man's extant knowledge on electricity and magnetism and introduced a series of four coherent and self-consistent equations which described the behavior of electric and magnetic fields on a classical level. This was the beginning of microwave engineering as presented in a treatise by Maxwell at that time. He predicted, purely from a mathematical and theoretical standpoint, a) the existence of electromagnetic wave propagation and b) that light was also a form of electromagnetic energy, both completely new concepts at the time.

From 1885 to 1887, Oliver Heaviside simplified Maxwell's work in his published papers. From 1887 to 1891, a German physics professor by the name of Heinrich Hertz, verified Maxwell's predictions experimentally and demonstrated the propagation of electromagnetic waves. He also investigated wave propagation phenomena along transmission lines and antennas and developed several useful structures. He could be called the first microwave engineer.

Marconi tried to commercialize Radio at a much lower frequency for long-distance communications, but he had a business interest in all of his work and developments. So this was not a purely scientific endeavor.

The possibility of electromagnetic wave propagation inside a hollow metal tube was never investigated by Hertz or Heaviside, since it was felt that two conductors were necessary for the transfer of electromagnetic waves or energy.

In 1897, Lord Rayleigh mathematically showed that electromagnetic wave propagation was possible in a waveguide, both circular and rectangular. He showed that there are infinite set of modes of the TE and TM type possible, each with its own cut-off frequency. These were all theoretical predictions with no experimental verifications.

From 1897 to 1936, waveguide was essentially forgotten until it was rediscovered by two men, George Southworth (AT&T) and W. L. Barron (MIT) who showed experimentally that waveguide could be used as a small bandwidth transmission media, capable of carrying high power signals.

With the invention of transistor in 1950s and the advent of microwave integrated circuits in 1960s, the concept of a microwave system on a chip became a reality. There has been many other developments, mostly in terms of application mass, which has made RF and microwaves an enormously useful and popular subject.

Maxwell equations lay the foundation and laws of the science of electromagnetics, of which the field of RF and microwaves is a small subset. Due to the exact and all-encompassing nature of these laws in predicting electromagnetic phenomena along with the great body of analytical and experimental investigations performed since then, we can consider the field of RF and microwave engineering a "mature discipline" at this time.

5.3 APPLICATIONS OF MAXWELL'S EQUATIONS

As indicated earlier in Chapter 2, standard circuit theory can not be used at RF and particularly at microwave frequencies. This is because the dimensions of the device or components are comparable to the wavelength, which means that the phase of an electrical signal (e.g. a current or voltage) changes significantly over the physical length of the device or component. Thus use of Maxwell's equations at these higher frequencies become imperative.

In contrast, the signal wavelengths at lower frequencies are so much larger than the device or component dimensions that there is negligible variation in phase across the dimensions of the circuit. Thus Maxwell's equation simplify into basic circuit theory as covered in Chapters 2 and 3.

At the other extreme of the frequency range lies the optical field, where the wavelength is much smaller than the device or circuit dimensions. In this case, Maxwell's equations simplify into a subject commonly referred to as geometrical optics which treats light as a ray traveling on a straight line. These optical techniques may be applied successfully to the analysis of very high microwave frequencies (e.g. high millimeter wave range), where they are referred to as "quasi-optical". Of course, it should be noted that further application of Maxwell's equations leads to an advanced field of optics called "physical optics or Fourier optics", which treats light as a wave and explains such phenomena as diffraction and interference, where geometrical fails completely.

The important conclusion to be drawn from this discussion is that Maxwell's equations present a unified theory of analysis for any system at any frequency, provided one uses appropriate simplifications when the wavelengths involved are a) much larger, b) comparable to, or c) much smaller than the circuit dimensions.

5.4 PROPERTIES OF RF AND MICROWAVES

An important property of signals at RF, and particularly at higher microwave frequencies is their great capacity in carrying information. This is due to the existence of large bandwidths that is available at these high frequencies. For example a 10% bandwidth at 60 MHz carrier signal is 6 MHz which is approximately one TV channel of information; on the other hand 10% of a microwave carrier signal at 60 GHz is 6 GHz which is equivalent to 1000 TV channels.

Another property of microwaves is that they travel by line of sight, very much like traveling of light rays as described in the field of geometrical optics. Furthermore, unlike the lower frequency signals, the microwave signals are not bent by the ionosphere. Thus use of line-of-sight communication towers or links on the ground and orbiting satellites around the Globe are a necessity for local or global communications.

A very important civilian as well as military instrument is Radar. The concept of Radar is based upon Radar cross-section which is the effective reflection area of the target. Target's visibility greatly depends on the target's electrical size which is a function of the incident signal's wavelength. Microwave frequencies form the ideal signal band for Radar applications.

Of course, another important advantage of use of microwaves in Radars is the availability of higher antenna gains as the frequency is increased for a given physical antenna size. This is because the antenna gain is proportional to the electrical size of the antenna, which becomes larger as frequency is increased in the microwave band. The key factor in all this is that microwave wavelengths are comparable to the physical size of the transmitting antenna as well as the target.

There is a fourth and yet a very important property of microwaves and that is the molecular, atomic and nuclear resonance of conductive materials and substances when exposed to microwave fields. This property creates a wide variety of applications. For example, since almost all biological units are composed of water predominantly, and as we know water is a good conductor, thus microwave gains tremendous importance in the field of detection, diagnostics and treatment of biological problems or investigations as in medicine (e.g. diathermy, scanning, etc.).

There are other areas that this basic property would create a variety of applications such as remote sensing, heating (e.g. industrial purification, cooking, etc.) and many others which are listed in a later section.

5.5 REASONS FOR USING RF/MICROWAVES

Over the past several decades, there has been a growing trend toward use of RF/Microwaves in system applications. The reasons are many, amongst which the following are prominent:

a. Wider bandwidths due to higher frequency
b. Smaller component size leading to smaller systems
c. More available and uncrowded frequency spectrum
d. Better resolution for Radars due to smaller wavelengths
e. Lower interference due to a lower signal crowdedness
f. Higher speed of operation
g. Higher antenna gain possible in a smaller space

On the other hand, there are some disadvantages in using RF/Microwaves such as: use of more expensive components; availability of lower power levels; existence of higher signal losses and use of high-speed semiconductors (such as GaAs or InP) along with their corresponding less-mature technology, relative to the traditional Silicon technology which is quite mature and less expensive at this time.

In many RF/Microwave applications the need for a system operating at these frequencies with all the above advantages, is so great that it outweighs these disadvantages aside and spurs the engineer forward into a high-frequency design.

5.6 RF/MICROWAVE APPLICATIONS

The major applications of RF/Microwave signals can be categorized as follows:

A. Communication

This application includes satellite, space, long-distance telephone, marine, cellular telephone, data, mobile phone, aircraft, vehicle, personal and Wireless Local Area Network (WLAN) and so on. There are two important sub-categories of applications that needs to be considered as follows:

A1. TV and Radio broadcast

In this application, RF/Microwaves are used as the carrier signal for the audio and video signals. An example is the Direct Broadcast Systems (DBS) which is designed to link satellites directly to home users.

A2. Optical Communications

In this application a microwave modulator is used in the transmitting side of a low-loss optical fiber with a microwave demodulator at the other end. The microwave signal acts as a modulating signal with the optical signal as the carrier. Optical communications is useful cases where a much larger number of frequency channels as well as lower interference from outside electromagnetic radiation are desired. Current applications include telephone cables, computer network links, low-noise transmission lines, etc.

B. Radar

This application includes air defense, aircraft/ship guidance, smart weapons, police, weather, collision avoidance, imaging, etc.

C. Navigation
This application is used for orientation and guidance of aircraft, ships and land vehicles. Particular applications in this area are:

C1. Microwave Landing System (MLS), which is used to guide aircraft to land properly in airports.

C2. Global Positioning Systems (GPS) which is used to find one's exact coordinates on the Globe.

D. Remote Sensing
In this application many satellites are used to monitor the Globe constantly for weather conditions, meteorology, ozone, soil moisture, agriculture, crop protection from frost, forests, snow thickness, icebergs and other factors such as natural resources monitoring and exploration, etc.

E. Domestic and industrial applications
This application includes microwave Ovens, microwave clothes dryer, fluid heating, moisture sensors, tank gauges, automatic door openers, automatic toll collection, Highway traffic monitoring and control, chip defect detection, flow meters, power transmission in space, food preservation, pest control, etc.

F. Medical applications
This application includes cautery, selective heating, Heart stimulation, Hemorrhaging control, sterilization, imaging, etc.

G. Surveillance
This application includes security systems, intruder detection, Electronic warfare (EW) receivers to monitor signal traffic, etc.

H. Astronomy and space exploration
In this application, gigantic dish antennas are used to monitor, collect and record incoming microwave signals from outer space, providing vital information about other planets, star, meteors, etc., in this or other galaxies.

I. Wireless applications
Short-distance communication inside as well as between buildings in a local area network (LAN) arrangement can be accomplished using RF and Microwaves.

Connecting buildings via cables (e.g. coax or fiber optic) creates serious problems in congested metropolitan areas, since the cable has to be run underground from upper floors of one building to upper floors of the other. However, this problem can be greatly alleviated using RF and microwave transmitter/receiver systems which are mounted on rooftops or in office windows (see Figure 5.1).

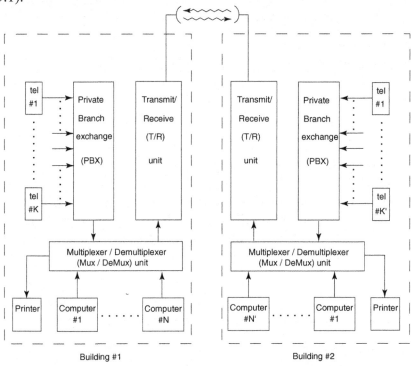

Building #1   Building #2

Figure 5.1 A typical local area network (LAN).

Furthermore inside buildings, RF and Microwaves can be used effectively to create a wireless LAN in order to connect telephones, computers and various LANs to each other. Using wireless LANs has a major advantage in office re-arrangement where phones, computers and partitions are easily moved with no change in wiring in the wall outlets. This creates enormous flexibility and cost saving features for any business entity.

A summary of RF and microwave applications is shown in table 5.1.

Category of Applications	Description
Astronomy and space exploration	-Deep space probes -Galactic explorations

Communication	-Optical communications
	  Telephone systems
	  Computer networks
	  Low-noise transmission media
	-TV and radio broadcast
	  Direct broadcast satellite
	  High definition TV

Domestic & industrial applications	-Agriculture
	  Moisture detection and soil treatment
	  Pesticides
	  Crop protection from freezing
	-Automobiles
	  Anti-theft radar or sensor
	  Automotive telecommunication
	  Blind spot radar
	  Collision avoidance radar
	  Near-obstacle detection
	  Radar speed sensors
	  Road to vehicle communication
	  Vehicle to vehicle communication
	-Highway
	  Automatic toll collection
	  Highway traffic control and monitoring
	  Range and speed detection
	  Structure inspection
	  Vehicle detection
	-Microwave Heating
	  Home microwave ovens
	  Microwave clothes dryer
	  Industrial heating
	-Microwave Imaging
	  Hidden weapon detection
	  Obstacle detection & Navigation
	-Office
	  Mail sorting
	  Wireless phones and computers
	-Power
	  Beamed power propulsion
	  Power transmission in space
	-Preservation
	  Food preservation
	  Treated manuscript drying
	-Production control

	Etching system production Industrial drying Moisture control
Medical applications	-Cautery -Heart stimulation -Hemorrhaging control -Hyperthermia -Microwave imaging -Sterilization -Thermography

Radar	-Air defense
	-Navigation & position information
	    Airport traffic control
	    Global positioning system (GPS)
	    Microwave landing system (MLS)
	-Police patrol (velocity measurement)
	-Smart weapons
	-Tracking
	-Weather forecast

Remote sensing	-Earth monitoring -Meteorology -Pollution control -Natural resources and exploration

Surveillance	-Security system
	    Intruder detection
	    Security system
	    Signal traffic monitoring

Wireless applications	-Wireless local area networks (LANs)

Table 5.1- Summary of applications of RF and microwaves

5.7 RADIO FREQUENCY (RF) WAVES

Having briefly reviewed many of the current applications of RF/Microwaves, we can see that this rapidly advancing field has great potential to be a fruitful source of many future applications.

As discussed earlier, electromagnetic (EM) waves are generated when electrical signals pass through a conductor. EM waves start to radiate more effectively from a conductor when the signal frequency is higher than the highest audio frequency which is approximately 15 to 20 kHz. Because of this radiating property, signals of such or higher frequencies are often known as radio frequency (RF) signals.

5.7.1 RF Spectrum Bands

Since it is not practical either a) to design a circuit that covers the entire frequency range, or b) to use all radio frequencies for all purposes, therefore the RF spectrum is broken down into various bands. Each band is used for a specific purpose and in general, RF circuits are designed to be used in one particular band. Table 5.2 shows the most common assignment of RF commercial bands.

NAME OF BAND	ABBREVIATION	FREQUENCY RANGE
Very low frequency	VLF	3-30 kHz
Low frequency	LF	30-300 kHz
Medium frequency	MF	300 kHz-3 MHz
High frequency	HF	3-30 MHz
Very high frequency	VHF	30-300 MHz
Ultra-high frequency	UHF	0.3-3 GHz
Super-high frequency	SHF	3-30 GHz
Extra-high frequency	EHF	30-300 GHz

Table 5.2- Commercial Radio Frequency Band

5.7.2 Definition of Microwaves

When the frequency of operation starts to increase toward approximately 1 GHz and above, a whole set of new phenomena occurs that is not present at lower frequencies. The radio waves at frequencies ranging from 1 GHz to 300 GHz are generally known as microwaves. Signals at these frequencies have wavelengths that range from 30 cm (at 1 GHz) to 1 millimeter (at 300 GHz). The special frequency range from 30 GHz to 300 GHz has a wavelength in the millimeter range thus is generally referred to as millimeter-waves.

NOTE: *It should be noted that in some texts, the range 300 MHz to 300 GHz is considered to be the microwave frequency range. This is in contrast with the microwave frequency range defined above, where the frequency range from 300 MHz to 1 GHz is referred as the RF range.*

5.7.3 Microwave Bands

The microwave frequency range consisting of the three main commercial frequency bands (UHF, SHF and EHF) can further be subdivided into several specific frequency ranges each with its own band designation. This band subdivision and designation facilitates

BAND DESIGNATION	FREQUENCY RANGE (GHz)
L Band	1.0-2.0
S band	2.0-4.0
C band	4.0-8.0
X band	8.0-12.0
Ku band	12.0-18.0
K band	18.0-26.5
Ka band (mmw)	26.5-40.0
Q band (mmw)	33.0-50.0
U band (mmw)	40.0-60.0
V band (mmw)	50.0-75.0
E band (mmw)	60.0-90.0
W band (mmw)	75.0-110.0
F band (mmw)	90.0-140.0
D band (mmw)	110.0-170.0
G band (mmw)	140.0-220.0

Table 5.3- IEEE and commercial Microwave band designations

the use of microwave signals for specific purposes and applications. In electronics industries and academic institutions, the most commonly used microwave bands are as set forth by the Institute of Electrical and Electronics Engineers (IEEE) and is shown in table 5.3. In this table the "Ka to G" are the millimeter-wave (mmw) bands.

5.8 RF AND MICROWAVE (MW) CIRCUIT DESIGN

Because of the behavior of waves at different frequencies, basic considerations in circuit design has evolved greatly over the last few decades and generally can be subdivided into two main categories:

a.   RF circuit design considerations, and

b.   Microwave (MW) circuit design considerations

Each category is briefly described next.

5.8.1 Low RF Circuit Design Steps

RF passive circuits have to go through a four step design process. In this design process the effect of wave propagation on the circuit operation is negligible and the following facts can be stated:

a. The length of the circuit (ℓ) is generally much smaller than the wavelength (i.e. $\ell << \lambda$)
b. Propagation delay time (t_d) is approximately zero (i.e. $t_d \approx 0$).
c. Maxwell's Equations simplify into all of the low frequency laws such as KVL, KCL, Ohm's law, etc. Therefore at RF frequencies (f<1 GHz), the delay time of propagation (t_d) is zero when $\ell << \lambda$ and all elements in the circuit can be considered to be lumped.

The design process for RF passive circuits has the following four steps:

Step 1. The design process starts with the required specifications as dictated by the problem set forth by the consumer. We need to know the load impedance as well as the source voltage and its impedance at this initial stage of the design.

Step 2. Next, a suitable technology that fits the parameters of the problem should be selected. For example, for low RF circuits, we need to use shielded transmission lines such as coaxial lines, etc. The characteristic impedance of the line may not be essential if the line is short and the frequency is sufficiently low.

Step 3. The third step consists of designing a lumped-element matching circuits that can transition the signal source at one end to the load at the other. Various design considerations particularly loss in the network, are included at this stage and must be incorporated in the design of the final matching network.

Step 4. In this final step, the entire circuit is put together in one seamless design to create a functional circuit. This circuit is now packaged properly by enclosing it in an appropriate box with correct connectors or terminals for communication to the outside world.

5.8.2 High RF and Microwave Circuits
To understand microwave circuits we should know that microwave circuits may have one or more lumped elements but should at least contain one distributed element. This last needs to be defined at this point:

DEFINITION- DISTRIBUTED ELEMENT: *Is defined to be an element whose property is spread out over an electrically significant length* *or area of a circuit instead of being concentrated at one location or within a specific component.*

EXAMPLE 5.1
Describe what a distributed inductor is?
Answer:
A distributed inductor would be an element whose inductance is spread out along the entire length of a conductor (such as self-inductance) as distinguished from an inductor whose inductance is concentrated within a coil.

EXAMPLE 5.2
Describe what a distributed capacitor is?
Answer:
A distributed capacitor is an element whose capacitance is spread out over a length of wire and not concentrated within a capacitor, such as the capacitance between the turns of a coil or between adjacent conductors of a circuit.

Working with distributed circuits, we need to know the following facts about them:

   a. The wave propagation concepts as set forth by the Maxwell Equations fully apply and,
   b. The circuit has a significant electrical length, i.e. its physical length is comparable to the wavelength of the signals propagating in the circuit.

This fact brings the next point into view:

   c. The time delay (t_d) due to signal propagation can no longer be neglected (i.e. $t_d \neq 0$).

To illustrate these points we will consider the following example.

EXAMPLE 5.3
How does a two-conductor transmission line (Such as a coaxial line, etc.) behave at low and high frequencies?

Answer:
At low frequencies this transmission line is considered to be a short piece of wire with a negligibly small distributed resistance which can be considered to be lumped for the purpose of analysis (since $t_d \approx 0$).

However at higher frequencies, the resistive, capacitive and inductive properties can no longer be separated and each infinitesimal length (Δx) of this transmission line exhibits these properties as shown in Figure 5.2.

From this Figure, we can see that the elements are series elements (R, L) and shunt elements (G ,C) which are defined as:
R= resistance per unit length in Ω/m
L = inductance per unit length in H/m
G = conductance per unit length in S/m
C = capacitance per unit length in F/m

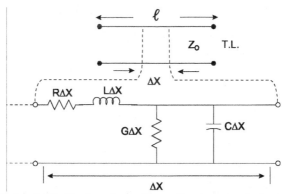

Figure 5.2 An infinitesimal portion of a transmission line (TL).

This equivalent circuit is referred to as a *distributed circuit model* of a two-conductor transmission line and will be used in the next example to derive the equivalent circuit model of a transmission line.

EXAMPLE 5.4
Using KVL and KCL derive the relationship between voltage and current in a transmission line at:
a. Low frequencies

b. High frequencies (i.e., RF/Microwave frequencies)
Solution:

    a. At low frequencies a transmission line (which can be lossy in general), can be represented as shown in Figure 5.3.

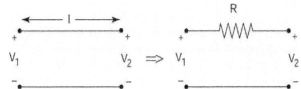

Figure 5.3 Equivalent circuit of a TL at low frequencies.

In this Figure, "R" is the distributed loss resistance of the line, which can be modeled as a lumped element. The voltage and current relationship can be written as:

$$V_1 = V_2 + IR$$

Note: *If the line is lossless, then we have:* $V_1 = V_2$

b. At high frequencies, based on Figure 5.2 a transmission line can be modeled as a distributed element as shown by the equivalent circuit in Figure 5.4.

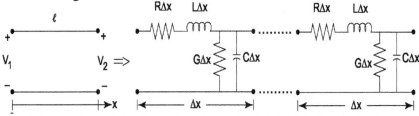

Figure 5.4 Equivalent circuit of a TL at high frequencies.

The analysis of this equivalent circuit will be postponed until later where we will examine one Δx section of a transmission line and will develop the governing equations of a transmission line in great depth.

5.8.3 High RF and Microwave Circuit Design Process

The microwave circuit design process is very similar to the low RF circuit design steps except for the wave propagation concepts, which should be taken into account.

The design process has the following four steps:

Step 1: The design process starts with the required specifications as dictated by the problem set forth by the consumer. We need to know the load impedance as well as the source voltage and its impedance at this initial stage of the design.

Step 2: Next, a suitable technology that fits the parameters of the problem should be selected. For example, for microwave ICs, we need to use planar transmission lines such as microstrip lines, etc. The characteristic impedance of the line must be established at this stage such that it is suitable and dovetails with the previous steps.

Step 3: The third step consists of designing a matching circuits that can transition the signal source at one end to the load at the other. A combination of reactive lumped elements and distributed elements may be employed in the design process. Other design considerations and criteria such as loss, VSWR, return loss, etc., may also be included at this stage and must be incorporated in the design of the final matching network.

Step 4. In this final step, the entire circuit is put together in one seamless design to create a functional circuit. This circuit is now packaged properly by enclosing it in an appropriate box with correct connectors or terminals for communication to the outside world.

Except for the fact that *one's familiarity with wave propagation* concepts becomes crucial, "Microwave Circuit Design" process is similar to the RF circuit design steps as delineated in Figure 5.5.

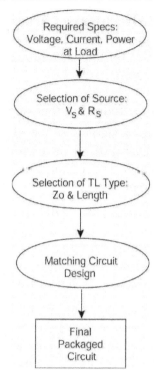

Figure 5.5 High RF and Microwave Circuit Design Steps

5.9 THE UNIVERSAL COMMUNICATION PRINCIPLE

Before we get into specific analysis and design of RF and microwave circuits, it is worthwhile first to examine a general communication system in which each circuit or component has a specific function in a bigger scheme of affairs. In general, any communication system is based upon a very simple and yet extremely fundamental truth, commonly referred to as the "universal communication principle".

The "Universal Communication Principle" is a fundamental concept which is at the heart of a wide sphere of existence called "life and livingness", or for that matter any of its subsets particularly the field of RF/Microwaves. This principle is intertwined throughout the entire field of RF/microwaves and thus plays an important role in our understanding of this subject. Therefore it behooves us well to define it at this juncture.

THE UNIVERSAL COMMUNICATION PRINCIPLE: *This principle states that communication is the process whereby information is transferred from one point in space and time (X_1, Y_1, Z_1, t_1), called the source point, to another point in space and time (X_2, Y_2, Z_2, t_2), called the receipt point. Usually, the receipt point at location (X_2, Y_2, Z_2) is separated by a distance (d) from the source point location (X_1, Y_1, Z_1) as shown below.*

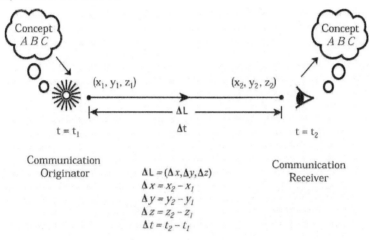

FIGURE 5.6   The universal communication principle.

The physical embodiment of the universal communication principle is a "communication system", which takes the information from the source point and delivers an exact replica of it to the receipt point (see Figure 5.7).

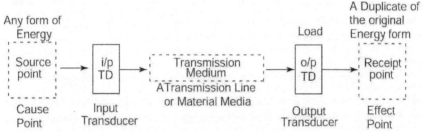

Figure 5.7 Depiction of a communication system

Thus in general, it can be seen that any communication system can be broken down into three essential elements:

1. Source point: *A point of emanation or generation of information.*
2. Receipt point: *A point of receipt of information.*
3. Distance (or Imposed space): *The space existing between the "Source point" and "Receipt point" where the information travels through.*

Furthermore, it can be observed that in order to achieve effective communication between two systems, we need to have three more factors present:
a) There must be intention on the part of the source point and the receipt point to emit and to receive the information, respectively,
b) source and receipt points must have attention on each other (i.e. both being ready for transmission and reception), and
c) duplication (i.e. an exact replica) must occur at the receipt point of what emanated from the source point.

Use of the universal communication principle in practice creates a one-way communication system (such as radio and TV broadcast, etc.), and forms one leg of a two-way communication system (such as CB radio, telephone, etc.), where this process is reversed to create the second leg of the communication action.

An important application of the universal communication principle is in a radar communication system where the source point (X_1, Y_1, Z_1) is at the same physical location as the receipt point (X_2, Y_2, Z_2), i.e., $X_1=X_2$, $Y_1=Y_2$, $Z_1= Z_2$; however the times of sending and reception are different ($t_1 \neq t_2$). Otherwise no communication would take place. This brings us to the obvious conclusion that one can not have a condition where the source and the receipt points are the same, simultaneously!

5.10 FUNDAMENTALS VERSUS STRUCTURE

Based on this simple concept of communication, the most complex communication systems can be understood, analyzed and designed.

It should be noted that the design and structure of any communication system can change and evolve into a more efficient system with time whereas the universal communication principle will never change.

Of course this should be no surprise to the workers in the field because as it turns out the foundation (which consists of fundamental postulates, axioms and natural laws) along with fundamental concepts (i.e., theorems, analytical techniques, theory of operation, etc.) of any science is far superior in importance to any designed circuitry, machinery, network, etc. This observation makes us realize that *the fundamentals are unchanging whereas the structure exists on a constant-change basis and is always evolving.* This brings us to the following conclusion:

Fundamentals of any science are superior and dictate the designed forms, structures or in general the entire application mass of that science, and not vice versa.

This is true in all aspects of design, i.e., while the underlying principle remains constant, the structure which is the electronic circuit, constantly undergoes improvements with new designs and evolves in time toward a more efficient circuitry.

This can best be described as "engineering principle as a constant" vs. "the application mass as a constantly evolving structure" where it approaches closer and closer to the underlying principle with each improvement.
Even though rarely new discoveries may bring about new underlying fundamentals to the forefront, nevertheless the fundamentals, as a general rule of thumb, remain invariant.

For example, circa 1864-1873 James clerk Maxwell interrelated all of the known data about electricity and magnetism, formulated and presented the classical laws of Electromagnetics. Since that time, which is over a century, tremendous technological changes and advances have happened all over the Globe and yet Maxwell's equations have not changed an iota. **This set of celebrated equations have remained timeless!**

Of course it should be noted that quantum mechanics, dealing with sub-atomic particles may be considered by some, to have generalized these equations and shown that energy is not continuous but quantized. Nevertheless, the Maxwell's equations at the classical level of observation have not been surpassed and are still true today and currently form the foundation of the "Electromagnetics" as a science -- the backbone of electronics and electrical engineering.

Now to build a communication system in the physical universe that works and is practical, one must satisfy two conditions:

1. First, it must be based on the fundamental concept of a) " the universal communication principle" and then b) "Maxwell's Equations"-- both in combination form a static which is unchanging!

2. Secondly, it must follow and conform to the current state of technology in terms of manufacturing, materials, device fabrication, circuit size and structure -- a kinetic and constantly evolving!
These two pre-requisites, in essence, clearly demonstrate and confirm the interplay of "static vs. kinetic" which is interwoven throughout our entire world of science and technology.

The above two steps of system design sets up the "Blueprint" for any "general engineering system design". One must heed these points carefully before one has gone very far in the quest for workable knowledge.

5.11 PASSIVE CIRCUIT BLOCK DIAGRAM
A passive circuit has four stages, which need to be understood well before a functional circuit is constructed (see Figure 5.8). A brief description of each stage can be stated as follows:

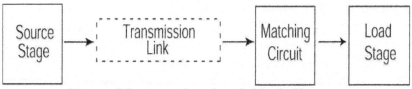

Figure 5.8 A passive circuit block diagram

1. **Source Stage:** This stage is a simple generator operating at a certain frequency and providing a certain output voltage. Using Thevenin's theorem, any generator can be modeled as a voltage source (open circuit voltage value of the generator) in series with a resistor (generator's internal resistance). An example would be the signal sent by a satellite and received at the antenna.

2. **Transmission Link:** This is the transmission media in which the microwave signal is transported from "cause or source point" to the "effect or the receipt point". An example would be the cable TV industry sending video signal via overhead cables, which are attached to utility poles.

3. **Matching Circuit Stage:** This stage matches the input signal from the feedline to the load. An example would be the circuit placed between the feed TV cable and the receiver, such that zero reflection occurs on the line.

4. **Load Stage:** This stage receives the signal and converts the electrical signal back to its original form (e.g. sound). An example for this stage could be a TV receiver box fed by an external cable. The processed signal from the receiver is finally detected and converted to audio and video signals at a TV monitor.

5.12 SUMMARY

To be proficient at higher frequency circuits (analysis or design), one needs to master, on a gradient scale, all of the underlying principles and develop a depth of knowledge before one can be called a skilled microwave practitioner.

One starts with the fundamental axioms of sciences, fundamental concepts in electromagnetics, Maxwell's equations and progresses toward high frequency circuit design by learning the DC and low frequency circuit concepts at first, then wave propagation concepts, matching circuit techniques and eventually arrives at the final destination of RF/MW active circuit design concepts, which was originally set forth as the goal of this book.

Knowing this progressive series of concepts will enable one to design complicated transmission line circuits with relative ease and proficiency at RF/MW frequencies.

CHAPTER 5- SYMBOL LIST

A symbol will not be repeated again, once it has been identified and defined in an earlier chapter, with its definition remaining unchanged.

ℓ – Length of the circuit

t_d – Time delay

λ - Wavelength

CHAPTER -5 PROBLEMS

5.1)   What are the differences and similarities between a lumped element and a distributed element?

5.2)   How many steps are required to design a) an RF circuit? b) A microwave circuit? Describe the steps.

5.3)   What are the similarities and difference(s) between an RF and a microwave circuit design procedure?

5.4)   Describe:
a) What is meant by "fundamentals vs. application mass"?
b) What is meant by timelessness of a fundamental truth?
c) What part of a system constantly evolves?
d) What are the pre-requisites for any general system design?
e) Give an example for (a-d) based on your own observations.

5.5)   Draw a) the design stages diagram and b) the block diagram of a passive microwave circuit. Provide a real-life example for each stage in (b).

5.6)   What are the main concepts one needs to master in order to design an RF or a microwave circuit?

5.7) Why is it necessary to understand the low frequency circuit concepts fully before trying to master RF/microwave circuits?

5.8) Provide five applications of microwaves in domestic and industrial applications by doing a brief research on the internet. Present description and diagrams for each of the applications.

5.9) Provide two examples of passive circuits that you have personally observed. Describe each.

5.10) Write an essay describing why RF and microwave engineering and its applications are essential in many areas? Briefly list the reasons and explain each.

CHAPTER 6

Plane Waves in Material Media

6.1 INTRODUCTION

The subject of "RF/Microwaves" primarily deals with electrical energy at high frequencies. Therefore to know microwaves, one needs to know the three qualities of energy in general.

6.2 Qualities of Energy

The following qualities apply to any and all types of energy whether electrical, mechanical, chemical, etc. at high or low frequencies. However, since we are dealing with electronics, we will narrow the following discussion to electrical energy and waves only.

A. QUALITY #1: EXISTING CHARACTERISTICS

These characteristics can be divided into three classes:

1. A Flow: is the transfer of energy from one point to another. The energy in a flow can have any type of waveform. So a flow is a transfer. This is shown in Figure 6.1.

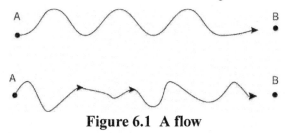

Figure 6.1 A flow

2. A divergence (also referred to as a "dispersal"): is a generalized case of a "flow" where a number of flows travel from or to a common center as shown in Figures 6.2 (a) and (b).

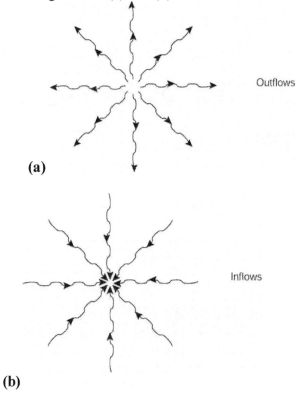

Figure 6.2 a) A net outflow, b) A net inflow.

NOTE: *"A divergence" is similar in concept but different (in definition) from "divergence of a vector quantity" which is an exact mathematical operation measuring the net outflux (or influx) of a vector quantity.*

3. A standing wave (also called a ridge of energy): is energy suspended in space and comes about when two flows or divergences of approximately equal magnitude and exact frequency impinge against one another with sufficient amplitude to cause an enduring state of energy, which may last after the flow itself has ceased. For example, a resonator or a cavity oscillator falls into the category of devices that generate this type of wave characteristic. A few examples are shown in Figures 6.3 (a) and (b).

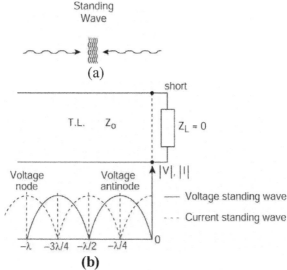

**Figure 6.3 Standing wave: a) Concept,
b) Voltage and current on a TL**

B. QUALITY #2: WAVELENGTH
Wavelength is a characteristic of an orderly flow of motion and describes its regular and repeated pattern by the distance between its peaks. Many motions are too random and too chaotic to have an orderly flow and thus have no wavelength.

DEFINITION- WAVELENGTH: *Is defined to be the physical distance between two points having the same phase in two consecutive cycles of a periodic wave along a line in the direction of propagation as shown in Figure 6.4.*

As frequency increases, the wavelength (λ) decreases as can be observed. Thus higher frequency waves have shorter wavelengths as already discussed in Chapter 5 (see Figure 6.4).

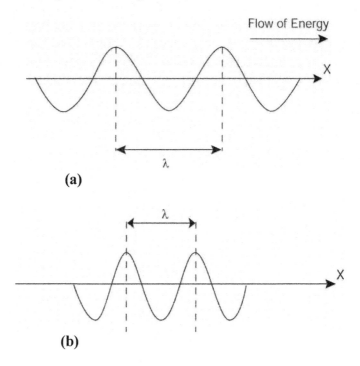

Figure 6.4 Wavelength for two cases: a) Lower frequency (larger λ), b) Higher frequency (smaller λ).

Wavelength has no bearing on the wave characteristics (quality #1) but applies to the repetition property of the wave flow. A standing wave has a potential flow when released, therefore may be considered to have a wavelength even though it is not a flow or a wave in the truest sense of the word.

If a random wave is periodic, it can be considered to have a wavelength using "Fourier theorem". It can be proven mathematically that through the use of Fourier analysis, any wave can be decomposed into its Fourier harmonics, provided that the wave is continuously flowing and periodic as shown in Figure 6.5.

Figure 6.5 Examples of Wave patterns.

C. QUALITY #3: A FLOW'S DIRECTION (OR ABSENCE THEREOF)

This quality describes the direction or the absence of direction of flow. A few examples are shown in Figure 6.6. This quality is an important one, since energy can have a flow with no net transfer of energy i.e. absence of the direction of flow.

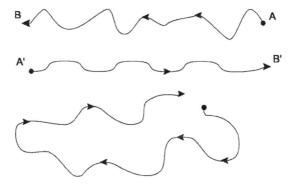

**Figure 6.6 A flow with a) a direction(A-B or A'-B'),
b) an absence of direction.**

For example, a wave traveling from a transmitter to a receiver, or electrons moving in a wire under the influence of an electric field is said to have a "direction of flow".

Examples of absence of direction include a) a free electron moving in the lattice of a solid at equilibrium (i.e. when no external field is applied) which is a flow with an absence of direction or b) an electron in an atom moving in an orbit around the nucleus. Both are flows without a net transfer of energy.

6.3 DEFINITION OF A WAVE

So far we have loosely used "a wave" to mean a special case of a flow of energy. Now we need to define it exactly:

DEFINITION- A WAVE: *Is a disturbance that propagates from one point in a medium to other points without giving the medium, as a whole, any permanent displacement.*

This general definition of a wave includes any and all disturbances that could be of electrical or non-electrical origins. However, now we further restrict our definition to a special class of waves which are of electrical origin. These waves are called electromagnetic (EM) waves. Now, we need to define an important term:

DEFINITION-AN ELECTROMAGNETIC (EM) WAVE: *Is a radiant energy flow produced by oscillation of an electric charge. In free space and away from the source (which is moving electric charges), EM rays of waves consist of vibrating electric and magnetic fields which move at the speed of light (in vacuum), are at right angles to each other and to the direction of motion.*

The propagation of a simple electromagnetic wave in free space is shown in Figure 6.7. EM waves propagate with no actual transport of matter and grow weaker in amplitude as they travel farther in space.

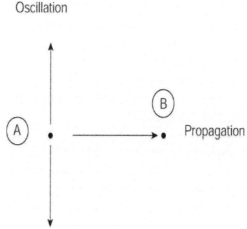

Figure 6.7 The propagation of a simple wave from A to B.

EM waves include Radio, microwaves, infrared, visible/ultraviolet light waves, X-, gamma- and cosmic- rays. (See Electromagnetic spectrum in Chapter 6).

These are all different types of electrical energy and all follow the same principles that we have discussed so far in this chapter (see Figures 6.8 and 6.9).

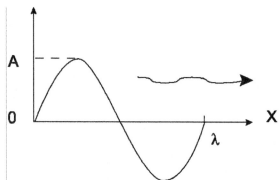

Figure 6.8 Wave amplitude in space.

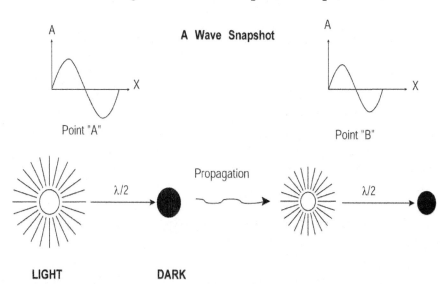

Figure 6.9 Reduction of wave amplitude as it propagates.

On a larger view of things, we can observe that RF and Microwaves are a special case of EM waves, which itself is a subset of larger field of study, i.e., waves. Of course, this last itself is a subset of a much larger sphere of existence known as "energy", as shown in Figure 6.10.

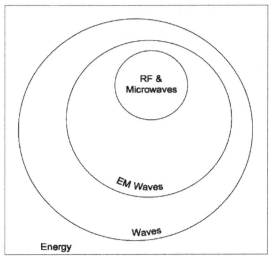

Figure 6.10 Relationship of RF and Microwaves to energy.

6.4 MATHEMATICAL FORM OF PROPAGATING WAVES

We know that $f(x-x_o)$ is the same function as $f(x)$ except shifted to the right a distance "x_o" along +x axis. If instead, we consider $f(x-vt)$ then the function $f(x)$ is shifted to the right a distance $x_o=vt$, where "v" and "t" can be considered to be the velocity of motion and the elapsed time, respectively. The distance (x_o) increases as time elapses, therefore the function is displaced continuously farther out along the +x axis as time elapses.

6.4.1 An Important Special Case: Sinusoidal Waves

Assume $f(x)$ is a sinusoidal function:

$f(x)=A \cos\beta x$ (6.1)

Where A is the amplitude and β is the phase constant. Then a sinusoidal wave propagating in +x direction would be represented   in time and phasor domain by:

a. Time domain form:

$\quad$**$f(x,t)= A\cos\beta(x-vt)$**

$\qquad$**$= A\cos(\beta x-\omega t)$**   (6.2)

Or,

b. in Phasor form:

$\quad$**$F=Ae^{-j\beta x}$**   (6.3)

Where ω $(=\beta v)$ is the angular frequency.

To find the wavelength (λ), we know that it is defined to be the physical distance between two peaks (or valleys). We note that at t=0, the wave's peak is at $x = 0$. The next peak is at $x = \lambda$ and the sinusoidal wave has a phase of 2π, thus:

$$\beta\lambda = 2\pi \Rightarrow \lambda = 2\pi/\beta \qquad (6.4)$$

For the wave propagating in the "-x" direction, the following can be written:

c. Time domain: $f(x,t)=A\cos(\beta x+\omega t)$ (6.5)

Or,

d. Phasor domain: $F=Ae^{j\beta x}$ (6.6)

The phase velocity (V_P), which is defined to be the velocity at which the plane of the constant phase propagates, can be obtained from:

$$\beta x-\omega t = B, \qquad (6.7a)$$

Where B is an arbitrary constant.

Differentiating Equation (6.7) with respect to time gives the phase velocity:

$$\beta dx/dt-\omega=dB/dt=0 \Rightarrow V_p=dx/dt=\omega/\beta \qquad (6.7b)$$

In an unrestricted or "free" space, a plane wave travels at velocity V_P which is given by:

$$\omega=1/\sqrt{\mu_0\varepsilon_0} \qquad (6.8)$$

Where μ_0 and ε_0 are the permeability and permittivity of free space.

Equations (6.2) and (6.5) show a simple wave that keeps its size and shape while propagating at a constant velocity V_P. This type of propagation is said to be undistorted and unattenuated since it is propagating in free space (or vacuum) which is a non-dispersive medium.

DEFINITION-A DISPERSIVE MEDIUM: *is a medium in which the phase velocity (V_P) of a wave is a function of its frequency.*

This means that a complex wave, consisting of several frequencies, travels through a dispersive medium at different velocities i.e. each frequency component travels at $V_p = \omega/\beta$ with different time delays. This would cause the wave to be distorted at the exit point.

For example a square-pulse waveform entering and traveling through a dispersive medium will lose its shape and will appear rounded at both of its edges when exiting the medium.

EM waves can have a "rise and fall" as well as an "advance and retreat" type of oscillation of the field quantity, as they propagate (see Figure 6.11).

6.4.2 Types of Waves

Waves are like fluids and propagate according to the medium in which they find themselves. If the medium is unrestricted, then it would be called "Free space wave propagation". When the source is a point and the medium of propagation is free space, waves have spherical wavefronts as shown in Figure 6.12.

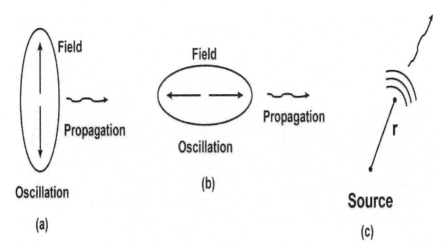

Figure 6.11 Propagation of an EM wave for a) A transverse field, b) A longitudinal field, and c) A wave a distance "r" from source.

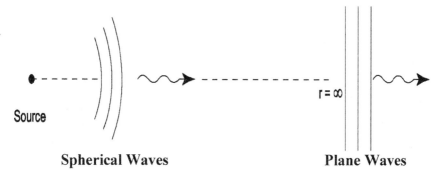

Figure 6.12 A spherical wave becoming a plane wave.

6.4.3 A Special Case: Plane Waves

When waves under consideration are at an infinite distance away from the source of disturbance, then the wavefront of each wave is a plane surface and these waves are called plane waves (see Figure 6.13). These plane waves are in the TEM mode of propagation.

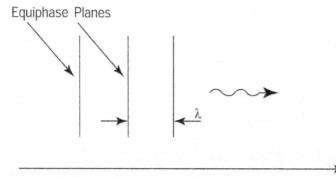

Figure 6.13 Propagation of a plane wave in x direction.

DEFINITION-TEM (TRANSVERSE ELECTRO-MAGNETIC) MODE: *Is defined to be waves having the electric and magnetic fields perpendicular to each other and to the direction of propagation. These waves have no field components in the direction of propagation.*

A typical TEM wave in free space is shown in Figure 6.14.

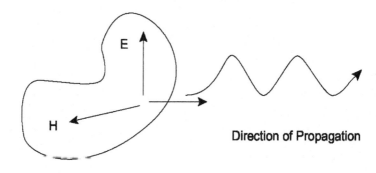

Field Oscillation

Figure 6.14   A typical TEM wave in free space.

The mathematical expression, **a(x,t),** for the plane wave propagation is defined below.

a. General time domain form is given by:

$$a(x,t)=A_o \, f(\omega t-\beta x) \qquad (6.9)$$

For a time harmonic wave, we can write:

$$a(x,t)=A_o cos(\omega t-\beta x)$$
$$=Re(A_o e^{-j\beta x} e^{j\omega t}) \qquad (6.10)$$

b. In phasor domain, we have:

$$A(x)= A_o e^{-j\beta x}, \qquad (6.11)$$

Which is a plane wave propagating in +x direction as shown in Figure 6.12 and 6.13.

6.5 PROPERTIES OF WAVES

There are several properties of waves that are worthy of consideration at the outset of this section:

Property #1: Flow property

This property is in common with quality #1 for energy. A wave is a flow. It goes from point "A" to point "B" and in doing so a transfer of energy takes place, of course with a reduced amplitude at the destination, as shown in Figure 6.15.

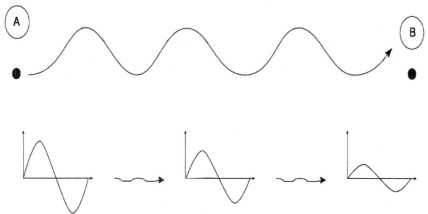

Figure 6.15 wave as a flow of energy showing a reduction of amplitude as it propagates.

Property #2: Wavelength Property

This property was discussed as quality #2 of energy. A wave with a regular and periodic (or repeating) waveform has a wavelength which is the physical distance between two peaks (or valleys) in two consecutive cycles as defined earlier in a more precise way. This concept is shown in Figure 6.16.

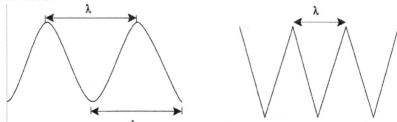

Figure 6.16 The concept of wavelength.

In order to derive wavelength (λ) we know that the speed of propagation (v) is uniform thus the distance (λ) traveled in one wave period (T=1/f) is:

$$\lambda = vT = v/f \tag{6.12}$$

At high RF and microwaves the wavelength ranges from one meter to one millimeter corresponding to a frequency of 300 MHz to 300 GHz.

NOTE: *For vacuum and air v=c=3x108 m/s.*
PROPERTY #3: REFLECTION AND TRANSMISSION PROPERTY
When a wave encounters an obstacle or a different medium, some of it reflects back (called a reflected wave) and the rest of it transmits through (called a transmitted wave). This is true for any and all types of waves.

EXAMPLE 6.1a: PERFECT REFLECTION
How does a perfect mirror behave for an incident wave?
Solution:
For a perfect mirror we have perfect reflection, i.e. 100% of the incident wave reflects back and zero transmission takes place as shown in Figure 6.17.

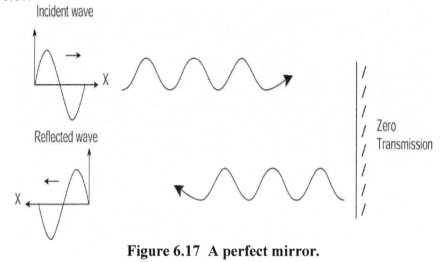

Figure 6.17 A perfect mirror.

Example 6.1b: Perfect transmission
What would constitute a perfect transmission condition?

Solution:
For a perfect transmission, the two media have to be identical in their electrical properties (such as permittivity, permeability, etc.) as shown in Figure 6.18. This means that for this condition to occur, the second medium has to continue to behave electrically the same as the first.

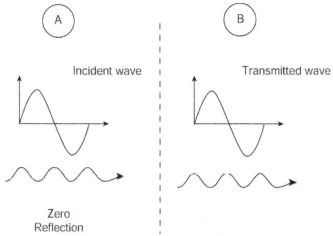

Figure 6.18 A perfect transmission.

Property #4) Standing-wave property
When two waves of exactly the same magnitude and frequency travel opposite to each other, the result is not a wave but an "Oscillation with no propagation" called a "Standing wave" which has a fixed location, as shown in Figure 6.19.

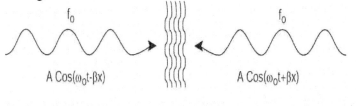

Figure 6.19 A standing wave.
The standing wave can be written mathematically in:
a. Phasor domain:

$$Ae^{-j\beta x} + Ae^{+j\beta x} = 2A\cos\beta x \qquad (6.13a)$$

b. Time domain:

$$2A\cos(\beta x)\cos(\omega t) \qquad (6.13b)$$

Since Equation (6.13b) is not of the form $f(\beta x - \omega t)$, thus it is not a wave but a pure oscillation at a fixed location!

NOTE: *A definite pre-requisite for a standing wave is two opposite waves of exact frequency. However, their amplitudes should be comparable, if* *not equal. The result would be a standing wave plus a traveling wave and not a pure standing wave as described above.*

6.6 BASIC PLANE WAVES IN LOSSLESS MEDIA

From Chapter 4 (section 4.10) we know that the General Wave Equation can be derived from the Maxwell's Equations in a lossless medium ($\sigma=0$) and is given by:

$$\nabla^2\overline{E} - \mu\varepsilon\frac{\partial^2\overline{E}}{\partial t^2} = 0$$

$$\nabla^2\overline{H} - \mu\varepsilon\frac{\partial^2\overline{H}}{\partial t^2} = 0$$

(6.14)

For sinusoidal electric field (E) and magnetic field (H) in the time domain are given by:

$$\overline{E} = \text{Re}(\overline{E}_o e^{j\omega t})$$ (6.15a)

$$\overline{H} = \text{Re}(\overline{H}_o e^{j\omega t})$$ (6.15b)

We can write the general wave equations in the phasor domain as:

$$\nabla^2\overline{E}_o + k^2\overline{E}_o = 0,$$ (6.16a)

$$\nabla^2\overline{H}_o + k^2\overline{H}_o = 0$$ (6.16b)

Where "k" is the Wave Number, and for non-conducting Media is defined as:

$$k = \omega\sqrt{\mu\varepsilon} = \omega/v_p = 2\pi/\lambda$$ (6.17)

A basic plane wave solution to the above equations can be found by considering a uniform plane wave (i.e., no amplitude variation in the x and y direction) propagating in the z-direction having electric and magnetic field components in the x- and y-directions respectively. Since there are no variation in the x and y direction, therefore we have:

$$\partial E_o/\partial x = \partial E_o/\partial y = 0$$

$$\overline{E}_o(z) = \overline{E}_x(z) = E_x(z)\hat{x}$$ (6.18)

$$\partial^2\overline{E}_x/\partial z^2 + k^2\overline{E}_x = 0,$$ (6.19)

By observation, the solution is of the exponential form, which generally can be written as:

$$E_x(z) = E^+ e^{-jkz} + E^- e^{jkz}$$

where E^- and E^+ are amplitude constants. This general solution (in phasor form) consists of two waves:
1. E^+e^{-jkz}: Representing an EM wave traveling in the +z direction, and
2. E^-e^{jkz} : representing an EM wave traveling in the –z direction.

Note: *The general equation for the magnitude of the E-field of a plane wave in phasor form is given by: $E(x,y,z)=|E|\,e^{-j\bar{k}\cdot\bar{r}}$, where wave vector $\bar{k}=k\hat{n}$, position vector $\bar{r}=x\hat{x}+y\hat{y}+z\hat{z}$ and $\hat{n}$ is a unit vector in the direction of propagation.*

In time domain, the above general solution can be written as:
$$\overline{E}(z,t)= [E^+\cos(\omega t-kz)+ E^-\cos(\omega t +kz)]\,\hat{x}$$

Using the results from chapter 4, the accompanying H field of the plane wave is given by:

$$\overline{E}_o(z) = \overline{E}_x(z) =E_x(z)\,\hat{x} \tag{6.20}$$
$$\nabla\times\overline{E} = -j\omega\mu\overline{H} \;\Rightarrow\; \overline{H} = (j/\omega\mu)\nabla\times\overline{E} \tag{6.21}$$
$$H_y(z)=H^+e^{-jkz} - H^-e^{jkz} \tag{6.22}$$
$$\text{Where } E^+/H^+=E^-/H^- =\omega\mu/k=\sqrt{\mu/\varepsilon}=\eta \tag{6.23}$$

The ratio of the E-field amplitude to that of the H-field is generally called the "wave impedance" of the wave, however, for plane waves it is called the "intrinsic impedance" of the medium and is represented by the symbol (η).

For plane waves in free space, we have:
$$\eta_o = \sqrt{\mu_o/\varepsilon_o} = 120\pi =377\,\Omega \tag{6.24}$$
For non free-space propagation, we have:
$$\eta=\eta_0/\sqrt{\varepsilon_r} \tag{6.25}$$

NOTE: *E- and H-field vectors are perpendicular to each other and both to the direction of propagation (z-direction), an important characteristic of Transverse Electromagnetic (TEM) waves.*

6.7 PLANE WAVES IN LOSSY MEDIA
If the medium is conductive (with a conductivity σ), the Maxwell's Equations in time domain can be written as:

$$\nabla^2 \overline{E} - \mu\varepsilon \frac{\partial^2 \overline{E}}{\partial t^2} - \mu\sigma \frac{\partial \overline{E}}{\partial t} = 0$$

$$\nabla^2 \overline{H} - \mu\varepsilon \frac{\partial^2 \overline{H}}{\partial t^2} = 0$$

(6.26)

In the phasor domain we have:

$$\nabla^2 \overline{E}_o + k^2 \overline{E}_o = 0,$$
(6.27a)

$$\nabla^2 \overline{H}_o + k^2 \overline{H}_o = 0$$
(6.27b)

Where "k" is the Wave Number, and for conducting media is a complex number defined as:

$$k = \omega\sqrt{\mu\varepsilon}(\sqrt{1 - j\sigma/\omega\varepsilon})$$
(6.28)

If we now define a complex propagation constant for TEM waves as:

$$\gamma = jk$$
(6.29)

Then we have:

$$\gamma = j\omega\sqrt{\mu\varepsilon}(\sqrt{1 - j\sigma/\omega\varepsilon}) = \alpha + j\beta$$
(6.30)

NOTE: *For the lossless case (i.e., when α=0), we get:*
$k=\beta$

If we now assume a uniform plane wave (i.e., no amplitude variation in the x and y direction) propagating in the z-direction having electric and magnetic field components in the x- and y-directions respectively, we can write:

$\partial E_o/\partial x = \partial E_o/\partial y = 0$ (i.e., no variation in the x and y directions)

$$\overline{E}_o(z) = \overline{E}_x(z) = E_x(z)\,\hat{x}$$
(6.31)

$$\partial^2 \overline{E}_x / \partial z^2 - \gamma^2 \overline{E}_x = 0,$$
(6.32)

By observation, the solution is of the exponential form, which generally can be written as:

$E_x(z) = E^+ e^{-\gamma z} + E^- e^{\gamma z}$

where E^- and E^+ are amplitude constants.

This general solution (in phasor form) consists of two waves:

1. $E^+e^{-\gamma z} = e^{-\alpha z}e^{-j\beta z}$: Representing an EM wave traveling in the +z direction, and

2. $E^-e^{\gamma z} = e^{\alpha z}e^{j\beta z}$: representing an EM wave traveling in the –z direction.

In time domain, the above general solution can be written as:

$$\overline{E}(z,t) = [E^+e^{-\alpha z}\cos(\omega t - \beta z) + E^-e^{\alpha z}\cos(\omega t + \beta z)]\ \hat{x} \qquad (6.33)$$

In the time domain, we can see that there is an exponential damping factor, with a rate of decay with distance given by the attenuation constant (α).

Using the results from chapter 4, the accompanying H field of the plane wave is given by:

$$\overline{E}_0(z) = E_x(z)\hat{x} \qquad (6.34)$$

$$\nabla \times \overline{E} = -j\omega\mu\overline{H} \qquad (6.35)$$

$$H_y(z) = H^+e^{-\gamma z} - H^-e^{\gamma z} \qquad (6.36)$$

Where $E^+/H^+ = E^-/H^- = j\omega\mu/\gamma = \eta \qquad (6.37)$

$$\eta = \sqrt{j\omega\mu/(\sigma + j\omega\varepsilon)} = \sqrt{\mu/\varepsilon}\sqrt{1/(1 - j\tan\delta)} = |\eta|\angle\delta/2 \quad (6.38)$$

$$|\eta| = (\sqrt{\mu/\varepsilon})/[1 + \tan^2\delta]^{1/4} \qquad (6.39)$$

Where
$$\tan\delta = \sigma/\omega\varepsilon \qquad (6.40)$$
is called the loss tangent of the medium.

6.7.1 Perfect Dielectrics

For a perfect dielectric, $\sigma = 0$, and thus $\tan\delta = 0$ leading to:

$$\eta = \sqrt{\mu/\varepsilon}\ , \qquad (6.41a)$$

and

$$\gamma = j\omega\sqrt{\mu\varepsilon} = \alpha + j\beta \qquad (6.41b)$$

Giving,
$\alpha = 0$ and $\beta = \omega\sqrt{(\mu\varepsilon)}$. $\qquad (6.41c)$

6.7.2 Good Conductors

Materials are considered to be good conductors if in the frequency range of interest:

$\tan\delta = \sigma/\omega\varepsilon \gg 1$

With this assumption, the propagation constant and intrinsic impedance simplify:

$$\alpha = \beta = \sqrt{\omega\mu\sigma/2} = \sqrt{\pi f\mu\sigma}, \tag{6.42a}$$

and

$$\eta = j\omega\mu/\gamma = \sqrt{\omega\mu/\sigma}\angle 45° \tag{6.42b}$$

Therefore, in this case E and H vectors are attenuated as they propagate and are out of phase by $45°$ at all times.

6.7.3 Perfect Conductors

For a perfect dielectric, $\sigma = \infty$, and thus $\tan\delta = \infty$, leading to:

$$\eta = 0, \tag{6.43}$$

and

$$\alpha = \beta = \infty, \tag{6.44}$$

Giving,

$$E = H = 0. \tag{6.45}$$

That is to say, no propagation is allowed in a perfect conductor and therefore it acts as a perfect shield for EM radiations.

6.7.4 Skin Depth

We define the distance that the wave attenuates to 1/e of its original value before entering the medium as the "depth of penetration or the skin depth (δ_s)" defined by:

$$e^{-\alpha\delta_s} = e^{-1} \rightarrow \delta_s = 1/\alpha = 1/\sqrt{\pi f\mu\sigma} \tag{6.46}$$

EXAMPLE 6.7

Assuming a TEM wave propagating in +z direction in a good conductor (such as copper or silver) with an E-field of amplitude E_o in the x direction, write down the E and the H fields in the phasor and time domain.

Solution:

$$\eta = \sqrt{\omega\mu/\sigma}\angle 45° = |\eta|\angle 45° = (1+j)/\sigma\,\delta_s \tag{6.47}$$

$$E_x(z) = E_o e^{-\gamma z} = E_o e^{-\alpha z} e^{-j\beta z} \tag{6.48}$$

$$H_y(z) = H^+ e^{-\gamma z} = E_o e^{-\alpha z} e^{-j(\beta z + 45°)}/|\eta| \tag{6.49}$$

In time domain, the above solution can be written as:

$$\overline{E}(z,t)= [E_o e^{-\alpha z}\cos(\omega t-\beta z)]\, \hat{x} \qquad (6.50a)$$

$$\overline{H}(z,t)= [(E_o e^{-\alpha z}/|\eta|)\cos(\omega t-\beta z-45°)]\, \hat{y} \qquad (6.50b)$$

Note: *The phase angle for a good conductor is 45°, whereas the phase angle for a lossless material is 0°. Therefore, we can see that the phase angle for any lossy medium which is not a good conductor lies somewhere between 0° and 45°.*

6.8 PLANE WAVES AT MEDIA INTERFACE

When a traveling plane wave reaches an interface between two different media (e.g., media 1 and), we observe that some of the wave energy reflects into the first media and the remaining is transmitted into the second as shown in Figure 6.20.

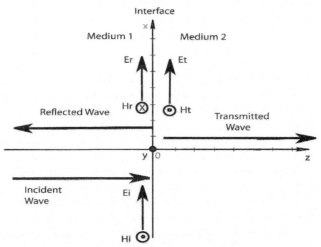

Figure 6.20 Normal incidence.

Of course, the amount of reflection and transmission of the wave into each media depends upon its electrical characteristics distinctly and precisely described by permittivity and permeability of the medium (ε, μ) relative to each other.

6.8.1 Boundary Conditions

If we assume a uniform plane wave (i.e., no amplitude variation in the x and y direction) propagating in the z-direction normal to the interface, having electric and magnetic field components in the x- and y-directions respectively, then we can write the E- and H-fields in the two regions (in the phasor domain) as:

$$E_{xi}(z)=E_i e^{-jk_1 z} \qquad (6.51a)$$

$$E_{xr}(z)=E_r e^{+jk_1 z} \qquad (6.51b)$$

$$E_{xt}(z)=E_t e^{-jk_2 z} \qquad (6.51c)$$

$$H_{yi}(z)=H_i e^{-jk_1 z} =E_i e^{-jk_1 z}/\eta_1 \qquad (6.51d)$$

$$H_{yr}(z)= H_r e^{+jk_1 z} = -E_r e^{+jk_1 z}/\eta_1 \qquad (6.51e)$$

$$H_{yt}(z)=H_t e^{-jk_2 z} =E_t e^{-jk_2 z}/\eta_2 \qquad (6.51f)$$

Where subscripts "i, r, t" signify "incident, reflected and transmitted," respectively, and wave numbers k_1 and k_2 are defined by:

$$k_1 = \omega\sqrt{\mu_1 \varepsilon_1} = \omega/ v_{P1} = 2\pi/\lambda_1 \qquad (6.52)$$

and

$$k_2 = \omega\sqrt{\mu_2 \varepsilon_2} = \omega/ v_{P2} = 2\pi/\lambda_2 \qquad (6.53)$$

Please note that E_i, E_r, E_t are complex numbers, in general. The minus sign in the H_{yr} equation is there to indicate the direction of power flow, which is in the –z direction. This is so because

$$\overline{P} = (\overline{E} \times \overline{H}) \qquad (6.54)$$

gives the direction of power flow, as discussed in depth in chapter 4.

From basic electromagnetic theory, we know that tangential E is continuous at the interface, thus:

$$E_i+E_r=E_t \qquad (6.55)$$

Furthermore, tangential H is also continuous at the interface (if there are no surface currents), thus we can write:

$$H_i+H_r=H_t \rightarrow E_i/\eta_1-E_r/\eta_1=E_t/\eta_2 \qquad (6.56)$$

Using these two equations we obtain the reflection coefficient (Γ) as:

$$\Gamma=E_r/E_i= (\eta_2-\eta_1)/(\eta_2 + \eta_1) \qquad (6.57)$$

And the transmission coefficient (T) as:

$$T=E_t/E_i= (2\eta_2)/(\eta_2 + \eta_1) \qquad (6.58)$$

Using the equation for Γ and T as given above, we obtain:

$$T = 1 + \Gamma \tag{6.59}$$

6.8.2 Summary of Analysis

Knowing the intrinsic impedance of the media in which the wave is propagating is crucial in determining its behavior and attenuation as time goes on.

For this reason, it is valuable to have a summary of the salient points of different types of media and their corresponding intrinsic impedance so that a quick analysis of the waves could be obtained. Rapid resolution of problems dealing with waves and the design of high frequency circuits that can create waves of a certain frequency, waveform and amplitude accurately could be called " wave engineering."

The intrinsic impedance for different types of media is different, thus these equations provide the percentage of reflection and transmission of waves as the incident wave strikes the interface. The values of the intrinsic impedance for some simple media is given below:

1. $\eta_o = \sqrt{\mu_o / \varepsilon_o} = 120\pi = 377 \ \Omega$ (free space)   (6.60a)

2. $\eta = \sqrt{\mu / \varepsilon} = \eta_o / \sqrt{\varepsilon_r}$ (perfect dielectric, $\sigma = 0$, $\mu_r = 1$)   (6.60b)

3. $\eta = \sqrt{\omega\mu / \sigma} \angle 45°$ (good conductor)   (6.60c)

4. $\eta = 0$ (perfect conductor, $\sigma = \infty$)   (6.60d)

5. $\eta = \sqrt{j\omega\mu / (\sigma + j\omega\varepsilon)} = |\eta| \angle \delta / 2$ (Partially conducting) (6.61)

Where $|\eta| = (\sqrt{\mu / \varepsilon}) / [1 + \tan^2 \delta]^{1/4}$,   (6.62)

and

$$\tan\delta = \sigma / \omega\varepsilon \tag{6.63}$$

6.9 STANDING WAVES

When an EM wave traveling in one medium encounters a discontinuity of any form or nature (such as another medium), then part of it will reflect (represented by Γ) and the remaining part will transmit to the other side (represented by T).

Assuming an initial lossless medium, the combination of the incident and reflected waves may be written as follows:

$$E_x(z)=E^+e^{-jkz}+ \Gamma E^+e^{jkz} = \Gamma E^+ (e^{-jkz} + e^{jkz})+ (1-\Gamma) E^+e^{-jkz} \qquad (6.64)$$

Yielding,
$$E_x(z)= 2\Gamma E^+ (Coskz)+ (1-\Gamma) E^+e^{-jkz} \qquad (6.65)$$
Conversion back into time domain gives:
$$E_x(z,t)= 2\Gamma E^+ (Coskz \; Cos\omega t)+ (1-\Gamma) E^+ Cos(\omega t -kz) \qquad (6.66)$$

The first term is a standing wave which is non-propagating, however the second term is a wave propagating in the +x direction. This mathematical result can be understood better by visualizing the reflecting wave locking up part of the incident wave into a standing wave, whereas the remaining portion of the wave continues to propagate.

6.9.1 Special Cases

A few special cases are of interest at this point and will bring a higher level of understanding to the subject of standing waves as follows:

a. Perfect Conductor (Γ=-1)

When the second medium is a perfect conductor, then
$$\sigma_2 =\infty \rightarrow \eta_2=0 \rightarrow \Gamma= -1$$
In this case we can write Equation 6.65 as:
$$E_x(z)= -2 \; E^+ (e^{-jkz} + e^{jkz})/2+ 2E^+e^{-jkz} \qquad (6.67)$$
Giving:
$$E_x(z)= E^+ (e^{-jkz} - e^{jkz})=-2j \; E^+ \; Sinkz = 2e^{-j\pi/2} E^+ \; Sinkz \qquad (6.68)$$
Converting to time domain yields:
$$E_x(z,t)= 2 \; E^+ \; Sinkz \; Cos \; (\omega t-\pi/2)=2 \; E^+ \; Sinkz \; Sin\omega t \qquad (6.69)$$

b. Same Impedance Medium (Γ=0)

When the second medium is the same or has the same electrical characteristics as that of the first medium (i.e., $\eta_1= \eta_2$), then there is no reflection and thus no standing waves and the only wave is the incident wave:
$$E_x(z)= E^+e^{-jkz} \qquad (6.70)$$

NOTE: *In order to get no standing waves, the second medium can be different than the first as long as the ratio of μ/ε remains the same* *(such as $\varepsilon_2 = n\varepsilon_1$, $\mu_2 = n\mu_1$, where n is a positive integer), even though the wave number would be different in the second medium. This would give us our first clue to the design of reflectionless and thus materials invisible to Radar.*

c. High Impedance Medium ($\Gamma=1$)

When the second medium has an intrinsic impedance much higher than the first one we obtain:

$\eta_2 \gg \eta_1 \rightarrow \eta_2 / \eta_1 \gg 1$

$\Gamma = (\eta_2 / \eta_1 - 1) / (\eta_2 / \eta_1 + 1) \approx 1$ (6.71a)

In this case the standing wave equation (6.65) becomes:

$E_x(z) = 2 E^+ (\text{Cos}kz)$ (6.71b)

d. Low Impedance Medium ($\Gamma = -1$)

When the second medium has an intrinsic impedance much lower than the first one we obtain:

$\eta_2 \ll \eta_1 \rightarrow \eta_2 / \eta_1 \ll 1$

$\Gamma = (\eta_2 / \eta_1 - 1) / (\eta_2 / \eta_1 + 1) \approx -1$ (6.72)

In this case we can write Equation 6.65 as:

$E_x(z) = -2 E^+ (e^{-jkz} + e^{jkz})/2 + 2E^+ e^{-jkz}$ (6.73a)

Giving:

$E_x(z) = E^+ (e^{-jkz} - e^{jkz}) = -2j E^+ \text{Sin}kz = 2e^{-j\pi/2} E^+ \text{Sin}kz$ (6.73b)

Converting to time domain yields:

$E_x(z,t) = 2 E^+ \text{Sin}kz \text{ Cos } (\omega t - \pi/2) = 2 E^+ \text{Sin}kz \text{ Sin}\omega t$ (6.73c)

This case is almost the same as in perfect conductor case above.

6.10 POWER AND THE POYNTING VECTOR

From a discussion in Chapter 4, we understand that the instantaneous rate of energy flow per unit area at any point in space is measured by the Poynting vector:

$$\overline{P}(t) = \overline{E}(t) \times \overline{H}(t)$$ (6.74a)

The Poynting vector gives the direction of energy flow in real time due to its vector nature. However, if we wish to find the time average value of $(\overline{P})$, then we need to use the phasor form of E and H as follows:

$$\overline{P}_{av} = 1 / 2 [\text{Re}(\overline{E} \times \overline{H}^*)]$$ (6.74b)

Where (H^*) designates the complex conjugate of H.

6.10.1 Lossless Medium

For *plane waves* propagating in the +z direction in a lossless medium, we can calculate the average power from the phasors for E and H fields as follows:

$$E_x(z) = E^+ e^{-jkz} \qquad (6.75a)$$
$$H_y(z) = H^+ e^{-jkz} \qquad (6.75b)$$

Where $E^+/H^+ = \sqrt{\mu/\varepsilon} = \eta$ (6.75c)

$$\overline{P}_{av} = \frac{1}{2\eta}|E^+|^2 \,\hat{z} \quad \text{W/m}^2 \qquad (6.75d)$$

6.10.2 Lossy Medium

For a lossy medium, a *plane wave* propagating in the +z direction, has an average power which is exponentially decreasing with increasing distance as given below:

$$E_x(z) = E^+ e^{-\gamma z} \qquad (6.76a)$$
$$H_y(z) = H^+ e^{-\gamma z} \qquad (6.76b)$$

Where

$$\gamma = j\omega\sqrt{\mu\varepsilon}(\sqrt{1 - j\sigma/\omega\varepsilon}) = \alpha + j\beta \qquad (6.76c)$$

and

$$E^+/H^+ = \eta \qquad (6.76d)$$

$$\eta = \sqrt{j\omega\mu/(\sigma + j\omega\varepsilon)} = \sqrt{\mu/\varepsilon}\sqrt{1/(1 - j\tan\delta)} = |\eta|\angle\delta/2 \quad (6.76e)$$

$$|\eta| = (\sqrt{\mu/\varepsilon})/[1 + \tan^2\delta]^{1/4} \qquad (6.76f)$$

Where

$$\tan\delta = \sigma/\omega\varepsilon \qquad (6.76g)$$

is called the loss tangent of the medium.

Therefore, the equations for E_x and H_y can be written as:

$$E_x(z) = E^+ e^{-\alpha z} e^{-j\beta z} \qquad (6.77a)$$
$$H_y(z) = E^+ e^{-\alpha z} e^{-j(\beta z + \delta/2)} /|\eta| \qquad (6.77b)$$

From the above equations for E_x and H_y, the average power for a lossy medium can be written as:

$$\overline{P}_{av} = 1/2\,\text{Re}(E_x . H_y^*)\hat{z}$$

Which gives,

$$\overline{P}_{av} = \frac{1}{2|\eta|}|E^+|^2 \, e^{-2\alpha z}\cos(\delta/2)\hat{z} \quad \text{W/m}^2 \qquad (6.78)$$

In the time domain, we can see that there is an exponential damping factor for power, with a rate of decay with distance given by the attenuation constant (α).

For a perfect conductor, we can see that:
$\sigma = \infty$,
$\alpha = \beta = \infty$,
Yielding,
$P_{av} = 0$ (6.79)
This means that no power is dissipated or absorbed in a perfect conductor.

Note: *The propagation constant can be rewritten as:*
$$\gamma = j\omega\sqrt{\mu\varepsilon}(\sqrt{1 - j\sigma/\omega\varepsilon}) = j\omega\sqrt{\mu(\varepsilon - j\sigma/\omega)}$$
We now define a complex permittivity (ε_{new}) as:
$\varepsilon_{new} = \varepsilon' - j\varepsilon'' = \varepsilon - j\sigma/\omega = \varepsilon(1 - j\sigma/\omega\varepsilon) = \varepsilon(1 - j\tan\delta)$
Where $\tan\delta = \sigma/\omega\varepsilon = \varepsilon''/\varepsilon'$
Thus we can write:
$\gamma = j\omega\sqrt{(\mu\varepsilon_{new})}$,
which has the same format as the lossless case.

In actual practice, however, the loss of many materials is caused not only by conductivity but also by the friction amongst polarized molecules as the electric field reverses direction billions of times per second at microwave frequencies. Therefore, the imaginary part of ε_{new} (i.e., ε'') could now be generalized to encompass all losses caused by conductivity and friction in the dielectric material's polarized molecules at high frequencies.

6.11 OBLIQUE INCIDENCE
When a wave's direction of propagation is perpendicular to a surface then the resultant reflection and transmitted waves will also be perpendicular to the surface. As it turns out, this is a special case of a more general case called "oblique incidence."

When a wave approaches an interface between two media at an angle other than 90°, then the resultant reflected and transmitted waves will also be propagating at angles that are no longer 90° to the interface as shown in Figure 6.21.

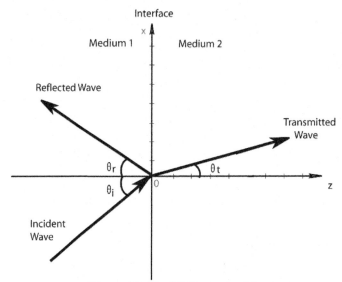

Figure 6.21 Oblique incidence.

We need to define an important term at this juncture:

DEFINITION: PLANE OF INCIDENCE- is the plane that contains the incident wave direction of propagation and the normal to the interface. The reflected wave and the transmitted wave will also be propagating in the plane of incidence.

If an incident wave, propagating in the medium #1 (characterized by ε_1 and μ_1) strikes the surface of a second medium (characterized by ε_2 and μ_2) at angle θ_i, then we will have two resulting waves as follows:

a. A **reflected wave** propagating in medium #1 at angle θ_r relative to the normal to the interface, given by Snell's law of reflection as:
$$\theta_r = \theta_i \tag{6.80}$$

b. A **transmitted wave** entering the medium #2 and propagating at angle θ_t relative to the normal to the interface, which can be found from the Snell's law of refraction as:
$$\sqrt{\varepsilon_1 \mu_1} \operatorname{Sin}\theta_i = \sqrt{\varepsilon_2 \mu_2} \operatorname{Sin}\theta_t \tag{6.81a}$$

NOTE: *In geometrics optics, Snell's law is written as :*
$$n_1 Sin\theta_i = n_2 Sin\theta_t \qquad (6.81b)$$
Where n_1 and n_2 are the refractive index of the media 1 and 2. With the advent of electromagnetic optics, it was found that:
$$n = \sqrt{(\varepsilon_r \mu_r)} \qquad (6.82)$$

Exercise 6.1 *Derive the Snell's law.*
Hint: Using the boundary condition equation for E, equate the tangential E-field phase for all x in each medium at z=0 plane.

Angles θ_r and θ_t only provide the direction of propagation for the reflected or transmitted waves, however, to obtain the magnitude of each wave we need to consider the polarization of the incident wave.

DEFINITION: POLARIZATION- *the orientation of the electric field (E) relative to a reference frame.*

Considering the polarization of the incident wave relative to the plane of incidence (as our reference frame), we obtain two possible cases:
Case #1: Perpendicular polarization
Case #2: Parallel polarization

Each of these two cases gives different magnitudes of reflection and transmission coefficients as discussed next.

6.11.1 Perpendicular Polarization
In this case the orientation of the electric field is perpendicular to the plane of incidence (the H-field is parallel to the plane of incidence) and therefore is parallel to the interface as shown in Figure 6.22.

The reflection coefficient (Γ) and the transmission coefficient (T) for the perpendicular polarization case can be derived to be:
$$\Gamma_1 = E_r/E_i = (\eta_2 Cos\theta_i - \eta_1 Cos\theta_t) / (\eta_2 Cos\theta_i + \eta_1 Cos\theta_t) \quad (6.83)$$
And,
$$T_1 = E_t/E_i = (2\eta_2 Cos\theta_i) / (\eta_2 Cos\theta_i + \eta_1 Cos\theta_t) \qquad (6.84)$$

Thus we can see that:
$$T_1 = 1 + \Gamma_1 \qquad (6.85)$$
This is the same relation as the normal incidence.

NOTE1: *For normal Incidence $\theta_i = \theta_t = 0°$, these expressions reduce to earlier results.*

NOTE2: *if $\mu_1 = \mu_2$, then using the Snell's law it can be shown that $\Gamma \neq 0$ for any θ_i. This means that a perpendicularly polarized wave is always reflected from a surface.*

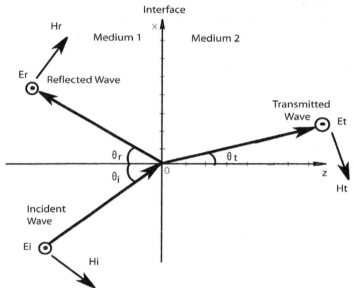

Figure 6.22- Perpendicular polarization

6.11.2 Parallel Polarization

In this case the orientation of the electric field is parallel to the plane of incidence (the H-field is perpendicular to the plane of incidence and therefore is parallel to the interface) as shown In Figure 6.23.

The reflection coefficient (Γ) and the transmission coefficient (T) for the perpendicular polarization case can be derived to be:

$$\Gamma_2 = E_r/E_i = (\eta_2 Cos\theta_t - \eta_1 Cos\theta_i) / (\eta_2 Cos\theta_t + \eta_1 Cos\theta_i) \qquad (6.86a)$$

And,

$$T_2 = E_t/E_i = (2\eta_2 Cos\theta_i) / (\eta_2 Cos\theta_t + \eta_1 Cos\theta_i) \qquad (6.86b)$$

Thus we can see that:

$T_2 = (1 + \Gamma_2)(Cos\theta_i / Cos\theta_t)$ (6.87)

NOTE3: *For normal Incidence $\theta_i = \theta_t = 0°$, these expressions reduce to earlier results.*

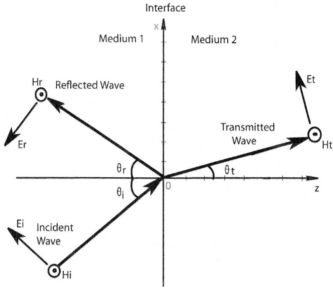

Figure 6.23- Parallel Polarization

NOTE4: *if $\mu_1 = \mu_2$, then using the Snell's law it can be shown that*
$\Gamma = 0$ *for* $tan\theta_i = (\varepsilon_2/\varepsilon_1)^{1/2}$ (6.88)
*This condition under which the reflected wave vanishes, gives rise to an angle normally referred to as the **Brewster angle** (θ_B) given by:*
$\theta_B = tan^{-1} (\varepsilon_2/\varepsilon_1)^{1/2}$ (6.89)

Chapter 6 –Problems

6.1) When an EM wave, with $\lambda = 0.1$ m in air, enters a perfect dielectric the wavelength is lowered to 0.045m. Determine ε and v of the dielectric if $\mu = \mu_0$.

6.2) What is the propagation constant at 800 MHz for a material with $\varepsilon_r=10$, $\mu_r=5$ and $\sigma =2$ S/m? Find the velocity of propagation and compare it to free-space velocity c.

6.3) Considering silver to have $\sigma =61.7$ MS/m, Find the frequency at which the depth of penetration is 0.1 mm.

6.4) At 1 GHz the amplitude of the E-field just inside a lossy medium is measured to be 1 V/m. Determine the amplitude and write an expression for the E-field and the H-field at a distance of 5 cm inside if the medium has: $\varepsilon_r=16$, $\mu_r=1$ and $\sigma =3$ S/m.

6.5) If the E-field of a uniform EM plane wave in free space is given by: $E_x(z,t)= 10 \sin (\omega t-kz)$ V/m
Calculate the total average power passing through a rectangular area of 50 cm by 100 cm in the z=0 plane. Write the expression for the H-field.

6.6) Determine the reflected and transmitted E- and H-fields at the interface of two media given by:
Medium #1: $\varepsilon_{r1}=1$, $\mu_{r1}=1$ and $\sigma_1 =0$ S/m
Medium #2: $\varepsilon_{r2}=10$, $\mu_{r2}=4$ and $\sigma_2 =0$ S/m

6.7) At the interface of air-Aluminum, the H-field in air is measured to be 0.1 A/m at a frequency of 900 MHz. Calculate the depth of penetration, α, β, and the magnitude of the E- and H-field in Aluminum.

6.8) A plane wave traveling in free space encounters a sheet of stainless steel of thickness 1 cm. Find the E- and H-fields just beyond the steel sheet if the H-field in air is 1 A/m. Write expressions for both E and H-fields.

6.9) At 1 GHz, a traveling EM wave in free space of amplitude $|E|=10$ V/m strikes the surface of a dielectric: $\varepsilon_{r2}=10$, $\mu_{r2}=4$ and $\sigma_2 =0.1$ S/m. a) Calculate the field magnitudes, b) Write expressions for the reflected and transmitted waves a distance "d=30 cm" from the interface in either direction, and c) Write the expression for the standing wave as a function of distance (z) in free space.

6.10) A plane wave, with $|E|=10$ V/m and f= 900 MHz, is normal incident from air at the surface of sea water with: $\varepsilon_{r2}=10$, $\mu_{r2}=5$ and $\sigma_2 =5$ S/m.

a) At what depth the E-field would reduce to 10% of its original value?

b) Calculate α and β.

c) If we change the frequency 10 times higher, what would be the new E and H fields at the depth found in part (a).

6.11) A parallel-polarized wave in air having an E-field with an amplitude of 5 v/m is incident at an angle of 40° on a medium with $\varepsilon_{r2}=3$, and $\mu_{r2}=1$, $\sigma_2 =0$ S/m. Determine:

a. The reflection and transmission coefficients,

b. Expressions for E and H fields in both media,

c. The reflected and transmitted waves at 2 meters away on either side of the interface.

d. The Brewster angle,

e. Repeat part (b) if $\sigma_2 =10$ S/m

6.12) A perpendicularly polarized wave (f=1 GHz) in air with an E-field of 10 v/m is incident at an interface at an angle of 30°. The second medium has $\varepsilon_{r2}=1.6$, and $\mu_{r2}=1$, $\sigma_2 =0$ S/m. Determine:

a. The reflection and transmission coefficients,

b. The expressions for E and H in the second medium,

c. The expression for the E-field standing wave in air.

6.13) If a parallel-polarized wave in air strikes a dielectric medium ($\varepsilon_{r2}=10$, and $\mu_{r2}=1$, $\sigma_2 =0$ S/m) at the Brewster angle, what would be the reflected and refraction angles? How about T_2 and Γ_2 values?

THE POSTULATES
OF
TEM TRANSMISSION
LINES

The postulates regarding TEM transmission lines are summarized as:
(Ref. Chapter 1, Section 1.10)

Postulate #1- The Uniformity Postulate: *A uniform transmission line consists of two straight parallel conductors.*

Postulate #2- The Longitudinal Current Postulate: *The currents in the line conductors flow only in the direction of the length of the line.*

Postulate #3- The Opposite Current Postulate: *At any point on the transmission line, the instantaneous total current in one conductor is equal but opposite to the current in the other conductor.*

Postulate #4- The Voltage Postulate: *At any point on the transmission line, there is a unique value of the potential difference between the two lines, which is the line integral of the electric field along any path traveling from one line to the other.*

Postulate #5- The Circuit Coefficient Postulate: *The electrical behavior of a transmission line is completely described by four electric circuit coefficients, whose values per unit length are constant everywhere on the line.*

Each infinitesimal length of the transmission line can be modeled by a total of four electric circuit coefficients, two series (R, L) and two shunt (G, C). These circuit coefficients are:

R=Resistance per unit length
L=Inductance per unit length
C=Capacitance per unit length
G= Conductance per unit length

CHAPTER 7

TRANSMISSION LINE FUNDAMENTALS

7.1 INTRODUCTION

The bridge between lumped-element circuits and distributed circuits is transmission lines that carry electrical signals between two points in a circuit. At RF and microwave frequencies, the purpose of transmission lines(TLs) are primarily for carrying information and secondarily power to other parts of the circuit.

Examples of commonly encountered TLs are telephone lines, fiber optics cables, video coaxial cables, microstrip lines miniaturized on a microwave IC chip as well as on printed circuit boards, cable TV lines, coaxial lines connecting the receiver set to the Satellite dish antenna, so on and so forth.

In this chapter, we will lay the conceptual foundation for understanding transmission lines and will compare several popular types of transmission lines. In the next chapter, we will take up the analysis of TLs in depth and will develop the mathematical foundation for understanding RF and microwave circuits .

7.2 TRANSMISSION MEDIA

When waves are constricted to a limited transmission space (also called a line, guide, channel, etc.), then the waves take on different forms and patterns according to the shape of the guide, just like fluid flow in a pipe.

7.2.1 TYPES OF TRANSMISSION MEDIA

A few examples of the wave patterns in different transmission media are: a) Coaxial line, b) two-wire transmission line, c) a waveguide, d) a microstrip line, e) a parallel plate waveguide, and f) a stripline, as shown in Figure 7.1.

Generally, any and all of these five transmission media could be called "transmission lines", but the terminology has been made more specific to convey more exact concepts, thus:

1. (a), (b), (e) and (f) are generally labeled as transmission lines (TLs).

2. (c) Is labeled a waveguide and,

3. (d) Is labeled a Microstrip line.

(a), (b), (e) and (f) all will support propagation of Transverse Electromagnetic (TEM) waves and will be used specifically in this book. An example of a TEM wave would be a single-frequency EM wave propagating in air as discussed earlier in Chapter 6, where the direction of propagation is perpendicular to the oscillating electric and magnetic fields.

NOTE 1: *Structure (d), a microstrip line, supports a quasi-TEM wave which is a wave with a small axial field. This type of transmission line has gained tremendous popularity in microwave integrated circuits due to its planar structure and ease of fabrication using printed circuit technology. Microstrip lines will be discussed in detail in a later chapter.*

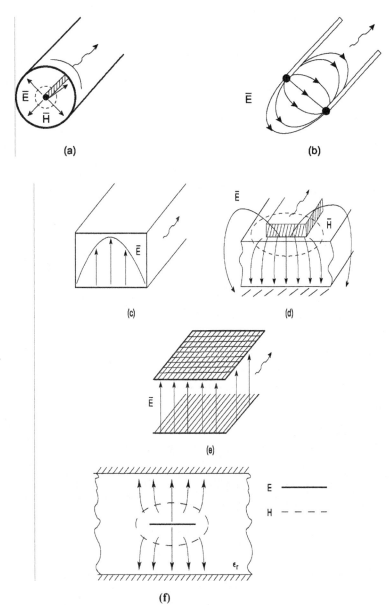

Figure 7.1 The E and H field patterns of waves in a: a) coaxial line, b) two-wire TL, c) waveguide, d)microstrip line, e) parallel plate TL, f) stripline.

NOTE 2: *Structures (a) and (c), a coaxial line and a waveguide, are closed structures and are preferred since they have much less radiation losses than the other three open structures.*

NOTE 3: *Structure (f), a stripline transmission line, can be thought of as a "flattened out" coaxial line, where both have a center conductor which is enclosed by an outer ground conductor with a uniform dielectric material filling the space between the two.*

Higher Order Transmission Lines (Non-TEM lines)

In this type of transmission lines, the propagating waves have at least one significant field component (E or H) along the length of the TL, which is the direction of propagation. Hollow metallic conducting waveguides (rectangular and cylindrical), dielectric waveguides or rods, optical fibers are in this class of TLs.

NOTE 4: *There are other types of transmission lines such as Slotline, Coplanar waveguide and Ridge waveguide, which have non-TEM modes of propagation and are beyond the scope of this book and can be found in advanced texts.*

A summary of Transmission media and their different characteristics is shown in table 7.1. The comparison made in this table can be roughly divided into two important general areas:

a. Electrical considerations: mode of propagation, dispersion, Bandwidth, Power loss and power capacity (items 1 through 5), and

b. Mechanical considerations: Physical size, ease of fabrication and ease of integration with other elements and components (items 6 through 8).

FEATURE	COAXIAL	STRIPLINE	MICROSTRIP	WAVEGUIDE
1) PROPAGATING MODE	Main: TEM Other: TM, TE	Main: TEM Other: TM, TE	Main: Quasi-TEM Other: TM, TE	Main: TE_{10} Other: TM, TE
2) DISPERSION	None	None	Low	Medium
3) BANDWIDTH	High	High	High	Low
4) POWER LOSS	Medium	High	High	Low
5) POWER CAPACITY	Medium	Low	Low	High
6) SIZE	Large	Medium	Small	Large
7) EASE OF FABRICATION	Medium	Easy	Easy	Medium
8) EASE OF INTEGRATION	Hard	Fair	Easy	Hard

Table 7.1 Comparison of various transmission media.

7.3 A SHORT HISTORY OF TRANSMISSION MEDIA

Waveguides were used for most microwave systems during 1930s and 1940s but they have a limited bandwidth, are bulky and expensive, even though they have the advantage of being able to handle high powers much needed for Radar applications.

During this same period, coaxial lines were also developed as a broadband and medium power transmission line, but they are difficult to integrate into or fabricate in the integrated circuit technology which is suited to planar type transmission lines.

Planar transmission lines received attention in 1950s. They are low cost compact and capable of being integrated with planar microwave integrated devices and circuits. Therefore, they play an important role in planar microwave technology for transmission of signals between devices, circuits and networks.

Examples of planar transmission lines include microstrip line (developed in 1952), stripline (developed circa 1955), slotline (developed in 1969).

Other planar transmission lines (e.g. coplanar waveguides, finlines, etc.) have also been developed through time. Overall and amongst all planar transmission lines, none have proven as popular as microstrip line technology, which has gained tremendous interest in planar circuit applications. For this reason microstrip lines are discussed and analyzed in depth in a later section in this chapter.

7.4 TRANSMISSION LINE PARAMETERS

At high frequencies, an infinitesimal length of a transmission line can be modeled by two series elements (R, L) in conjunction with two shunt elements (G, C) as shown in Figure 7.2.

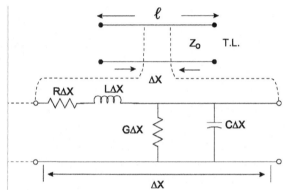

FIGURE 7.2   An infinitesimal portion of a transmission line (TL).

Juxtaposing an infinite number of this infinitesimal model into a long chain, will create a workable model for a transmission line as shown in Figure 7.3.

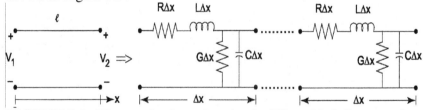

FIGURE 7.3   The equivalent circuit of a TL at high frequencies.

The derivation of the governing differential equations of a TEM Transmission Line (TL), which can be obtained by examining one Δx section of its length (Figure 7.2), is relegated to the next chapter.

From Figure 7.2 we can see that the electrical properties of a TL at any given frequency can be completely characterized by four distributed parameters (R, L, G, and C).

As noted from Figure 7.1, the three main TEM type TLs are:
  a. Coaxial line
  b. Two-wire line
  c. Parallel plate line

In this chapter, we list the equations necessary to calculate these four parameters for the three basic types of TLs.

7.4.1 The Basic Assumption
The basic assumption used in the derivation of the four equations for each type of line is that the conductivity of the conductors in a TL is usually high enough to justify our neglect of the effect of the series resistance "R" on the calculation of the complex propagation constant (γ).

Using this basic assumption in the derivation process, makes the axial field along the TL disappear and thus the propagating waves become approximately TEM.

From the last Chapter, we know that for a TEM wave propagating in a medium (ε, μ, and σ) we can write in general :

$$\gamma = \alpha + j\beta = j\omega\sqrt{\mu\varepsilon}(\sqrt{1 - j\sigma/\omega\varepsilon}) \tag{7.1}$$

As will be seen in the next chapter, the complex propagation constant (γ) for a TEM wave propagating on a TL can be derived to be:

$$\gamma = \alpha + j\beta = \sqrt{(R + j\omega L)(G + j\omega C)} \tag{7.2}$$

If we neglect R in equation (7.2), we can write:

$$\gamma = \alpha + j\beta \approx j\omega\sqrt{L/C}\sqrt{(1 + G/j\omega C)} \tag{7.3}$$

Comparing equation (7.3) with (7.1), we can see the following identities between material properties (ε, μ, σ) and electrical properties (L, C):

$G/C= \sigma/\varepsilon,$ (7.4)

And

$LC=\mu\varepsilon$ (7.5)

Combining equations (7.4) and (7.5), we obtain:

$\Rightarrow GL=\mu\sigma$ (7.6)

From equations (7.4) through (7.6), we can see that if for example L is derived through analytical methods, then we can quickly determine G and C without any further analysis. However, to determine R we need to use the equation for power loss along the conductor.

7.4.2 Parameter Expressions

The expressions for the line parameters (R, L, G and C) are provided in table 7.1 for the three types of TEM TLs as shown in Figure 7.4. The derivation of these expressions are not necessary at this stage of our work and for simplicity has been omitted. However, if one has an intense passion for derivations, more advanced texts on this subject could be consulted!

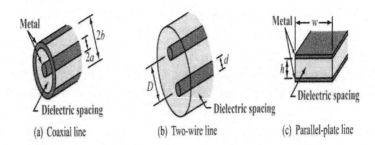

(a) Coaxial line   (b) Two-wire line   (c) Parallel-plate line

FIGURE 7.4   The three types of TLs for TEM waves.

From table 7.1, it is interesting to note that each of the presented expressions are functions of two sets of parameters:

a. Geometric parameters that define the *cross-sectional* dimensions of the TL, such as radius or width of conductors, height of the dielectric, distance between conductors, etc.

b. Material parameters characterizing the *conductor* and the *dielectric* material of the TL (i.e., the constitutive parameters: ε, μ, and σ).

We use the following definitions of symbols in table 7.1:

DEFINITIONS:

1. $R_s=(\pi f \mu_c/\sigma_c)^{1/2}$, **Surface resistance (Resistance of a unit length at depth δ).**

2. $\delta=(\pi f \mu_c \sigma_c)^{-1/2}$, **Skin Depth (depth where amplitude drops to 1/e of surface value).**

3. $A=\ln\{(D/d)+[(D/d)^2-1]^{1/2}\}$

4. ε, μ, and σ pertain to the dielectric material.

5. μ_c and σ_c pertain to the conductor.

parameter	Coaxial	Two-wire	Parallel-Plate	Unit
R	$R_s(1/a+1/b)/2\pi$	$2R_s/\pi d$	$2R_s/w$	Ω/m
L	$\mu\ln(b/a)/2\pi$	$\mu A/\pi$	$\mu h/w$	H/m
G	$\mu\,\sigma/L$	$\mu\,\sigma/L$	$\mu\,\sigma/L$	S/m
C	$\mu\varepsilon/L$	$\mu\varepsilon/L$	$\mu\varepsilon/L$	F/m

Table 7.1 Expressions for the R, L, G and C parameters for three types of TLs.

NOTE: *R, L, G, and C represent the* **combined** *effect of both conductors per unit length of TL. For example, R represents the combined resistance of both conductors per unit length in Ω/m.*

Chapter 7 –Problems

7.1) A lossless parallel-plate TL, operating at 1 GHz, has a 1.5 cm width of copper ($\mu_c=\mu_o$, $\sigma_c=5.8\times10^7$ S/m) over a substrate ($\varepsilon_r=2.25$, μ_o, $\sigma=0$) which has a thickness of 0.2 cm. Determine the parameters per unit length: R, L, G, C as well as γ for the TL.

7.2) Consider a coaxial TL with inner and outer conductor (copper) diameters of 0.75 cm and 1.5 cm, respectively. If the dielectric between the two conductors has $\varepsilon_r=5$, μ_o, $\sigma =10^{-3}$ S/m. Calculate the line parameters at 1 GHz and 10 GHz. Which parameters changed due to an increase in frequency ? Explain the reason.

7.3) A two-wire copper ($\mu_c=\mu_o$, $\sigma_c=5.8 \times 10^7$ S/m) TL is operating at 5 GHz. The wires are separated by 4 cm with each having a diameter of 3 mm. The dielectric surrounding the conductors has $\varepsilon_r=3$, μ_o, $\sigma=10^{-5}$ S/cm. Calculate the line parameters.

7.4) Write an essay describing what TEM and non-TEM transmission lines are and provide two examples for each with application diagrams. What are the basic differences between these two classes of TLs?

7.5) Write an essay by doing a brief research on advantages, disadvantages and applications of:
    a. Coaxial lines
    b. Metallic Waveguides
    c. Dielectric waveguides

7.6) Calculate the line parameters and the propagation constant at 1 GHz for a coaxial line with inner and outer conductor radii of 0.5 cm and 1 cm, respectively for the following two cases and determine which one is a better TL:
    a. Dielectric: $\varepsilon_r=2.25$, μ_o, $\sigma =0$ (perfect dielectric); and conductor: $\mu_c=\mu_o$, $\sigma_c=5.8 \times 10^7$ S/m (lossy metal).
    b. Dielectric: $\varepsilon_r=2.25$, μ_o, $\sigma =10^{-3}$ S/m (lossy material); and conductor: $\mu_c=\mu_o$, $\sigma_c=\infty$ S/m (perfect conductor).

7.7) Consider a lossless transmission line of length 2 m connected to a signal generator. If two sine waves each having one volt amplitude with two different frequencies: $f_1=1.5$ GHz and $f_2=9$ GHz are sent at t=0, determine the following at the other end of the line:
a) Time delay for each wave,
b) Phase delay for each wave,
c) Voltage equations of each wave as a function of time
d) Voltage value detected, assuming no reflection at the end.

CHAPTER 8

Lossless Transmission Lines

8.1 INTRODUCTION

Unguided propagation of waves was studied in chapter 6, the guided EM waves, using a two-conductor transmission line (TL), was introduced in Chapter 7 and is now explored further. The exact analysis of these TLs require field theory (E- and H-fields) and wave analysis as prescribed by the Maxwell's equations discussed in chapter 4.

However, a TL can be modeled using distributed parameters and with the help of voltage and current on the line (scalar quantities) to replace the E- and H-fields (vector quantities), we are able to simplify the analysis of TLs considerably.

8.2 WAVES ON A TRANSMISSION LINE (TEM MODE)

When we mention a "transmission line", it is commonly understood to be any system of conductors suitable for conducting TEM-mode electromagnetic waves efficiently between two or more terminals. Common examples of TEM-mode transmissions lines are telephone lines, power lines, coaxial lines, parallel plate lines, etc.

At lower frequencies the length of the line is much smaller than the signal wavelength and thus the transmission line can be treated as a "lumped element" with almost zero loss and no time delay for signal propagation between two points.

However, at high RF/microwave frequencies the length of the line is comparable to the signal wavelength and the time delay of propagation (and the corresponding signal phase shift) can no longer be ignored.

Under these conditions, the "distributed circuit model" is used to analyze a transmission line. Such a model provides the governing differential equations for voltage and current waves propagating along a transmission line without a need to resort to Maxwell's equations to solve for the electromagnetic field quantities.

NOTE: *The TL is considered to be a **uniform** element, meaning that its properties do not change and thus stay constant along the length of the line.*

8.3 The Governing Equations

At high frequencies, an infinitesimal length of a transmission line can be modeled by two series elements (R, L) in conjunction with two shunt elements (G, C) as shown in Figure 8.1.

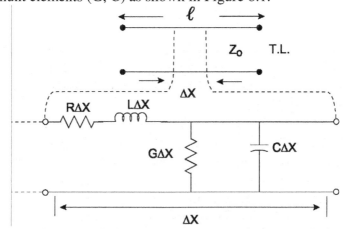

FIGURE 8.1   An infinitesimal portion of a transmission line (TL).

Juxtaposing an infinite number of this infinitesimal model into a long chain, will create a workable model for a transmission line as shown in Figure 8.2.

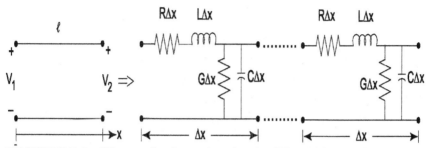

FIGURE 8.2   The equivalent circuit of a TL at high frequencies.

To develop the governing differential equations, we will examine one Δx section of a transmission line as shown in Figure 8.3.

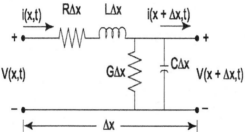

FIGURE 8.3 Voltage and current in an infinitesimal length of TL.

Using KVL for the Δx section, we can write:

v(x,t)= i(x,t) RΔx+ LΔx ∂i(x,t)/∂t +v(x+Δx,t)   (8.1a)

Upon rearranging terms and dividing both sides by Δx, we obtain:

$$-\frac{v(x+\Delta x)-v(x,t)}{\Delta x}=Ri(x,t)+L\frac{\partial i(x,t)}{\partial t}$$

Letting Δx→0, yields:

$$-\frac{\partial v(x,t)}{\partial x}=Ri(x,t)+L\frac{\partial i(x,t)}{\partial t}$$ (8.1b)

Similarly, using KCL we can write:

$$i(x,t) = v(x+\Delta x,t)\, G\Delta x + C\Delta x\, \frac{\partial v(x+\Delta x,t)}{\partial t} + i(x+\Delta x,t) \qquad (8.2a)$$

Upon rearranging terms, dividing by Δx and letting $\Delta x \to 0$, we have:

$$-\frac{\partial i(x,t)}{\partial x} = Gv(x,t) + C\frac{\partial v(x,t)}{\partial t} \qquad (8.2b)$$

Equations (8.1b) and (8.2b) are two cross-coupled equations in terms of v and i. These two equations can be separated by first differentiating both equations with respect to "x" and then properly substituting for the terms, which leads to:

$$-\frac{\partial^2 v(x,t)}{\partial x^2} = R\frac{\partial i(x,t)}{\partial x} + L\frac{\partial^2 i(x,t)}{\partial x \partial t}$$

$$= -R\left(Gv(x,t) + C\frac{\partial v(x,t)}{\partial t}\right) - L\left(G\frac{\partial v(x,t)}{\partial t} + C\frac{\partial^2 v(x,t)}{\partial t^2}\right)$$

Or,

$$\frac{\partial^2 v(x,t)}{\partial x^2} = LC\frac{\partial^2 v(x,t)}{\partial t^2} + (RC+LG)\frac{\partial v(x,t)}{\partial x} + RGv(x,t)$$

$$(8.3a)$$

Similarly for "i," we can write:

$$\frac{\partial^2 i(x,t)}{\partial x^2} = LC\frac{\partial^2 i(x,t)}{\partial t^2} + (RC+LG)\frac{\partial i(x,t)}{\partial x} + RGi(x,t)$$

$$(8.3b)$$

For sinusoidal signal variation for "v" and "i", we can write the corresponding Phasors as follows:

$$v(x,t) = Re[V(x)e^{j\omega t}]$$
$$i(x,t) = Re[I(x)e^{j\omega t}]$$

Using phasor differentiation results from Chapter 3, Equations (8.3a) and (8.3b) can be written as:

$$\frac{d^2 V(x)}{dx^2} - \gamma^2 V(x) = 0 \qquad (8.4a)$$

$$\frac{d^2 I(x)}{dx^2} - \gamma^2 I(x) = 0 \qquad (8.4b)$$

Where

$$\gamma = \alpha + j\beta = \sqrt{(R + j\omega L)(G + j\omega C)} \qquad (8.5)$$

γ is the **propagation constant**, with real part (α) and imaginary part (β), called the **attenuation constant** (Np/m) and **phase constant** (rad/m), respectively.

The solution to the second order differential equations as given by Equations (8.4a) and (8.4b), can be observed to be of exponential type format ($e^{\pm\gamma x}$). Thus we can write the general solutions for $V(x)$ as follows:

$$V(x) = V_0^+ e^{-\gamma x} + V_0^- e^{\gamma x} \qquad (8.6a)$$

Where the complex constants V_0^+ and V_0^- are determined from the boundary conditions imposed by the source voltage and the load value.

Similarly, $I(x)$ can be obtained from $V(x)$ as:

$$I(x) = \left(\frac{-1}{R + j\omega L}\right)\frac{dV(x)}{dx} = \frac{V_0^+ e^{-\gamma x} - V_0^- e^{\gamma x}}{Z_0} \qquad (8.6b)$$

Where,

$$Z_0 = \sqrt{\frac{R + j\omega L}{G + j\omega C}} \qquad (8.7)$$

is the characteristic impedance of the transmission line.

SPECIAL CASE: A LOSSLESS TRANSMISSION LINE

For this case, we have R=G=0. This yields the following simplifications:

$$\gamma = j\omega\sqrt{LC} = j\beta, \qquad (8.8a)$$

$$Z_0 = \sqrt{\frac{L}{C}} \qquad (8.8b)$$

Where $\beta = \omega\sqrt{LC}$ is the phase constant.

In this case Equations 8.4 can be written as:

$$\frac{d^2V(x)}{dx^2} + \beta^2 V(x) = 0 \qquad (8.9a)$$

$$\frac{d^2I(x)}{dx^2}+\beta^2I(x)=0 \tag{8.9b}$$

The solutions to Equations 8.9 are given by:

$$V(x)=V_0^+ \, e^{-j\beta x}+V_0^- \, e^{j\beta x} \tag{8.10a}$$

$$I(x)= \frac{V_0^+ e^{-j\beta x} - V_0^- e^{j\beta x}}{Z_0} \tag{8.10b}$$

NOTE 1: *Transmission line Equations could have all been derived using the Maxwell's equations directly from the field quantities E and H as delineated in earlier chapters (see Chapters 2,4).*

The term $e^{-\gamma x}$ [or $e^{-j\beta x}$] represents a propagating wave in "+x" direction while $e^{\gamma x}$ [or $e^{j\beta x}$] represents a propagating wave in "-x" direction on a transmission line. The combination of the two waves propagating in opposite directions to each other, forms a standing wave on the transmission line.

NOTE 2: *Based on a given set of boundary conditions for the source and the load, we can find the constants in the equations 8.10. For example, if the source voltage (at x=0) is known to be V=V_g and the load voltage (at x= ℓ) is V=V_L, then the constants V_0^+ and V_0^- can easily be found from the following two equations:*

$$x=0, \quad V_g=Vo^+ +Vo^- \tag{8.11}$$
$$x=\ell, \quad V_L=Vo^+ e^{-j\beta\ell} +Vo^- e^{j\beta\ell} \tag{8.12}$$

EXERCISE 8.1
a. Derive expressions for Vo⁺ and Vo⁻ from equations 8.11 and 8.12 in terms of V_g and V_L.
b. Given the load value as $Z=Z_L$, find Vo⁺ and Vo⁻ in terms of V_g and Z_L [as in part (a)].
  Hint: Use $V_L= Z_L \, [Vo^+ e^{-j\beta\ell} -Vo^- e^{j\beta\ell}]/Z_0$

8.4 SINUSOIDAL WAVE PROPAGATION ON A TRANSMISSION LINE

Consider a transmission line as shown in Figure 8.4. Assuming a sinusoidal signal excitation, the propagating voltage and current waves on a transmission line are also sinusoidal and can be expressed as:

$$v(x,t)=Re[V(x)e^{j\omega t}] \tag{8.13}$$
$$i(x,t)=Re[I(x)e^{j\omega t}] \tag{8.14}$$

Where complex quantities $V(x)$ and $I(x)$ are phasor quantities.

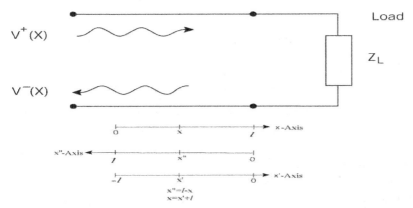

FIGURE 8.4 Incident and reflected waves on a transmission line.

Using the distributed circuit model of a transmission line and its corresponding equivalent circuit, the following differential equations for $I(x)$ and $V(X)$ can be derived for an infinitesimal length of a transmission line:

$$\frac{d^2V(x)}{dx^2} - \gamma^2 V(x) = 0 \tag{8.15a}$$

$$\frac{d^2I(x)}{dx^2} - \gamma^2 I(x) = 0 \tag{8.15b}$$

Where γ is the complex propagation constants given by:

$$\gamma = \alpha + j\beta = [(R+j\omega L)(G+j\omega C)]^{1/2} \tag{8.16}$$

Where:

α = **attenuation constant (in Nepers/m)**
β = **phase constant (in radians/m)**
R = resistance per unit length in Ω/m
L = inductance per unit length in H/m

G = conductance per unit length in S/m
C = capacitance per unit length in F/m

By observation, we notice that the general solution to the problem is of exponential form, therefore we can write:

$$V_1(x)= V_o^+ e^{-\gamma x} \quad \Rightarrow \quad I_1(x)= \frac{V_o^+}{Z_O} e^{-\gamma x} \text{ (Incident waves)} \qquad (8.17a)$$

$$V_2(x)= V_o^- e^{\gamma x}, \quad \Rightarrow \quad I_2(x)= - \frac{V_o^-}{Z_O} e^{\gamma x} \text{ (Reflected waves)} \quad (8.17b)$$

Where Z_0 is the characteristic impedance of the transmission line; V_o^+ and V_o^- are complex constants in general, whose values depend upon the source and the transmission line characteristics, as will be seen shortly.

Since we are dealing with a linear system, the general solution for voltage and current is obtained using the superposition theorem as follows:

$$V(x)=V_1(x)+V_2(x)= V_o^+ e^{-\gamma x} + V_o^- e^{\gamma x} \qquad (8.17c)$$

$$I(x)=I_1(x)+I_2(x)= \frac{V_o^+}{Z_O} e^{-\gamma x} - \frac{V_o^-}{Z_O} e^{\gamma x} \qquad (8.17d)$$

From Equations (8.17c,d), we observe that voltage and current are a pair of waves co-existing and are inseparable for a distributed circuit. Each solution for voltage or current consists of two waves which will be labeled as follows:

a. An incident wave: $e^{-\gamma x} = e^{-\alpha x} e^{-j\beta x}$ $\qquad\qquad\qquad$ (8.18a)
b. A reflected wave: $e^{\gamma x} = e^{\alpha x} e^{j\beta x}$ $\qquad\qquad\qquad\qquad$ (8.18b)
Where "βx" is referred to as the electrical length.

As already mentioned, each wave travels at the phase velocity (V_P) given by:
$$V_P = \omega/\beta = c/(\mu_r\varepsilon_r)^{1/2} \qquad (8.19)$$
Where c is the speed of light in vacuum given by:
$$c = 1/(\mu_o\varepsilon_o)^{1/2} = 2.9988 \times 10^8 \approx 3 \times 10^8 \text{ m/s.}$$

The time-average incident power propagating along a transmission line is given by (assuming Z_O is a real number):

$$P^+(x) = \frac{1}{2} \text{Re}\left[V^+(x)I^+(x)*\right] = \frac{|V_o^+|^2}{2Z_O} e^{-2\alpha x} \qquad (8.20)$$

The same can be written for the reflected power propagating back to the source.

Approximation for Small Loss Case:

If α is small, we can it through another method, that is to say, by using the law of conservation of energy. This law requires that the rate of decrease of propagating power P(x) along the line should equal the average power loss per unit length (P_{loss}). Thus we can write:

$$-\frac{\partial P(x)}{\partial x} = P_{loss} = 2\alpha P(x)$$

Since the loss is small, we can linearize the slope as follows:

$$\alpha = \frac{P_{loss}}{2P(x)} \approx \frac{-\Delta P/\Delta x}{2P} = \frac{-[P(x+\Delta x)-P(x)]/\Delta x}{2P(x)} \quad \text{(Np/m)}$$

$$(8.21)$$

Since the power is decreasing as the distance increases, therefore the slope is negative and we use a negative sign for the slope to make P_{loss} a positive quantity.

Equation (8.21) shows an interesting and yet very practical way to measure the actual attenuation constant (α). This method is particularly helpful if one is trying to establish the integrity of a faulty line, since a simple comparison of the measured (α) with the nominal (α) would reveal the needed information. The following example elucidates this point further.

Note: *Because the slope has been linearized, this method is only valid for small distances and small α. If the loss is large, we need to use a more exact method as discussed further in a later chapter on lossy lines.*

EXAMPLE 8.3

The microwave power at one point (P_1) on a transmission line is measured to be 10 mW. At a distance of $d=50$ m away, another power measurement (P_2) indicates a power of 7 mW. Determine the attenuation constant of the transmission line.

Solution:

Since the loss is small and the distance large, we can use this approximate method:

$$\alpha = \frac{P_{loss}}{2P(x)} \approx \frac{-\Delta P / \Delta x}{2P} = \frac{-[P(x+\Delta x) - P(x)]/\Delta x}{2P(x)}$$

Where

$\Delta P / \Delta x = (P_2 - P_1)/d$

Thus we have:

$$\alpha = \frac{-(P_2 - P_1)/d}{2P_1} = \frac{-(7-10)/50}{2 \times 10} = 0.003 \ Np/m$$

8.5   THE CONCEPT OF THE REFLECTION COEFFICIENT

Any time an incident wave encounters a second medium different than the first, it is partly reflected (creating a reflected wave) while the remaining is transmitted through (creating a transmitted wave). The reflected wave encountering the incident wave forms a standing wave as described earlier. Thus we can see that there are four possible waves in a transmission line:

a. An incident wave,

b. A reflected wave,

c. A transmitted wave, and

d. A standing wave.

8.5.1 The Reflection Coefficient

Let us now define an important term:

DEFINITION- REFLECTION COEFFICIENT: *Is defined to be the ratio of the reflected wave phasor to the incident wave phasor.*

In the special case of a uniform transmission line when the incident wave encounters a second medium such as a termination (load) or a discontinuity, then under these conditions, the ratio of the reflected wave phasor to the incident wave phasor is "The reflection coefficient".

To illustrate this concept, consider a transmission line circuit with a load (Z_L) located at $x=\ell$, as shown earlier in Figure 8.4.

$$V^+(x) = V_0^+ e^{-\gamma x} \tag{8.22a}$$

$$V^-(x) = V_0^- e^{\gamma x} \tag{8.22b}$$

At the load end $(x = \ell)$, $V^+(\ell)$ is given by:

$$V^+(\ell) = V_0^+ e^{-\gamma \ell} \tag{8.23a}$$

However to find $V^-(\ell)$, we need to realize that the reflected wave reflects from the load by a factor of Γ_L (i.e., Γ_L is the load reflection coefficient at $x=\ell$):

$$V^-(\ell) = \Gamma_L V_0^+ e^{-\gamma \ell} \tag{8.23b}$$

The reflected wave travels back a distance of $x'' = \ell - x$ towards the source as:

$$V^-(x'') = V^-(\ell-x) = \Gamma_L V_0^+ e^{-\gamma \ell} e^{-\gamma x''} = \Gamma_L V_0^+ e^{-\gamma \ell} e^{-\gamma(\ell-x)} \tag{8.23c}$$

where x'' is an imaginary reference frame set up at the load $(x''=0)$ and is directed toward the source $(x'' = \ell)$. Thus $V^-(x)$ can be written as:

$$V^-(x) = \Gamma_L V_0^+ e^{-2\gamma \ell} e^{\gamma x} = V_0^- e^{\gamma x} \tag{8.23d}$$

The reflection coefficient can now be defined as:

$$\Gamma(x) = \frac{V^-(x)}{V^+(x)} = \frac{V_0^- e^{\gamma x}}{V_0^+ e^{-\gamma x}} = \frac{V_0^-}{V_0^+} e^{2\gamma x} = \Gamma_L e^{-2\gamma \ell} e^{2\gamma x} \tag{8.23e}$$

8.5.2 The Current Reflection Coefficient

The reflection coefficient [given by $\Gamma(x)$ or more precisely $\Gamma_v(x)$] is normally defined in terms of voltage waves, however, if we desire to find the current reflection coefficient, then it can be obtained by the following relationship:

$$\Gamma_i(x) = \frac{I^-(x)}{I^+(x)} = \frac{-V^-(x)/Z_0}{V^+(x)/Z_0} = \frac{-V_0^- e^{\gamma x}}{V_0^+ e^{-\gamma x}} = -\Gamma_L e^{-2\gamma \ell} e^{2\gamma x} = -\Gamma_v(x)$$

$$\tag{8.23f}$$

Thus we have:

$$\Gamma_i(x) = -\Gamma_v(x) \tag{8.23g}$$

8.5.3 The Input Impedance

The total voltage and current phasors [V(x), I(x)] along the transmission line can be written as:

$$V(x) = V^+(x) + V^-(x) = V_o^+ e^{-\gamma x} + V_o^- e^{\gamma x} \tag{8.24a}$$

Or,

$$V(x) = V_o^+ \left(e^{-\gamma x} + \frac{V_o^-}{V_o^+} e^{\gamma x} \right) = V_o^+ \left(e^{-\gamma x} + \Gamma_L e^{-2\gamma \ell} e^{\gamma x} \right) \tag{8.24b}$$

Similarly,

$$I(x) = I^+(x) - I^-(x) = V^+(x)/Z_o - V^-(x)/Z_o \tag{8.25a}$$

Or,

$$I(x) = \frac{V_o^+}{Z_O} \left(e^{-\gamma x} - \Gamma_L e^{-2\gamma \ell} e^{\gamma x} \right). \tag{8.25b}$$

The input impedance, $Z_{IN}(x)$, at any point along the transmission line is obtained through dividing equation 8.24b over 8.25b and is given by:

$$Z_{IN}(x) = \frac{V(x)}{I(x)} = Z_O \frac{e^{-\gamma x} + \Gamma_L e^{-2\gamma \ell} e^{\gamma x}}{e^{-\gamma x} - \Gamma_L e^{-2\gamma \ell} e^{\gamma x}} \tag{8.26}$$

A Special Case:

At the load end (where $x = \ell$), the following is observed:

$$Z_{in}(\ell) = Z_L = Z_O \frac{1 + \Gamma_L}{1 - \Gamma_L} \tag{8.27a}$$

$$\Rightarrow \Gamma_L = \frac{Z_L - Z_O}{Z_L + Z_O} \tag{8.27b}$$

We can generalize equation (8.27b) for any arbitrary point along the transmission line with an input impedance (Z_{in}), and write the reflection coefficient (Γ_{IN}) at that point as:

$$\Gamma_{IN} = \frac{Z_{IN} - Z_O}{Z_{IN} + Z_O} \tag{8.27c}$$

Using Equation (8.27b) and letting the distance from the load as **d=ℓ-x,** Equation (8.26) can be written as:

$$Z_{IN}(d) = Z_O \frac{Z_L + Z_O \tanh \gamma d}{Z_O + Z_L \tanh \gamma d} \qquad (8.28)$$

8.6 LOSSLESS TRANSMISSION LINES

Since most of the transmission lines at RF/microwave frequencies have negligible losses, we will focus exclusively on lossless transmission lines.

In a lossless transmission line, there is no series resistance (R) or shunt leakage conductance (G). Thus the energy propagating on the line does not get attenuated in strength (or power). Considering Figure 8.5, the following simplifications can be made:

$\alpha = 0$,

$\gamma = j\beta$,

$$Z_o = \sqrt{\frac{L}{C}} \qquad (8.29a)$$

$V_P = \omega/\beta = 1/(LC)^{1/2}$ (8.29b)

$\lambda = V_P/f = 2\pi/\beta$ (8.29c)

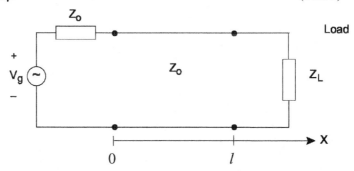

FIGURE 8.5 A lossless Transmission line.

Using Equation (8.23e), we can write:

$$\Gamma(x) = = \frac{V^-(x)}{V^+(x)} = \frac{V_o{}^- e^{j\beta x}}{V_o{}^+ e^{-j\beta x}} = \frac{V_o{}^-}{V_o{}^+} e^{j2\beta x} = \Gamma_L e^{-j2\beta \ell} e^{j2\beta x} \qquad (8.30a)$$

Using equations (8.24b) and (8.25b), we can write the voltage and current on a lossless transmission line as:

$V(x) = V^+(x) + V^-(x) = V_o{}^+ e^{-j\beta x} + V_o{}^- e^{j\beta x}$ (8.30b)

$$V(x)= V_0^+ e^{-j\beta x} \left(1 + \frac{V_0^-}{V_0^+} e^{j2\beta x} \right)$$

Or,

$$V(x)= V_0^+ e^{-j\beta x}[1+\Gamma(x)] \tag{8.31a}$$

Similarly, I(x) can be written as:

$$I(x)= I^+(x)-I^-(x)= \frac{V_0^+}{Z_0} e^{-j\beta x} - \frac{V_0^-}{Z_0} e^{j\beta x}$$

$$I(x)= \frac{V_0^+}{Z_0} e^{-j\beta x}[1-\Gamma(x)] \tag{8.31b}$$

The input impedance at any point (x) on the transmission line from Equations 8.31 can now be written as:

$$Z_{IN}(x)=Z_0 \frac{1+\Gamma(x)}{1-\Gamma(x)} \tag{8.32}$$

Using Equation (8.30) and letting the distance from the load as **d=ℓ-x**, Equation (8.32) can be written as:

$$Z_{IN}(d) = Z_0 \frac{Z_L + jZ_0 \tan\beta d}{Z_0 + jZ_L \tan\beta d} \tag{8.33}$$

The time-average incident (P_i or P^+), reflected (P_r or P^-) and transmitted (P_t or P_L) powers propagating along a transmission line are given by (assuming Z_O is a real number, $\alpha=0$):

$$P^+(x) = \frac{1}{2} \mathrm{Re}\left[V^+(x)I^+(x)^*\right] = \frac{\left|V_o^+\right|^2}{2Z_O} \tag{8.34a}$$

$$P^-(x) = \frac{1}{2} \mathrm{Re}\left[V^-(x)I^-(x)^*\right] = \left|\Gamma_L\right|^2 \frac{\left|V_o^+\right|^2}{2Z_O}, \tag{8.34b}$$

$$P_i(x) = P^+(x) - P^-(x) = (1-\left|\Gamma_L\right|^2)\frac{\left|V_o^+\right|^2}{2Z_O} = P_L, \tag{8.34c}$$

Where P_L is given by:

$$P_L = \frac{1}{2} Re(V_L I_L^*) = \frac{1}{2} Re(V_L V_L^* / Z_L^*) = |V_L|^2 \frac{Re(Z_L)}{2|Z_L|^2} \quad (8.34d)$$

8.7 DETERMINATION OF V_o^+ AND V_o^-

From the earlier discussion, we know that the incident wave is given by:
$$V^+(x) = V_o^+ e^{-j\beta x} \tag{8.34e}$$

To find V_o^+ we need to look at the source end (x =0), where we have:
$$V(0) = V_g - Z_o I(0) \tag{8.34f}$$
Where,
$$V(0) = V_o^+ [1 + \Gamma(0)]$$

$$I(0) = \frac{V_o^+}{Z_O} [1 - \Gamma(0)]$$

Upon substitution for V(0) and I(0) in Equation 8.34f, we have:
$$V_o^+ = (V_g/2) \quad \text{(for x=0 at source)} \tag{8.34g}$$

Equation (8.34g) is simply stating a voltage division of the source voltage between the source impedance (Z_g) and the characteristic impedance of the line (Z_o), where $Z_g = Z_o$. This can be easily visualized by noting that the incident wave does not see the load at first but only Z_o, thus the voltage division!

Moreover, we know that the reflected wave is given by:
$$V^-(x) = V_o^- e^{j\beta x} \tag{8.34h}$$
To find V_o^- we need to visualize the incident wave traveling toward the load with a magnitude of $V_g/2$ given by:
$$V^+(x) = (V_g/2) e^{-j\beta x}$$

At the load (x=ℓ), the incident wave reflects back to the source by a factor of Γ_L. This is called the reflected wave and is given by:
$$V^+(\ell) = (V_g/2) e^{-j\beta \ell}$$
$$V^-(\ell) = \Gamma_L (V_g/2) e^{-j\beta \ell}$$

The reflected wave travels back a distance of x"= ℓ-x and arrives at the source as:
$$V^-(\ell) = \Gamma_L (V_g/2) e^{-j\beta \ell} e^{-j\beta x"} = \Gamma_L (V_g/2) e^{-j\beta \ell} e^{-j\beta(\ell-x)} = (V_g/2) \Gamma_L e^{-j2\beta \ell} e^{j\beta x}$$
$$\tag{8.34i}$$

where x" is an imaginary reference frame set up at the load (x"=0) and is directed toward the source (x"= ℓ). Comparing 8.34i with 8.34h, we obtain:

$$V_o^- = (V_g/2)\, \Gamma_L\, e^{-j2\beta\ell} \quad \text{(for x=0 at source)} \tag{8.34j}$$

Therefore using Equations (8.34g) and (8.34j) in Equation (8.30b), the total voltage at each point (x) along the transmission line can be written as:

$$V(x)= V_o^+ e^{-j\beta x} + V_o^- e^{j\beta x} =(V_g/2)\, e^{-j\beta x} + (V_g/2)\Gamma_L\, e^{-j2\beta\ell}\, e^{j\beta x}$$

Or,

$$V(x)= (V_g/2)\, e^{-j\beta x}[1 + \Gamma_L\, e^{-j2\beta\ell}\, e^{j2\beta x}]= (V_g/2)e^{-j\beta x}[1+\Gamma(x)] \tag{8.34k}$$

It should be noted that Equation (8.34k) is the same as Equation (8.31a) derived earlier.

8.8 A SUMMARY OF ANALYSIS

Let us now recapitulate what we have developed for the incident and reflected waves mathematically and write:

$$V^+(x)= (V_g/2)e^{-j\beta x} =(V_g/2)\angle -\beta x \tag{8.34m}$$

$$V^-(x)= V_o^- e^{j\beta x} =(V_g/2)\Gamma_L\, e^{-j2\beta\ell}\, e^{j\beta x}=(V_g/2)\Gamma_L\angle -2\beta\ell+\beta x \tag{8.34n}$$

At the source end (x=0) we have:

$$V^+(0)= (V_g/2) =(V_g/2)\angle 0° \tag{8.34o}$$

$$V^-(x)= (V_g/2)\Gamma_L\angle -2\beta\ell \tag{8.34p}$$

At the load end (x=ℓ) we have:

$$V^+(x)= (V_g/2)e^{-j\beta\ell} =(V_g/2)\angle -\beta\,\ell \tag{8.34q}$$

$$V^-(x)= (V_g/2)\Gamma_L\, e^{-j2\beta\ell}\, e^{j\beta x} = (V_g/2)\Gamma_L\angle -\beta\ell \tag{8.34r}$$

What we have presented so far can be summarized in one diagram, which reveals all of the complexities of transmission line analysis and makes them into great simplicities. Figure 8.6 shows these simplicities clearly and makes the analysis or design of any complex transmission line an expedient task!

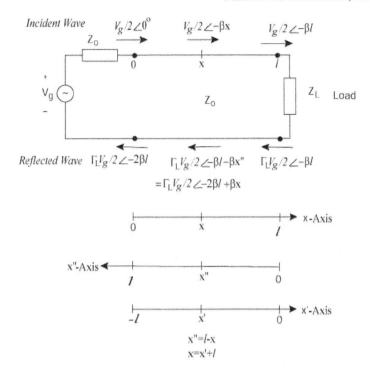

FIGURE 8.6   A summary of transmission line key points.

8.9 VOLTAGE STANDING WAVE RATIO (VSWR)

As described earlier, a standing wave results from two waves having the same frequency traveling in opposite directions on a transmission line. The meeting of these two waves produces a standing wave pattern of voltage and current on a transmission line.

The maximum value of voltage anywhere along the transmission line is given by:

$$V_{max}=|V(x)|_{max}=|V_o^+|+|V_o^-|=|V_o^+|(1+|\Gamma_L|) \tag{8.35}$$

The minimum value of the voltage is given by:

$$V_{min}=|V(x)|_{min}=|V_o^+|-|V_o^-|=|V_o^+|(1-|\Gamma_L|) \tag{8.36}$$

Similarly, for the current standing wave we have:

$$I_{max}=|I(x)|_{max}=|I_o^+|+|I_o^-|=\frac{|V_o^+|}{Z_O}+\frac{|V_o^-|}{Z_O}$$

$$=\frac{|V_o^+|}{Z_O}\left(1+|\Gamma_L|\right) \tag{8.37}$$

$$I_{min}=|I(x)|_{min}=|I_o^+|-|I_o^-|=\frac{|V_o^+|}{Z_O}-\frac{|V_o^-|}{Z_O}$$

$$=\frac{|V_o^+|}{Z_O}\left(1-|\Gamma_L|\right) \tag{8.38}$$

Equations (8.35) to (8.38) are used to define the standing wave ratio (SWR), often referred to as voltage standing wave ratio "VSWR", as follows:

$$\text{VSWR}=\frac{V_{max}}{V_{min}}=\frac{I_{max}}{I_{min}}=\frac{1+|\Gamma_L|}{1-|\Gamma_L|} \tag{8.39}$$

Or,

$$|\Gamma_L|=\frac{\text{VSWR}-1}{\text{VSWR}+1} \tag{8.40}$$

EXAMPLE 8.4
What is the VSWR for a matched transmission line ($Z_o=50\Omega$)?
Solution:
$Z_L=Z_o \Rightarrow \Gamma_L=0$
VSWR=(1+0)/(1-0)=1

EXAMPLE 8.5
What is the VSWR for:
a. An open load ($Z_L=\infty$),
b. A short load ($Z_L=0$)? Assume $Z_o=50\ \Omega$.
Solution:
a) $Z_L=\infty \Rightarrow \Gamma_L=\lim_{ZL\to\infty}(Z_L-50)/(Z_L+50)=1$
VSWR=(1+1)/(1-1)=∞
b) $Z_L=0$
$\Rightarrow \Gamma_L=(0-50)/(0+50)=-1 \Rightarrow |\Gamma_L|=1$

VSWR=(1+1)/(1-1)=∞

Conclusion: From examples 8.2 and 8.3, we can see that:

$$1 \leq \text{VSWR} \leq \infty \qquad (8.41)$$

EXAMPLE 8.6

What is the Z_{IN} of a TL at x=0 (d=ℓ-x = ℓ) for an open circuit load?

Solution:

For $Z_L=\infty$, (8.34) can be written as:

$$Z_{OC} = Z_{IN}(\ell) = \lim_{Z_L \to \infty} Z_0 \frac{Z_L + jZ_0 \tan\beta\ell}{Z_0 + jZ_L \tan\beta\ell} \qquad (8.42a)$$

$$Z_{OC} = -jZ_0 \cot\beta\ell \qquad (8.42b)$$

EXAMPLE 8.7

What is the Z_{IN} of a TL at x=0 (d=ℓ-x = ℓ) for an short circuit load?

Solution:

For $Z_L=0$, (8.34) can be written as:

$$Z_{SC} = Z_{IN}(\ell) = Z_0 \frac{0 + jZ_0 \tan\beta\ell}{Z_0 + 0}$$

$$Z_{SC} = jZ_0\tan\beta\ell \qquad (8.43)$$

8.10 QUARTER-WAVE TRANSFORMERS

The two main functions of any transmission line at any frequency, are two-folded as follows:

a.   Transmission of power, and/or

b.   Transmission of information.

At RF/microwave frequencies, it becomes essential that all lines be matched to each other, to the source and finally to the load. This is due to the obvious fact that reflections due to mismatch or discontinuities (e.g. at a connection, at a junction, etc.) will result in echoes and will reduce the transmitted power and will distort the information carrying signal.

A simple method for matching a resistive load Z_L to a lossless feed line (having a real characteristic impedance Z_O) is the use of a quarter-wave transformer which is a piece of a transmission line having a $\lambda/4$ length and a characteristic impedance of $(Z_O')_{\lambda/4}$.

The characteristic impedance of the quarter-wave transformer $(Z_O')_{\lambda/4}$ terminated in a real load Z_L can be derived as follows:

8.10.1 Derivation of Z_O for $\lambda/4$ TLs

Considering Figure 8.7, we observe that:

$x=0 \Rightarrow d=\ell-x = \ell$

$d=\lambda/4 \Rightarrow \beta d=(2\pi/\lambda)(\lambda/4)= \pi/2 \Rightarrow \tan\beta d=\infty$

Thus the input impedance of the quarter-wave transformer (Equation 8.33b) terminated in a real load Z_L can be written as:

$d=\lambda/4$

$$Z_{in} = \lim_{\ell \to \lambda/4}(Z'_O)\frac{Z_L + jZ'_O \tan\beta\ell}{Z'_O+jZ_L \tan\beta\ell} = (Z'_O)\frac{jZ'_O \tan\beta\ell}{jZ_L \tan\beta\ell}$$

$$\Rightarrow Z_{in} = \frac{Z'^2_O}{Z_L} \qquad\qquad (8.44)$$

Thus, if we choose Z_O' as follows, then $\Gamma_{in}=0$:

$$(Z'_O)_{\lambda/4} = \sqrt{Z_{in}Z_L} \qquad\qquad (8.45)$$

This case is shown in Figure 8.7.

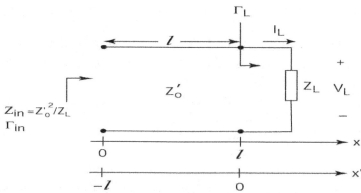

FIGURE 8.7 A quarter wave transformer input impedance ($\Gamma_{in}=0$).

POINT OF CAUTION: *This simple method of matching is applicable on when both of the following conditions are met:*

a) *The feed transmission line is lossless (this leads to a characteristic impedance value which is a real number), and*
b) *The load is resistive*

Note: *There are cases where the load is a complex number, and thus at first glance a quarter-wave transformer does not seem to lend itself for matching purposes. However, in such a case the load should first be converted into a real number by adding a reactance having the same value as the load's reactance but with the opposite sign. The resultant load is resistive and can then be transformed to the feed line's characteristic impedance through the use of a quarter-wave transformer as described above.*

The following example further elucidates this-simple method of matching.

EXAMPLE 8.8

What is $(Z_T)_{\lambda/4}$ of a quarter-wave transformer to transform a load of 100 Ω to a 50 Ω feed line as shown in Figure 8.8?

Solution:

To create a match, we require that Z_{in} to be the same as the characteristic impedance of the feed line, i.e., Z_{in}=50 Ω. Using (8.45), we can write:

$(Z_T)_{\lambda/4}=(Z_L Z_{in})^{1/2}$ $=>\Gamma_{in}=0$

Thus we obtain:

$(Z_T)_{\lambda/4}=(100 \times 50)^{1/2}=70.7\ \Omega$

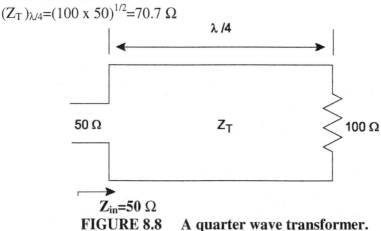

$Z_{in}=50\ \Omega$

FIGURE 8.8   A quarter wave transformer.

NOTE 1: *Example 8.8 clearly shows why these types of shorted transformers are ideal for electrically isolating the RF circuitry from the DC bias source in an active circuit (e.g., an amplifier, etc.). This is because the RF circuitry is connected at the input side of the transformer while DC bias source is at the short-circuited end of the transformer (of course, the short circuit is created by the use of a high-value capacitor to ground). In this fashion, the RF signal "sees" an open circuit at the RF side and would not be able to travel to the DC bias source, while the DC bias "sees" a direct connection (i.e. a short circuit) to the RF circuitry.*

NOTE 2: *The λ/4 TL match is only valid at one frequency! The frequency response and further analysis of quarter-wave TLs will be relegated to Chapter 13. In that chapter, we will see that the prime function of a λ/4 TL is "impedance inversion," $Z_{in} = (Z_o')^2{}_{\lambda/4}/Z_L$, however, under the special condition of "purely resistive loads," this function could be classified as impedance transformation.*

8.11   A GENERALIZED LOSSLESS TRANSMISSION LINE CIRCUIT

In the previous examples, the main focus has been on the effects of a load on the current and voltage waves traveling on a transmission line. However the source of the waves, which is the generator located at the other end, plays an important role in the propagation of the waves along the transmission line.

Up to this point in our discussion, the generator's internal impedance has been a real number equal to the characteristic of the transmission line. In effect, the generator was matched to the line and only the effects of the mismatch of the load was studied so far. Obviously, this is a special case. The most general case is having mismatches at both ends (i.e., at the generator and at the load ends), which will now be discussed in detail.

8.11.1 Voltage and Current Waves

Consider a finite lossless transmission line (T.L.) of length (ℓ) with a characteristic impedance (Z_O) driven by a generator (V_g) with an internal impedance (Z_g) at x=0 and terminated in a load (Z_L) at x=ℓ as shown in Figure 8.9.

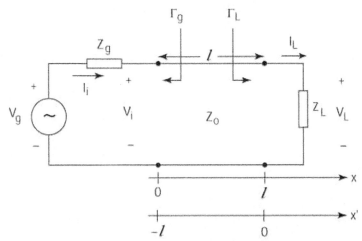

FIGURE 8.9   A general transmission line circuit.

The boundary condition (B.C.) at each end can be written as:

a. B.C. #1-Voltage and current at x=0 is given by:
$V_i = V_g - Z_g I_i$

b. B.C. #2-Voltage and current at x=ℓ is given by:
$V_L = Z_L I_L$

c. Voltage and current on the T.L. for 0≤ x ≤ℓ, from (8.31) and (8.32) is given by:
$V(x) = V^+(x) + V^-(x)$
$$V(x) = V_o^+ e^{-j\beta x}[1 + \Gamma(x)] \qquad (8.46a)$$

$$I(x) = I^+(x) - I^-(x) = \frac{V_o^+}{Z_0} e^{-j\beta x}[1 - \Gamma(x)] \qquad (8.46b)$$

Where, from (8.30), $\Gamma(x)$ is given by:
$$\Gamma(x) = \frac{V^-(x)}{V^+(x)} = \frac{V_o^- e^{j\beta x}}{V_o^+ e^{-j\beta x}} = \frac{V_o^-}{V_o^+} e^{j2\beta x} = \Gamma_L\ e^{j2\beta(x-\ell)} \qquad (8.46c)$$

Applying the boundary condition given by (a), we can solve for V^+ as follows:

$$V_i=V(0)=V_0^{+}[1+\Gamma(0)]= Vg- Z_g\frac{V_0^{+}}{Z_O}[1-\Gamma(0)] \tag{8.47}$$

Where
$$\Gamma(0)=\Gamma_L\, e^{-j2\beta\ell}$$

From Equation 8.47, we can solve for V_0^{+} in terms of V_g to obtain:

$$V_0^{+} = \frac{Z_O V_g}{Z_O + Z_g}\left(\frac{e^{j\beta\ell}}{1-\Gamma_L\Gamma_g e^{-j2\beta\ell}}\right) \tag{8.48a}$$

where

$$\Gamma_g = \frac{Z_g - Z_O}{Z_g + Z_O} \tag{8.48b}$$

Thus $V(x)$ and $I(x)$ under this general condition may be obtained by substituting for V_0^{+} from Equation (8.48a) in (8.46a,b) as follows:

$$V(x) = \frac{Z_O V_g}{Z_O + Z_g} e^{-j\beta x}\left(\frac{1+\Gamma_L e^{j2\beta(x-\ell)}}{1-\Gamma_L\Gamma_g e^{-j2\beta\ell}}\right) \tag{8.49a}$$

$$I(x) = \frac{V_g}{Z_O + Z_g} e^{-j\beta x}\left(\frac{1-\Gamma_L e^{j2\beta(x-\ell)}}{1-\Gamma_L\Gamma_g e^{-j2\beta\ell}}\right) \tag{8.49b}$$

NOTE: *Equations (8.49a,b) show phasor expressions for the voltage and current due to a sinusoidal voltage source (V_g) feeding a finite transmission line, which is terminated in a general load(Z_L).*

These equations represent the summation of infinite number of reflections from both ends of the transmission line, i.e.,

$$V(x)=V_1^{+}+V_1^{-}+V_2^{+}+V_2^{-}+...= \sum_{i=1}^{\infty}(V_i^{+}+V_i^{-}) \tag{8.50a}$$

where
$$|V_1^{+}|=|V_0^{'+}|,$$
$$|V_1^{-}|=|\Gamma_L|\,|V_0^{'+}|,$$
$$|V_2^{+}|=|\Gamma_g||\Gamma_L|\,|V_0^{'+}|,$$
$$|V_2^{-}|=|\Gamma_g||\Gamma_L|^{2}\,|V_0^{'+}|, ...,$$
$$V_0^{'+} = V_g[Z_O/(Z_O+Z_g)]$$

EXERCISE 8.2

Prove that the summation of infinite number of voltage reflections as shown by Equation 8.50a converges to Equation 8.49a.
HINT: Note that:

$$\sum_{n=0}^{\infty} x^n = 1 + x + x^2 + \ldots + x^n + \ldots = 1/(1-x), \quad |x| < 1 \tag{8.50b}$$

From Equation (8.49) we can derive several special useful cases as shown as discussed below.

8.11.2 Case I-Matched at Both Ends

This case is shown in Figure 8.10 below.

$Z_g = Z_L = Z_O$
$\Gamma_g = \Gamma_L = 0$
$V_o^+ = (V_g/2)$ (for x=0 at source)

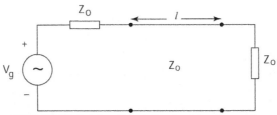

FIGURE 8.10   Matched at both ends.

Since $\Gamma_L = 0$, there is no reflected wave from the load, and thus Equation 8.49 can be written as:

$$V(x) = \frac{V_g}{2} e^{-j\beta x} \tag{8.51a}$$

$$I(x) = \frac{V_g}{2Z_O} e^{-j\beta x} \tag{8.51b}$$

At the source end (x=0), we have:

$$V(0) = V_i = \frac{V_g}{2} \qquad (8.51c)$$

$$I(0) = I_i = \frac{V_g}{2Z_0} \qquad (8.51d)$$

and at the load end (x=ℓ), we can write:

$$V(\ell) = V_L = \frac{V_g}{2} e^{-j\beta\ell} \qquad (8.51e)$$

$$I(\ell) = I_L = \frac{V_g}{2Z_0} e^{-j\beta\ell} \qquad (8.51f)$$

In this case there are no standing waves on the transmission line and magnitude of the voltage and current is the same everywhere on the line, that is,

$$|V_i|=|V_L|=|V(x)|=\frac{V_g}{2} \qquad (8.51g)$$

$$|I_i|=|I_L|=|I(x)|=\frac{V_g}{2Z_0} \qquad (8.51h)$$

NOTE: *In some texts, the reference for length is located at the load end rather than the generator end. This axis is designated by the x'-axis in figure 8.9. This means that there is a shift in the x-axis (by +ℓ), i.e.,*

x=x'+ℓ   (8.51i)

Thus Equations (8.51a,b) can now be written in terms x' as:

$$V(x')= (Vg/2)e^{-j\beta(x'+\ell)} \qquad \text{(for x'=0 at load)}$$

Or,

$$V(x') = \frac{V_g}{2} e^{-j\beta\ell} e^{-j\beta x'} \qquad (8.51j)$$

$$I(x') = \frac{V_g}{2Z_O}e^{-j\beta\ell}e^{-j\beta x'} \qquad (8.51k)$$

8.11.3 Case II-Matched at the Source End
This case is shown in Figure 8.11 below.

$Z_g= Z_O$, $Z_L\neq Z_O$

$\Gamma_g =0$

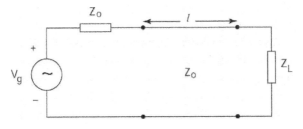

FIGURE 8.11   Matched at source end only.

Since $\Gamma_g=0$, there is no reflected wave from the source, but there is a reflected wave from the load. Thus Equation 8.49 can be written as:

$$V(x) = \frac{V_g}{2}e^{-j\beta x}\left(1+\Gamma_L e^{2j\beta(x-\ell)}\right) \qquad (8.52a)$$

$$I(x) = \frac{V_g}{2Z_O}e^{-j\beta x}\left(1-\Gamma_L e^{j2\beta(x-\ell)}\right) \qquad (8.52b)$$

In terms of the shifted axis (x=x'+ℓ), we can write Equations (8.52) as:

$$V(x') = \frac{V_g}{2}e^{-j\beta(x'+\ell)}\left(1+\Gamma_L e^{j2\beta x'}\right) \qquad (8.52c)$$

$$I(x') = \frac{V_g}{2Z_O}e^{-j\beta(x'+\ell)}\left(1-\Gamma_L e^{j2\beta x'}\right) \qquad (8.52d)$$

At the generator end (x'=-ℓ), we have:

$$V(-\ell) = V_i = \frac{V_g}{2}\left(1+\Gamma_L e^{-j2\beta\ell}\right) \qquad (8.52e)$$

$$I(-\ell) = I_i = \frac{V_g}{2Z_O}\left(1-\Gamma_L e^{-j2\beta\ell}\right) \qquad (8.52f)$$

At the load end (x'=0) we have:

$$V(0) = V_L = \frac{V_g}{2} e^{-j\beta\ell} (1 + \Gamma_L)$$

(8.52g)

$$I(0) = I_L = \frac{V_g}{2Z_0} e^{-j\beta\ell} (1 - \Gamma_L)$$

(8.52h)

It should be noted that Equation (8.52g) is the same as Equation (8.34k) when x=ℓ.

8.11.4 Case III-Matched at the Load End
This case is shown in Figure 8.12 below.

$Z_g \neq Z_O$, $Z_L = Z_O$

$\Gamma_L = 0$

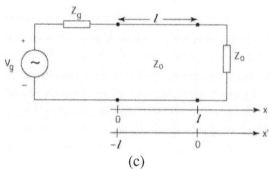

(c)

FIGURE 8.12   Matched at load end only.

Using Equation 8.49, we can write:

$$V(x) = \frac{Z_0 V_g}{Z_0 + Z_g} e^{-j\beta x}$$

(8.53a)

$$I(x) = \frac{V_g}{Z_0 + Z_g} e^{-j\beta x}$$

(8.53b)

At the generator end (x=0), we have:

$$V(0) = V_i = \frac{Z_0 V_g}{Z_0 + Z_g}$$

(8.53c)

This result could have easily be written using the voltage division principle, without using Equation (8.49). In other words, this case reduces to a simple voltage division between the source internal impedance (Z_g) and the transmission line presenting a constant input impedance of (Z_o).

$$I(0) = I_i = \frac{V_g}{Z_O + Z_g} \qquad (8.53d)$$

And at the load end $(x=\ell)$ we have:

$$V(0) = V_L = \frac{Z_O V_g}{Z_O + Z_g} e^{-j\beta\ell} \qquad (8.53e)$$

$$I(0) = I_L = \frac{V_g}{Z_O + Z_g} e^{-j\beta\ell} \qquad (8.53f)$$

The voltage and current on the transmission line have the same magnitude except for a phase shift with length:

$$V_L = V_i e^{-j\beta\ell} \quad \text{for } x=\ell \qquad (8.53g)$$

Or in general,

$$V(x) = V_i e^{-j\beta x} \qquad (8.53h)$$

Similarly, we can write for current:

$$I_L = I_i e^{-j\beta\ell} \quad \text{for } x=\ell \qquad (8.53i)$$

Or in general,

$$I(x) = I_i e^{-j\beta x} \qquad (8.53j)$$

Equations (8.53a) and (8.53b) can be written in terms of the shifted axis $(x=x'+\ell)$ as:

$$V(x') = V_i e^{-j\beta(x'+\ell)} \qquad (8.53k)$$

$$I(x') = I_i e^{-j\beta(x'+\ell)} \qquad (8.53\ell)$$

EXAMPLE 8.9

Consider a 50 Ω lossless transmission line of length $\ell=1$ m, connected to a generator operating at $f=1$ GHz and having $V_g=10$ V and $Z_g=50$ Ω at one end and to a load $Z_L=100$ Ω at the other (see Figure 8.13).

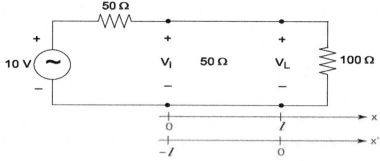

FIGURE 8.13 Circuit for Example 8.9.

Determine:
a. The Voltage and current at any point on the transmission line.
b. The voltage at the generator (V_i) and load (V_L) ends.
c. The reflection coefficient and VSWR at any point on the line.
d. The average power delivered to the load.

Solution:

a. Since $Z_g=Z_O=50\ \Omega \Rightarrow \Gamma_g=0$

Since $\Gamma_g=0$, special case II above applies here. Thus we can write:

$\beta=\omega/c=2\pi x 10^9/3x10^8=20\pi/3$

$$\Gamma_L = \frac{Z_L - Z_O}{Z_L + Z_O} = \frac{100-50}{100+50} = \frac{1}{3}$$

$$V(x) = \frac{V_g}{2}e^{-j\beta x}\left(1+\Gamma_L e^{j2\beta(x-\ell)}\right)=5e^{-j20\pi x/3}\left(1+\frac{1}{3}e^{j40\pi(x-1)/3}\right)$$

$$I(x) = \frac{V_g}{2Z_O}e^{-j\beta x}\left(1-\Gamma_L e^{j2\beta(x-\ell)}\right)=0.1e^{-j20\pi x/3}\left(1-\frac{1}{3}e^{j40\pi(x-1)/3}\right)$$

b. At the generator end (x=0 m), we have:

$$V_i = V(-1) = 5\left(1+\frac{1}{3}e^{-j40\pi/3}\right)=-4.16+j1.44\ \text{V}$$

At the load end (x=1 m), we have:

$$V_L = V(1) = 5e^{-j20\pi/3}\left(1+\frac{1}{3}\right)=\frac{20}{3}e^{-j20\pi/3}$$

c. The reflection coefficient and VSWR are as follows:

$$\Gamma(x) =\Gamma_L\ e^{j2\beta(x-1)}=\frac{1}{3}e^{j40\pi(x-1)/3}$$

$$VSWR = \frac{1+|\Gamma_L|}{1-|\Gamma_L|} = \frac{1+1/3}{1-1/3} = 2$$

d. The average power delivered to the load is:

$\alpha=0$

$$P(x) = \frac{1}{2} \mathrm{Re}\left[V_L(x)I_L^*(x)\right] = \frac{|V_L|^2}{2Z_L} = \frac{\left|20e^{-j20\pi/3}/3\right|^2}{2x100} = \frac{2}{9} = 0.22 \ W$$

NOTE: *If the load was completely matched to the line the power delivered to the load would have been:*

$Z_L=50 \ \Omega$

$|V_i|=|V_L|=V_g/2=5 \ V$

$$\left(P_{av}\right)_{max} = \frac{|V_L|^2}{2Z_L} = \frac{5^2}{2x50} = 0.25 \ W$$

Since there is no reflected power, $(p_{av})_{max}$ is also the incident power (P_i) which is higher than the (P_{av}) calculated earlier under unmatched conditions. The difference in the two powers is due to the reflected power back to the source:

$P_r=|\Gamma_L|^2P_i=(1/9)(0.25)=0.03 \ W$

Chapter 8- Symbol List

A symbol will not be repeated again, once it has been identified and defined in an earlier chapter, with its definition remaining unchanged.

C_0 - Capacitance per unit length

EM – Electro-Magnetic

k – Arbitrary constant

TEM – Transverse Electro-Magnetic

TL – Transmission Line

v – Velocity of motion

V_P - Phase velocity

V^+ - Incident voltage

V^- - Reflected voltage

Z_0 – Characteristic Impedance

Z_{OC} - Open circuit impedance

Z_{SC} - Short circuit impedance

$Z_{\lambda/4}$ - Impedance at the location $\lambda/4$.

β - Phase constant

Γ - Reflection coefficient

Γ_L - Reflection coefficient at the load

$\Gamma(x)$ - Reflection coefficient at location x

ε – Dielectric permittivity

ε_{ff} – Effective relative dielectric constant

ε_o – Permittivity of vacuum (8.85×10^{-12} F/m)

ε_r – Dielectric constant of a material

γ - Propagation constant

λ_o - Wavelength in free space

ω - Angular frequency ($\omega = \beta v$)

CHAPTER -8 PROBLEMS

8.1)   In the two-port network shown in Figure P8.1, assume that $(V_S)_{RMS}=20\angle 0°$ V, and $Z_L=50+j50$ Ω.

a) Find $V^+(0)$, $V^+(\lambda/8)$, $V^-(0)$, $V^-(\lambda/8)$.

b) Calculate net voltages: $V(0)$, $V(\lambda/8)$, $I(0)$ and $I(\lambda/8)$.

c) Calculate the input powers at x=0, $\lambda/8$ independently and show: $P(0)=P(\lambda/8)$.

d) Find $Z_{IN}(0)$

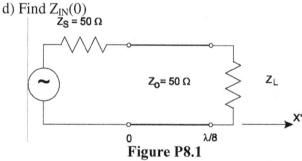

Figure P8.1

8.2)   Find the input impedance and the reflected power at Port(1) and the power delivered to the load at port(2) for the circuit shown in Figure P8.2. Assume $V_s=\cos 2\pi x 10^9 t$ Volts.

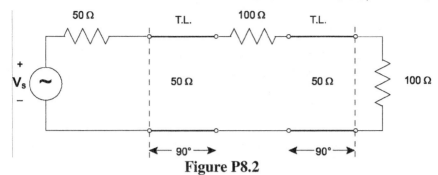

Figure P8.2

8.2) In the lossless transmission line circuit shown in Figure P8.3, calculate the incident power, the reflected power and the power transmitted into the 75 Ω line. Show that:
$P_{INC}=P_{REF}+P_{TRANS}$

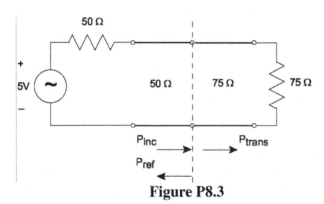

Figure P8.3

8.4) A lossless transmission line (l=0.6λ) is terminated in a load impedance ($Z_L=40+j20$ Ω). Find the reflection coefficient at the load, the input impedance of the line and the VSWR on the line.

8.5) In the circuit shown in Figure P8.5, calculate the reflection coefficient at the load, the VSWR on the line and the power to load.

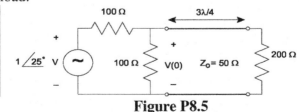

Figure P8.5

8.6)   Consider the lossless transmission line circuit shown in Figure P8.6. Assuming x=0 at the source, calculate:
a) The load impedance (Z_L)?
b) The reflection coefficient at the input of the line.
c) The VSWR on the line.
d) If the source is $V_s=10\cos(2\pi x10^9t+45°)$ Volts, find V(0).

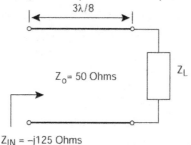

$3\lambda/8$

Z_0= 50 Ohms

Z_L

Z_{IN} = –j125 Ohms

Figure P8.6

8.7)   A lossless transmission line is terminated with a 200 Ω load if the VSWR on the line is 2.0, find the possible values for the line's Z_0. If Vs=5 V, find the voltage at the source and load for the higher Z_0 . What is the power delivered to the load?

8.8)   For a lossless transmission line, terminated in a reactive load ($Z_L=jX$), find the reflection coefficient and the VSWR. What is $|\Gamma|$? Write equations for voltage and current at the load and source if x=0 is at the load.

8.9)   In a TL circuit (Z_0=75 Ω, ℓ=50 cm) operating at f=20 GHz, assume that $V_S=10\angle60°$ V, and $Z_L=100-j50$ Ω,
a) Find $V^+(0)$, $V^+(\lambda/4)$, $V^-(0)$, $V^-(\lambda/8)$, $V^-(\ell)$, $\Gamma^+(0)$, $\Gamma(0)$ and $\Gamma(\lambda/4)$.
b) Calculate net voltages: V(0), V($\lambda/4$), V(ℓ), I(0) and I($\lambda/4$).
c) Calculate the input powers at x=0, and ℓ independently and show: P(0)=P(ℓ). Assume x=0 at source end.
d) At what frequency the input impedance would be a real number? Find Z_{IN} and Γ_{IN}.

CHAPTER 9

Standing Waves & The Smith Chart

9.1 INTRODUCTION

One of the most valuable and yet pervasive graphical tools in all of microwave engineering is the "Smith chart", originally developed in 1939 by P. Smith at the Bell Telephone Laboratories. This chart is the reflection coefficient-to-impedance/admittance converter or vice versa and can greatly simplify the analysis of complex design problems involving transmission lines or lumped elements.

Furthermore, the smith chart provides valuable information about the circuit's performance when line lengths change or new elements are added to the circuit, particularly where obtaining the same amount of information through mathematical models and calculations would be very tedious and time consuming.

Over the years, it has proven itself to be a most useful tool and is thus employed frequently in all stages of circuit analysis or design whether done through manual methods or computer-aided-design (CAD) Software techniques.

9.2 A VALUABLE GRAPHICAL AID

Considering the equation for the reflection coefficient (as given earlier in Chapter 8) we have:

$$\Gamma = \frac{Z - Z_O}{Z + Z_O} = \frac{Z_N - 1}{Z_N + 1} \tag{9.1}$$

where $Z_N = \dfrac{Z}{Z_O} = r + jx$ is the normalized impedance and Z_O is the characteristic impedance of the transmission line or a reference impedance value.

Based on (9.1), the Smith chart can be derived mathematically as discussed in the next section. This chart is a plot of Γ for different normalized resistance and reactance values, where the circuit is assumed to be passive i.e. Re(Z)≥0.

It can be shown that the loci of constant resistance values are circles centered on the horizontal (or real) axis while the loci of constant reactance values are circles centered on the vertical (or imaginary) axis offset by one unit.

9.3 DERIVATION OF SMITH CHART

The Smith chart is a plot of

$$\Gamma = \frac{Z_N - 1}{Z_N + 1} \tag{9.2}$$

in the Γ-plane as a function of r and x. Using (9.2) and separating Γ in terms of its real part (U) and imaginary part (V) we obtain:

$Z_N = r + jx$

$$\Gamma = \frac{r + jx - 1}{r + jx + 1} = U + jV \tag{9.3}$$

$$U = \frac{r^2 - 1 + x^2}{(r+1)^2 + x^2} \tag{9.4}$$

$$V = \frac{2x}{(r+1)^2 + x^2} \qquad (9.5)$$

At this juncture we note that by using (9.4) and (9.5), we can obtain two families of circles which when superimposed on each other will make up the entire Smith chart. The procedures to obtain these two families of circles are described next.

9.3.1 Constant-r Circles

The first family of circles is obtained by eliminating "x" from (9.4) and (9.5) which gives:

$$\left(U - \frac{r}{r+1}\right)^2 + V^2 = \left(\frac{1}{r+1}\right)^2 \qquad (9.6)$$

Equation (9.6) represents a family of circles with a center located at

$$(U_o, V_o) = \left(\frac{r}{r+1}, 0\right), \qquad (9.7a)$$

with a radius of

$$R = \left(\frac{1}{r+1}\right). \qquad (9.7b)$$

From Equations (9.7) we can observe that all constant-r circles are centered on the real axis with a shrinking size as "r" is increased. In this regard, we note that r=0 circle is the most-outer circle of the Smith chart while r=∞ circle is reduced to a point at (0,1). Figure 9.1 depicts this concept further.

9.3.2 Constant-x Circle

The second family of circles is obtained by eliminating "r" from (9.4) and (9.5) which gives:

$$(U - 1)^2 + \left(V - \frac{1}{x}\right)^2 = \left(\frac{1}{x}\right)^2 \qquad (9.8)$$

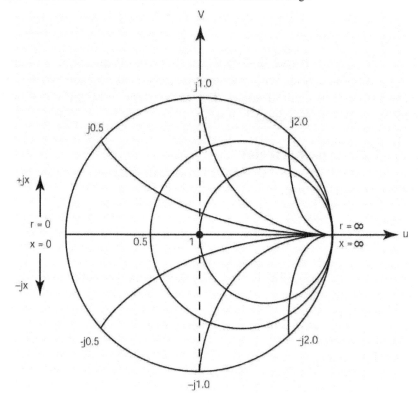

Figure 9.1 Construction of a standard Smith Chart

Equation (9.8) represents a family of circles with a center located at

$$(U_o', V_o') = \left(1, \frac{1}{x}\right) \tag{9.9a}$$

with a radius of

$$R' = \left(\frac{1}{x}\right) \tag{9.9b}$$

From Equations (9.9) we can observe that all constant-x circles are centered on a shifted line parallel to the imaginary axis (by +1 unit to the right), with a shrinking size as "x" increases. In this regard, we note that x=0 circle is the real axis of the Smith chart while x= ±∞ circles are reduced to a point at (1,0). This case is shown in Figure 9.2.

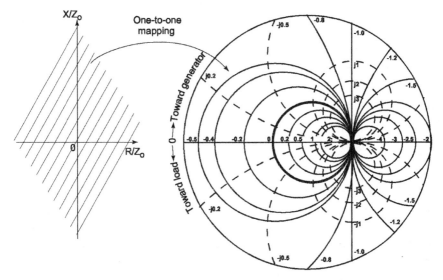

FIGURE 9.2 The whole impedance plane mapping into a compressed Smith chart.

As described earlier, plotting the two families of circles as represented by (9.6) and (9.8) for all values of (r,x) creates a circular chart commonly known as the Smith chart.

The standard Smith chart is a one-to-one correspondence between points in the normalized impedance (Z_N) plane [where $r=\text{Re}(Z_N) \geq 0$] and points in the reflection coefficient (Γ) plane. The upper half of the chart represents normalized impedance values with positive reactances while the lower half corresponds to negative reactances $(x \leq 0)$

NOTE: *The Smith chart could have also been developed based on normalized admittance (Y_N) as follows:*

$$Y_N = \frac{Y}{Y_O} = g + jb \qquad (9.10a)$$

Where $Y_O = 1/Z_O$ is the normalized characteristic admittance or a reference admittance value.

Thus we can write Equation (9.2) as:

$$\Gamma = \frac{Z_N - 1}{Z_N + 1} = \frac{\dfrac{1}{Y_N} - 1}{\dfrac{1}{Y_N} + 1} = -\left(\frac{Y_N - 1}{Y_N + 1}\right) \tag{9.10b}$$

Now using the transformation:

$$\Gamma' = \left(\frac{Y_N - 1}{Y_N + 1}\right) \tag{9.10c}$$

we obtain the same results as for impedance except that the transformation will be from Y_N-plane into Γ'-plane where

$$\Gamma' = -\Gamma = \Gamma e^{j180°} \tag{9.11}$$

Equation (9.11) indicates that Γ' and Γ are only $180°$ apart but have the same magnitude, which means that when dealing with admittances and impedances on the same chart we need to keep in mind the $180°$ phase adjustment every time we convert Z_N to Y_N or vice versa. Therefore a Smith chart can be used as an impedance chart (Z-Smith chart) or equally as an admittance chart (Y-Smith chart).

SUMMARY: *In summary, using a Smith chart requires awareness and an understanding of the following transformations:*

$Z_N \leftrightarrow \Gamma$

$Y_N \leftrightarrow \Gamma'$

$\Gamma' \leftrightarrow \Gamma e^{j180°}$

The magic of the Smith chart lies in the fact that through the use of the above transformation, a semi-infinite and an unbounded region (i.e. $0 \le r \le \infty$, $-\infty \le x \le +\infty$) is transformed into a finite and workable region (i.e., $0 \le \Gamma \le 1$) which creates easily understood graphical solutions to many complex microwave problems.

9.4 DESCRIPTION OF THE SMITH CHART

As discussed in the previous sections, instead of plotting contours of constant reflection coefficient, contours of constant normalized resistance and reactance are plotted in the Γ-plane. A selected collection of these contours (which are circles), plotted in the Γ-

plane, comprise the entire smith chart (commonly known as the "compressed smith chart") which includes impedances with both positive and negative real parts (see Figure 9.1). The "compressed smith chart" is obtained when the entire impedance plane is mapped on a one-to-one basis onto the reflection coefficient plane as shown in Figure 9.2.

The "compressed smith chart", even though very general and applies to both active and passive circuits, is yet impractical and is seldom used in design. Instead, a more useful part of this chart (called a standard smith chart) is used in practice for all passive networks where $Re(Z) \geq 0$, which corresponds to mapping only the right-hand side half of the impedance plane into a circle in the reflection coefficient plane with radius $|\Gamma| \leq 1$ as shown in Figure 9.3.

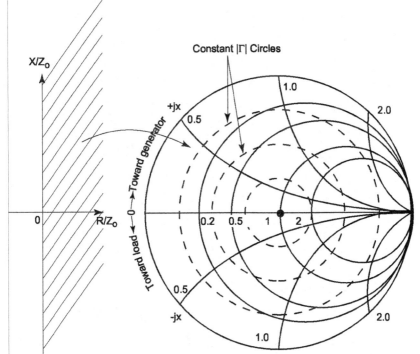

FIGURE 9.3 Positive half of impedance plane mapping into a standard Smith chart.

Standard Smith chart represents a graphical display of impedance-to-reflection coefficient transformation, in which all values of impedance with Re(Z)≥0 (representing a semi-infinite region of the resistance-reactance rectangular plane) is mapped one-to-one into a circle with the radius of one unit in the reflection coefficient plane. A full blown-out version of the standard smith chart is shown in Figure 9.4 where each circle is marked with its corresponding resistance or reactance value.

IMPEDANCE OR ADMITTANCE COORDINATES

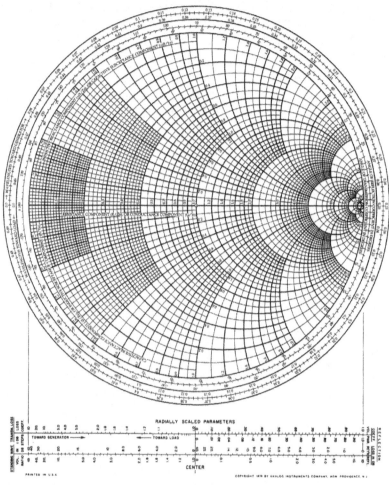

Figure 9.4 The Standard Smith Chart

Thus the Smith chart is comprised of many circles either fully or partially enclosed within the outermost circle ($|\Gamma|=1$) of the standard Smith chart.

The set of circles centered on the horizontal (or real) axis are circles of constant normalized resistance with values ranging from zero (extreme far left) to infinity (extreme far right) on the chart with each circle having a variable reactance.

On the other hand, the set of circles centered on the vertical axis which is offset by one unit from the center, represents circles of constant normalized reactances with values ranging from $-\infty$ to $+\infty$ with each circle having a variable positive resistance. These are shown as partial-circles starting from the right-hand side of the chart and going above the real axis (representing normalized positive reactances) and below (representing normalized negative reactances); the center real axis (horizontal line) represents the zero reactance circle with an infinite radius.

The markings for the positive and negative normalized reactances can be seen on the Smith chart close to the outermost circle.

The key to understanding the Smith chart is realizing that it is a polar plot of the reflection coefficient:
$$\Gamma=|\Gamma|e^{j\theta}, \quad 0\le\theta\le 180° \tag{9.12}$$
with the reference of zero degrees at the right side of horizontal semi-axis.

All passive networks ($|\Gamma| \le 1$) have impedance values with $Re(Z)\ge 0$ which when normalized by the characteristic impedance of the transmission line (to which they are connected) can be represented uniquely on the Smith chart.

The real usefulness of the Smith chart lies in its ability to provide a one-to-one correspondence between reflection coefficient and input normalized impedance (or admittance) values.

Furthermore, moving a distance "ℓ" toward the load along a lossless transmission line corresponds to a change in the reflection coefficient by a factor of $e^{-2j\beta\ell}$ which corresponds to a counter-clockwise rotation of $2\beta\ell$ on the Smith chart as shown in Figure 9.5.

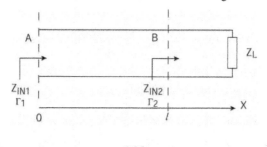

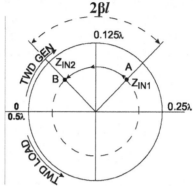

Figure 9.5 Traveling on a lossless transmission line b)Smith chart solution

9.5 SMITH CHART'S CIRCULAR SCALES

Consider a standard smith chart as shown in Figure 9.4. Any specific normalized impedance (z=r+jx) value can be uniquely located on this chart for r≥0. The r-values would be on the resistance circles and x-values on the partial circles for reactance. The positive reactance would be on the upper half of the chart whereas negative reactance values are plotted on the lower half of the chart.

Traveling on a transmission line toward the generator corresponds to moving clockwise on the Smith chart, whereas traveling toward the load corresponds to moving in a counter-clockwise direction as indicated by arrows on the left hand side outer-edge of the Smith chart.

The phase relationship and electrical length along a transmission line are shown on the outer edge of the Smith chart in terms of two secondary scales: One is graduated in fractional wavelength (l/λ) and the other in degrees.

9.5.1 Wavelength Scale

Since the impedance value on a transmission line repeats itself every half wavelength, a complete revolution on the wavelength scale is equivalent to a half wavelength on the Smith chart.

9.5.2 Degree Scale

The degree scale goes through 180 degrees positive and 180 degrees negative with 0 degrees being on the right-hand semi-axis. This scale shows that in a complete revolution of the chart, the reflection coefficient's phase changes 360 degrees corresponding to a half wavelength on the wavelength scale.

These two scales (i.e. the wavelength & the degree scales) are important because they show that when a transmission line is terminated in a load impedance not equal to the line's characteristic impedance, the resulting impedance value on the line varies cyclically every half wavelength (this is of course due to the periodic nature of the standing wave pattern on the line). This fact is built into the Smith chart through these two scales and thus facilitates impedance calculations at various points along a line after the chart has been entered for a specific impedance value.

9.6 SMITH CHART'S RADIAL SCALES

A number of radially marked scales, at the bottom of the Smith chart, are placed in such a manner that they can be radially set off and their values read off from the center of the Smith chart by using a pair of dividers or compass. These scales are described as follows:

9.6.1 Reflection

Starting with the scale on the right hand side, this scale is designed to show the ratio of the reflected wave to the incident wave and is further sub-divided into four scales in the following manner:

1. REFL. COEF. is the reflection coefficient and has the following two sub-scales:

   a. **VOL**: is the voltage reflection coefficient magnitude and is defined as:

$$|\Gamma|=|V^-/V^+| \qquad\qquad (9.13)$$

This scale starts from 0 at the center and ends at 1 at the outer rim of the chart.

b. PWR: is the power reflection coefficient and is defined to be:

$$|\Gamma|^2 = |V^-/V^+|^2 \tag{9.14}$$

Similar to 1(a) above, this scale starts at 0 at the center and ends at 1 at the outer edge of the chart.

2. LOSS IN DB is the loss due to reflection and is expressed in dB with the following two sub-scales:

a. RETN: is the return loss and is defined as the ratio of the incident power to the reflected power at any point on the transmission line, expressed in dB and is equal to:

$$R_{loss}(dB) = 10 \ \log_{10}(P_i/P_O) = 10 \ \log_{10}(1/|\Gamma|^2)$$
$$\Rightarrow R_{loss}(dB) = -20 \ \log_{10}|\Gamma| \tag{9.15}$$

This scale starts from 0 (corresponding to $|\Gamma| = 1$) at the outer edge of the chart and approaches infinity at the center of the chart (where $|\Gamma| = 0$) which indicates that the more perfect the load, the less reflection from the load and higher the return loss.

b. REFL: (Reflected loss or Mismatch loss) is the loss caused by reflection and is equal to the ratio of incident power to the difference between incident and reflected power expressed in decibels as follows:

$$M_{loss}(dB) = 10 \ \log_{10}[P_i/(P_i-P_O)] = -10 \ \log_{10}(1-|\Gamma|^2) \tag{9.16}$$

This scale starts from zero at the center and approaches to infinity as $|\Gamma|$ approaches unity at the outer edge of the chart.

9.6.2 Standing Wave

This scale shows the voltage standing wave ratio (VSWR) as follows:

1. VOL. RATIO: (voltage ratio) this scale plots the VSWR as a ratio of maximum voltage to minimum voltage as given by the following equation:

$$VSWR = \frac{V_{max}}{V_{min}} = \frac{1+|\Gamma|}{1-|\Gamma|} \tag{9.17}$$

The "VOL. RATIO" scale progresses from 1 at the center of the chart ($|\Gamma|= 0$) to infinity at the left-hand margin ($|\Gamma|= 1$).

2. IN DB: This scale expresses VSWR in dB by the relation:

$$(VSWR)_{dB}=20 \log_{10} (VSWR)_{ratio} \hspace{2cm} (9.18)$$

EXAMPLE 9.2
What does VSWR= 2.0 on the "Voltage ratio" scale correspond in dB?
Solution:
Using the adjacent dB scale, we read a value of 6.0 dB on it.

In the next chapter we will discuss the applications of the smith chart which are of great importance to the design of RF and microwave circuits.

9.7 THE ZY SMITH CHART

By superimposing two Smith charts, with one 180° rotated, we obtain a normalized impedance-admittance Smith chart (also known as a ZY Smith chart) as shown in Figure 9.6. The rotated represents the admittance, whereas the other chart represents impedance. The proof for 180° chart rotation to obtain admittance values, is presented in a later chapter.

The ZY Smith chart has therefore two markings: one for impedance chart and another for the admittance chart. Symbols $-X_S$ and $+X_S$ are used on the left hand side for the impedance chart and $-B_P$ and $+B_P$ are used for admittance chart, respectively. From These markings, we can see that positive reactances ($+X_S$) are on the upper half of the chart while negative reactances ($-X_S$) are on the lower half of the chart, respectively. This situation is reversed for the admittance chart, where positive susceptances ($+B_P$) are located on the lower half and the negative susceptances ($-B_P$) are on the upper half of the chart.

Each point on a ZY Smith chart represents the impedance and the corresponding admittance value simultaneously, whereby one can read off these values by a simple glance at the chart. This means that given an impedance (or admittance) value, its corresponding admittance (or impedance) value can readily be read off from the chart without any resort to calculations.

This is an important feature and a major improvement over a standard Smith chart, since it greatly facilitates the circuit design process, particularly where complicated designs are desired. As will be seen later, the ZY Smith chart is an essential analytical tool and will be extensively used for RF/Microwave matching circuit design.

Chapter 9- Symbol List

A symbol will not be repeated again, once it has been identified and defined in an earlier chapter, with its definition remaining unchanged.

P_i – Power incident

P_r – power reflected

PWR – Power reflection coefficient

REFL – Reflection loss or mismatch loss

REFL COEF – Reflection coefficient

RETN – Return loss

R_{loss} - Return loss

R_N - Normalized resistance

VOL – Voltage reflection coefficient magnitude

VSWR – Voltage Standing Wave Ratio

X_N - Normalize reactance

Z_0 – Characteristic impedance

Z_N – Normalized impedance

Γ_g - Reflection coefficient at the generator/source

Γ_L - Reflection coefficient at the load

The Complete Smith Chart (ZY)

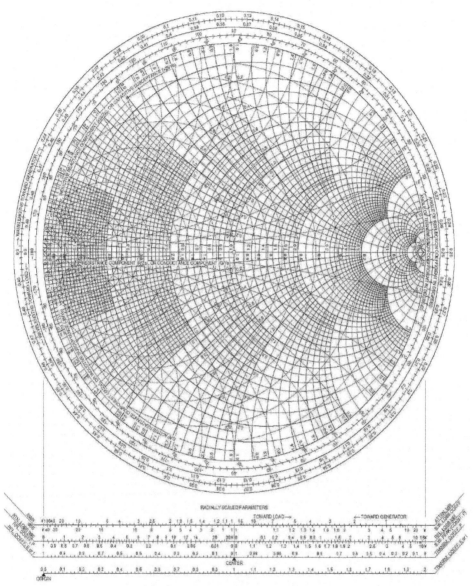

FIGURE 9.6 The ZY Chart

CHAPTER-9 PROBLEMS

9.1)   What is a standard Smith chart? What range of resistor and reactive values is mapped into a standard Smith chart?

9.2)   What resistor values get mapped into a compressed Smith chart? Show by drawing a diagram.

9.3)   A lossless transmission line ($Z_o=75$ Ω) is connected to a load $Z_L=100+j100$ Ω. Using a Smith chart:
a) Determine the reflection coefficient at the load
b) Calculate the return loss.
c) Find the VSWR on the line.
d) Determine the reflection coefficient and the input impedance $3\lambda/8$ away from the load.

9.4)   Using a smith chart find Z_L for:
a) $\Gamma=0.9$ $e^{j60°}$
b) $\Gamma= -0.75$
c) $\Gamma=0.6-j0.6$

9.5)   VSWR on a lossless transmission line ($Z_O=50$ Ω) is measured to be 2.0. Using a Smith chart determine:
a) The magnitude of the reflection coefficient in "ratio" and in "dB".
b) The return loss in dB.
c) The mismatch loss in dB
d) If the load is resistive($R>Z_o$) and is located $5\lambda/8$ away from the source, determine the load impedance value, the input impedance of the transmission line and the reflection coefficients at the load and at the source (see Figure P9.5).
e) Perform part (d) if $R< Z_o$.

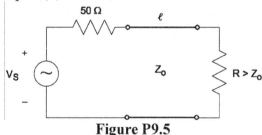

Figure P9.5

9.6)   A lossless transmission line ($Z_o=200$ Ω) is connected to a load $Z_L=100-j200$ Ω. If $\ell=2.25\lambda$, using a Smith chart:

a) Determine the reflection coefficient and the return loss at
   the source,
b) Write the equation for voltage and current at TL's two
   endpoints as well as its midpoint (x=0 at source),
c) Find the VSWR on the line in ratio and dB,
d) Determine the reflection coefficient and the input
   impedance $7\lambda/4$ away from the load.

CHAPTER 10

Lossy Transmission Lines

10.1 INTRODUCTION

All transmission lines have some form of a loss while EM waves are being transmitted along their length. The losses are caused by:
   a.   Finite conductivity of the conductors, and
   b.   Lossy dielectric materials between the conducting metals.

Even though these losses are small and in most practical problems, they can be ignored, however, there are cases that the transmission line loss is significant and needs to be understood and calculated.

In this chapter we will study the losses in a transmission line and present exact methods to calculate the attenuation constant.

10.2 PROPAGATION CONSTANT FOR LOSSY LINES

The general expression for the complex propagation constant (from chapter 8) can be written as:

$$\gamma = \alpha + j\beta = \sqrt{(R + j\omega L)(G + j\omega C)} \qquad (10.1)$$

Where γ is the **propagation constant**, with real part (α) and imaginary part (β), called the **attenuation constant** (Np/m) and **phase constant** (rad/m), respectively.

Equation 10.1 can be further rearranged and written as:

$$\gamma = \alpha + j\beta = \sqrt{(j\omega L)(j\omega C)(1 + R/j\omega L)(1 + G/j\omega C)}$$
$$= j\omega\sqrt{LC}\sqrt{1 - j(R/\omega L + G/\omega C) - RG/\omega^2 LC} \qquad (10.2)$$

10.2.1 A Special Case: Low-Loss Line

If the line is low-loss, then the series resistance (R) is negligibly small relative to the inductive reactance (ωL), and so is the shunt conductance (G) relative to the capacitive susceptances (ωC), i.e.,

$R \ll \omega L$ (10.3a)

$G \ll \omega C$ (10.3b)

Which yields:

$RG \ll \omega^2 LC$ (10.3c)

Using the approximation given by 10.3, equation 10.2 reduces to the following approximation:

$$\gamma \approx j\omega\sqrt{LC}\sqrt{1 - j(R/\omega L + G/\omega C)} \qquad (10.4)$$

We know that from Taylor series expansion that:

$(1+x)^{1/2} \approx 1 + x/2, \quad \text{if } x \ll 1$ (10.5)

Therefore Equation (10.4) can be further approximated as:

$$\gamma \approx j\omega\sqrt{LC}[1 - j(R/\omega L + G/\omega C)/2]$$
$$= (R\sqrt{C/L} + G\sqrt{L/C})/2 + j\omega\sqrt{LC} = \alpha + j\beta \qquad (10.6)$$

From Equation 10.6 we obtain:

$$\alpha \approx (R\sqrt{C/L} + G\sqrt{L/C})/2 = (R/Z_0 + GZ_0)/2 \qquad (10.7)$$

$$\beta \approx \omega\sqrt{LC} \qquad (10.8)$$

Where $Z_0 = \sqrt{L/C}$ is the characteristic impedance of a lossless line.

Note: *The equation for β for a low-loss line is the same as the one for lossless line!*

10.3 THE CHARACTERISTIC IMPEDANCE FOR LOSSY LINES

Using the results obtained in chapter 8, we know that the general equation for Z_o is given by:

$$Z_o = \sqrt{\frac{R + j\omega L}{G + j\omega C}} \qquad (10.9)$$

From this equation, we observe that the characteristic impedance for a lossy line is a complex number in general.

10.3.1 Low-Loss Line

However, if the losses are small as given by equations (10.3a,b), then we can approximate equation (10.9) as follows:

$$Z_o = \sqrt{\frac{R + j\omega L}{G + j\omega C}} = \sqrt{\frac{j\omega L(1 + R/j\omega L)}{j\omega C(1 + G/j\omega C)}} \approx \sqrt{L/C} \qquad (10.10)$$

Note: *The equation for Z_o for a low-loss line is the same as the one for lossless line!*

10.4 ANALYSIS OF LOSSY LINES

For sinusoidal signal variation for "v" and "i", we can write the corresponding Phasors as follows:

$$v(x,t) = Re[V(x)e^{j\omega t}] \qquad (10.11a)$$
$$i(x,t) = Re[I(x)e^{j\omega t}] \qquad (10.11b)$$

Using phasor differentiation results from Chapter 3, the transmission line equations for $V(x)$ and $I(x)$ were derived in chapter 8 as follows:

$$\frac{d^2V(x)}{dx^2} - \gamma^2 V(x) = 0 \qquad (10.12a)$$

$$\frac{d^2I(x)}{dx^2} - \gamma^2 I(x) = 0 \qquad (10.12b)$$

Where

$$\gamma = \alpha + j\beta = \sqrt{(R + j\omega L)(G + j\omega C)} \qquad (10.13)$$

γ is the **propagation constant**, with real part (α) and imaginary part (β), called the **attenuation constant** (Np/m) and **phase constant** (rad/m), respectively.

The solution to the second order differential equations as given by these two equations can be observed to be of exponential type format ($e^{\pm\gamma x}$). Thus we can write the general solutions for $V(x)$ as follows:

$$V(x)=V_0^+ \, e^{-\gamma x}+V_0^- \, e^{\gamma x} \qquad (10.14a)$$

Where the complex constants V_0^+ and V_0^- are determined from the boundary conditions imposed by the source voltage and the load value.

Similarly, $I(x)$ can be obtained from $V(x)$ (see Chapter 8) as:

$$I(x)=\left(\frac{-1}{R+j\omega L}\right)\frac{dV(x)}{dx}=\frac{V_0^+ e^{-\gamma x}-V_0^- e^{\gamma x}}{Z_0} \qquad (10.14b)$$

Where,

$$Z_0=\sqrt{\frac{R+j\omega L}{G+j\omega C}} \qquad (10.14c)$$

is the characteristic impedance of the transmission line.

NOTE 1: *Transmission line Equations could have also been derived using the Maxwell's equations by using the vector quantities: the E- and H-field. Dealing with vectors, however, would have rendered this derivation a more tedious and laborious task.*

We observe that the term $e^{-\gamma x}$ represents a propagating wave in the "+x" direction while $e^{\gamma x}$ represents a propagating wave in the "-x" direction on a transmission line. The combination of the two waves propagating in opposite directions to each other, forms a standing wave on the transmission line, which will lead to standing wave patterns most elegantly depicted by the Smith chart plots as discussed in chapter 9.

NOTE 2: *Based on a given set of boundary conditions for the source and the load, we can find the constants in the equations 10.14ℓ-m. For example, if the source voltage (at x=0) is known to be $V=V_g$ and the load voltage (at x= ℓ) is $V=V_L$, then the constants V_o^+ and V_o^- can easily be found from the following two equations:*

x=0, $V_g=Vo^+ +Vo^-$ (10.14d)

x=ℓ, $V_L=Vo^+ e^{-\gamma\ell} +Vo^- e^{\gamma\ell}$ (10.14e)

EXERCISE 10.1

a. Find Z_o and α when R/L=10(G/C), γ=α+j100 rad/s, R=0.9 Ω/m, C=0.5 nF/m and f =1 GHz.

b. Given Z_L=100 Ω, Vg=10 V, and ℓ= 1m find Vo$^+$ and Vo$^-$. Use part (a) results.

Hint: Use $V_L= Z_L [Vo^+ e^{-\gamma\ell} -Vo^- e^{\gamma\ell}]/Z_o$

10.5 SINUSOIDAL WAVE PROPAGATION ON A TRANSMISSION LINE

Consider a transmission line as shown in Figure 10.1. Assuming a sinusoidal signal excitation, the propagating voltage and current waves on a transmission line are also sinusoidal and can be expressed as:

$v(x,t)=Re[V(x)e^{j\omega t}]$ (10.14e)

$i(x,t)=Re[I(x)e^{j\omega t}]$ (10.14f)

Where complex quantities V(x) and I(x) are phasor quantities.

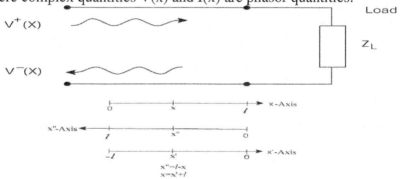

FIGURE 10.1 Incident and reflected waves on a transmission line.
Using the distributed circuit model of a transmission line and its corresponding equivalent circuit, the following differential equations for

I(x) and V (X) can be derived for an infinitesimal length of a transmission line:

$$\frac{d^2V(x)}{dx^2} - \gamma^2 V(x) = 0 \qquad (10.15a)$$

$$\frac{d^2I(x)}{dx^2} - \gamma^2 I(x) = 0 \qquad (10.15b)$$

Where γ is the complex propagation constants given by:

$$\gamma = \alpha + j\beta = [(R+j\omega L)(G+j\omega C)]^{1/2} \qquad (10.16)$$

Where:

α = **attenuation constant (in Nepers/m)**
β = **phase constant (in radian/m)**
R = resistance per unit length in Ω/m
L = inductance per unit length in H/m
G = conductance per unit length in S/m
C = capacitance per unit length in F/m

By observation, we notice that the general solution to the problem is of exponential form, therefore we can write:

$$V_1(x) = V_o^+ e^{-\gamma x} \quad \Rightarrow \quad I_1(x) = \frac{V_o^+}{Z_O} e^{-\gamma x} \qquad (10.17a)$$

$$V_2(x) = V_o^- e^{\gamma x}, \quad \Rightarrow \quad I_2(x) = - \frac{V_o^-}{Z_O} e^{\gamma x} \qquad (10.17b)$$

Where Z_0 is the characteristic impedance of the transmission line; V_o^+ and V_o^- are complex constants in general, whose values depend upon the source and the transmission line characteristics, as will be seen shortly.

Since we are dealing with a linear system, the general solution for voltage and current is obtained using the superposition theorem as follows:

$$V(x) = V_1(x) + V_2(x) = V_o^+ e^{-\gamma x} + V_o^- e^{\gamma x} \qquad (10.17c)$$

$$I(x) = I_1(x) + I_2(x) = \frac{V_o^+}{Z_O} e^{-\gamma x} - \frac{V_o^-}{Z_O} e^{\gamma x} \qquad (10.17d)$$

From Equation (10.17), we observe that voltage and current are a pair of waves co-existing and are inseparable for a distributed circuit. Each solution for voltage or current consists of two waves which will be labeled as follows:

a. An incident wave: $e^{-\gamma x}=e^{-\alpha x}\,e^{-j\beta x}$ (10.18a)
b. A reflected wave: $e^{\gamma x}=e^{\alpha x}\,e^{j\beta x}$ (10.18b)
Where "βx" is referred to as the electrical length.

As already mentioned, each wave travels at the phase velocity (V_P) given by:
$V_P= \omega/\beta = c$ **(air),** (10.19a)
Where c is the speed of light in vacuum given by:
$c = 1/(\mu_0\varepsilon_0)^{1/2} =2.9988 \times 10^8 \approx 3 \times 10^8$ **m/s.** (10.19b)

The time-average incident power propagating along a transmission line, in the absence of reflection, is given by (assuming Z_O is a real number):

$$P^+(x) = \frac{1}{2}\text{Re}\!\left[V^+(x)I^+(x)\,^*\right]=\frac{V_0^{+^2}}{2Z_O}e^{-2\alpha x}=P_1e^{-2\alpha x}$$ (10.20a)

Where P_1 is the power at x=0.

Note: *The same can be written for the reflected power propagating back to the source.*

The coefficient α can be calculated by two methods:

α calculation-Exact Method:
If we let $P^+(x)=P_2$, and x=d, then we can write:
$P_2=P_1e^{-2\alpha x}$ (10.20b)
$2\alpha d =\ln(P_1/P_2)$
$\alpha =\ln(P_1/P_2)\,/2d$ (Np/m) (10.20c)

α calculation-Approximation (small loss case):
If α is small or distance (d) is not large so that the exponential curve of power decay is almost linear, then we can find α through another method, that is to say, by using the law of conservation of energy. This law requires that the rate of decrease of propagating power P(x) along the line should equal the average power loss per unit length (P_{loss}). Thus we can write:

$$-\frac{\partial P(x)}{\partial x} = P_{loss} = 2\alpha P(x)$$

Since the loss is small, we can linearize the slope as follows:

$$\alpha = \frac{P_{loss}}{2P(x)} \approx \frac{-\Delta P / \Delta x}{2P} = \frac{-[P(x+\Delta x)-P(x)]/\Delta x}{2P(x)} \quad (Np/m) \quad (10.21)$$

Since the power is decreasing as the distance increases, therefore the slope is negative and we use a negative sign for the slope to make P_{loss} a positive quantity.

Equation (10.21) shows an interesting and yet very practical way to measure the actual attenuation constant (α). This method is particularly helpful if one is trying to establish the integrity of a faulty line, since a simple comparison of the measured (α) with the nominal (α) would reveal the needed information. The following example elucidates this point further.

Note: *Since the slope has been linearized, this method is only valid for small distances and small α. Otherwise, only the exact method:*
$\alpha = ln(P_1/P_2)/(2d)$
should be used.

EXAMPLE 10.3
The microwave power at one point (P_1) on a transmission line is measured to be 20 mW. At a distance of d=25 cm away, another power measurement (P_2) indicates a power of 10 mW. Determine the attenuation constant of the transmission line.
Solution:
Since the loss on the line is large and is occurring over a small distance, we have to use the exact method:
$\alpha = ln(P_1/P_2) /2d = ln(20/10)/(2x0.25)$
$\alpha = 1.39$ Np/m

10.6 REFLECTION COEFFICIENT DEFINED

Any time an incident wave encounters a second medium different than the first, it is partly reflected (creating a reflected wave) while the remaining is transmitted through (creating a transmitted wave).   The reflected wave encountering the incident wave forms a standing wave as described earlier. Thus we can see that there are four possible waves in a transmission line:

a. *An incident wave,*
b. *A reflected wave,*
c. *A transmitted wave, and*
d. *A standing wave.*

Let us now define an important term:

DEFINITION- REFLECTION COEFFICIENT: *Is defined to be the ratio of the reflected wave phasor to the incident wave phasor.*

In the special case of a uniform transmission line when the incident wave encounters a second medium such as a termination (load) or a discontinuity, then under these conditions, the ratio of the reflected wave phasor to the incident wave phasor is "The reflection coefficient".

To illustrate this concept, consider a transmission line circuit with a load (Z_L) located at $x=\ell$, as shown earlier in Figure 10.1.

$$V^+(x)= V_0^+ e^{-\gamma x} \tag{10.22a}$$

$$V^-(x)= V_0^- e^{\gamma x} \tag{10.22b}$$

Where V_0^+ and V_0^- are the amplitude of the waves at the source end.

At the load end $(x =\ell)$, $V^+(\ell)$ is given by:

$$V^+(\ell)= V_0^+ e^{-\gamma \ell} \tag{10.23c}$$

However to find $V^-(\ell)$, we need to realize that the reflected wave reflects from the load by a factor of Γ_L (i.e., Γ_L is the load reflection coefficient at $x=\ell$):

$$V^-(\ell)= \Gamma_L V_0^+ e^{-\gamma \ell} \tag{10.23d}$$

The reflected wave travels back a distance of x"= ℓ-x towards the source as:

$$V^{-}(x")= V^{-}(\ell-x)= \Gamma_L\ V_0^{+}e^{-\gamma\ell}\ e^{-\gamma x"} = \Gamma_L\ V_0^{+}e^{-\gamma\ell}\ e^{-\gamma(\ell-x)} \qquad (10.23e)$$

where x" is an imaginary reference frame set up at the load (x"=0) and is directed toward the source (x"= ℓ). Thus V⁻(x) can be written as:

$$V^{-}(x)= \Gamma_L\ V_0^{+}e^{-2\gamma\ell}\ e^{\gamma x}= V_0^{-}e^{\gamma x} \qquad (10.23f)$$

The reflection coefficient can now be defined as:

$$\Gamma(x)=\frac{V^{-}(x)}{V^{+}(x)} = \frac{V_0^{-}e^{\gamma x}}{V_0^{+}e^{-\gamma x}} = \frac{V_0^{-}}{V_0^{+}}e^{2\gamma x} = \Gamma_L e^{-2\gamma\ell}e^{2\gamma x} \qquad (10.23g)$$

Thus the total voltage and current phasors [V(x), I(x)] along the transmission line can now be written as:

$$V(x)= V^{+}(x)+V^{-}(x)= V_0^{+}e^{-\gamma x} + V_0^{-}e^{\gamma x}$$

Or,

$$V(x)= V_0^{+}\ (e^{-\gamma x} +\frac{V_0^{-}}{V_0^{+}}\ e^{\gamma x})= V_0^{+}\ (e^{-\gamma x} +\Gamma_L\ e^{-2\gamma\ell}\ e^{\gamma x}) \qquad (10.24)$$

Similarly,

$$I(x)= I^{+}(x)-I^{-}(x)=V^{+}(x)/Z_0 -V^{-}(x)/Z_0$$

Or,

$$I(x)=\frac{V_0^{+}}{Z_0}\ (e^{-\gamma x} -\Gamma_L\ e^{-2\gamma\ell}e^{\gamma x}). \qquad (10.25)$$

The input impedance, $Z_{IN}(x)$, at any point along the transmission line is obtained through dividing equation 10.24 over 10.25 and is given by:

$$Z_{IN}(x) = \frac{V(x)}{I(x)} = Z_0\ \frac{e^{-\gamma x} +\Gamma_L e^{-2\gamma\ell}e^{\gamma x}}{e^{-\gamma x} -\Gamma_L e^{-2\gamma\ell}e^{\gamma x}} \qquad (10.26a)$$

A special case:

At the load end (where x = ℓ), the following is observed:

$$Z_{in}(\ell)= Z_L = Z_0\ \frac{1+\Gamma_L}{1-\Gamma_L} \qquad (10.26b)$$

$$\Rightarrow \Gamma_L = \frac{Z_L - Z_0}{Z_L + Z_0} \tag{10.27a}$$

We can generalize equation (10.27a) for any arbitrary point along the transmission line with an input impedance (Z_{in}), and write the reflection coefficient (Γ_{IN}) at that point as:

$$\Gamma_{IN} = \frac{Z_{IN} - Z_0}{Z_{IN} + Z_0} \tag{10.27b}$$

Using Equation (10.27a) and letting the distance from the load as **d=ℓ-x,** Equation (10.26) can be written as:

$$Z_{IN}(d) = Z_0 \frac{Z_L + Z_0 \tanh \gamma d}{Z_0 + Z_L \tanh \gamma d} \tag{10.28}$$

10.7 Summary of the Lossy Line Analysis
Consider a terminated lossy line as shown in Figure 10.2.

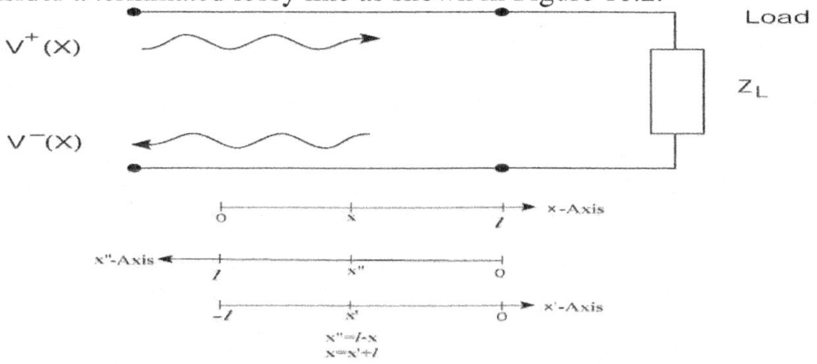

FIGURE 10.2 Incident and reflected waves on a transmission line.

From the discussion presented above on the waves on a terminated lossy lines, we can write the net voltage and current waves at any arbitrary point (x) on the line as:

$V(x) = V^+(x) + V^-(x) = V_0^+ e^{-\gamma x} + V_0^- e^{\gamma x}$

Or,

$$V(x) = V_0^+ (e^{-\gamma x} + \frac{V_0^-}{V_0^+} e^{\gamma x}) = V_0^+ (e^{-\gamma x} + \Gamma_L e^{-2\gamma \ell} e^{\gamma x})$$

$$= V_0^+ e^{-\gamma x}(1 + \Gamma_L e^{-2\gamma \ell} e^{2\gamma x}) = V_0^+ e^{-\gamma x}(1 + \Gamma_L e^{-2\gamma d}) \tag{10.29}$$

Where "d" is the distance from the load given by:

d=ℓ-x

Similarly,
$$I(x) = I^+(x) - I^-(x) = V^+(x)/Z_0 - V^-(x)/Z_0$$
Or,

$$I(x) = \frac{V_o^+}{Z_0}(e^{-\gamma x} - \Gamma_L e^{-2\gamma\ell}e^{\gamma x}) = V_o^+ e^{-\gamma x}(1 - \Gamma_L e^{-2\gamma\ell} e^{2\gamma x})/Z_0$$

$$= V_o^+ e^{-\gamma x}(1 - \Gamma_L e^{-2\gamma d})/Z_0 \qquad (10.30)$$

The reflection coefficient and the input impedance at any point (x) is given by:

$$\Gamma(x) = \frac{V^-(x)}{V^+(x)} = \frac{V_o^- e^{\gamma x}}{V_o^+ e^{-\gamma x}} = \frac{V_o^-}{V_o^+}e^{2\gamma x} = \Gamma_L e^{-2\gamma\ell}e^{2\gamma x} \qquad (10.31)$$

Thus in terms of "d", we can write:
$$\Gamma(d) = \Gamma_L e^{-2\gamma d}$$
$$|\Gamma(d)| = |\Gamma_L e^{-2\gamma d}| = |\Gamma_L| e^{-2\alpha d}$$
Where "d" is the distance from the load given by:
d=ℓ-x
$$(VSWR)_{lossy} = (1+|\Gamma(d)|)/(1-|\Gamma(d)|) = (1+|\Gamma_L|e^{-2\alpha d})/(1-|\Gamma_L|e^{-2\alpha d}) \qquad (10.32)$$

From this equation, we can see that as distance from load increases, the reflection coefficient, $\Gamma(d)$, for a lossy line decreases causing an attenuation in the reflected wave and a subsequent decrease in the VSWR. Thus a simple attenuator could be used to bring down the input VSWR of a device with loss of power as the trade-off.

Note: *If the line were lossless, then Z_o would have been a real number and the reflection coefficient would have increased by a factor of $e^{2\alpha d}$.*

10.8 POWER ANALYSIS OF LOSSY LINES
The incident power generated by the source and delivered to the input of the transmission line (at x=0) is given by:

$$P^+(x=0) = \frac{1}{2}Re[V^+(0)I^+(0)^*] = \frac{|V_o^+|^2}{2Z_O} \qquad (10.33)$$

The reflected power at the input of the TL (at x=0) is given by:

$$P^-(x=0) = \frac{1}{2}\mathrm{Re}\left[V^-(0)I^-(0)*\right] = \frac{|\Gamma(0)|^2|V_o^+|^2}{2Z_O}e^{-2\alpha\ell} \qquad (10.34)$$

$$P_{in}(x=0)=P^+ - P^- = \frac{|V_o^+|^2}{2Z_O}[1-|\Gamma(0)|^2]$$

Where $\Gamma(0) = \Gamma_L e^{-2\gamma\ell}$ with a magnitude of: $|\Gamma(0)| = |\Gamma_L|e^{-2\alpha\ell}$.

At the other end where the load is located ($x=\ell$), the power actually delivered to the load is the difference between the incident and reflected powers and thus can be similarly written as:

$$P_L = P^+(\ell) - P^-(\ell) = \frac{1}{2}\mathrm{Re}\left[V^+(\ell)I^+(\ell)* - V^-(\ell)I^-(\ell)*\right] = \frac{1}{2}\mathrm{Re}[V(\ell)I(\ell)*]$$

$$= \frac{|V_o^+ e^{-\alpha\ell}|^2}{2Z_O}(1-|\Gamma_L|^2) = \frac{|V_o^+|^2}{2Z_O}(1-|\Gamma_L|^2)e^{-2\alpha\ell}$$

$$(10.35)$$

The difference between the power at the input and the power absorbed by the load is power lost in the line (P_{loss}) and is given by:

$$P_{loss} = P_{in} - P_L = \frac{|V_o^+|^2}{2Z_O}[(1-|\Gamma_L|^2 e^{-4\alpha\ell}) - (1-|\Gamma_L|^2)e^{-2\alpha\ell}]$$

$$= P_o[(1-e^{-2\alpha\ell}) + |\Gamma_L|^2 e^{-2\alpha\ell}(1-e^{-2\alpha\ell})]$$

$$(10.36)$$

Where $P_o = |V_o^+|^2/2Z_O$.

The first term represents the power loss due to the incident wave, whereas the second represents the power loss due to the reflected power caused by load.

10.9 DISTORTIONLESS LINES
For a lossy TL, the phase constant (β) of a TL is no longer linear but a nonlinear function of frequency $g(\omega)$, due to the losses present, i.e.,
$\beta = g(\omega) \neq \omega/c$, $\qquad (10.37a)$
where "c" is the speed of light, a constant value for a given medium.

The phase velocity is a nonlinear function of "ω" and is given by:
$V_P = \omega/\beta = \omega/g(\omega)$ $\qquad (10.37b)$

V_P will no longer be a constant value and will be different as frequency varies over any given bandwidth. This means that frequency components of a wideband signal will travel at different speeds while propagating on the TL and so will arrive at different times at the load end. This effect is called dispersion, which leads to signal distortion and is not generally desirable.

There is a special case of a lossy line, which can lead to a linearity for β if we choose the TL parameters properly. Such a case is called the "distortionless line" and is analyzed further below.

10.9.1 Design of TL Parameters

As we noted earlier, the propagation constant of a lossy TL is given by:

$$\gamma = \alpha + j\beta = [(R+j\omega L)(G+j\omega C)]^{1/2} \tag{10.38}$$

By rearranging the terms, we obtain:

$$\gamma = [\,(j\omega L \cdot j\omega C\,)\,(1+R/j\omega L)(1+G/j\omega C)]^{1/2}$$
$$= j\omega(LC\,)^{1/2}\,[\,1-j(R/\omega L+ G/\omega C)-RG/\omega^2 LC]^{1/2}$$

If we choose the TL parameters such that:

R/L= G/C

Then we have:

$$\gamma = j\omega(LC\,)^{1/2}\,[\,1- j(R/\omega L+ R/\omega L)-R^2/\omega^2 L^2]^{1/2}$$

Which simplifies into:

$$\gamma = j\omega(LC\,)^{1/2}\,[\,(1- jR/\omega L)^2]^{1/2} = j\omega(LC\,)^{1/2}\,(1- jR/\omega L)$$

Thus we obtain:

$$\gamma = \alpha + j\beta = R(C/L)^{1/2} + j\omega(LC)^{1/2} \tag{10.39}$$
$$\alpha = R(C/L)^{1/2}$$
$$\beta = \omega(LC)^{1/2}$$

From the last equation we obtain a linear relationship for β, which was the desired target of analysis.

To satisfy the parameter choice for a distortionless line, we usually require that loading coils to be added periodically throughout the length of the line so as L is increased in such a way that desired ratio R/L= G/C is achieved.

NOTE: *The distortionless line is not lossless because $\alpha = R(C/L)^{1/2}$ is not zero. However, since α is not a function of frequency, therefore all frequency components of the signal passes through the TL with the same amount of attenuation, leading to no distortion of the original signal waveform.*

10.10 THE LOW-LOSS LINE

In actual practice all lines have loss due to finite conductivity of the conductors and presence of lossy dielectric materials. However, if the length of the TL is small, then the losses involved are usually negligible and can be ignored to simplify the analysis of the propagating signals. This is the case of lossless line that we have studied earlier in Chapter 8.

If the loss is small, then one can usually obtain an approximate value of the loss based on a first-order analysis as follows.

The propagation constant of a lossy TL from an earlier analysis is given by:

$$\gamma = \alpha + j\beta = [(R+j\omega L)(G+j\omega C)]^{1/2} \qquad (10.40)$$
$$= j\omega(LC)^{1/2} [1-j(R/\omega L+ G/\omega C)-RG/\omega^2 LC]^{1/2}$$

If the line is low-loss, then R and G are negligible compared to the reactive elements, L and C, that is to say:

$R \ll \omega L$

$G \ll \omega C$

Thus we have:

$RG \ll \omega^2 LC$

Using this approximation, the equation for γ simplifies:

$$\gamma = j\omega(LC)^{1/2} [1-j(R/\omega L+ G/\omega C)]^{1/2} \qquad (10.41)$$

If we now use the binomial expansion given by the Taylor series when $x \ll 1$, we obtain:

$$(1+x)^{1/2}=1+x/2+x^2/4+\ldots \ldots \approx 1+x/2 \qquad (10.42)$$

Thus we can write:

$$\gamma = \alpha + j\beta \approx j\omega(LC)^{1/2} [1-j(R/\omega L+ G/\omega C)/2] \qquad (10.43a)$$
$$\alpha \approx [R(C/L)^{1/2}+ G(L/C)^{1/2}]/2=[R/Zo+ GZo]/2 \qquad (10.43b)$$
$$\beta \approx \omega(LC)^{1/2} \qquad (10.43c)$$

Where $Z_o=(L/C)^{1/2}$ is the characteristic impedance of the TL in the absence of loss.

NOTE1: *β for a low-loss TL is approximately the same as the lossless case.*

The approximate equation for the characteristic impedance of a lossy TL can be obtained as:

$$Z_o=\sqrt{\frac{R+j\omega L}{G+j\omega C}}$$

$$=(j\omega L/\ j\omega C\ )\ [(1+R/j\omega L)/(1+G/j\omega C)]^{1/2} \tag{10.44}$$

Using the low loss approximations, we obtain:

$R<<\omega L$

$G<<\omega C$

$$Z_o \approx (L/C)^{1/2} \tag{10.45}$$

Therefore, Z_o for a low-loss case is approximately a real quantity and not a complex number as generally expected.

NOTE2: *Z_o for a low-loss TL is approximately the same as the lossless case.*

10.11 AN EXAMPLE OF A LOSSY LINE

The following example further illustrates how to solve a typical lossy line problem.

EXAMPLE 10.1

A lossy Transmission line has a length of 2.9 m and is operating at $\omega=3x10^4$ rad/sec with V(0)=100 V, as shown in Figure 10.3. The lossy line has the following parameters:

L=10 mH/m, C=1 μF/m, R=20 Ω/m, G=0, Z_L=300 Ω.

Calculate Z_o, γ, V_p, I(0), V_L, I_L, P(0), P_L, Γ(0), input VSWR, Z(0) and the power lost in the line (P_{loss}). Assume the generator has a zero phase at the sending end.

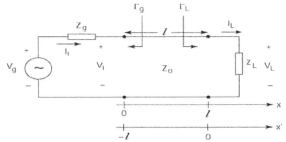

FIGURE 10.3 Incident and reflected waves on a transmission line.

Solution:

a) $Z_o = \sqrt{\dfrac{R + j\omega L}{G + j\omega C}}$

$\omega L = (3 \times 10^4)(10 \times 10^{-3}) = 300\ \Omega$

$\omega C = (3 \times 10^4)(1 \times 10^{-6}) = 0.03\ S$

Therefore,

$Z_o = \sqrt{\dfrac{20 + j300}{0 + j0.03}} = 100\angle -2° = 100\text{-}j3.3\ \Omega$

b) $\gamma = \alpha + j\beta = [(R + j\omega L)(G + j\omega C)]^{1/2}$ $= [(20 + j300)(j0.03)]^{1/2} = 0.1 + j3$

$\alpha = 0.1\ Np/m$

$\beta = 3\ rad/m$

c) $Vp = \omega/\beta = 3 \times 10^4/3 = 10^4\ m/s$

$\beta\ell = 3 \times 2.9 = 8.7\ rad \approx 140°$

d) $V(x) = V^+(x) + V^-(x) = V_o^+ e^{-\gamma x} + V_o^- e^{\gamma x} = V_o^+ e^{-\gamma x}(1 + \Gamma_L e^{-2\gamma d})$

Where "d" is the distance from the load given by: **d=ℓ-x**

$I(x) = I^+(x) - I^-(x) = V^+(x)/Z_o - V^-(x)/Z_o = V_o^+ e^{-\gamma x}(1 - \Gamma_L e^{-2\gamma d})/Z_o$

$\Gamma_L = \dfrac{Z_L - Z_o}{Z_L + Z_o} = (300 - 100 + j3.3)/(300 + 100 - j3.3)$

$= 0.5\angle 1.4° = 0.5\angle 0.0245\ rad$

e) Signal attenuates one way from source to load (and by the same factor back to source) by a factor of :

ATT factor$= e^{-\alpha d} = e^{-0.1 \times 2.9} \approx 0.75$

$|V(0)| = 100 = |V_o^+|\,|(1 + 0.5e^{j0.024}\ x\ e^{-2x(0.1 + j3)x2.9})|$

$\Rightarrow |V_o^+| = 100/1.075 = 93\ V$

Since the generator has a zero phase, thus $V_o^+ = |V_o^+| = 93\angle 0°\ V$

Thus the sending end voltage is:

$V_S = V(0) = 100\angle 15°\ V$

f) $I_S=I(0)= V^+(0)/Z_o -V^-(0)/Z_o$

$= 93/100\angle2° -(93x0.75x0.75x0.5/100\angle-280°+1.4°+2°)$

$= 0.93\angle-14.5°$ A

g) $V_L= V^+(\ell) +V^-(\ell)=93x0.75\angle-140° x(1+0.5\angle1.4°)\approx104.5\angle-140°$ V

$I^+(\ell)= V_o^+ e^{-\gamma\ell}/Z_o=93 e^{-(0.1+j3)x2.9}/100\angle-2°=0.93x0.75\angle-138°$

$= 0.70\angle-138°$ A

$I^-(\ell)= \Gamma_L I^+(\ell) =0.35\angle-136.6°$ A

$I_L= I^+(\ell) -I^-(\ell)=0.35\angle-139.5°$ A

h) $Z(0)=V(0)/I(0)= 100\angle15°/0.93\angle-14.5°=107.5\angle29.5°=94.5+j52.5$ Ω

$\Gamma (0)=V^-(0)/V^+(0)= 93x0.75x0.75x0.5\angle-280°+1.4°/93\angle0°$

$=0.28\angle-278.6°$

$VSWR=(1+|\Gamma (0)|)/(1-|\Gamma (0)|)=(1+0.28)/(1-0.28)=1.78$

Note: *If the line were lossless, then Z_o would have been a real number and the reflection coefficient would have increased by a factor of $e^{2\alpha d}=(1/0.75)^2=1.78$ as follows:*

$\Gamma(0)=V^-(0)/V^+(0)= 1.78x0.28\angle-280°=0.5\angle-280°$

$VSWR=(1+|\Gamma(0)|)/ (1-|\Gamma(0)|)=(1+0.5)/(1-0.5)=3$

This example clearly shows that a lossy line improves the VSWR on the line by a factor of 1.7 (i.e., 3/1.78=1.7).

i) Power lost in the line is found as follows:

$P_{loss}=P(0)-P(\ell)$

$P(0)=Re(100\angle15°) x (0.93\angle-14.5°)^*/2=40.4$ W

$P(\ell)=Re(104.5\angle-140°) x (0.35\angle-139.5°)^*/2=18.3$ W

Thus:

$P_{loss}=40.4-18.3=22.1$ W

Transmission Line Efficiency (TLE) $=P_{out}/P_{in} =18.3/40.4=45\%$

Note: *For a lossless TL ($P_{loss}=0$), $P_{out}=P_{in}$, thus TLE=1=100%.*

This example shows that losses on a line, especially for long lines, can quickly add up and weaken the signal considerably. Thus the use of relay point amplifiers (or boosters), to re-establish the original power on the line become imperative for industries specializing in transmission of signals via long lengths of cable; examples include cable TV lines, fiber optics cables, etc.

Note: *We could have calculated P_{loss} by the equation derived earlier as follows:*

$$P_{loss} = P_{in} - P_L = \frac{|V_0^+|^2}{2Z_O}[(1-|\Gamma_L|^2 e^{-4\alpha\ell}) - (1-|\Gamma_L|^2)e^{-2\alpha\ell}]$$

$$= P_0[(1-e^{-2\alpha\ell}) + |\Gamma_L|^2 e^{-2\alpha\ell}(1-e^{-2\alpha\ell})]$$

Where $P_0 = |V_0^+|^2/2Z_0$.

$P_{loss} = (93^2/2 \times 100)[(1-0.75^2) + 0.5^2 \times 0.75^2(1-0.75^2)]$
$\qquad = 43.25[0.44 + 0.14 \times 0.44] \approx 22$ W,   (same value as earlier).

10.12 LOSS CALCULATIONS USING SMITH CHART

Using a Smith chart, we can calculate the losses on a lossy Transmission line. The radial scale at the bottom of a Smith chart has a "Transm Loss" scale which is discussed next.

10.12.1 TRANSM Loss

"Transm Loss" is the transmission loss and is used primarily for lossy transmission lines and has two scales:

a. LOSS COEF: is the transmission loss coefficient and is used as a correction factors for the additional line losses created in a lossy transmission line due to high VSWR. A high VSWR on a line creates peaks of high current densities alternated with high voltage density peaks. Since resistive losses are proportional to the current value squared and dielectric losses are proportional to voltage value squared, the locale where these peaks of energy lie create additional losses on the line which is not accounted for through ordinary calculations.

Thus a correction factor is needed to provide a more accurate estimation of line losses when a high VSWR exists on the lossy transmission line. The "LOSS COEF" scale provides the much needed correction factor when the VSWR on the line is greater than unity. The correction factor provided by this scale would increase the calculated line losses which will affect the attenuation factor calculations.

For example, when the VSWR is 1 (i.e. A matched case) the correction factor from this scale is read to be one. On the other hand, when the VSWR of the line is increased to 4 (due to a load mismatch), then the correction factor is read off to be approximately 2.1, which means that the line losses have more than doubled due to this high VSWR.

b. 1 DB STEPS: is the transmission loss in 1-dB steps and is used to calculate VSWR on a lossy transmission line. Graphically, a lossy line can no longer be represented by a constant VSWR circle, instead by a spiral on the Smith chart due to the attenuation of both the incident wave's amplitude traveling "toward the load" and the reflected wave's amplitude back to the generator. This power loss is shown in Figure 10.4 on a Semi-Log scale. From this Figure, it can be seen that:

$$|\Gamma_g|^2 = P_r/P_i \text{ (at the source end)} \tag{10.46}$$

$$|\Gamma_L|^2 = P_r^{'}/P_i^{'} \text{ (at the load end)} \tag{10.47}$$
$$\Rightarrow |\Gamma_g| < |\Gamma_L|,$$

This would hold true as long as the line remains lossy.

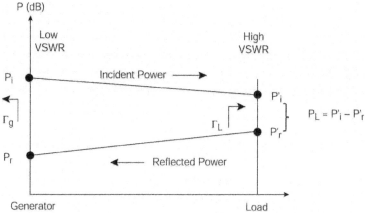

Figure 10.4 Power attenuation on a lossy line.

It is important to note that as the measurement plane moves toward the generator and away from the load, the reflection coefficient becomes smaller and thus VSWR is reduced as illustrated in the next example.

EXAMPLE 10.2
Consider an unknown load connected to a lossy 50 Ω cable (with 2 dB of insertion loss) connected to a generator. The VSWR at the generator end is measured to be 2.0. What is the VSWR at the load?

Solution:
We first plot the VSWR circles at the generator end by dropping a vertical line from the constant-VSWR circle to intersect the "1 dB Step" scale at point A (see Figure 10.5). Now we add 2 dB correction to this value "toward load" as indicated on the scale to obtain point B. The radius related to point B is that of the load VSWR and is found by drawing a vertical line from point B to intersect the left hand semi-axis on the Smith chart. By swinging this radius around, it is seen that the new VSWR circle has a VSWR=3.2 at the load end.

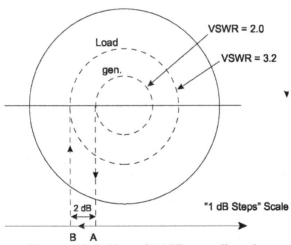

Figure 10.5 Use of "1dB steps" scale.

As can be seen from Example 10.1, a lossy line can improve the VSWR at the generator end at the expense of power loss, which may not always be desirable.

We also note from this example that moving away from the center (i.e. higher $|\Gamma|$) on this scale is labeled as "Toward Load" while moving toward the center of the chart (i.e. lower $|\Gamma|$) is labeled as "Toward generator".

NOTE: *Incidentally, it is interesting to note that the values on "the transmission loss (in one dB steps)" are one-half of the values on the "Return loss in dB" scales. This factor of "One-half" is caused by the fact that the "return loss scale" indicates two-way power attenuation through a given piece of cable, whereas the transmission loss is defined as merely a one-way attenuation loss.*

CHAPTER-10 PROBLEMS

10.1)   A 50 m long lossy TL at 10 kHz has $\alpha=0.9$ Nepers/m and $\beta=0.60$ rad/m with a $Z_o=150-j75$ Ω. If the line is connected to an RF source with an amplitude of 5 V and internal resistance of 150 Ω, and is terminated in a 100+j100 Ω load, determine:
a) The input voltage, current and power,
b) The load voltage and current
c) The first-time reflected power at the source.

10.2)   A line is 2 km long and is connected to a 100 kHz source with an amplitude of 10 V. If the line has:
R=0.86 Ω/m, G=0, L=6 µH/m, C=0.4 nF
If the load is 250+j250 Ω, determine
a) α, β and Zo,
b) The input power
c) Load voltage, current and absorbed power

10.3)   A 250 m transmission line with $\alpha=0.004$ Np/m, $\beta=0.06$ rad/m and $Z_o=100$ Ω is connected to a 2 MHz source with an

amplitude of 30V and an internal resistance of 100 Ω. It is terminated in a 200 Ω load.
a) Determine the sending-end voltage and power,
b) Determine the receiving-end voltage and power,
c) Find the reflected power from the load, and
d) VSWR at the sending end.

10.4) A 3 km long line with $\alpha=0.1$ Nepers/m and $\beta=0.04$ rad/m and Zo=200 Ω is connected to 10 kHz generator with an amplitude of 40 V and an internal resistance of 200 Ω. If the load is 200 Ω,
a) find the magnitude and phase of the sending and received voltages at the load,
b) The sending and received powers, and
c) If the line is opened at the load, what is the sending and receiving end voltages.

10.5) VSWR on a 20 m lossy transmission line with $\alpha=0.1$ Nepers/m, $\beta=0.04$ rad/m and $Z_O=50$ Ω is measured to be 3.0 at the load end.
a) Find the magnitude of the reflection coefficient in "ratio" and in "dB" at the load.
b) VSWR at the source
c) The return loss in dB.

CHAPTER 11

Lumped Elements On The Smith Chart

11.1 INTRODUCTION

As discussed earlier, The Smith chart is an extremely powerful tool for the analysis and design of RF and microwave circuits. The Smith chart applications in the analysis or design of RF and microwave circuits can be subdivided into three categories:

a. Circuits containing "lumped elements".

b. Circuits containing primarily "distributed elements", particularly transmission lines (TLs).

c. Circuits containing "Distributed and lumped elements" in combination.

In this chapter, we will treat lumped element circuits in depth and relegate distributed-element circuit analysis and their combinations with lumped elements to the next chapter.

11.2 LUMPED ELEMENT CIRCUIT APPLICATIONS

Before we proceed into different Smith chart applications, it would serve us well, at the outset, if we define, the following notations which will be used throughout this book:

Impedance: $Z=R+jX$ (Ω) (11.1)

Admittance: $Y=G+jB$ (S) (11.2)

The normalized values are given by:

$(Z)_N=Z/Z_O= R/Z_O+jX/Z_O =r+jx$ (11.3)

$(Y)_N=Y/Y_O=G/Y_O +jB/Y_O=g+jb$ (11.4)

Where,

$r=R/Z_O,$ (11.5)

$x=X/Z_O,$ (11.6)

$g=G/Y_O,$ (11.7)

$b=B/Y_O,$ (11.8)

$Y_O=1/Z_O$ (11.9)

Where "Z_O" is a reference impedance value selected such that all normalized values can easily be placed on the Smith chart. It should be noted that in the absence of transmission lines "Z_O" is no longer the characteristic impedance of the transmission line as discussed before.

The lumped elements employed in the design of RF and microwave circuits are usually lossless reactive elements (such as inductors or capacitors) and are added either in series or in parallel in the circuit as will be seen shortly.

11.3 INPUT IMPEDANCE FOR SERIES ELEMENTS

Consider the circuit shown in Figure 11.1 where a load (Z_L) is in series with a series element (Z_S). The lumped element can be reactive (lossless), resistive (lossy) or a combination of both. In this application we consider a very general lumped element consisting of both resistive and reactive components.

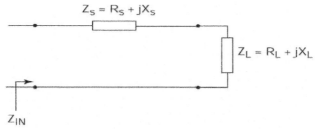

Figure 11.1 Circuit for series lumped element.

Since the lumped element is in series with the load, we need to consider only the Z-chart markings of the ZY-Smith chart (or only a Z-chart), in order to determine Z_{in}. We know mathematically that:
$Z_{in}=Z_L+Z_S$
Thus:
$$(Z_{in})_N=(r_L+r_S)+j(x_L+x_S) \tag{11.10}$$

The purpose of this application is to show how to achieve this result graphically where the exact steps are delineated below:

a. Locate $(Z_L)_N$ on the Smith chart(see point "A" in Figure 11.2)

b. Moving on the constant resistance circle that passes through Z_L, add a reactance of jx_S to arrive at point "B".

c. Now moving on a constant reactance circle that passes through point "B", add a resistance of r_S to arrive at point "C".

d. The input impedance value is read off at point "C", using the Z-chart markings.

11.3.1 Alternate procedure
Point "C" could have equally been reached by the following steps (see Figure 11.2):

a. Move on a constant reactance circle (that passes through "A" and add the resistance of r_S to arrive at point B' (see Figure 11.2)
b. Now moving on a constant resistance circle (that passes through point B'), add the reactance of jx_S to arrive at point "C".

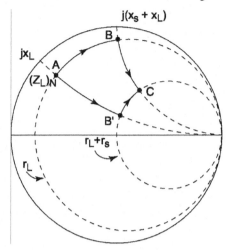

Figure 11.2 Graphical solution.

11.4 INPUT ADMITTANCE FOR SHUNT ELEMENTS

Consider the circuit shown in Figure 11.3, where a load (Y_L) is in parallel with a shunt element (Y_P). In general, The lumped element is considered to have both resistive and reactive components.

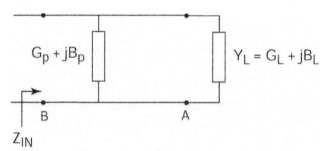

Figure 11.3 Circuit for shunt lumped element.

Since the lumped element is in parallel with the load, only the Y-chart markings of the ZY-Smith chart need be considered.

The total admittance is given mathematically by:

$Y_{in} = Y_L + Y_P$

$(Y_{in})_N = (g_L + g_P) + j(b_L + b_P)$

We now present the procedure to determine $(Y_{in})_N$ graphically:
a.   Locate $(Y_L)_N$ on the Y-chart at point "A" in Figure 11.4.

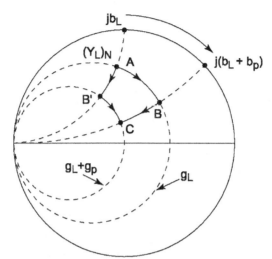

Figure 11.4 Smith chart solution.

b. Move on the constant conductance circle [that passes through $(Y_L)_N$] and add a susceptance of "jb_P" to arrive at point "B".
c. Move on the constant susceptance circle (passing through "B") by adding a conductance of "g_P" to arrive at point "C".
d. The input admittance is read off at point "C" using the Y-chart markings.

11.4.1 Alternate Procedure
As discussed earlier, the input admittance equally could have been determined by:

a. Moving on a constant susceptance circle and adding g_P to arrive at point "B' " as shown in Figure 11.4.

b. Now add jb_P on a constant conductance circle to arrive at point "C".

11.5 INPUT IMPEDANCE FOR REACTIVE ELEMENTS

This is a special case where the series or the shunt elements are lossless (i.e. purely reactive). In this case there are 4 possible combinations (see Fig. 11.5) as follows:

1. Series L
2. Series C
3. Shunt L
4. Shunt C

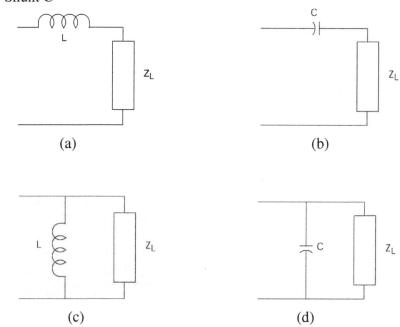

Figure 11.5 Four cases: a) series L, b) series C, c) shunt L, and d) shunt C.

To find the input impedance, we first calculate the normalized series reactance ($jx=jX/Z_O$) or normalized shunt susceptance value ($jb=jB/Y_O$) of the lumped element before entering the Smith chart. Next, we locate $(Z_L)_N$ on the chart as point "A" (see Figure 11.6). Now starting from point "A", the following steps are applied:

1. To add a series L: on a constant resistance circle, move up by $jx_S = j\omega L/Z_O$.
2. To add a Series C: on a constant resistance circle, move down by $jx_S = -j/\omega C Z_O$.
3. To add a shunt L: on a constant conductance circle, move up by $jb_P = -j/\omega L Y_O$.
4. To add a shunt C: on a constant conductance circle, move down by $jb_P = j\omega C/Y_O$.

These are all shown in Fig. 11.6.

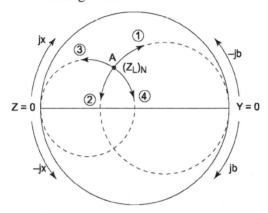

Figure 11.6 A graphical representation of 4 reactive-element configurations on the Smith chart.

11.5.1 Rule of Thumb

Upon close observation of these four cases, it appears that for the majority of load values, adding series (or shunt) inductor would move point "A" upward on the constant resistance (or conductance) circle while adding a series (or shunt) capacitance would move point A downward.

However, it should be noted that the above is a good rule of thumb to follow when dealing with purely reactive elements, but should never be generalized outside the scope of this discussion. This rule of thumb is limited but workable and will never actually replace the reasoning and the understanding that goes into making it.

Example 11.1

Calculate the total input admittance of a combination of a load $Z_L=50+j50 \ \Omega$ with a shunt inductor of $L=8 \ nH$ at $f_0=1 \ GHz$ as shown in Fig. 11.7. Assume a 50 Ω system.

Solution:

$Z_O=50 \ \Omega \Rightarrow Y_O=0.02 \ S$

a. We first find the susceptance of the shunt inductor:

$jB_P=-j/(\omega_O L)=-j0.02 \ S \Rightarrow jb_P=jB_P/Y_O=-j1$

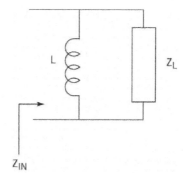

Figure 11.7 Circuit for example 11.1.

b. Locate $(Z_L)_N=Z_L/Z_O=1+j1$ on the smith chart at point "A" in Figure 11.8.

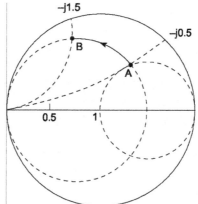

Figure 11.8 Smith chart solution for example 11.1.

c. Since this is an inductor, we need to move upwards from point "A" on a constant conductance circle by -j1 to arrive at point "B".

d. The normalized input admittance is read off at point "B" as:

$(Y_{in})_N=0.5-j1.5$

$Y_{in}=Y_O(Y_{in})_N=0.01-j0.03$ S

Or,

$Z_{in}=1/Y_{in}=10+j30$ Ω

11.6   COMBINATION OF SERIES AND SHUNT ELEMENTS

In this application, we will consider the case where there are several series and shunt elements in combination with the load (as shown in Figure 11.9).

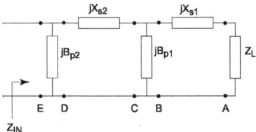

Figure 11.9 Combination of series and shunt reactive elements.

The standard method, discussed in section 11.5, can be used repeatedly to arrive at the total input impedance as described in the following steps:

a.   Since the first element adjacent to the load is connected in series, we start with $(Z_L)_N$ and locate it on the Z-chart (see point "A" in Figure 11.10),

b.   On the constant resistance circle passing through $(Z_L)_N$, a reactance of $jx_{S1}= jX_{S1}/Z_O$ is added to arrive at point "B".

c.   Now switching to the Y-chart, we move on the constant conductance circle and add a susceptance of $jb_P=jB_{P1}/Y_O$ to arrive at point "C".

d.   Since the next element is in series, we switch back to the Z-chart and move on a constant resistance circle by adding a reactance of $jx_{S2}=jX_{S2}/Z_O$ to arrive at point "D".

e.   The final element is in parallel, so we switch to the Y chart and add a susceptance of $jb_{P2}=jB_{p2}/Y_O$ to arrive at "E".

f.   The total impedance is now read off on the Z-chart at point "E" as shown in Figure 11.10.

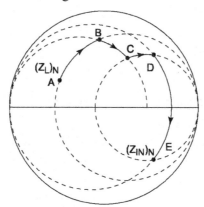

Figure 11.10 The Smith chart solution.

Example 11.2
Find the input impedance at f=100 MHz for the circuit shown in Figure 11.11.

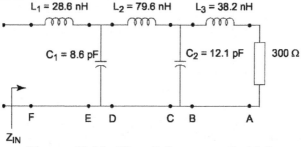

Figure 11.11 Circuit for example 11.2.

Solution:
First, we choose the normalizing factor arbitrarily to be:
$Z_O=50 \ \Omega$,
And,
$Y_O=0.02$ S.
Then we normalize all impedance and admittance values:
$jx_{S1}=(jX_1)_N=j\omega L_1/Z_O=j0.36$
$jb_{P1}=(jB_1)_N=j\omega C_1/Y_O=j0.27$
$jx_{S2}=(jX_2)_N=j\omega L_2/Z_O=j1.0$

$jb_{P2}=(jB_2)_N=j\omega C_2/Y_O=j0.38$
$jx_{S3}=(jX_3)_N=j\omega L_3/Z_O=j0.48$
$(Z_L)_N=300/50=6$

a) Locate $(Z_L)_N$ on the smith chart(point "A" in Figure 11.12).

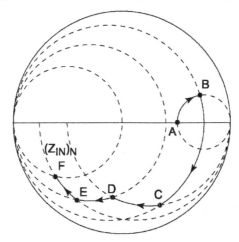

Figure 11.12 Smith chart solution for example 11.2.

b) Since the first element (L_3) adjacent to the load is a series inductor, we move upward from point "A" on a constant resistance circle by a reactance of j0.36 to arrive at point "B".

c) Now switch to constant conductance circle, add the next shunt element by moving downward by j0.27 to arrive at point "C".

d) For the next series inductor, switch to the constant resistance circle and move upward by j1.0 to arrive at point "D".

e) Next, for the shunt capacitor, switch to a constant conductance circle and move downward by j0.38 to arrive at point "E".

f) Finally, for the series inductor, switch to the constant conductance circle and move upward by j0.48 to arrive at point "F".

g) Now we read off the value of the normalized input impedance at point "F" as:
$(Z_{in})_N=Z_{in}/Z_O=0.4-j1.0 \Rightarrow Z_{in}=20-j50 \ \Omega$

Chapter 11- Symbol List

A symbol will not be repeated again, once it has been identified and defined in an earlier chapter, with its definition remaining unchanged.

b - Normalized susceptance, $b=B/Z_0$

b_L - Normalized susceptance at the load

b_P - Normalized susceptance at the parallel element

g - Normalized conductance, $g=G/Z_0$

g_L - Load Normalized conductance

g_P - Shunt Normalized conductance

I_{max} - Maximum current on a transmission line.

I_{min} - Minimum current on a transmission line.

ℓ_{max} – location of Z_{max} on the transmission line

ℓ_{min} – location of Z_{min} on the transmission line

r - Normalized resistance, $r=R/Z_0$

x- Normalized reactance, $x=X/Z_0$

V_{max} - Maximum voltage on a transmission line.

V_{min} - Minimum voltage on a transmission line

Y_0 - Characteristic admittance

Z_0 - Characteristic impedance

Z_D - Device impedance

Z_{in} - Input impedance

$(Z_{in})_N$ - Normalized input impedance

Z_{max} - Maximum impedance, corresponding to the location of the peak of the voltage and the valley of the current in a standing wave pattern on a transmission line.

Z_{min} - Minimum impedance, corresponding to the location of the valley of voltage and the peak of the current in a standing wave pattern on a transmission line.

Γ_D -Device reflection coefficient

CHAPTER-11 PROBLEMS

11.1) Using a Smith chart, determine Z_{in} for the circuit shown in Figure P11.2. Assume $f_o=1$ GHz.

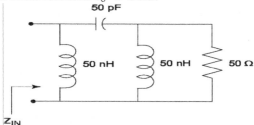

Figure P11.1

11.2) Determine the input impedance of the lumped-element network shown in Figure P11.2 (all values are in Ω).

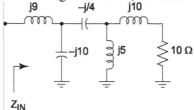

Figure P11.2

11.3) A 100 Ω TL is to be matched to a load $Z_L=25-j25$ Ω using lumped elements at f= 5 GHz.
a) Determine the simplest matching network that will block DC to the load.
b) Design a more sophisticated matching network having five lumped elements. Determine the element values.

11.4) A 50 Ω lossless TL is terminated in a 85 Ω resistor in series with an unknown capacitor. At 20 MHz the VSWR is measured to be 2.50, find the unknown capacitor value.

11.5) Find the input impedance of a load that consists of a 200 Ω resistor that is connected in series with a j50 Ω inductor. The load is connected to a shunt capacitor having –j75 Ω reactance. This is followed by a series inductor (j100 –j75 Ω) and a shunt capacitor with –j50 Ω reactance.

11.6) What is the impedance (Z_D) of a device having $\Gamma_D = 5\angle 150°$? Assume $Z_O = 50\ \Omega$. If this device is connected first to a series element having $Z_S = 150 + j75\ \Omega$, and then to a parallel element $Z_p = 100 - j50\ \Omega$, find the input impedance of the whole circuit using a Smith chart.

11.7) A 75 Ω lossless TL is terminated in a 150 Ω resistor in series with an unknown inductor. At 50 MHz the VSWR is measured to be 4, find the unknown inductor value.

CHAPTER 12

Distributed Elements On The Smith Chart

12.1 INTRODUCTION

The Smith chart applications in the analysis or design of RF and microwave circuits containing "lumped elements" was discussed in the previous chapter.

In this chapter we will study circuits containing primarily "distributed elements", particularly transmission lines (TLs). In the final section, we will discuss circuits containing "Distributed and lumped elements" in combination.

12.2 DISTRIBUTED CIRCUIT APPLICATIONS

The most common distributed circuit element is a transmission line (TL) and the Smith chart can be used effectively for calculation of values of its different parameters. Before we proceed into different Smith chart applications, it would serve us well, at the outset, if we define, the following notations which will be used throughout this book:

Impedance: $Z=R+jX$ (Ω) $\qquad$ (12.1)

Admittance: $Y=G+jB$ (S) $\qquad$ (12.2)

The normalized values are given by:

$(Z)_N=Z/Z_O= R/Z_O+jX/Z_O =r+jx$ $\qquad$ (12.3)

$(Y)_N=Y/Y_O=G/Y_O +jB/Y_O=g+jb$ (12.4)

Where,

$r=R/Z_O,$ (12.5)

$x=X/Z_O,$ (12.6)

$g=G/Y_O,$ (12.7)

$b=B/Y_O$ (12.8)

$Y_O=1/Z_O$ (12.9)

Where "Z_O" is the characteristic impedance of the transmission line (for distributed elements) or a reference impedance value (for lumped elements).

12.3 INPUT IMPEDANCE USING A KNOWN LOAD (Z_L)

The input impedance (Z_{in}) at any point on a transmission line, a distance "l" away from the load (Z_L), can be calculated by the following procedure:

a. Plot the normalized load impedance $[(Z_L)_N=Z_L/Z_0)]$ on the Smith chart,

b. Draw the constant VSWR circle that goes through $(Z_L)_N$,

c. Starting from $(Z_L)_N$, move "toward generator" on the constant VSWR circle a distance "l/λ",

d. Read off the normalized input impedance value (Z_{in}/Z_o) from the chart as shown in Figure 12.1.

This process can be reversed easily when the input impedance (Z_{in}) is known and the load impedance is unknown (Z_L). In this case, starting from $(Z_{in})_N$, one moves "Toward load" a distance "l/λ" on the constant VSWR circle to arrive at $(Z_L)_N$.

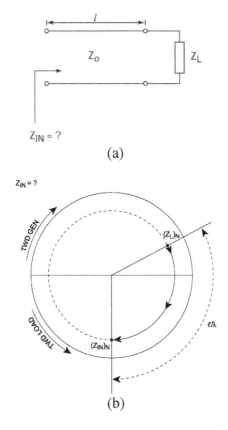

Figure 12.1 a) TL circuit, b) Smith chart solution.

EXAMPLE 12.1

Find the input impedance of a transmission line ($Z_O=50$ Ω) that has a length of $\lambda/8$ and is connected to a load impedance of $Z_L=50+j50\Omega$?

Solution:

a. Locate $(Z_L)_N=Z_L/Z_O=1+j1$ on the smith chart.

b. Draw the constant VSWR circle as shown in Figure 12.2.

c. Now move "toward Generator" on the constant VSWR

Circle a distance of $\lambda/8$ (or $90°$) to obtain:

$(Z_{in})_N=2-j1 \Rightarrow Z_{in}=Z_O(Z_{in})_N=100-j50$ Ω.

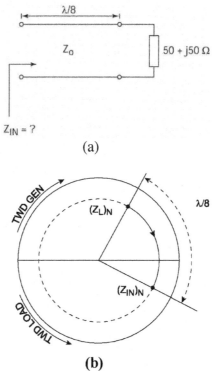

(b)
Figure 12.2 a) TL circuit, b) Smith chart solution
(Example 12.1).

12.4 INPUT IMPEDANCE USING REFLECTION
COEFFICIENT ($|\Gamma_{IN}| \leq 1$)

When the reflection coefficient at any point on a transmission line is known, the input impedance at that point can be calculated as follows:

a. Locate $\Gamma_{IN} = |\Gamma_{IN}| e^{j\theta}$ on the Smith chart; The magnitude of $|\Gamma|$ can be read off the "Reflection coefficient voltage" radial scale at the bottom of the chart while "θ" is read off the circular scale (See Figure 12.3).

b. Normalized values of resistance and reactance (r,x) can be read off the Smith chart at point "A", giving Z_{in} as:

$$Z_{in} = Z_0(r+jx)$$

NOTE 1: *If conversely, the input impedance (Z_{in}) is known and the corresponding reflection coefficient is desired to be found, the procedure would be as follows:*

a. Plot the normalized input impedance (Z_{in})_N on the Smith chart and read off the angle "θ" on the circular scale.
b. Draw the constant VSWR circle,
c. The intersection of this circle with the right-hand horizontal axis is found and dropped off onto the "reflection coef." radial scale at the bottom and the |Γ| value is read off as shown in Figure 12.3.

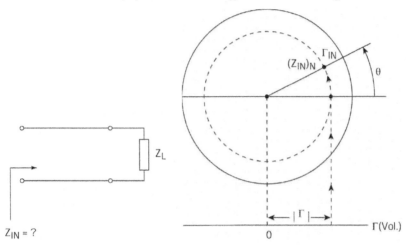

Figure 12.3 a) TL circuit, b) Smith chart solution.

NOTE 2: *If the value of Z_{in} at a distance ℓ from the reflection coefficient location is sought, one needs to use the procedure described in application #1.*

12.5 IMPEDANCE DETERMINATION USING NEGATIVE RESISTANCE (|Γ| > 1)

When the magnitude of the reflection coefficient is greater than unity, the corresponding impedance has a negative resistance value and thus maps outside the standard Smith chart. In this case, another type of chart called a compressed Smith chart (as discussed earlier) should be used. This chart includes the standard Smith chart (|Γ|≤ 1) and ($|\Gamma|>1$) region which corresponds to the negative resistance region.

An alternate way of determining an impedance (Z) having ($|\Gamma|>1$), is by using a standard smith chart with the help of the following procedure:

a. Obtain the complex conjugate of the reflection coefficient at point "B", ($\Gamma^*=|\Gamma|\angle-\theta$).
b. Plot $1/\Gamma^*$ on the standard Smith chart (see point "C" in Figure 12.4)

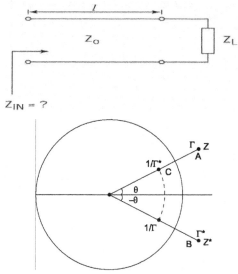

Figure 12.4 a) TL circuit, b) Smith chart solution.

c. Read off the normalized impedance value (r+jx, corresponding to $1/\Gamma^*$) on the Smith chart.
d. The impedance (Z) value corresponding to Γ is obtained by negating "r" and keeping "x" intact, i.e.,
    Z=Z₀(-r+jx)

This procedure can be proven as shown below.

12.5.1 Proof of Procedure
Assuming Z_O is a real number, the normalized impedance (Z/Z_O) corresponding to Γ is given by (see point A in Figure 12.4):

$Z/Z_0 = -r+jx, \quad r>0$ (12.10)

Where "r" and "x" are normalized values of resistance and reactance, respectively.

Knowing that $\Gamma = |\Gamma| \angle \theta$, we can write:

$\Gamma \leftrightarrow -r+jx$

$\Gamma = (Z-Z_0)/(Z+Z_O) = (-r+jx-1)/(-r+jx+1)$ (12.11)

$\Gamma^* = |\Gamma| \angle -\theta$

$\quad = (r+jx+1)/(r+jx-1)$ (12.12)

Thus we have:

$1/\Gamma^* = (r+jx-1)/(r+jx+1) = (Z'/Z_0-1)/(Z'/Z_0+1)$ (12.13)

Where $Z'/Z_0 = r+jx$ is the impedance corresponding to $1/\Gamma^*$, that is to say,

$$1/\Gamma^* = \frac{1}{|\Gamma|} \angle \theta \leftrightarrow r+jx$$ (12.14)

From Equation (12.13a) we can see that $1/\Gamma^*$ (shown at point B in Figure 12.4) has the same angle as Γ, namely, they are on the same vector. Therefore from Equations (12.11) and (12.14) we conclude that the impedance corresponding to Γ is simply obtained by reversing the sign of the real part of Z', i.e.,

$Z = Z'|_{(r,x) \to (-r,x)}$ (12.15)

EXAMPLE 12.2

What is the impedance (Z_D) of a device having $\Gamma_D = 2.23 \angle 26.5°$? Assume $Z_O = 50 \; \Omega$.

Solution:

a. We find $\Gamma_D^* = 2.23 \angle -26.5°$

b. Plot $1/\Gamma_D^* = 0.447 \angle 26.5°$ on the smith chart. From the chart we obtain:

   $Z_D' = 50(2+j1) = 100+j50 \; \Omega$

c. Using Z_D' from step (b), we can write Z_D as:

   $Z_D = -100+j50 \; \Omega$

12.6 ADMITTANCE (Y) FROM IMPEDANCE (Z)

As discussed in Chapter 7, we know that the reflection coefficient [$\Gamma(x)$], the normalized input impedance [$Z_N(x)$] and the normalized input admittance $[Y_N(x)]$ at any point on the line are given by:

$$Z_N(x)=[1+\Gamma(x)]/[1-\Gamma(x)] \tag{12.16}$$

and,

$$Y_N(x)= 1/Z_N(x)=[1-\Gamma(x)]/[1+\Gamma(x)] \tag{12.17}$$

Where,

$$\Gamma(x)= \Gamma_L\, e^{j2\beta x} \tag{12.18}$$

is the reflection coefficient at any point (x) on the transmission line.

From the expression for $\Gamma(x)$, we note that for every phase change of $2\beta l=\pi$ (i.e. every $\ell =\lambda/4$), $\Gamma(x)$ changes sign which leads to the inversion of the expressions given in (12.17) and (12.18) causing $Z_N(x)$ to become $Y_N(x)$ and vice versa. This observation indicates that Y_N is located 180 degrees opposite to Z_N on the VSWR circle as shown below in Figure 12.5.

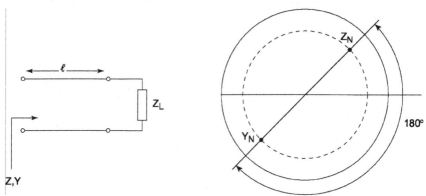

Figure 12.5 a) TL circuit, b) Smith chart solution.

Example 12.3
Find the admittance value for an impedance value of Z= 50+j50 Ω, in a 50 Ω system.

Solution:
$Z_O=50\ \Omega \Rightarrow Y_O=1/50=0.02\ S$
$Z_N=Z/Z_O=1+j1$

Using the smith chart, Y_N can be read off at 180° away on the constant VSWR circle:
$Y_N=0.5-j0.5$

$Y=Y_OY_N \Rightarrow Y=0.01-j0.01$ S

NOTE 1: *Z to Y conversion can also be obtained by rotating the Z-chart by 180° and super-imposing it on the original chart, which will give a ZY-Smith chart. The Y-chart has negative susceptance on the upper half and positive susceptance on the lower half, exactly opposite of the Z-chart. The Z-Y chart is shown in Figure 12.6.*

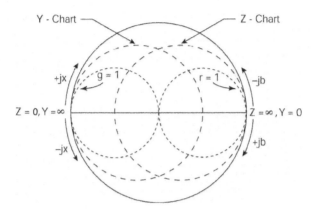

Figure 12.6 ZY Smith chart.

NOTE 2: *The standard Smith chart may be considered to be a Y- or Z-chart depending on the first time of entrance of values in it, being either admittance (Y) or impedance (Z).*

NOTE 3: *When working with **series elements,** the concept of impedance becomes important and we need to use the **Z-chart**. On the other hand when working with **parallel (or shunt) elements**, the concept of admittance becomes paramount and therefore we switch to the **Y-chart**.*

12.7 Z_{max} AND Z_{min} ON A TL

The following procedures can be used to calculate Z_{max} and Z_{min} values and locations:

a. Z_{max} and Z_{min} Value

Given a known load $(Z_L)_N$, the VSWR circle can be drawn (see Figure 12.7). Furthermore, using the results for Γ and Z_{in} from Chapter 7, we can write:

$\Gamma(x) = \Gamma_L \, e^{j2\beta x}$,   (12.19)

Where $\Gamma_L = |\Gamma_L| \, e^{j\theta}$.

Therefore we can write:

$\Gamma(x) = |\Gamma_L| \, e^{j\phi(x)}$, $\phi(x) = 2\beta x + \theta$ (12.20)

and,

$[Z_{in}(x)]_N = Z_{in}(x)/Z_O = [1 + \Gamma(x)]/[1 - \Gamma(x)]$ (12.21)

From Equation (12.21) we note that maximum input impedance $(Z_{max})_N$ occurs when the numerator is maximum and denominator is minimum. By observation, this condition occurs when $\Gamma(x) = |\Gamma_L| \, e^{j\phi(x)}$ is a positive real number i.e. $\phi(x) = 0$, which gives $(Z_{max})_N$ as:

$(Z_{max})_N = [1 + |\Gamma_L|]/[1 - |\Gamma_L|]$ (12.22)

This value can be read off the chart at the intersection of the VSWR circle with the right hand horizontal axis (where $\phi = 0$) as shown in Figure 12.7.

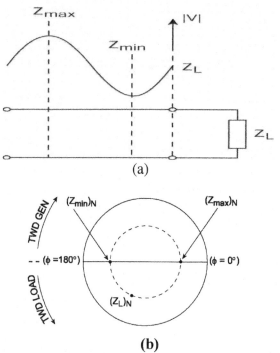

(a)

(b)

Figure 12.7 a) Location of Z_{max} and Z_{min} on the TL, b) Smith chart solution.

From Equation (12.21) we can observe that minimum input impedance $(Z_{min})_N$, being the inverse of $(Z_{max})_N$, occurs when $\Gamma(x)$ is a negative real number (i.e., $\phi=180°$):

$$(Z_{min})_N=1/(Z_{max})_N \quad =[1-|\Gamma_L|]/[1+|\Gamma_L|] \tag{12.23}$$

This value can be read off the chart where the VSWR circle intersects the left semi-axis, (see Figure 12.7)

NOTE: *Since $(Z_{min})_N= 1/(Z_{max})_N=(Y_{max})_N$, thus the value and location of $(Z_{min})_N$ could have easily been found (using the application #4) by locating it $180°$ away from $(Z_{max})_N$ on the VSWR circle.*

b. Z_{max} and Z_{min} location (distance from load)
1. Z_{max} distance from load
Starting from the load on the VSWR circle, we now move "Toward generator" to arrive at $\phi = 0°$ where $(Z_{max})_N$ is located. The distance "ℓ_{max}" can now be read off using the circular scale on the outer edge of the Smith chart as shown in Figure 12.8.

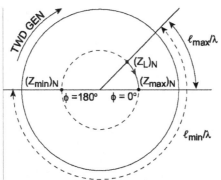

Figure 12.8 Smith chart solution.

2. Z_{min} distance from load
Starting from the load, we now travel "Toward generator" on the VSWR circle to arrive at $\phi = 180°$ where $(Z_{min})_N$ is located. The distance traveled is "ℓ_{min}/λ" which can be read off on the outer circular scale (see Figure 12.8).

From Smith chart we can observe that the length difference between the locations of Z_{max} and Z_{min} is $\lambda/4$, i.e.

$|\ell_{max} - \ell_{min}| = \lambda/4$ (12.24)

This observation is further confirmed by our earlier discussion of the transmission line and Smith chart where we noted that the input impedance at any point on a line (e.g. Z_{max}) repeats itself every $\lambda/2$. Since Z_{min} is located one half of the distance between the two repeating maxima, thus the distance between Z_{max} and Z_{min} should be $\lambda/4$ (as shown in Figure 12.9), as indicated by (12.15).

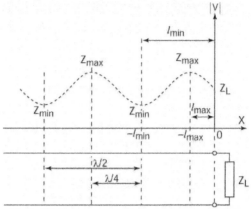

Figure 12.9 Voltage standing wave on a TL circuit.

For example, if ℓ_{max} is known and is nearest to the load, then ℓ_{min} is simply given by:

$\ell_{min} = \ell_{max} + \lambda/4$ (12.25)

Without having to resort to the chart; and vice versa if ℓ_{min} is known and is nearest to the load then :

$\ell_{max} = \ell_{min} + \lambda/4$ (12.26)

12.7.1 Lines With Purely Resistive Loads

When a transmission line with a real characteristic impedance (Z_O) is terminated in a resistive load (i.e. has no reactive component, $Z_L = R_L$), then there are two possible cases:

Case I: $R_L > Z_O$

In this case, the maximum impedance on the line equals the load value and is located at the load repeating every $\lambda/2$, that is:

$Z_{max} = R_L,$ (12.27)

$\ell_{max} = n(\lambda/2), \quad n = 0, 1, 2, ...$ (12.28)

The minimum line impedance (Z_{min}) is located $\lambda/4$ away from the load and repeats itself every $\lambda/2$, i.e.,

$$\ell_{min}=\lambda/4 + n(\lambda/2), \quad n=0,1,2,... \tag{12.29}$$

Furthermore, we can write:

$$(Z_{min})_N=1/(Z_{max})_N \Rightarrow Z_{min}/Z_O=Z_O/Z_{max}$$
$$Z_{min}=Z_O^2/Z_{max} \tag{12.30}$$

Or,

$$Z_{min}=Z_O^2/R_L \tag{12.31}$$

These are shown in Figure 12.10.

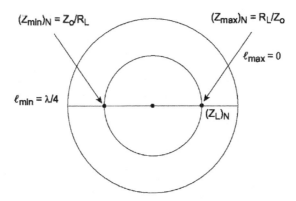

Figure 12.10 Smith chart solution.

EXAMPLE 12.4

A microwave signal is traveling on a transmission line which has $Z_O= 50 \ \Omega$ and a load value of $Z_L = 100 \ \Omega$. Find the values of Z_{max} and Z_{min} and their location on the transmission line.

Solution:

Since $R_L>Z_O$, the maximum voltage and thus maximum impedance occurs at the load, i.e.,

$Z_{max}=R_L=100 \ \Omega$

$\ell_{max}=0,$

The minimum impedance occurs $\lambda/4$ away from the load :

$\ell_{min}=\lambda/4$

$Z_{min}=50^2/100=25 \ \Omega$

This is shown in Figure 12.11.

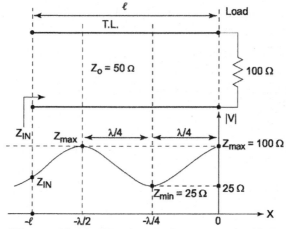

Figure 12.11 TL circuit for example 12.4.

Case II: $R_L < Z_O$
In this case, the minimum impedance on the line is located at the load and repeats every $\lambda/2$, i.e.,

$$Z_{min}=R_L, \tag{12.32}$$
$$\ell_{min}=n(\lambda/2), \quad n=0,1,2,... \tag{12.33}$$

The maximum line impedance is located $\lambda/4$ away from the load and also repeats every $\lambda/2$ as shown in Figure 12.12. Thus using Equation (12.22) we can write:

$$(Z_{min})_N=1/(Z_{max})_N$$
$$Z_{max}=Z_O^2/Z_{min}=Z_O^2/R_L, \tag{12.34}$$
$$\ell_{max}= \lambda/4+n(\lambda/2) \quad , \quad n=0,1,2,... \tag{12.35}$$

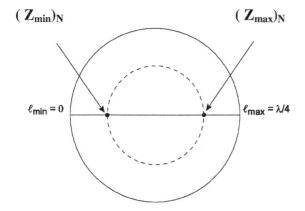

Figure 12.12 Smith chart solution.

EXAMPLE 12.5
A microwave signal at a frequency of f=1 GHz, is traveling on a transmission line having Z_O= 50 Ω, and terminated in a load of Z_L = 20 Ω. Find the values of Z_{max} and Z_{min} and their location on the transmission line.

Solution:
Since $R_L < Z_O$, the minimum voltage or impedance on the line occurs at the load, i.e.,
$Z_{min} = 20 \ \Omega$,
$\ell_{min} = 0$.

From Equation (12.34) and (12.35), the value and location of Z_{max} is given by:
$Z_{max} = Z_O^2/R_L = 50^2/20 = 125 \ \Omega$
$\lambda = c/f \implies \lambda(cm) = 30/f(GHz) = 30 \ cm$
The first maximum occurs at: $\ell_{max} = \lambda/4 = 7.5$ cm away from the load as shown in Figure 12.13.

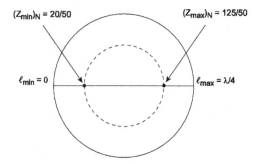

Figure 12.13 Smith chart solution.

The standing wave pattern is plotted in Figure 12.14.

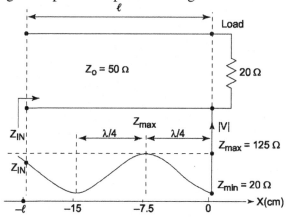

Figure 12.14 Plot of the standing wave on the TL circuit.

12.8 VSWR OF A KNOWN LOAD

There are two methods to find the VSWR on a transmission line with a given load (Z_L or Γ_L) as follows:

Method #1:
Using $|\Gamma_L|$ as the radius, draw the constant VSWR circle. From the intersection of this circle with the left-hand horizontal axis drop a vertical line onto the VSWR scale on the bottom of the chart to find the VSWR as shown in Figure 12.15.

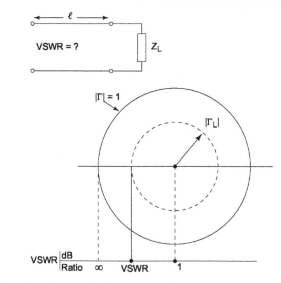

Figure 12.15 TL circuit and the Smith chart solution.

Method #2:

For a lossless transmission line we know that $|\Gamma|=|\Gamma_L|$ anywhere on the line, which is the radius of the VSWR circle. Therefore VSWR can be calculated by:

$$VSWR = \frac{1+|\Gamma_L|}{1-|\Gamma_L|} \tag{12.36}$$

$$|\Gamma_L| = \left| \frac{Z_L - Z_O}{Z_L + Z_O} \right| \tag{12.37a}$$

From Application #5 we have:

$$(Z_{max})_N = 1/(Z_{min})_N = \frac{1+|\Gamma_L|}{1-|\Gamma_L|} = VSWR \tag{12.37b}$$

Thus:

$$Z_{max} = Z_O(VSWR), \tag{12.38a}$$

and,

$$Z_{min} = Z_O/VSWR \tag{12.38b}$$

The VSWR value can be read off from the VSWR circle intersection with the horizontal semi-axis at $\theta = 0°$ (where Z_{max} is located) as shown in Figure 12.16.

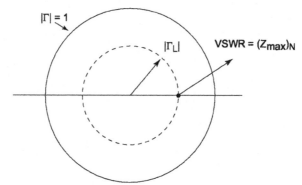

Figure 12.16 Smith chart solution.

12.9 PLOT OF STANDING WAVE PATTERN

As discussed in Chapter 7, when the incident wave encounters a discontinuity of any kind (such as a load), which is different than the characteristic impedance of the propagating media, a portion (or all) of the wave will be reflected.

The reflected wave when combined with the incident wave will create a standing wave pattern in voltage and current.

Voltage and current waves simultaneously coexist and each have their own standing wave patterns with peaks and valleys occurring at different points along the line as shown in Figure 12.17.

Use of the Smith chart will help us determine the exact standing wave pattern for voltage and current for a known load with a relatively good degree of accuracy.

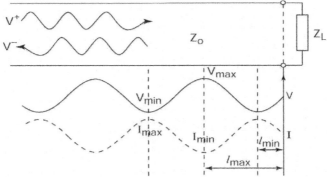

Figure 12.17 Voltage and current standing waves on a TL circuit.

To determine the standing wave pattern let us consider an incident voltage wave (V^+) causing an incident current wave (I^+) traveling toward the load Z_L on a lossless transmission line (Z_O).   The reflected voltage and current waves (V^-, I^-) will interact with the incident voltage and current waves (V^+, I^+) to create the standing wave pattern.

To get an exact pattern determination in terms of its peak and valley magnitude and location, the following procedure can be used:

a. Locate $(Z_L)_N = Z_L/Z_O$ on the Smith chart, draw the constant-VSWR circle and determine the VSWR on the line.

b. Determine the location and value of Z_{max} (ℓ_{max} away from the load). The location of Z_{max} corresponds to the location of the peak of that voltage standing wave pattern (V_{max}) and the valley of the current standing wave pattern (I_{min}) because:
$$Z_{max} = V_{max}/I_{min} \qquad (12.39)$$

12.9.1 V_{max} Calculation
Furthermore, to calculate the magnitude of the maximum voltage (V_{max}) on the line, we note that:
$$V_{max}=|V^+|+|V^-|=|V^+|(1+|V^-/V^+|)=|V^+|(1+|\Gamma_L|) \qquad (12.40)$$
From Equation (12.37) we can write:
$$|\Gamma_L|=\left(\frac{VSWR-1}{VSWR+1}\right) \qquad (12.41)$$

Substituting (12.41) in (12.40), we get:

$$V_{max} = |V^+| \left(\frac{2VSWR}{VSWR + 1} \right) \qquad (12.42)$$

Similarly, I_{min} is given by:

$$I_{min} = V_{max}/Z_{max} = |I^+| - |I^-| = |V^+|/Z_O - |\Gamma_L||V^+|/Z_O$$

$$= \frac{|V^+|}{Z_O} (1 - |\Gamma_L|)/Z_O = \frac{|V^+|}{Z_O} \left(\frac{2}{VSWR + 1} \right) \qquad (12.43)$$

Thus the location and magnitude of V_{max} and I_{min} can easily be determined once the load value (Z_L, or Γ_L) and the incident voltage value ($|V^+|$) are known.

12.9.2 V_{min} Calculation

The location and value of Z_{min} (ℓ_{min} away from the load) can be determined from the Smith chart. The location of Z_{min} corresponds to the valley of the voltage standing wave pattern (V_{min}) and the peak of the current standing wave pattern (I_{max}), because:

$$Z_{min} = V_{min}/I_{max} \qquad (12.44)$$

To calculate the value of V_{min} and I_{max} in terms of the magnitude of the incident voltage $|V^+|$ and the load, we note that:

$$V_{min} = |V^+| - |V^-| = |V^+|(1 - |V^+/V^-|) = |V^+|(1 - |\Gamma_L|) \qquad (12.45)$$

Using Equation (12.41) in (12.45), we get:

$$V_{min} = |V^+| \left(\frac{2}{VSWR + 1} \right) \qquad (12.46)$$

Similarly, I_{max} is given by:

$$I_{max} = V_{min}/Z_{min} = |I^+| + |I^-| = |V^+|/Z_O + |\Gamma_L||V^+|/Z_O$$

$$= |V^+|(1 + |\Gamma_L|)/Z_O$$

$$= \frac{|V^+|}{Z_O} \left(\frac{2VSWR}{VSWR + 1} \right) \qquad (12.47)$$

NOTE: *Utilizing equations (12.42) and (12.47), we can see that:*

$I_{max}=V_{max}/Z_O$
And similarly, from Equations (12.43) and (12.45) we can write:
$I_{min}=V_{min}/Z_O$
This would give an alternate way to find I_{max} and I_{min}.

Knowing the value and location of V_{max}, V_{min}, I_{max} and I_{min}, the patterns for voltage and current can now be plotted easily. Figure 12.18 shows the standing wave pattern for voltage and current on a transmission line.

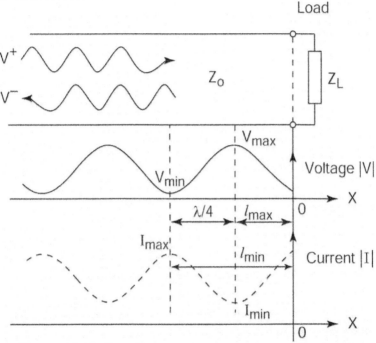

Figure 12.18 Standing wave patterns on a TL circuit.

The following example may further help to illustrate the concept of standing waves.

EXAMPLE 12.6
Determine the standing wave pattern on a transmission line ($Z_O=50$ Ω) terminated in $Z_L=100+j100$ Ω with an incident voltage of $V^+=1\angle 0°$ as shown in Figure 12.19.

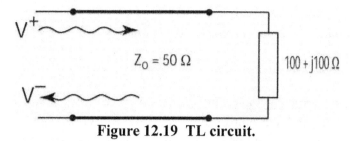

Figure 12.19 TL circuit.

Solution:

a. Locate $(Z_L)_N = Z_L/Z_O = 2+j2$ on the smith chart and draw the constant VSWR circle as shown in Figure 12.20.

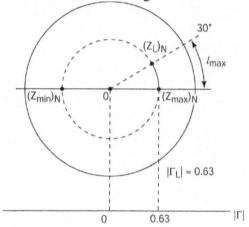

Figure 12.20 Smith chart solution.

From this Figure we can read off [VSWR $=4.4$ at $(Z_{max})_N$] and calculate the following:

$VSWR=(Z_{max})_N=4.4$

$Z_{max}=4.4 \times 50=220 \ \Omega$

$\ell_{max}=0.292-0.250=0.042\lambda$

Thus from (12.39) to (12.43), V_{max} and I_{min} are given by:

$V_{max}=[2 \times 4.4/(1+4.4)]=1.63$ V

$I_{min}=V_{max}/Z_{max}=1.63/220=7.4$ mA

Similarly, from the VSWR circle we can write:

$(Z_{min})_N=1/(Z_{max})_N=1/4.4$

$Z_{min}=50(1/4.4)=12 \ \Omega$

$\ell_{min}=0.042\lambda+\lambda/4=0.292\lambda$

Thus from (12.44) to (12.47), V_{min} and I_{max} are given by:

$V_{min}=[2/(1+4.4)]=0.37$ V

$I_{max}=V_{min}/Z_{min}=0.37/12=30.9$ mA

The final standing wave pattern is plotted in Figure 12.21.

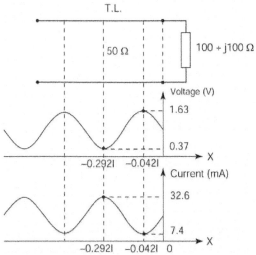

Figure 12.21 Final standing wave pattern on the TL circuit.

NOTE: *An alternate method would be to calculate V_{max} and V_{min} using the VSWR value and then find I_{max} and I_{min} as follows:*

VSWR=4.4

$V_{max}=2\times4.4/(1+4.4)=1.63$ v

$V_{min}=2/(1+4.4)=0.37$ v

$I_{max}=V_{max}/Z_O=1.63/50=30.9$ mA

$I_{min}=V_{min}/Z_O=0.37/50=7.4$ mA

These are the same values that were obtained earlier.

12.10 INPUT IMPEDANCE FOR SINGLE STUBS

DEFINITION-STUB: *A stub is defined to be a short section of a transmission line (usually terminated in either an open or a short) often connected in parallel and sometimes in series with a feed transmission line in order to transform the load to a desired value.*

In general, the stub can have any general termination (Z_L'), however in practice as explained above, Z_L' is either a short or an open circuit as shown in Figure 12.22.

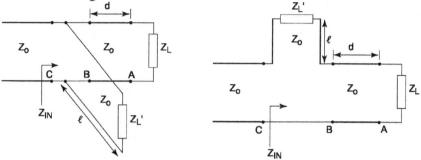

Figure 12.22 a) Parallel stub, b) Series stub.

There are two cases that will be considered separately as follows:
a. Parallel stubs, and
b. Series stubs

12.10.1 Parallel (or Shunt) Stubs

Consider the stub located a distance "d" away from a load (Z_L) as shown in Figure 12.22a. We would like to determine the input impedance of the combination.

Before we proceed to find the input impedance, we need to determine the stub's susceptance. Since the stub is connected in parallel, we use the smith chart as a Y-chart. The stub has a length (l) which can be used to determine its input admittance (or susceptance).

If the stub is terminated in a short, we use the Y-chart and start from $Y = \infty$ (see point "A" in Figure 12.23c) and travel "l" toward generator to arrive at point "B". We read off the stub's susceptance from the chart. In a similar fashion, an open stub's susceptance can be found except we should start at $Y=0$ on the opposite side (see Figures 12.23 and 12.24).

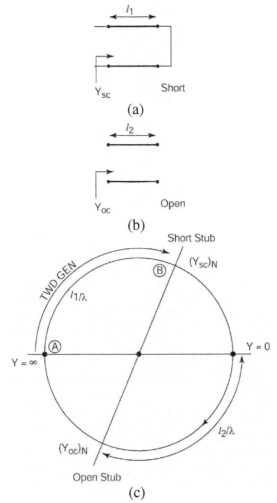

Figure 12.23 a) Short stub, b) Open stub, and c) Smith chart solution.

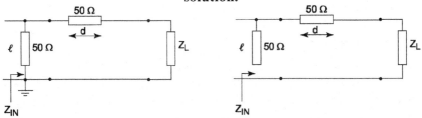

Figure 12.24 Shorthand schematic for a) Short shunt stub, b) Open shunt stub.

To find the input impedance, the following steps are carried out:
1. Locate Z_L on the Smith chart (use a ZY-chart)at point "A" in Figure 12.25.

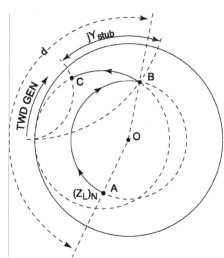

Figure 12.25 Smith chart solution for a shunt stub.

2. Draw the constant VSWR circle.
3. Travel a distance (d) toward the generator on the VSWR circle to arrive at point "B",
4. Now since we are adding the parallel stub, we must switch to the Y-chart and travel on a constant conductance circle an amount equal to the susceptance of the stub to arrive at point "C", as shown in Figure 12.25.
5. To find the input impedance, we switch back to the Z-chart and read off the normalized values (r,x) at point "C" corresponding to $(Z_{in})_N$. The total input impedance is given by:
$Z_{in} = Z_O(Z_{in})_N$

12.10.2 Series Stubs

Consider a series stub located a distance (d) away from the load (Z_L) as shown in Figure 12.26. Similar to the parallel stub case, we need to know the series stub's reactance (jX) based on its electrical length $(\beta \ell)$.

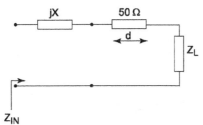

Figure 12.26 A series stub TL circuit.

Since the stub is in series, we use the smith chart as a Z-chart. If the stub is terminated in a short, start from Z = 0 (point "A" in Figure 12.27c) and travel a distance of l/λ "toward generator" to arrive at point "B". Read off the normalized stub's reactance (jx=jX/Z$_O$) from the chart as shown in Figure 12.27b. Similarly, an open stub's reactance can be determined by following the above procedure except by starting from Z=∞ on the chart as shown in Figure 12.27c.

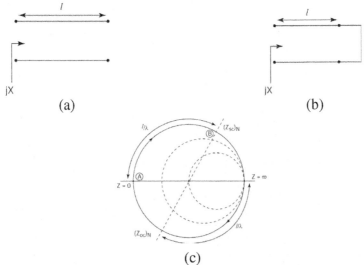

(a)   (b)

(c)

Figure 12.27 a) Open stub, b) Short stub, c) Smith chart solution.

To find the input impedance, the following steps are carried out:
1. Locate (Z$_L$)$_N$ on the Smith chart at point "A" as shown in Figure 12.28 (use a Z-chart).
2. Draw the constant VSWR circle,

3. From $(Z_L)_N$, travel a distance (d) toward the generator on the VSWR circle to arrive at point "B",

4. Now, since we are adding the series stub, we travel on a constant resistance circle an amount equal to the reactance of the stub, jx, to arrive at point "C".

5. The input impedance is read off at point "C" in Figure 12.28

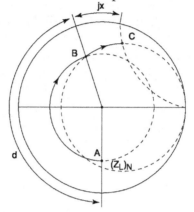

Figure 12.28 Smith chart solution.

EXAMPLE 12.7

Consider a transmission line (Z_O=50 Ω) terminated in a load Z_L=15+j10 Ω as shown in Figure 12.29. Calculate the input impedance of the line where the shunt open stub is located a distance of d=0.044λ From the load and has a length of ℓ=0.147λ.

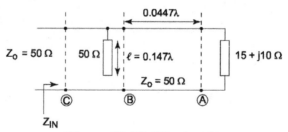

Figure 12.29 TL circuit.

Solution:

   a. The susceptance of the open stub is first calculated by

moving on a smith chart from Y=0 and moving a distance of 0.147λ toward generator to arrive at $(Y_{OC})_N = j1.33$ as shown in Figure 12.30.

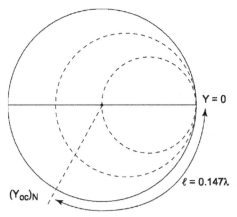

Figure 12.30 Shunt open stub on the Smith chart.

Next, the input impedance is found by :
  b. Locate$(Z_L)_N = (15+j10)/50 = 0.3+j0.2$ on the smith chart (see point "A" in Figure 12.31):
  c. Draw the constant VSWR circle.
  d. From Z_L, travel a distance of 0.044λ to arrive at point "B". The admittance is read off to be:
     $(Y_B)_N = 1-j1.33$ (point "B" in Figure 12.31)

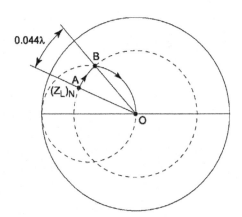

Figure 12.31 Smith chart solution.

e.   Adding an open shunt stub of length $\ell=0.147\lambda$ with $(Y_{OC})_N=j1.33$ gives:

$(Y_{in})_N=(Y_B)_N+(Y_{OC})_N=(1-j1.33)+j1.33=1$

$(Z_{in})_N=1/(Y_{in})_N=1 \Rightarrow Z_{in}=Z_O=50\ \Omega$

Adding the shunt stub on the smith chart results in arriving at point "O", which is obtained by moving on r=1 constant resistance circle by -j1.33.

NOTE: *Use of Application #8 in the design of circuits to bring about reflection-less loads are widely explored in the next chapter, where matching circuits are treated in depth.*

EXAMPLE 12.8

Consider a transmission line ($Z_O=50\ \Omega$) with $Z_L=100\ \Omega$ as shown in Figure 12.32. Calculate the input impedance of the line where the shorted series stub is located a distance of $d=\lambda/4$ from the load and has a length $l=\lambda/8$.

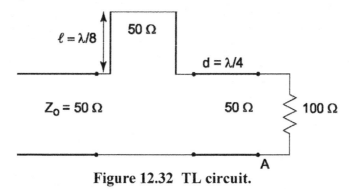

Figure 12.32 TL circuit.

Solution:

a. The reactance of the series shorted stub is first calculated by moving on a smith chart from Z=0 a distance of 0.125λ toward generator to arrive at $(Z_{SC})_N=j1$ as shown in Figure 12.33. Next, to find the input impedance we perform the following steps.

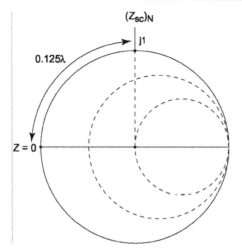

Figure 12.33 Short series stub on the Smith chart.

b. Locate$(Z_L)_N$=100/50=2 on the smith chart (see point "A" in Figure 12.34):

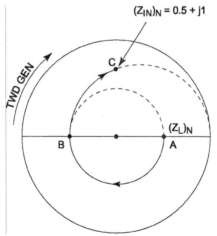

Figure 12.34 Smith chart solution.

c. Draw the constant VSWR circle. From Z_L, travel a distance of 0.25λ to arrive at point "B". The impedance is read off to be: $(Z_B)_N$=0.5 (at point "B")

NOTE: *Since the load is resistive and has a value more than Z_O, the $(Z_L)_N$ value and location corresponds to $(Z_{max})_N$ (at point "A") and Z_B corresponds to $(Z_{min})_N$ (for more details, see application #5).*

d. From point "B", move toward generator on a constant resistance circle to 0.5+j1 (point "C" in Figure 12.34) which corresponds to adding a series stub of length $\ell=0.125\lambda$ or $(Z_{SC})_N=j1$, giving:

$(Z_{in})_N=(Z_B)_N+(Z_{SC})_N=0.5+j1$

$Z_{in}=Z_O(Z_{in})_N =25+j50 \ \Omega$

NOTE: *This example shows that there are infinite number of resonances that can occur for a "distributed circuit" which is in contrast with "lumped circuits" that have a finite number of resonances.*

12.11 COMBINATION OF DISTRIBUTED AND LUMPED ELEMENTS

This final Application deals with circuits having distributed elements (such as transmission lines) and lossless lumped elements (such as capacitors and inductors).

To obtain the input impedance (or admittance) we use the following two rules:

a. *When dealing with distributed elements, for ease and convenience we start from the load end. Then we travel on a constant VSWR circle a length (ℓ) towards the generator.*

b. *When dealing with lossless lumped elements, we also start from the load end but move on a constant resistance (or conductance circle) depending on whether the lumped element is in series (or shunt) with the rest of the circuit.*

The overall procedure is the same as delineated in the previous applications. The example below will illustrate this concept further.

Example 12.13

In the circuit shown below (Figure 12.35), determine the input impedance at f = 10 GHz.

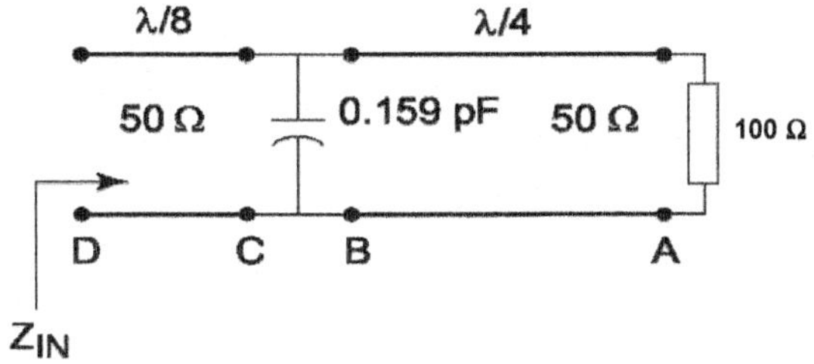

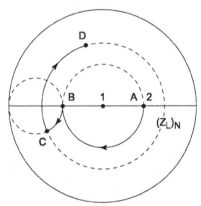

Figure 12.35 TL circuit.

Solution:
To find Z_{in} we perform the following steps:
a) Locate $(Z_L)_N=100/50=2$ on the smith chart (see Figure 12.36).

b) Since the first element adjacent to the load is a series transmission line we draw the constant VSWR transmission line.

c) Starting from $(Z_L)_N$, at point "A", we move on this circle a length of $\lambda/4$ "toward generator" to arrive at point "B".

d) Now since the next element is a shunt capacitor, we switch to the Y-chart and move on the constant conductance circle to arrive at point "C". The shunt capacitor has a susceptance of:
$jB=j2\pi \times 10^{10} \times 0.318 \times 10^{-12}=j0.02 \ \Omega$

Figure 12.36 Smith chart solution.

e) The next element is a series transmission line, so we switch back to the Z-chart and draw the constant VSWR circle that passes through "C".

f) Now from point "C" we move a distance of $\lambda/8$ "toward generator" to arrive at point "D" as shown in Figure 12.62.

g) The value of the input impedance is read off at point "D" as:

$(Z_{in})_N = 0.4 + j0.55 \Rightarrow Z_{in} = 20 + j27.5\ \Omega$

Chapter 12- Symbol List

A symbol will not be repeated again, once it has been identified and defined in an earlier chapter, with its definition remaining unchanged.

b - Normalized susceptance, $b = B/Z_0$

b_L - Normalized susceptance at the load

b_P - Normalized susceptance at the parallel element

g - Normalized conductance, $g = G/Z_0$

g_L - Load Normalized conductance

g_P - Shunt Normalized conductance

I_{max} - Maximum current on a transmission line.

I_{min} - Minimum current on a transmission line.

ℓ_{max} – location of Z_{max} on the transmission line

ℓ_{min} – location of Z_{min} on the transmission line

r - Normalized resistance, $r = R/Z_0$

x- Normalized reactance, $x = X/Z_0$

V_{max} - Maximum voltage on a transmission line.

V_{min} - Minimum voltage on a transmission line

Y_0 - Characteristic admittance

Z_0 - Characteristic impedance

Z_D - Device impedance

Z_{in} - Input impedance

$(Z_{in})_N$ - Normalized input impedance

Z_{max} - Maximum impedance, corresponding to the location of the peak of the voltage and the valley of the current in a standing wave pattern on a transmission line.

Z_{min} - Minimum impedance, corresponding to the location of the valley of voltage and the peak of the current in a standing wave pattern on a transmission line.

Γ_D -Device reflection coefficient

CHAPTER-12 PROBLEMS

12.1) A lossless transmission line (Z_O=50 Ω) is terminated in a load (Z_L=100+j100 Ω).   A single shorted stub (ℓ=λ/8, 50Ω) is inserted λ/4 away from the load as shown in Figure P12.1. Using a Smith chart, determine the line's input impedance (Z_{IN}).

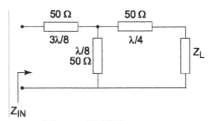

Figure P12.1

12.2) A lossless transmission line (Z_O=75 Ω) is terminated in an unknown load as shown below. Determine the load if the VSWR on the line is found to be 2 and the adjacent voltage maxima are at x= -15 cm and -35 cm where the load is located at x=0.

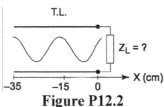

Figure P12.2

12.3) Determine the input impedance and reflection coefficient of a transmission line (Z_O=50 Ω) at a distance of 2cm from the load impedance (Z_L=75-j50 Ω) if the wavelength on the transmission line is found to be 16 cm. What is the VSWR on the line?

12.4) Find the input impedance of the transmission line circuit in a 50 Ω system (as shown in Figure P12.4) for Z_L=25+j25 Ω, d_1=3λ/8, d_2=λ/4 and l=λ/8. What is the VSWR at the input terminals?

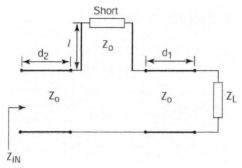

Figure P12.4

12.5) Find the input impedance of a double-stub shunt tuner as shown in Figure P12.5. Assume that the stubs are short circuited and $l_1=0.23\lambda$, $l_2=0.1\lambda$, $d=\lambda/8$ and $Z_O=50\ \Omega$. What is the reflection coefficient at the input terminals when f=1 GHz?

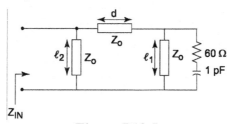

Figure P12.5

CHAPTER 13

Frequency Response of Networks

13.1 INTRODUCTION
The Smith chart can be used effectively to plot out the course of input impedance variation over a frequency range (f_2-f_1) as frequency is increased from f_1 to f_2. Vice versa, from the frequency response plot of a complex circuit in the Smith chart, one can develop an equivalent circuit model

13.2 FREQUENCY RESPONSE OF RLC NETWORKS
Of all possible combinations of three elements (R, L and C), there are 4 non-trivial combinations that are of interest and therefore are discussed in the next few sections.

13.2.1 Series RC + Shunt L Combination
This combination is shown in Figure 13.1.

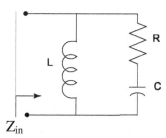

Figure 13.1 Series RC+shunt L combination.

In the "series RC + shunt L" combination, we see that "series RC", being a capacitive load, is located on the lower half of the Smith chart at f=f₁ (point "A" on the Smith chart in Figure 13.2).

As frequency is increased (from f₁), the capacitive reactance magnitude decreases and point "A" moves on a constant resistance circle toward the real axis to arrive at point "B" where f=f₂.

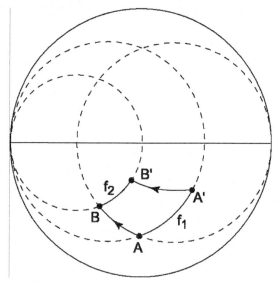

Figure 13.2 Smith chart solution.

Now adding a shunt inductor (with a susceptance of 1/ωL) would move points A and B more toward the real axis (to points A' and B') as frequency is increased form f₁ to f₂.

These points move on the constant conductance circles that pass through points A and B to arrive at points A' and B'. Connecting points A' and B' would map the course of the frequency response for this RLC combination in the f_2-f_1 frequency range (see Figure 13.2).

13.2.2 Series RL+Shunt C Combination
This combination is shown in Figure 13.3.

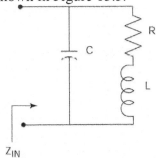

Figure 13.3 Series RL+shunt C combination.

In the "series RL + shunt C" combination, the "series RL", being an inductive load, is located on the upper half of the ZY-chart as shown at point "A" in Figure 13.4).

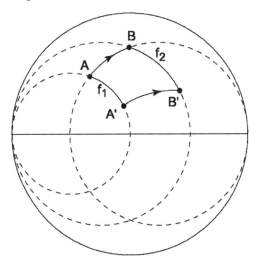

Figure 13.4 Smith chart solution.

As frequency is increased from f_1 to f_2, the inductive reactance magnitude (ωL) increases and point "A" at $f=f_1$ moves on a constant resistance circle away from the real axis to point "B" at $f=f_2$. Adding a shunt capacitor (with a susceptance value of ωC) would move points A (for $f=f_1$) and B (for $f=f_2$) on constant conductance circles to points A' and B' as shown in Figure 13.50. Similar to case 1, connecting points A' and B' would yield the input impedance (or admittance) variation in the frequency range (f_2-f_1).

13.2.3 Shunt RC + Series L Combination

For the "parallel RC+ series L" combination, we need to consider the Y-chart (see Figure 13.5).

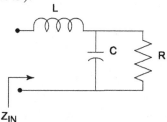

Figure 13.5 Shunt RC+series L combination.

Since we are interested in its performance in the frequency range (f_2-f_1), thus we first plot the admittance of the parallel RC combination at $f=f_1$ at point "A" as shown in Figure 13.6 (located on the lower half of the Y-chart, due to being a capacitive load).

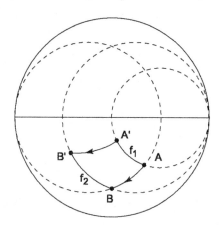

Figure 13.6 Smith chart solution.

As frequency increases from f_1 to f_2, the capacitive susceptance magnitude (ωC) increases and point "A" (at $f=f_1$) moves on a constant conductance circle to point "B" (at $f=f_2$).

Adding a series L (having a reactance "ωL") will move points A and B on constant resistance circles to points A' and B'.

Connecting points A' and B' provides the plot of input impedance frequency response on the Smith chart as shown in Figure 13.6.

13.2.4 Shunt RL + Series C Combination

For the "parallel RL + series C" combination, we need to consider the Y-chart (see Figure 13.7).

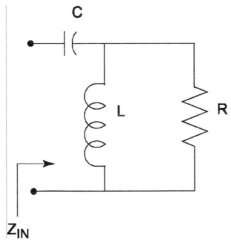

Figure 13.7 Smith chart solution.

We are interested in its performance in the frequency range (f_2-f_1), therefore we first plot the admittance of the parallel RL combination at $f=f_1$ at point "A" as shown in Figure 13.8 (located on the upper half of the Y-chart, due to being an inductive load).

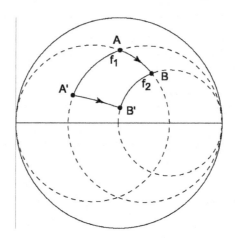

Figure 13.8 Smith chart solution.

As frequency increases from f_1 toward f_2, point "A" would move on a constant conductance circle toward the real axis to point "B". This is because the magnitude of the inductive susceptance $(1/\omega L)$ decreases with frequency.

Now adding a series C (with a reactance of $-1/\omega C$) will move points A and B on constant resistance circles to points A' and B'. Connecting A' to B', provides the plot of the input impedance frequency response of this RCL combination on the Smith chart (see Figure 13.8).

OBSERVATION: *By looking at the Smith chart plots (cases 1 through 4) we note that the input impedance moves clockwise in the Smith chart as the frequency is increased. This observation is actually based upon a much deeper concept which is the "Foster's Reactance Theorem". This theorem is briefly discussed in the next section.*

13.3 FOSTER'S REACTANCE THEOREM

The Foster's reactance theorem can be stated as:

For a passive lossless one-Port network, the reactance and susceptance are strictly and monotonically increasing functions of the frequency.

This theorem, in essence, states that:

The slope of the reactance function x(ω) or the susceptance function B(ω), is always positive, i.e.,

$$\partial X(\omega)/\partial\omega > 0 \quad \text{for } 0 < \omega < \infty \qquad (13.1)$$
$$\partial B(\omega)/\partial\omega > 0 \quad \text{for } 0 < \omega < \infty \qquad (13.2)$$

This positive-slope condition means that the impedance or admittance frequency response of a passive lossless one-port network moves in a clockwise direction in the Smith chart as frequency is increased.

This is a general concept and applies to both lumped or distributed elements as illustrated in the next two examples.

Example 13.1 (Lumped circuit)
Plot the frequency response (of the input admittance) for a parallel LC lumped circuit, as shown in Figure 13.9.

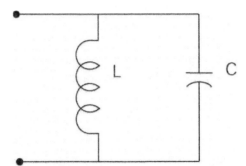

Figure 13.9 Circuit for example 13.1.

Solution:
$$Y_{in} = jB = j(\omega C - 1/\omega L)$$
$$\partial B(\omega)/\partial\omega = C + 1/\omega^2 L > 0$$

The input admittance (or susceptance) as a function of ω is sketched in Figure 13.10.

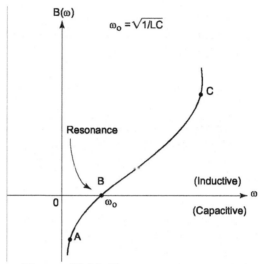

Figure 13.10 Frequency response.

Setting $B(\omega)$ equal to zero, yields the resonant frequency (ω_0) as:
$\omega_0 = 1/\sqrt{LC}$

Furthermore, as the frequency increases the impedance goes from point "A", through point "B"(resonance) and then to point "C". This can be plotted on a smith chart on the outermost circle (r=0) circle as shown in Figure 13.11.

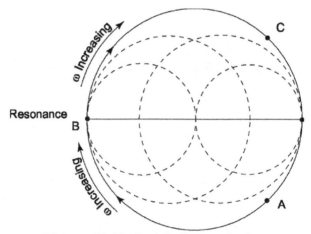

Figure 13.11 Smith chart solution.

13.4 FREQUENCY RESPONSE OF DISTRIBUTED CIRCUITS

For a TL circuit, terminated in a load (Z_L), the input impedance from earlier chapter is found to be:

$$Z_{IN}(d) = Z_0 \frac{Z_L + jZ_0 \tan \beta d}{Z_0 + jZ_L \tan \beta d} \qquad (13.3)$$

Where "d" is the distance from the point of observation to the load.

There are four cases that are worthy of note for their ease of analysis. These four cases are:

    a. Half-wavelength TLs
    b. Short-circuited TLs
    c. Open-circuited TLs
    d. Quarter-wave TLs

Each of these cases are studied below.

13.4.1 Half-Wavelength TLs

We know that the impedance on a lossless TL repeats itself every $\lambda/2$. This is also evident from the Smith chart, which has a total outer parameter length of $\lambda/2$. Therefore, the input impedance is the same as the load, i.e.,

$Z_{in}=Z_L$ for $\ell=n \lambda/2$, n=0,1,2,... $\qquad (13.4)$

This means that the line impedance will remain unchanged as multiples of half-wavelength are added to a TL.

13.4.2 Short-Circuited TLs

The input impedance for a short-circuited line ($Z_L=0$), is found to be:

$Z_{in}=jZ_0 \tan\beta d= jZ_0 \tan\theta=jX_s \qquad (13.5)$

Where $\theta=\beta d$ and $X_s=Z_0 \tan\theta$. Since the point of observation is the end of the line, thus $d=\ell$.

From this equation we see that a short circuited TL behaves purely as a reactive element whose type (inductive or capacitive) depends upon θ, as follows:

a. Inductive reactance: $X_s > 0$, for $0° < \theta < 90°$

b. Capacitive reactance: $X_s < 0$, for $90° < \theta < 180°$

Note 1: *At $\theta = 90°$ the input impedance of a short-circuit becomes infinite, that is to say, the short load gets converted to an open circuit due to impedance inversion property of a quarter wave TL.*

Note 2: *If the length of the TL is short, it behaves like a variable inductor, i.e.,*

$\ell/\lambda \le 0.1 \Rightarrow \theta = 2\pi\ell/\lambda \le 0.628\ rad \Rightarrow \theta \le 32°$

Then $\tan\theta \approx \theta$ (rad). Thus the inductance value can be written as:

$X_S = L\omega \approx Z_o \theta \Rightarrow L = Z_o \theta / \omega \Rightarrow L = Z_o (2\pi\ell/\lambda)/2\pi f$

$L = (Z_o \ell)/f\lambda = (Z_o \ell)/V_p$

Where $V_p = f\lambda$ is the phase velocity of the propagating waves.

Example 13. 2 (Distributed Circuit)

Plot the frequency response of the input impedance of a shorted transmission line as shown in Figure 13.12.

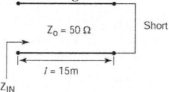

$Z_0 = 50\ \Omega$ Short

$l = 15\text{m}$

Z_{IN}

Figure 13.12 Circuit for example 13.2.

Solution:

$Z_{in} = j Z_O \tan\beta\ell$,

Where,

$\beta = 2\pi/\lambda$,

$\lambda = c/f = 300/f(\text{MHz})$ (m)

Therefore we can write:

$\beta\ell = 2\pi/\lambda \times 0.15 = (\pi/10)f$, (f in MHz)   (13.6)

In order to get resonance at a frequency $f = f_O$, "Z_{in}" must approach infinity (∞). But Since "Z_{in}" is proportional to "$\tan\beta l$", therefore we can write:

$\tan\beta\ell = \infty \Rightarrow \beta\ell = (2n+1)\pi/2$, $n = 0,1,2,3$ (13.7)

Substituting for "$\beta\ell$" from (13.6) in (13.7), we have:

$(\pi/10)f_O = (2n+1)\pi/2 \Rightarrow f_O = 5(2n+1)$ MHz, $n = 0,1,2,3$

Thus there are infinite number of frequencies at which the circuit resonates. The resonant frequencies occur at: f=5,15,25,....(MHz). These resonant frequencies are shown in Figure 13.13 in the frequency domain and on the smith chart as shown in Figure 13.14.

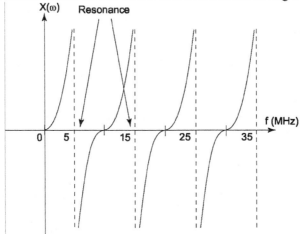

Figure 13.13 Plot of X vs. frequency.

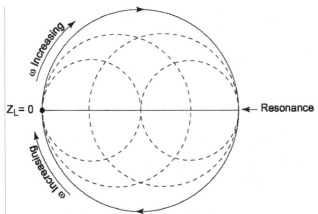

Figure 13.14 Smith chart solution.

NOTE: *This example shows that there are infinite number of resonances that can occur for a "distributed circuit" which is in contrast with "lumped circuits" that have a finite number of resonances.*

13.4.3 Open-Circuited TLs

The input impedance for an open-circuited line ($Z_L=\infty$), is found to be:

$Z_{in}=-jZ_o/\tan\beta d= -jZ_o/\tan\theta= -jZ_o\cot\theta =jX_s$ (13.8)

Where $\theta=\beta d$ and $X_s= -Z_o\cot\theta$. Since the point of observation is the end of the line, thus $d=\ell$.

From this equation we see that a short circuited TL behaves purely as a reactive element whose type (inductive or capacitive) depends upon θ, as follows:

a. Capacitive reactance: $X_s>0$, for $0°<\theta<90°$
b. Inductive reactance: $X_s<0$, for $90°<\theta<180°$

Note 1: *At $\theta=90°$ the input impedance of an open-circuit becomes zero, that is to say the open load gets converted to a short circuit due to impedance inversion property of a quarter wave TL.*

Note 2: *If the length of the TL is short, it behaves like a variable capacitor, i.e.,*

$\ell/\lambda \leq 0.1 => \theta= 2\pi\ell/\lambda \leq 0.628 \text{ rad} => \theta \leq 32°$

Then $\cot\theta =1/\tan\theta \approx 1/\theta$ (rad). Therefore, the capacitance value can be written as:

$X_S=-1/C\omega \approx -Z_o/\theta =>C= \theta/\omega Z_o = (2\pi\ell/\lambda)/(2\pi f Z_o)$
$C= \ell/f\lambda Z_o = \ell/Z_oV_p$
Where $V_p=f\lambda$ is the phase velocity of the propagating waves.

13.5 QUARTER-WAVE TLs

The input impedance for a $\lambda/4$ length of a TL (also called a quarter-wave transformer) which has an electrical length (θ) of 90°, is found to be:

$Z_{in}=Z_o^2/Z_L => (Z_{in})_N=1/(Z_L)_N$ (13.8)

Where $(Z_{in})_N= Z_{in}/Z_o$ and $(Z_L)_N = Z_L/Z_o$.

For this reason a quarter-wave line ($\theta=90°$) is often called an impedance inverter.

From this equation we see that the input impedance of the TL is equal to the normalized admittance of the load, i.e.,

$(Z_{in})_N = (Y_L)_N$ (13.9)
Where $(Y_L)_N = Y_L/Y_o$ and $Y_o = 1/Z_o$.

This inversion property will change any reactive element to its opposite type. For example, if $Z_L = 25 + j25$ (resistor+inductive reactance) in a 50 Ω system, then Z_{in} is given by:
$Z_{in}/Z_o = Z_o/Z_L => Z_{in} = 50 - j50 \ \Omega$
The result is a resistor in series with a capacitive reactance!

NOTE: *This impedance inverting property occurs not just for $\lambda/4$ length of a TL but for all lengths that are odd multiples of $\lambda/4$, i.e.,*
$(Z_{in})_N = (Y_L)_N$ *for* $\ell = (2n+1)\lambda/4$ $n=0,1,2,..$ (13.10)

The transforming property of a quarter-wave line becomes pronounced and of significant importance when the load is a resistive load ($Z_L = R_L$). In such a case, its transforming property overshadows the inversion property, as Z_{in} now becomes purely a resistive value (R_{in}). To utilize the transforming property effectively, we need only select a quarter-wave line of appropriate Zo that is given by:
$Z_o = (R_{in}R_L)^{1/2}$ (13.11)

For example, if a resistor of 25 Ω is desired to be transformed to a 100 Ω value, we need to connect it as load to a quarter-wave line ($\theta = 90°$) such that its input impedance provides the desired value (100 Ω). The appropriate Z_o for the $\lambda/4$ TL is given by:
$Z_o = (R_{in}R_L)^{1/2} = (100 \times 25)^{1/2} = 50 \ \Omega$

Conclusion: *A quarter-wave line ($\theta = 90°$) is first and foremost an impedance inverter, and only under a special condition of resistive loads can be utilized as an impedance transformer. Such a transforming property occurs only at one frequency ideally and usually over a narrow bandwidth as will be seen shortly.*

13.5.1   Quarter-Wave Transformer Bandwidth
A quarter–wave transformer is has a length of $\lambda_o/4$ only at one specific frequency (f_o) and if we use it for matching networks, it no

longer provides a perfect match at other frequencies since the length is no longer $\lambda_o/4$.

To develop an equation for the useful bandwidth of a quarter-wave transformer, we consider the input impedance equation of a TL terminated in a load Z_L as given by:

$$Z_{IN}(d) = Z_0 \frac{Z_L + jZ_0 \tan \beta d}{Z_0 + jZ_L \tan \beta d} \qquad (13.12)$$

If we let:

$t = \tan \beta d = \tan \theta$,

$Z_L = R_L$,

Z_0 (feed TL),

Z_0' ($\lambda/4$ TL),

$Z_0' = (Z_0 R_L)^{1/2}$ at $f = f_o$, and

$\theta_o = \beta_o d = 2\pi d/\lambda_o = 90°$ (A perfect match)

Where $\lambda_o = Vp/f_o$ (TEM lines).

Thus we can write:

$2\pi d/(Vp/f_o) = \pi/2 \implies d = Vp/4f_o \qquad (13.13)$

For any frequency (f), we can write:

$Z_{in} = Z_0'(R_L + jZ_0't)/(Z_0' + jR_Lt) \qquad (13.14)$

And

$\Gamma_{in} = (Z_{in} - Z_0)/(Z_{in} + Z_0) = (R_L - Z_0)/[R_L + Z_0 + j2t(Z_0 R_L)^{1/2}] \qquad (13.15)$

The reflection coefficient magnitude can be derived from this equation as:

$|\Gamma_{in}| = \{1 + [4Z_0 R_L/(R_L - Z_0)^2] \sec^2\theta\}^{-1/2} \qquad (13.16)$

where $\sec^2\theta = 1/\cos^2\theta$

We can observe that at $f = f_o$ the term $\sec^2\theta$ becomes a large number because:

$\theta = 90° \implies \sec^2 90° = 1/\cos^2 90° \approx \infty$

Thus we can write an approximate equation for $|\Gamma_{in}|$ as:

$|\Gamma_{in}| \approx |R_L - Z_0| \, |\cos\theta|/2(Z_0 R_L)^{-1/2} \qquad (13.17)$

A simple sketch of this equation is shown in Figure 13.15:

The bandwidth of the quarter-wave transformer can now be calculated based upon the maximum value of a specified $|\Gamma_m|$ that can be tolerated satisfactorily, such that:

$$|\Gamma_{in}| \leq |\Gamma_m| \tag{13.18}$$

From Figure 13.10, we can see that the variation $|\Gamma_{in}|$ plot is symmetrical around $\theta=\pi/2$ and $\Gamma_{in}=\Gamma_m$ at two values:

a) $\theta_1=\theta_m$ at $f=f_{m1}$,   (13.19a)

and

b) $\theta_2= \theta_1+\Delta\theta =\pi- \theta_m$ at $f=f_{m2}$ (13.19b)

Where $\Delta0=2(\pi/2 - \theta_m)$

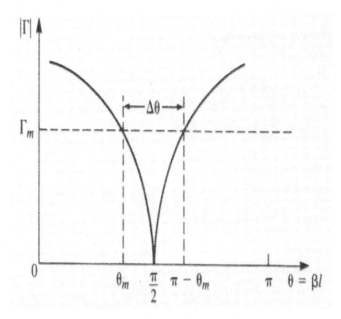

Figure 13.10 The frequency response of a quarter-wave transformer near its design frequency (f_o).

Using the exact expression, we can find Γ_m as follows:

$1/\Gamma_m^2=1+[2(Z_oR_L)^{1/2} \sec\theta_m/(R_L-Z_o)]^2$

$=> \cos\theta_m = 2\Gamma_m (Z_oR_L)^{1/2} / [(1-\Gamma_m^2)^{1/2} . |R_L-Z_o|]$ (13.20)

For TEM lines, we have:

$$\theta_m=\beta_m d=2\pi f_m d/\lambda_m \tag{13.21}$$

Where $\lambda_m = Vp/f_m$ and $d = Vp/4f_o$. Therefore, we can write:
$$\theta_m = \pi f_m /2f_o \Rightarrow f_m = 2f_o\theta_m/\pi \tag{13.22}$$

Due to symmetry of the Γ_{in} plot, the bandwidth for the $\lambda/4$ transformer for $|\Gamma_{in}| \leq |\Gamma_m|$ can be calculated as:
$$\Delta f = f_{m2} - f_{m1} = 2(f_o - f_{m1}) = 2f_o(1 - 2\theta_m/\pi) \tag{13.23}$$

Figure 13.11 shows frequency response (variation of $|\Gamma_{in}|$ vs. f) of a quarter-wave transformer for several load mismatches. From this Figure, we can see that as the load mismatch value (Z_L/Z_o) deviates greatly from unity in either direction (e.g., 10 or 0.1), the bandwidth shrinks, as expected due to higher reflected waves. Vice versa, as the load mismatch value decreases toward unity (e.g., 2, 0.5), then the reflected waves reduce and the bandwidth increases until a perfect match is achieved, i.e.,
$$Z_L = Z_o \Rightarrow \Gamma_{in} = 0$$
at which moment we obtain an infinite bandwidth theoretically.

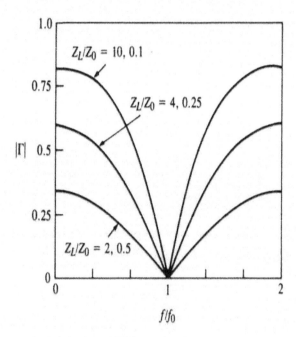

Figure 13.11 Variation of $|\Gamma_{in}|$ vs. f, for a quarter-wave transformer with several load mismatches.

Example 13. 3
Design a quarter-wave transformer to match a 10 Ω load to a 50 Ω Feed TL at f_o= 3 GHz. Find the bandwidth if we desire VSWR ≤ 1.5.
Solution:
The matching transformer has a Z_o' given by:
$Z_o'=(Z_oR_L)^{1/2} = (50×10)^{1/2} ≈ 22.4$ Ω

To calculate the bandwidth we proceed as follows:
VSWR = 1.5 => Γ_m=(1.5-1)/(1.5+1)=0.2
Δf=2f_o (1-2θ_m/π)
$\cos\theta_m$ = 2Γ_m $(Z_oR_L)^{1/2}$ / $[(1-\Gamma_m^2)^{1/2} . |R_L-Z_o|]$
=>θ_m=77°=1.34 rad
Δf=2f_o (1-2θ_m/π) ≈0.88 GHz
Therefore, the frequency range of interest would be between 2.56 GHz and 3.44 GHz, which represents a fractional bandwidth ($\Delta f/f_o$) of 29%.

CHAPTER-13 PROBLEMS

13.1) A load impedance Z_L=120+j100 Ω is to be matched to a 75 Ω feed TL using lumped elements at f=5 GHz.
a) Determine the possible solutions for the matching networks
b) If the frequency increases by 1 GHz, determine the new input impedance using the Smith Chart.

13.2) Design quarter-wave transformer to match a 300 Ω to a 100 Ω feed TL. For VSWR≤2, determine the useful bandwidth at f_o=10 GHz. What is the percent bandwidth?

13.3) Design a lumped L-section matching network that will match an RL load consisting of R_L=100 Ω and L=7 nH to a 50 Ω TL at 3 GHz. a) If there is a ±10% change in frequency, plot $|\Gamma_{in}|$ vs. frequency to determine its variation vs. frequency, b) for part (a) determine the region on the Smith chart which shows the corresponding variation in the input impedance.

13.4) Using the impedance inversion property of a 50 Ω quarter-wave TL:

a) Determine its input impedance on the Smith chart if it is connected to a 50+j50 Ω load fo=20 GHz.

b) If the frequency is increased to 25 GHz, determine the new input impedance.

c) What lumped element should be added at the input of the λ/4 TL in part (b) to create a match?

13.5) Consider an open-circuited 75 Ω transmission line having a length of 20 m:

a) Calculate and plot the frequency response of the input impedance.

b) What are the resonant frequencies and at what lengths do they occur?

c) How would Foster's reactance theorem apply here?

13.6) The normalized impedance of an unknown device is measured (from 1 to 2 GHz) to have a frequency response as plotted in Figure P13.6. Determine an equivalent circuit for the unknown device with all element values correctly calculated (assume Z_0=50 Ω, f=1 GHz).

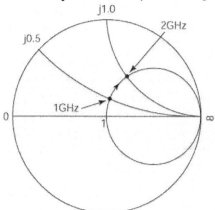

Figure P13.6

13.7) Design a quarter-wave transformer to match a 150 Ω load to a 50 Ω Feed TL at f_o= 5 GHz.
a) Find the bandwidth if we desire VSWR $\leq$ 1.2.
b) If the frequency changes by ±5%, what is the change in $|\Gamma_{in}|$ and VSWR?
c) Plot the frequency response of the transformer as a function of frequency ($|\Gamma_{in}|$ vs. f).

13.8) Consider an short-circuited 100 Ω transmission line having a length of 50 m:
a) Calculate and plot the frequency response of the input impedance.
b) What are the resonant frequencies and at what lengths do they occur?
c) How would Foster's reactance theorem apply here?

13.9) A load impedance Z_L=100-j200 Ω is to be matched to a 50 Ω feed TL using lumped elements at f=10 GHz.
a) Determine the possible solutions for the matching networks,
b) If the frequency changes by ±10%, determine the new input impedance value using the Smith Chart.

13.10) Design quarter-wave transformer to match a 200 Ω to a 50 Ω feed TL. For VSWR$\leq$1.5, determine the useful bandwidth at f_o=20 GHz. What is the percent bandwidth for this case?

13.11) Design a lumped L-section matching network that will match an RC load consisting of R_L=150 Ω and C=0.005 pF to a 50 Ω TL at 100 GHz. Plot $|\Gamma_{in}|$ vs. frequency to determine the bandwidth for which $|\Gamma_{in}|$<0.2. Determine the region on the Smith chart which shows the corresponding variation in the input impedance.

PART III

CIRCUIT DESIGN ESSENTIALS

CHAPTER 14

Lumped Matching Network Design

14.1 INTRODUCTION

Having studied the Smith chart in full detail and seen the ease and simplicity that it brings to the analysis of distributed or lumped element circuits, we now turn to the design of matching networks.

Applications in the last few chapters have in reality set the stage for most of the possible ways a Smith chart could be used as an essential tool in RF/microwave circuit analysis and more importantly in network design.

Many of these applications will be cited as reference throughout the rest of this chapter in order to simplify and further speed up the process of the design of a matching network, which is an essential part of any modern active circuit.

14.2 DEFINITION OF IMPEDANCE MATCHING

At the outset of this section, we will define an important nomenclature:

DEFINITION- MATCHING: *is defined to be connecting two circuits (source and load) together via a coupling device or network in such* *a way that the maximum transfer of energy occurs between the two circuits.*

This is one of the most important design concepts in amplifier and oscillator design as shown in Figure 14.1.

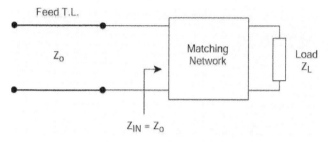

Figure 14.1 The concept of matching.

The concept of Impedance matching (also referred to as "tuning") is an important step in the overall design process of passive networks at RF/microwave frequencies for two reasons:

a. Maximum power transfer to occur from source to load, and

b. Signal-to-noise ratio to be improved because matching causes an increase in the signal level.

(a) and (b) are the primary reasons to employ tuning in practically all RF/microwave active circuit design. To get a conceptual understanding of why a matching network is needed in a circuit in general, we can visualize an active circuit in which a load impedance is different from the transmission line characteristic impedance causing power reflections back to the source.

To alleviate this problem and bring about zero power reflection from the load (i.e. maximum power transfer) a matching network needs to be inserted between the transmission line and the load.

Ideally, the matching network is lossless to prevent further loss of power to the load. It acts as an intermediary circuit between the two non-identical impedances in such a way that the feeding transmission line sees a perfect match (eliminating all possible reflections) while the multiple reflections existing between the load and the matching network will be unseen by the source.

14.3 SELECTION OF A MATCHING NETWORK

Selection of a lossless matching network is always possible as long as the load impedance is not purely imaginary and has in fact a non-zero real part.

There are many considerations in selecting a matching network including:

14.3.1 Simplicity

The simplest design is usually highly preferable since simpler matching networks have fewer elements, require less work to manufacture, are cheaper, are less lossy and more reliable compared to a more complicated and involved design.

14.3.2 Bandwidth

Any matching network can provide zero reflection at a single frequency, however, to achieve impedance matching over a frequency band more complex designs need to be used. Thus, there is a trade-off between design simplicity and matching bandwidth and eventually the network price as shown in Figure 14.2

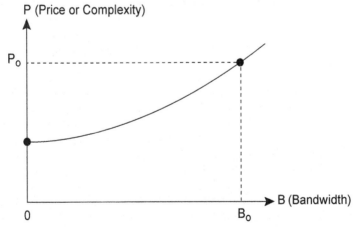

Figure 14.2 Relationship of price with frequency bandwidth.

14.3.3 Feasibility of Manufacturing

To manufacture a certain design, one needs to consider first the type of transmission line technology that the matching network will be implemented with. This means that before the matching circuit is designed one needs to know before-hand whether it is a microstrip or coaxial line type technology, So that the matching circuit will be designed properly to integrate most efficiently with the rest of the network.

For example, in microstrip line technology due to its planar configuration, the use of quarter-wave transformers, stubs and chip lumped elements for matching are feasible. On the other hand, in waveguide technology, implementing tuning stubs for matching purposes is more predominant than lumped elements or $\lambda/4$ multi-section transformers.

14.3.4 Ease of Tunability

Variable loads require variable tuning. Thus the matching network design and implementation should account for this. To implement such an adjustable matching network may require a more complex design or even switching to a different type of transmission line technology in order to accommodate such a requirement.

These four considerations form the backbone of all design criteria. However, for the sake of clarity and ease, we will focus only on the first consideration, i.e., "simplicity", for the rest of this work and leave the other three considerations to more advanced texts.

NOTE: *There are cases where the matching network has two or more solutions for the same load impedance. The preference of one design over the other would greatly depend upon bringing the other three considerations into view, which will place the ensuing discussions outside the scope of this work.*

14.4 THE GOAL OF IMPEDANCE MATCHING

The most important design tool in amplifier and oscillator design is the concept of impedance matching. The goal of impedance matching in all of its different forms can be summed up into one issue, and that is:

GOAL OF IMPEDANCE MATCHING: *Making the input impedance of the load and the added matching network theoretically equal to the characteristic impedance of the feeding transmission line, thus allowing maximum amount of power to transfer to the load.*

Next section will delineate conditions under which maximum power transfer does take place.

14.5 TRANSFER OF MAXIMUM AVERAGE POWER

Consider the circuit as shown in Figure 14.3, which is a problem of great practical importance. In this circuit, source impedance (Z_S) is a known and fixed value, V_S is the phasor representation of the source sinusoidal voltage at angular frequency (ω):

$$V_S = Re(|V_S|e^{j\omega t}) \tag{14.1}$$

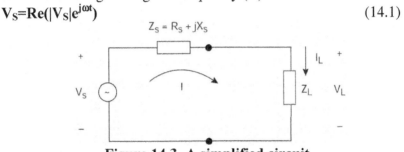

Figure 14.3 A simplified circuit .

The problem is to select the load impedance (Z_L) such that the maximum average power (P_{av}), at steady state, is obtained from the source and fed to the load. This problem can be easily solved with the help of the following theorem:

14.5.1 Maximum Power Transfer Theorem

Consider the general circuit having a known source impedance and an unknown load as shown in Figure 14.3. The maximum power transfer theorem states that the maximum power that can be delivered to a load is only feasible when the load has an optimum impedance value ($Z_L)_{opt}$ equal to the complex conjugate of the source impedance value ($Z_{S,}$), i.e.,

$$(Z_L)_{opt} = Z_S^* \qquad\qquad (14.2)$$

From Equation (14.2) we can see that:
$$R_L = R_S$$
$$X_L = -X_S$$

Considering the maximum power transfer as the cornerstone of matching, we can make the following conclusive observation about the goal of matching:

The goal of matching is adding a matching network to a load (Z_L) in such a way that the input impedance (Z_{in}) of the total combination will be located at the center of the Smith chart (i.e., $Z_{in}=Z_o$, where Z_o is a real number).

14.5.2 Proof of Maximum Power Transfer Theorem
The average power delivered to the load can be written as:
$$V_L = Z_L I_L$$
$$I_L = \frac{V_S}{Z_S + Z_L}$$
$$P_{av} = \frac{1}{2}\text{Re}(V_L I_L^*) = \frac{1}{2}\text{Re}(Z_L|I_L|^2) = |V_S|^2\frac{\text{Re}(Z_L)}{2|Z_S + Z_L|^2} \qquad (14.3)$$

Where V_S, $Z_S = R_S + jX_S$ and $Z_L = R_L + jX_L$ are the source voltage phasor, source impedance and load impedance, respectively.

Substitution in Equation (14.3) gives:
$$P_{av} = |V_S|^2\frac{R_L}{2[(R_S + R_L)^2 + (X_S + X_L)^2]} \qquad (14.4a)$$

In Equation (14.4), V_S, R_S and X_S are given, R_L and X_L are to be chosen such that their value will maximize P_{av}. The reactance X_L is found by differentiating P_{av} with respect to X_L and setting it to zero, which yields:

$$\partial P_{av}/\partial X_L = 0 \quad \Rightarrow X_L = -X_S \qquad\qquad (14.4b)$$

With this choice, the term $(X_L+X_S)^2$ in the denominator becomes zero, which minimizes the denominator and maximizes the expression with respect to X_L. Thus Equation (14.4) can now be written as:

$$P_{av} = |V_S|^2 \frac{R_L}{2(R_S + R_L)^2} \tag{14.5}$$

Now to determine optimum R_L, we set the partial derivative of P_{av} with respect to R_L equal to zero, i.e.,

$$\frac{\partial P_{av}}{\partial R_L} = 0 \tag{14.6}$$

Upon differentiation and setting it equal to zero, we obtain:
$$R_L = R_S \tag{14.7}$$
Q.E.D. – which was to be proven!

Using $Z_L = Z_S^*$ (referred to as a conjugately matched load), from Equation (14.4) we obtain the maximum power delivered to the load $(P_{av})_{max}$ as:

$$\left(P_{av}\right)_{max} = \frac{|V_S|^2}{8R_S} \tag{14.8}$$

Furthermore, under these conditions the power produced by the source is given by:

$$P_S = \frac{1}{2}\text{Re}\left(V_S I_L^*\right) = \frac{1}{2}\text{Re}\left(\frac{|V_S|^2}{Z_S + Z_L}\right) = \frac{|V_S|^2}{4R_S} \tag{14.9}$$

Thus we have:

$$P_S = \frac{|V_S|^2}{4R_S} = 2\left(P_{av}\right)_{max} \tag{14.10a}$$

From Equation (14.10), we can observe that the efficiency of a conjugately matched load is 50%, i.e.

$$\frac{\left(P_{av}\right)_{max}}{P_S} = 0.5 = 50\% \qquad \text{for } Z_L = Z_S^* \tag{14.10b}$$

NOTE 1: *For RF and microwave engineers this fact (i.e. 50% efficiency) is of much significance since the energy in the incoming electromagnetic waves would have been lost if it were not absorbed by a conjugately matched load (which is the first or "front-end stage" of a receiver).*

NOTE 2: *For power engineers and electric power companies, this situation is never allowed to occur and in fact the reverse is desired. This is because they are extremely interested in efficiency and want to deliver as much of the average power as possible to the load (i.e. the customer). Thus, huge power generators are never conjugately matched.*

NOTE 3: *The "maximum power transfer theorem" assumes that the source impedance (Z_S) is a fixed and known quantity while the load impedance is a variable and unknown quantity (Z_L), whose value can be varied to the complex conjugate of Z_S, to achieve a maximum power transfer. Under this condition due to the complex conjugate condition, the total resistance in the circuit is given by:*

$$Z_{tot} = Z_S + Z_L = 2R_S = 2R_L$$

NOTE 4: *If the reverse is true, namely the load impedance (Z_L) is a known and fixed quantity and the source impedance (Z_S) a variable quantity, the requirement that source and load impedances be complex conjugate of each other is no longer valid and does not apply in this case.*

Furthermore, to obtain maximum power transfer from the source to the load for this case, it can easily be observed that we need to have minimum loss in the source. Thus, we can write the following for the source:

$$R_S = 0$$
$$X_S = -X_L$$

Under this condition, since the reactances cancel out, the total resistance in the circuit is given by:
$$Z_{tot} = Z_S + Z_L = R_L$$

14.6 LUMPED ELEMENT DESIGN OF MATCHING CIRCUITS

Considering the size of most modern RF/microwave circuits, actual discrete lumped element capacitors and inductors are used in the design process at low RF/microwave frequencies (up to around 1-2 GHz) or at higher frequencies (up to 60 GHz) if the circuit size is much smaller than the wavelength ($\ell<\lambda/10$)

Although microwave integrated circuit (MIC) technology has pushed the frequency limitation of lumped elements into the high microwave range, there are a large number of circuits whose size has become comparable with the signal wavelength at higher frequency ranges where using lumped elements would become completely impractical.

Thus one of the biggest limitations of the use of lumped elements is in circuits whose size has become comparable with the signal wavelength.

Furthermore, if the length (ℓ) of the lumped component is below ($\lambda/10$) as mentioned above, then they can be used in "hybrid" or "Monolithic" Microwave Integrated Circuits (MICs) at frequencies up to 60 GHz. At these high frequencies, electrical elements can be realized via several methods. These methods for each component can be summarized as follows:

1. CAPACITORS:
a. A single-gap capacitor (C<0.5 pF)
b. An inter-digital gap capacitor in a microstrip line (C<0.5 pF)
c. A short or open transmission line stub (C<0.1 pF)
d. A chip capacitor
e. A metal-insulator-metal(MIM) capacitor (C<25 pF)

These are shown in Figure 14.4.

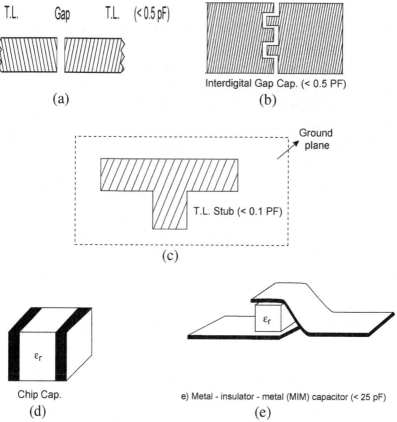

**Figure 14.4 Several types of capacitors, a) single-gap,
b) interdigital, c) TL stub, d)chip, and e) metal-insulator-metal
(MIM).**

2. RESISTORS:

a. Thin film technology using NiChrome or doped semiconductor material

b. Chip resistor

These are shown in Figures 14.5 (a) and (b).

Lossy Film

T.L.   T.L.

a) Planar resistor

ε_r

b) Chip resistor

Figure 14.5 Two types of resistors, a) planar, and b) chip.

3. Inductors
a. A loop of a transmission line
b. A short length of a transmission line
c. A spiral inductor using an air bridge

These are shown in Figures 14.6 (a), (b), and (c).

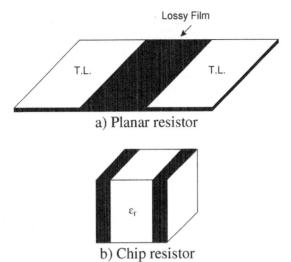

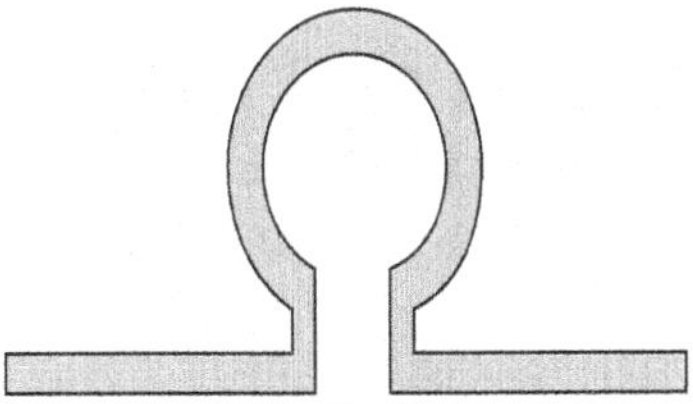

Ground plane

(a) Loop Inductor 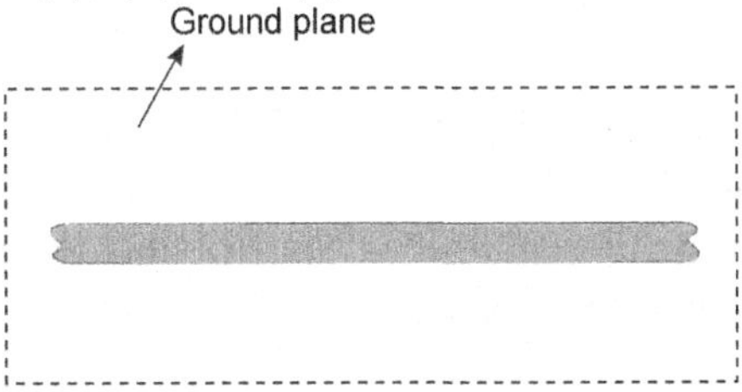   (b) TL Inductor

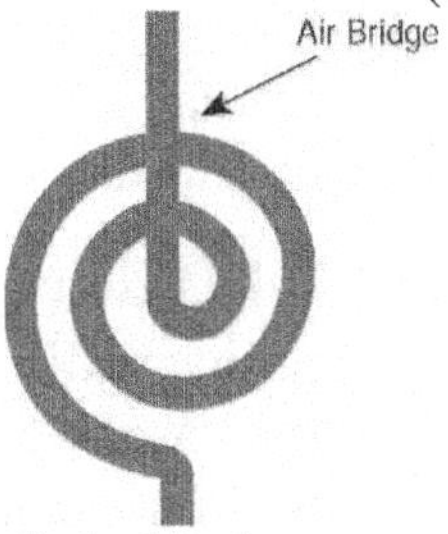

Air Bridge

(c) Spiral Inductor

Figure 14.6 Three types of inductors.

14.6.1 Matching Network Design Using L-Sections

As already discussed in Chapter 6, the simplest type of matching network is the L(ell)- section consisting of two reactive elements that match a load to a transmission line. The actual configuration is of the form of an inverted L. The two possibilities are shown in Figure 14.7.

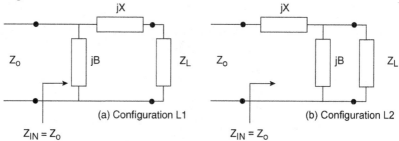

Figure 14.7 Two possibilities of an L-section, a) L1, b) L2.

Considering the fact that either of the two reactive elements can be an inductor or a capacitor, circuit configurations L1 and L2 provide a total of eight different possibilities for a given load. The location of the load on the "smith chart" determines the useful configuration as discussed in the next section.

14.7 DESIGN BASED ON THE LOAD LOCATION

Depending on the location of the normalized load impedance on the Smith chart, one or both of the two configurations L1 and L2 may become practical.

The location of the load becomes crucial in the choice of circuit configuration for the purpose of matching. The load location can have three distinct possibilities:

14.7.1 Case I-The Load is Inside (1+jx) Circle

Case I is when the load is located inside the (1+jx) Circle (Resistance Unity Circle). In this case, we can see from Figure 14.8 that the first element has to be a shunt element thus configuration L2 is the only practical one.

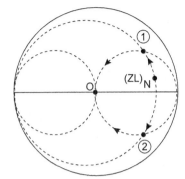

Figure 14.8 Smith chart solution.

Using configuration L2, two possible solutions exist:

- **Solution (1): shunt L & series C**
- **Solution (2): shunt C & series L**

These are shown in Figure 14.9.

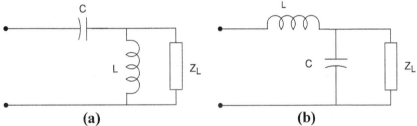

(a)   (b)

Figure 14.9 Two circuit solutions for case I.

14.7.2 Case II- The Load is Inside (1+ jb) Circle

Case II is when the load is inside the (1+ jb) circle (Conductance Unity Circle). In this case, from Figure 14.10 we can see that the first element has to be a series element thus only configuration L1 becomes useful.

Similar to case 1, there are two solutions possible as shown below:

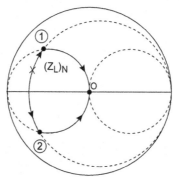

Figure 14.10 Smith chart solutions.

- **Solution (1): series L & shunt C**
- **Solution (2): series C & shunt L**

The circuits for these two solutions are shown in Figure 14.11.

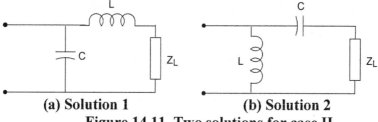

| (a) Solution 1 | (b) Solution 2 |

Figure 14.11 Two solutions for case II.

14.7.3 Case III- The Load is Outside (1+ jx) & (1+ jb) Circle

Case III is when the load is outside the $(1+ jx)$ and $(1+ jb)$ circle. In this case, there are four solutions possible as shown in Figure 14.12. These four possibilities are summarized below.

Solutions (1) and (2): both require a series element first which makes configuration L1 the only practical one. Thus the solutions are:

- **Solution (1): series C & shunt C**
- **Solution (2): series C & shunt L**

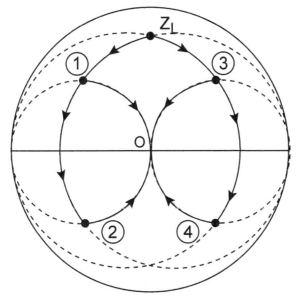

Figure 14.12 Smith chart solutions for case III.

The circuits for the two solutions are shown in Figure 14.13.

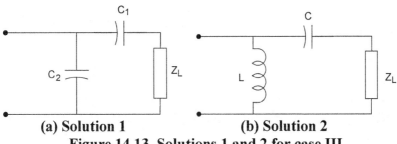

(a) Solution 1   (b) Solution 2
Figure 14.13 Solutions 1 and 2 for case III.

Solutions (3) and (4) below, both require a shunt element inserted first, which makes configuration L2 useful. These two solutions are:

- **Solution (3): shunt C & series L**
- **Solution (4): shunt C & series L**

These are shown in Figure 14.14.

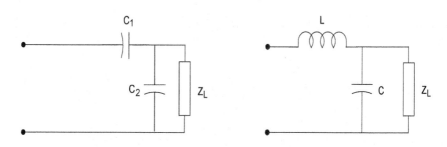

(a) Solution 3   (b) Solution 4

Figure 14.14 Solutions 3 and 4 for case III.

14.7.4 Design Flexibility

Considering all three cases (i.e. I, II and III), it appears that case III has the highest flexibility since when the load is located outside the unity circle, we have the highest amount of design flexibility to suit the designer's needs.

If the load falls inside any of the unity circles, one may be able to add a reactive element to the load in such a way as to bring the combined load to the outside of the unity circle and then take advantage of the matching possibilities that are available at the outside of these two unity circles.

EXAMPLE 14.1

Consider a load $(Z_L)_N$ located inside the $(1+jb)$ circle. Discuss the matching possibilities for this load.

Solution:
This load obviously has two matching possibilities (1 and 2) as discussed earlier in case II.
Let us add a series "L" to take the load Z_L to Z_L' outside the $(1+jB)$ circle as shown in Figure 14.15.

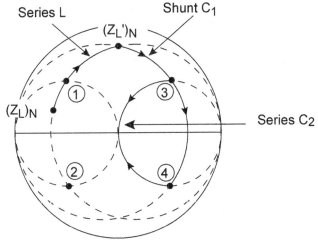

Figure 14.15 Smith chart solutions.

Now since $(Z_L')_N$ is outside, we have two additional possibilities (3 and 4) which may be more suitable for our design needs.

Selecting solution "3", we can see that the final matching circuit will have the following three elements as shown in Figure 14.16.

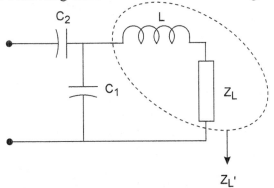

Figure 14.16 Adding L to convert to case III for extra solutions.

As discussed earlier, there seems to be four main considerations that govern the matching circuit design process i.e.: simplicity, bandwidth, feasibility of manufacturing and ease of tunability. These four criteria heavily influence one's decision in the choice of the matching circuit's design.

Therefore, even though from the simplicity point of view solution (3) in the above example seems to be more complex than a simple L-design, there are instances where the other three considerations would become paramount and thus make this design a valuable one.

14.8 DESIGN RULES FOR LUMPED MATCHING NETWORKS

Based on the discussion presented in the previous two sections, there are certain rules that if followed would simplify and even speed up the matching circuit design process. These rules can be summarized as follows:

Rule #1. Use a ZY Smith chart at all times.

Rule #2. Always start off from the load end and travel "toward Generator" (in order to prevent uncertainty and confusion about the starting point).

Rule #3. Always move on a constant-R or constant-G circle in such a way as to arrive eventually at the center of the Smith chart.

Rule #4. Each motion along a constant-R or constant-G circle gives the value of a reactive element.

Rule #5. Moving on a constant-R circle yields series reactive elements, whereas moving on a constant-G circle yields shunt reactive elements.

Rule #6. The direction of travel (or motion) on a constant-R or constant-G circle determines the type of element to be used, i.e. a capacitor or an inductor.

Rules 5 and 6 lead to the following additional two rules.

Rule #7. When the motion is upward, in most cases it corresponds to a series or a shunt inductor.

Rule #8. When the motion is downward, in most cases it corresponds to a series or a shunt capacitor.

NOTE: *These rules are merely a guideline to be followed in the matching circuit design process. They will never replace the theoretical and practical understandings that goes into making them. These understandings as contained in this work, are the essentials from which all of these rules have been derived.*

EXAMPLE 14.2
Given the circuit shown in Figure 14.17, design a lumped element matching network at 1 GHz that would transform $Z_L=10+j10$ Ω into a 50 Ω transmission line.

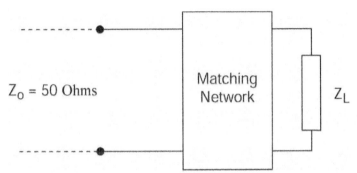

Figure 14.17 Circuit for example 14.2.

Solution:
a. $Z_O=50$ Ω, $Y_O=0.02$ S
   $(Z_L)_N=(10+j10)/50=0.2+j0.2$

b. Locate $(Z_L)_N$ on the smith chart as shown in Figure 14.18.

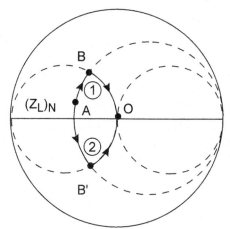

Figure 14.18 Smith chart solutions.

c. Since $(Z_L)_N$ is inside the unity conductance circle, this would correspond to case II and has two possible solutions.

SOLUTION (1):
-Start from load on a constant-R circle and move up from point "A" to "B". This Yields Series L:
$j\omega L = j0.2 \times 50 \Rightarrow L = 1.59$ nH

-Now starting from point "B", a motion downward on the unity conductance circle yields a shunt C:
$j\omega C = j2.0 \times 0.2 \Rightarrow C = 6.37$ pF

-The final circuit schematic is shown in Figure 14.19.

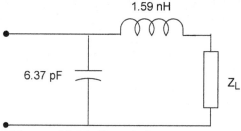

1.59 nH

6.37 pF

Z_L

Figure 14.19 Circuit for solution 1.

SOLUTION (2):
Starting from load, move downward on a constant-R circle

(series C) to point "B'" and the upward (shunt L) to arrive at "C" s follows:

Series C $\Rightarrow$ 1/jωC=-j0.6 X 50 $\Rightarrow$ C=5.3 pF

Shunt L $\Rightarrow$ 1/jωL =-j2 x 0.02 $\Rightarrow$ L=3.98 nH

The schematic for solution (2) is shown in Figure 14.20.

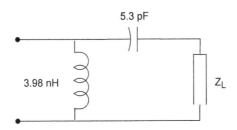

Figure 14.20 Circuit for solution 2.

Chapter 14- Symbol list

A symbol will not be repeated again, once it has been identified and defined in an earlier chapter, with its definition remaining unchanged.

P_{av} - Average power

$(P_{av})_{max}$ - Maximum average power

$(Z_L)_{opt}$ - Optimum load impedance

CHAPTER-14 PROBLEMS

14.1) Design a lumped element matching circuit that transforms a load (Z_L=150+j150 Ω) to a 75 transmission line such that a DC signal is blocked in reaching the load at f= 1 GHz.

14.2) Design a lumped matching network to match the load Y_L=(4-j6)x10^{-3} S to a transmission line (Z_O=100 Ω) as shown below. Find the element values at 10 GHz.

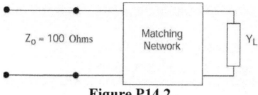

Figure P14.2

14.3) Design a matching network to transform the load, $Z_L=100+j100 \ \Omega$, to a $50+j50 \ \Omega$ impedance at f= 5 GHz.

14.4) Design a matching network to transform a load impedance $(Z_L=100+j50\Omega)$ to the input impedance $(Z_{in}=75-j50 \ \Omega)$ at 15 GHz as shown in Figure P14.4 by using lumped elements

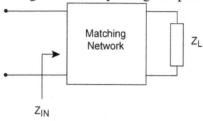

Figure P14.4

14.5) Design a lumped element matching network that will match a 200 Ω load to an input reflection coefficient of $\Gamma_{in}=0.5\angle150°$ in a 50 Ω system as shown in Figure P14.5. The matching network should allow a DC signal to reach the load.

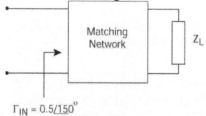

Figure P14.5

14.6) A certain microwave device has $Z_d=15-j60 \ \Omega$ as shown below. Design a matching network to match the device impedance to a 75 Ω system using lumped elements at 20 GHz. Present the element values for all possible solutions.

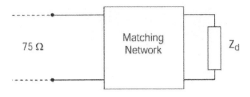

Figure P14.6

14.8) A lossless feed transmission line (Z_O=50 Ω) is to be matched to a load, Z_L=25-j10, by means of a lumped element matching circuit.

a) How many solutions are possible? Determine the element values for all possible solutions.

b) By adding an inductor to the load, how many solutions are possible now? Determine the inductor value as well as the element values for all possible solutions.

14.9) Design a matching network having three elements to transform the load, Z_L=25-j25 Ω, to a feed TL with Z_O=50 Ω at f= 10 GHz. Realize all possible values and choose the most practical and compact design for implementation in a Microwave Integrated Circuit (MIC).

CHAPTER 15

Distributed Matching Network Design

15.1 INTRODUCTION

At higher frequencies where the component or circuit size is comparable with wavelength, distributed components may be used to match the load to the transmission line.

15.2 DISTRIBUTED MATCHING NETWORK DESIGN

The most common technique in this type of design is the use of a single open-circuited or short-circuited length of transmission line (called a stub) connected either in parallel or in series with the transmission feed line at a certain distance from the load as shown in Figure 15.1.

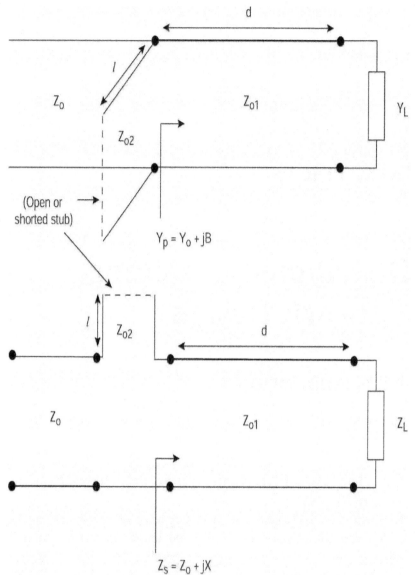

Figure 15.1 A stub at a distance d, a) shunt stub, b) series stub.

Rather than using a two-wire transmission line schematic, alternate microstrip line schematic for short- and open-stubs can be drawn more effectively as shown in Figure 15.2 (a),(b),(c) and (d).

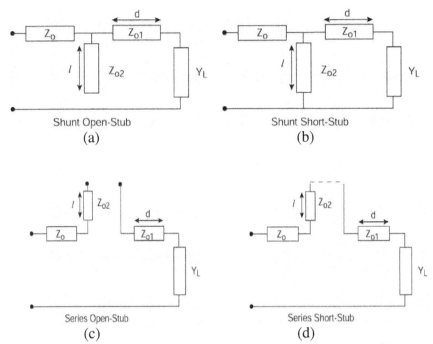

**Figure 15.2 Microstrip-line schematic for shunt (a,b)
and series (c,d) stubs.**

Such a matching network is easy to build using microstrip or stripline technology. In single-stub matching networks, the two variable parameters are the distance "d" (from load to stub) and the length "ℓ" (stub's length) which provides the value of stub susceptance or reactance.

Selection of distance "d" is crucial for both shunt and series stub as explained below:

a. For the shunt stub case, "d" should be chosen such that the input admittance Y_P (seen looking into the line before adding the stub) is of the form $Y_P = Y_O + jB$ with the stub susceptance selected as $(-jB)$ resulting in a matched condition.

b. for the series stub case, "d" should be chosen such that the impedance Z_S (seen looking into the line before addition of the stub) is of the form $Z_S = Z_O + jX$ with the stub reactance selected as $-jX$, resulting in a matched condition.

15.3 Choice of Short- or Open-Circuited Stubs

With a $\lambda/4$ difference in length between the two, a short or open transmission line with proper length, can provide any value of reactance or susceptance needed for the design.

Structural considerations behind choice of a short- versus an open-stub are as follows:

a. OPEN STUBS: For microstrip and stripline technology use of open stubs are preferred. Use of short stubs require a via-hole through the substrate to the ground plane, which adds extra work and can be eliminated through the use of open circuits.

b. SHORT STUBS: For coaxial line or waveguide as a transmission line media,   use of short stubs are preferred because the open stubs may radiate causing power losses thus making the stub no longer a purely reactive element.

15.4 DESIGN STEPS FOR SINGLE STUB MATCHING (SAME Z_o)

The Smith chart can be used effectively to design the distance "d" of the stub to the load and the length "ℓ" of the stub to create the proper value of susceptance or reactance (for more details see application #8, Chapter 10).

There are two circuit configurations where the stub is either in parallel or in series. Each case needs to be treated separately as follows:

15.4.1 Parallel Stub Design

This is shown in Figure 15.23. The design process has the following steps:

Step 1. Plot $(Y_L)_N$ on the ZY chart
(Please note that a single Y-chart could also be used as well but the load impedance has to be inverted first)

Step 2. Draw the appropriate VSWR circle which goes through $(Z_L)_N$

Step 3. On the VSWR circle, move (toward generator) to intersect the (1+jb) conductance unity circle at two solutions located at points "A1" and "A2" as shown in Figure 15.23:

- **Solution #1: $Y_1 = 1+ jb_1$ (distance d_1)**
- **Solution #2: $Y_2 = 1+ jb_2$ (distance d_2)**

Step 4. Now add a shunt susceptance of either $-jb_1$(solution #1) or $-jb_2$ (solution #2) to arrive at the center of the chart.

Step 5. To determine lengths ℓ_1 and ℓ_2, we first locate $-jb_1$ and $-jb_2$ on the Smith chart as shown in Figure 15.24a.

Then starting from $Z = \infty$ (for open stubs) or $Z = 0$ (for short stubs), we travel along the outer edge of the chart "toward generator" to arrive at $-jb_1$ (for open) or $-jb_2$ (for short) stubs. The lengths can be read off on the circular scale on the outer edge of the chart. These are shown in Figures 15.24b and 15.24c.

EXAMPLE 15.1 (PARALLEL STUB DESIGN)

Design a matching network using a single shunt open stub as a tuning element to match a load impedance $Z_L=15+j10\ \Omega$ to a 50 Ω transmission line(see Figure 15.3)

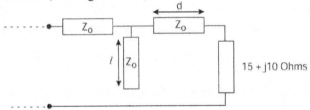

Figure 15.3 Circuit for example 15.1.

Solution:

a. Plot $(Z_L)_N=(15+j10)/50=0.3+j0.2$ on the ZY-chart

b. Draw the VSWR circle through $(Z_L)_N$ as shown in Figure 15.4.

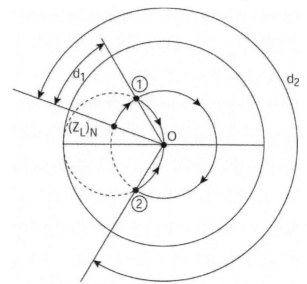

Figure 15.4 Smith chart solutions.

c. Move toward generator to meet the $(1+jb)$ circle at two points, giving two solutions:

$(Y_1)_N = 1 - j1.33$ with $d_1 = 0.044\lambda$ and $-jb_1 = j1.33$

$(Y_2)_N = 1 + j1.33$ with $d_2 = 0.387\lambda$ and $-jb_2 = -j1.33$

d. From Figure 15.5 we can read off ℓ_1 and ℓ_2 as:

$\ell_1 = 0.147\lambda$

$\ell_2 = 0.353\lambda$

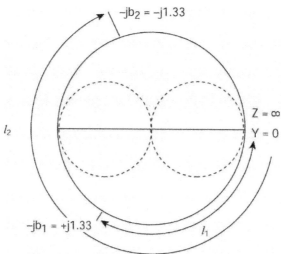

Figure 15.5 Smith chart solutions for stub lengths.

The two possible design schematics are shown in Figures 15.6.

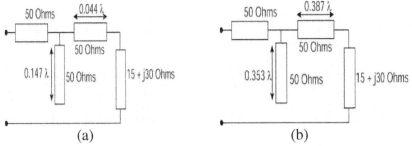

(a)   (b)

Figure 15.6 Two possible circuit designs.

NOTE: *Design #1 is more desirable Since it is usually preferred to keep the matching stub as close as possible to the load (i.e. smaller "d") in order to improve:*
- ❀ *The sensitivity of the matching network to frequency and thus   providing a larger bandwidth,*
- ❀ *The standing wave losses occurring on the line between the stub and the load possibly due to a high VSWR.*

15.4.2 Series Stub Design

From Figure 15.7, the design steps are as follows:

Step 1. Plot $(Z_L)_N$ on the ZY-chart.

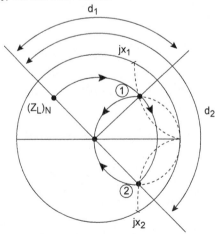

Figure 15.7 Smith chart solutions.

Step 2. Draw the appropriate VSWR circle.

Step 3. Move "toward generator" to intersect the $(1+jx)$, unity resistance circle, at two points (1) and (2) as shown in Figure 15.29:

- Solution #1: $Z_1 = 1+ jx_1$ (distance d_1), $Z_{1stub}=-jx_1$
- Solution #2: $Z_2 = 1+ jx_2$ (distance d_2) $Z_{2stub}=-jx_2$

Step 4. Now add a series reactance of either $-jx_1$ for solution #1 (or $-jx_2$ for solution #2) to cancel the existing reactance.

Step 5. stub lengths ℓ_1 (or ℓ_2) is now calculated by first locating reactance $-jx_1$ (or $-jx_2$) on the Smith chart (see Figures 15.30a,b).

For a series open stub, start from $Z = \infty$ and travel on the outer edge of the chart "Toward generator" to arrive at $-jx_1$ for solution #1 (or $-jx_2$ for solution #2). On the other hand, for a series short stub, repeat the above procedure except start from $Z = 0$ as shown in Figure 15.8.

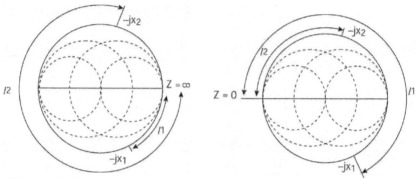

Figure 15.8 Smith chart solutions for stub lengths, a) open stub, b) short stub.

EXAMPLE 15.2 (SERIES STUB DESIGN)
Using a single series open stub, design a matching network that will transform a load impedance $Z_L=100+j80$ Ω to a 50 Ω Feed transmission line as shown in Figure, 15.9.

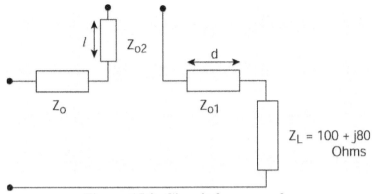

Figure 15.9 Circuit for example .

Solution:

a. Plot $(Z_L)_N=(100+j80)/50=2+j1.3$ on the smith chart.

b. Draw the VSWR circle (see Figure 15.10)

c. Move "toward generator" to intersect $(1+jx)$ circle at two points (1) and (2) giving:

$Z_1=1-j1.33$ with $d_1=0.120\lambda$ and $Z_{1stub}=j1.33$

$Z_2=1+j1.33$ with $d_2=0.463\lambda$ and $Z_{2stub}=-j1.33$

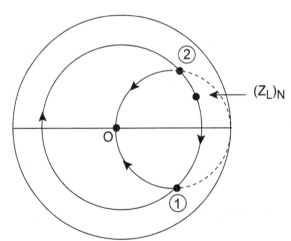

Figure 15.10 Smith chart solutions.

d. Lengths ℓ_1 and ℓ_2 can be read off from Figure 15.11 as:

$\ell_1=0.397\lambda$

$\ell_2=0.103\lambda$

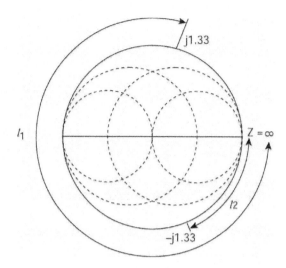

Figure 15.11 Smith chart solutions for stub lengths.

The two possible design schematics are shown in Figure 15.12.

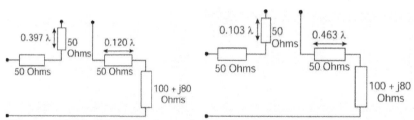

Figure 15.12 Final design schematics, a) design 1, b) design 2.

15.5 DESIGN OF SINGLE STUB MATCHING (DIFFERENT Z_O)

As can be seen from the previous two examples, the stub, the feed transmission line, and the line between the load and the stub all have the same characteristic impedance (Z_O).

However, if a characteristic impedance other than Z_O is desired, the location and length of the stub will now be different. The following technique can be used effectively to solve for this situation.

15.5.1 Part I

Add a stub at the load such that it will reduce the load to a purely resistive value (see Figure 15.13 for a shunt stub case). The following two types of stubs (each with the possibility of being short- or open-circuited) should be considered:

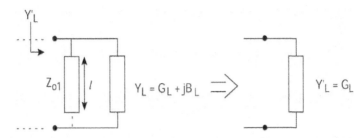

Figure 15.13 Conversion of the load to a purely resistive load using a shunt stub.

A1. Shunt Stub (see Figure 15.13):

Load: $Y_L = G_L + jB_L$

Stub: $-jB_L$

Giving: $Y_L' = G_L$

The new load (Y_L') is purely resistive. To determine the length of the stub, we have to specify the stub termination as being short or open:

-SHORT SHUNT STUB(Z_{O1})

$$Y_{SC} = -jY_{O1}/\tan\beta\ell = -jB_L \qquad (15.1)$$

$$\Rightarrow Y_{O1} = B_L\tan\beta\ell,$$

$$Z_{O1} = 1/Y_{O1} = 1/B_L\tan\beta\ell \qquad (15.2)$$

By proper choice of stub length(ℓ), any positive value of stub characteristic impedance can be realized; for example:

$$\ell = \lambda/8 \Rightarrow Z_{O1} = 1/B_L \quad \text{(for } B_L > 0) \qquad (15.3)$$

$$\ell = 3\lambda/8 \Rightarrow Z_{O1} = -1/B_L \quad \text{(for } B_L < 0) \qquad (15.4)$$

-OPEN SHUNT STUB(Z_{O1})

$$Y_{OC} = jY_{O1}\tan\beta\ell = -jB_L \qquad (15.5)$$

$$\Rightarrow Y_{O1} = -B_L/\tan\beta\ell,$$

$$Z_{O1} = 1/Y_{O1} = -\tan\beta\ell/B_L \qquad (15.6)$$

By proper choice of stub length(ℓ), any positive value of stub characteristic impedance can be realized; for example:

$\ell=\lambda/8 \Rightarrow Z_{O1}=-1/B_L$ (for $B_L<0$) (15.7)

$\ell=3\lambda/8 \Rightarrow Z_{O1}=1/B_L$ (for $B_L>0$) (15.8)

A2. Series stub:

Load: $Z_L = R_L + jX_L$

Stub: $-jX_L$

Giving: $Z_L' = R_L$

The new load (Z_L') is purely resistive. To determine the length of the stub, we have to specify the stub termination as being short or open:

-SHORT SERIES STUB (Z_{O1})

$Z_{SC}=-jZ_{O1}\tan\beta\ell=-jX_L$ (15.9a)

$\Rightarrow Z_{O1}=X_L/\tan\beta\ell,$ (15.9b)

By proper choice of stub length(ℓ), any positive value of stub characteristic impedance can be realized; for example:

$\ell=\lambda/8 \Rightarrow Z_{O1}=X_L$ (for $X_L>0$) (15.10)

$\ell=3\lambda/8 \Rightarrow Z_{O1}=-X_L$ (for $X_L<0$) (15.11)

-OPEN SERIES STUB (Z_{O1})

$Z_{OC}=jZ_{O1}/\tan\beta\ell=-jX_L$ (15.12a)

$\Rightarrow Z_{O1}=-X_L\tan\beta\ell,$ (15.12b)

By proper choice of stub length (ℓ), any positive value of stub characteristic impedance can be realized; for example:

$\ell=\lambda/8 \Rightarrow Z_{O1}=-X_L$ (for $X_L<0$) (15.13)

$\ell=3\lambda/8 \Rightarrow Z_{O1}=X_L$ (for $X_L>0$) (15.14)

15.5.2 Part II

Considering that the new load (Y_L' or Z_L') is now purely resistive (G_L or R_L), a simple quarter-wave ($\lambda/4$) transformer (Z_O') can be used efficiently to transform (Y_L' or Z_L') to Z_O. The $\lambda/4$ transformer has a characteristic impedance of:

Shunt stub: $Z_O'=(Z_O /Y_L')^{1/2} =(Z_O/G_L)^{1/2}$

Or,

Series stub: $\mathbf{Z_O'=(Z_L'Z_O)^{1/2}=(R_LZ_O)^{1/2}}$

Where Z_O is the characteristic impedance of the feed line (assumed to be lossless), and is a positive real number. This method in its entirety (parts 1 and 2) is depicted on the Smith chart, as shown in Figure 15.14.

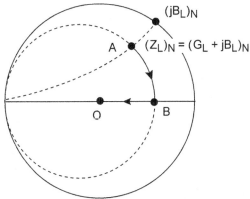

Figure 15.14 Smith chart solution.

Starting from point "A", we travel on a constant conductance circle to point "B" (located on the purely resistive axis). A quarter-wave transformer would then take it from point "B" to "O", the center of the chart.

c) The final circuit schematic for the matching network is shown below in Figure 15.15.

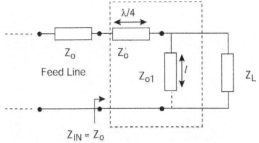

Figure 15.15 Final circuit schematic.

Example 15.3

Design a matching network using a quarter-wave transformer that would transform a 50 Ω load to $\Gamma_{in}=0.68\angle 97°$ as shown in Figure 15.16.

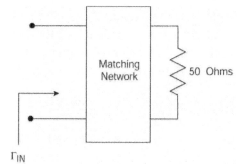

Figure 15.16 Circuit for example 15.3.

Solution:
To design the matching network we need first transform the load to the resistive part of Γ_{in} and then add a reactance equal to the reactance of Γ_{in} as follows:

a) Plot $\Gamma_{in} = 0.68\angle 97°$ on the smith chart as shown in Figure 15.17 and read off $(Y_{in})_N$:
$(Y_{in})_N = (0.4 - j1.05) \Rightarrow Y_{in} = Y_0(Y_{in})_N = 0.008 - j0.021$ S

b) Starting from the center of the chart (i.e. load at point "O"), A quarter-wave transformer (Z_{O1}) is now added to transform 50 Ω to ($R_{in} = 1/0.008 = 125$ Ω) (point "A" in Figure 15.17) :
$Z_{O1} = (50/0.008)^{1/2} = 79$ Ω

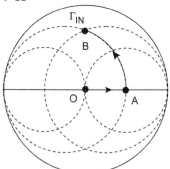

Figure 15.17 Smith chart solution.

c) The reactive part $(B_L = -j0.021)$ can now be synthesized by using an open circuited shunt stub of length $\ell = 3\lambda/8$ to arrive at point "B". The characteristic impedance is given by:
$Z_{O2} = 1/0.021 = 47.6$ Ω

(Note: $Y_{OC}=jY_{O2}\tan\beta\ell=-j/47.6$ since $\tan\beta\ell=-1$)

d) The final circuit schematic is shown in Figure 15.18.

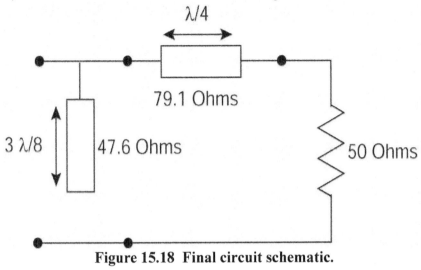

Figure 15.18 Final circuit schematic.

15.6 GENERALIZED IMPEDANCE MATCHING TECHNIQUES

When the input and the output reflection coefficients are both non-zero, then the matching network would transform the load impedance to a point (other than the center of the chart) corresponding to the desired input reflection coefficient.

This case is a very generalized concept of a matching network and is in contrast with the case where either the input or the output reflection coefficient was at the center of the chart.

This type of matching network could occur for example in an intermediate matching stage of a two-stage amplifier. Figure 15.19 show the generalized concept of a matching network along with the plot of the input and output reflection coefficients in the Smith chart.

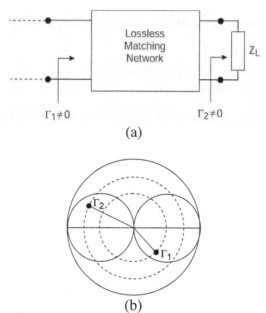

(a)

(b)

Figure 15.19 a) Generalized concept of matching, b) Smith chart solution.

There are a number of possible solutions which would lead to the desired matching network.

15.6.1 Technique #1

Assuming the input and output reflection coefficients to be Γ_1 and Γ_2, respectively, an obvious solution is to convert the load (Γ_2) to 50 Ω first and then match Γ_1 to 50 Ω, which is located at the center of the chart as shown in Figure 15.20a.

To realize the matching circuit, we start from the load at point A and travel "toward generator" on the constant VSWR circle to arrive at point B. Adding an opposite shunt stub
at this point will move this point to the center of the Smith chart ($\Gamma_2'=0$) which is the new load at point "O" as shown.

Now starting from point "O", add a series stub (to arrive at point "C") and then a series transmission line to end up at Γ_1 which is the input reflection coefficient. The resulting distributed circuit is shown in Figure 15.20b.

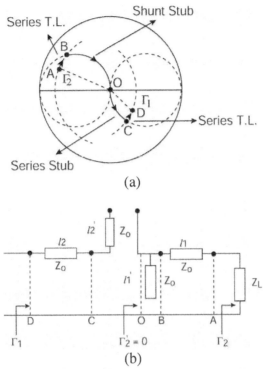

(a)

(b)

Figure 15.20 Technique #1, a) Smith chart solution, b) Circuit schematic.

NOTE 1: *As described earlier, it is best to keep the matching philosophy of moving from the load impedance toward the center of the chart which means to move from the output (load) and progress backward to the input end.*

NOTE 2: *The matching network above could have been alternately realized with lumped elements using the constant conductance or resistance circle (as described in the "Lumped element design" section) rather than the distributed element design.*

15.6.2 Technique #2

First we draw the constant VSWR circle for (Γ_1) as shown in Figure 15.21. Then starting from (Γ_2) at point "A", we travel on a constant conductance circle to intersect the (Γ_1) VSWR circle at point B. This corresponds to a shunt stub element.

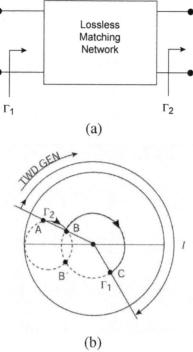

(a)

(b)

Figure 15.21 Technique #2, a) Circuit block diagram, a) Smith chart solution.

Next, we travel on the constant VSWR circle "toward generator " (clockwise) to arrive at point "C". This would correspond to a series transmission line of length "ℓ", as shown in the schematic in Figure 15.22.

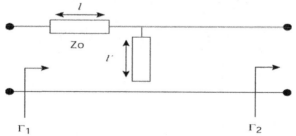

Figure 15.22 Technique #2, Circuit schematic (two-element design).

NOTE 1: *There is a second solution which uses the second intersection of the constant-G circle with the constant VSWR circle at point B' leading to a similar design procedure as described above.*

NOTE 2: *Solutions #2 provide only two elements (compared to four elements given by solution #1 which usually results in the best bandwidth for the interstage design.*

POINT OF INTEREST: *In some cases it is more convenient to work with the equivalent problem of conjugate reflection coefficient which functionally yields an equivalent circuit as shown in Figures 15.23 and 15.24.*

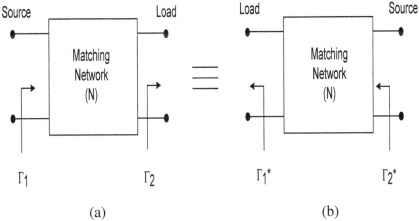

(a)   (b)

Figure 15.23 An equivalent representation of reflection coefficients at the terminals.

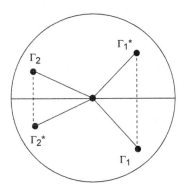

Figure 15.24 Conjugate reflection coefficients on the Smith chart solutions.

In Figure 15.25, since one is matching Γ_1^* to Γ_2^*, we have to start from Γ_1^* (as the load) and progress backwards to Γ_2^* at the other end.

Traveling from point "A" to "B" gives a series transmission line, followed by going from "B" to "C" (producing a shunt stub), which is identical to what was obtained earlier.

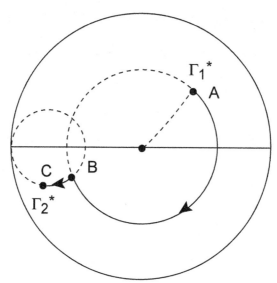

Figure 15.25 Smith chart solution.

15.7 STUB REALIZATION USING MICROSTRIP LINES

Series transmission lines and shunt stubs (short or open) can easily be realized using design steps for microstrip line technology (as outlined in Chapter 7).

Given a dielectric constant (ε_r), its height (h) and a certain characteristic impedance value (Z_O), the width of the microstrip line (W) can be calculated.

For example, a series transmission line and an open/short shunt stub in microstrip schematic is shown in Figure 15.26.

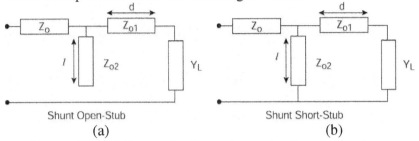

Shunt Open-Stub   Shunt Short-Stub
(a)   (b)

Figure 15.26 Microstrip-line schematics for a) shunt-open and b) shunt-short stubs.

The two solutions are shown on the smith chart in Figure 15.27 and are labeled as A1 and A2.

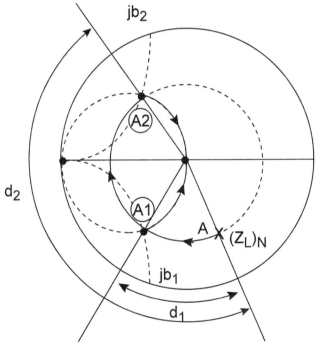

Figure 15.27 Smith chart solution.

The stub lengths can be calculated using a Smith chart as shown in Figure 15.28.

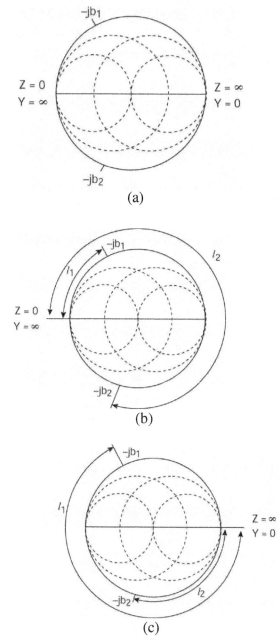

**Figure 15.28 Smith chart solutions for stub length, a) ZY chart,
b) short stub length, c) open stub length.**

15.7.1 Balanced Stubs vs. Unbalanced Single Stubs

To minimize the microstrip transition interaction and improve the input VSWR, many designers use a balanced approach for shunt stubs rather than a single stub.

Using the balanced shunt stubs technique, two stubs of the same length (as the single stub) but twice the characteristic impedance are placed in parallel. That is,

$$\ell_2'=\ell_2 \tag{15.15a}$$

$$Z_{O2}'=2Z_{O2} \tag{15.15b}$$

The reason we use twice the characteristic impedance for each open shunt stub is due to the fact that each half of the balanced stub (Y_{stub}) must provide half the total admittance (Y_{tot}), i.e.,

$$Y_{stub}= jY_{O2}' \tan\beta\ell_2'= \frac{1}{2} Y_{tot} \tag{15.16a}$$

Where

$$Y_{tot}=j\, Y_{O2}\, \tan\beta\ell_2 \tag{15.16b}$$

Thus substituting Equation (15.14) in (15.13), we have:

$$Y_{O2}'\, \tan\beta\ell_2'=\frac{1}{2}\, Y_{O2}\, \tan\beta\ell_2 \tag{15.16c}$$

Choosing $\ell_2'=\ell_2$ yields:

$$Y_{O2}'=\frac{1}{2} Y_{O2} \tag{15.16d}$$

Or,

$$Z_{O2}'=2Z_{O2} \tag{15.16e}$$

A similar discussion applies to a short shunt stub with the similar conclusions.

Example 15.4

Give an example of application of open single stubs and double stubs in active networks. Discuss the conversion of a single into double stubs with proper length and characteristic impedance relationships for two cases: a) same Z_o, and b) different Z_o.

Solution:

A practical example is shown in Figure 15.29.

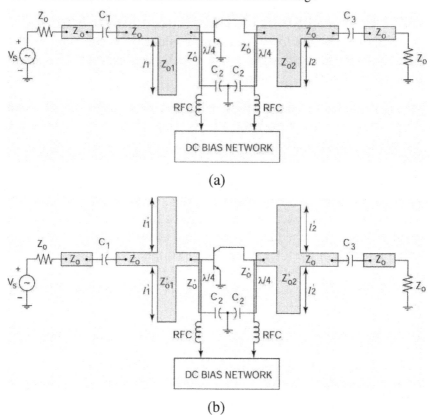

(a)

(b)

Figure 15.29 a) single stubs, and b) corresponding double-stubs conversion.

We will now summarize the two possible cases for the design of balanced shunt stubs:

a) Case I - Same characteristic impedances

$Z'_{o1} = Z_{o1} = Z_o$

$Z'_{o2} = Z_{o2} = Z_o$

To obtain the stub lengths l'_1 and l'_2, we utilize the smith chart and read off the length values for $(Y_{stub})_{bal}$ such that:

$(Y_{stub})_{bal} = (Y_{stub})_{unbal}/2$

$(Y_{stub})_{unbal}$ is the single stub admittance value, whereas $(Y_{stub})_{bal}$ refers to one of the double stub admittance values.

b) Case II - Different characteristic impedances

$l'_1 = l_1,$ $\qquad l'_2 = l_2$

$Z'_{o1} = 2Z_{o1},$ $\qquad Z'_{o2} = 2Z_{o2}$

CHAPTER-15 PROBLEMS

15.1) Design a single stub matching circuit (see Figure P15.1) that transforms a load (Z_L=30+j50 Ω) to a transmission line as follows (use a 100 Ω system) :

a) Assume $Z_{O1}=Z_{O2}$=100 Ω.

b) Assume Z_{O1}=100 Ω and Z_{O2}=200 Ω

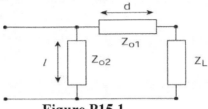

Figure P15.1

15.2) Using TLs, design the matching network shown in Figure P15.2 to match the load, Z_L=100-j100 Ω to a 50 Ω transmission line. Assume Z_{o1}=75 Ω and f= 15 GHz.

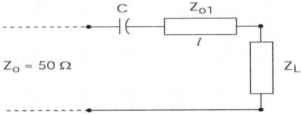

Figure P15.2

15.3) Design a Distributed element matching network to transform a load impedance (Z_L=75+j75Ω) to the input impedance (Z_{in}=50-j50 Ω) at 10 GHz as shown in Figure P15.3.

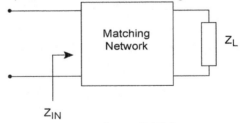

Figure P15.3

15.4) Design a matching network that will match a 50 Ω load to an input reflection coefficient of Γ_{in}=0.5∠150° in a 50 Ω system as shown in Figure P15.5. The matching network should use a quarter-wave transformer.

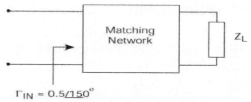

$\Gamma_{IN} = 0.5 \underline{/150^\circ}$

Figure P15.4

15.5) In the circuit shown below, a load $Z_L=90+j60$ Ω is to be matched to a 30 Ω line as shown in Figure P16.6. If Z_1 represents a stub of length "l" having a 50 Ω characteristic impedance, Determine d, Z_{O1} and l.

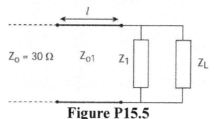

Figure P15.5

15.6) A certain microwave device has $Z_d=100-j100$ Ω as shown below. Design a matching network to match the device impedance to a 75 Ω system using distributed elements.

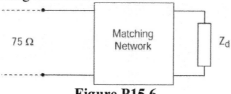

Figure P15.6

15.7) A lossless transmission line ($Z_O=50$ Ω) is to be matched to a load, $Z_L=5.5-j10.5$, by means of a short circuited stub($Z_{O1}=100$ Ω) as shown in Figure P11.8. Determine the position and length of the stub.

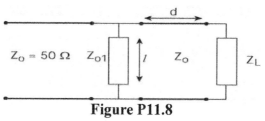

Figure P11.8

CHAPTER 16

Quasi-TEM Transmission Lines

16.1 INTRODUCTION

Amongst all planar transmission lines, microstrip line has gained much popularity and importance in microwave planar circuit technology, and thus will be considered and analyzed in this section.

16.2 MICROSTRIP LINE

A microstrip line is a transmission line consisting of a strip of conductor of thickness (t), width (w) and a ground plane separated by a dielectric medium of thickness (h) as shown in Figure 16.1.

Since it is an open conduit for wave transmission, not all of the electric or magnetic fields will be confined in the structure. This fact along with the existence of a small axial E-field, leads to a not-purely TEM wave propagation, but a quasi-TEM mode of propagation.

These types of transmission lines are very popular and are used extensively in microwave planar circuit design and microwave integrated circuit (MIC) technology. Use of printed circuit board technology and its simplicity of fabrication, along with ease of placement and interconnection of lumped elements and components has made this type of transmission line very popular and much superior to other types of planar transmission lines

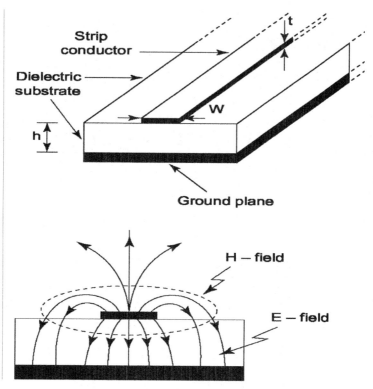

Figure 16.1 Microstrip line, a) geometry, and b) E and H fields plot.

16.3 WAVE PROPAGATION IN MICROSTRIP LINES

The dielectrics used in the fabrication of the Microstrip line are characterized by a dielectric constant (ε_r) defined by:

$$\varepsilon_r = \varepsilon/\varepsilon_o, \tag{16.1}$$

$$\varepsilon_o = 8.854 \times 10^{-12} \text{ F/m}$$

where ε and ε_o are the dielectric's and vacuum's permittivity, respectively. Some of the most popular dielectrics are: Duroid (three values: $\varepsilon_r = 2.23$, 6, 10.5), alumina ($\varepsilon_r = 9.5$-10), Quartz ($\varepsilon_r = 3.7$), silicon ($\varepsilon_r = 11.9$), etc.

The EM-wave propagation in a microstrip line is approximately non-dispersive below a cut-off frequency (f_o), which is given by:

$$f_o \text{(GHz)} = 0.3 \sqrt{\frac{Z_O}{h\sqrt{\varepsilon_r - 1}}} \qquad (16.2)$$

Where h is in centimeters.

The phase velocity for a quasi-TEM is given by:

$V_P = c/\sqrt{\varepsilon_{ff}}$

Where c is the speed of light and ε_{ff} is the effective relative dielectric constant.

Since the field lines are not contained in the structure and some exist in the air (see Figure 16.1), the effective dielectric constant satisfies the following relation:

$1 < \varepsilon_{ff} < \varepsilon_r$

In general, the effective dielectric constant (ε_{ff}) is a function of not only the substrate material (ε_r) but also of the dielectric thickness (h) and conductor width (W).

The characteristic impedance (Z_o) is given by:

$$Z_O = \frac{1}{V_P C_O} \qquad (16.3)$$

Where C_o is the capacitance per unit length.

The wavelength (λ) of a propagating wave in the microstrip line is given by:

$\lambda = V_P/f = \lambda_o/\sqrt{\varepsilon_{ff}}$ \qquad (16.4)

where $\lambda_o = c/f$ is the wavelength in free space.

NOTE: *The wavelength of a TEM wave (λ_{TEM}) propagating in the dielectric material is different than the wavelength (λ_o) of a propagating wave in free space as follows:*

$\lambda_{TEM} = \lambda_o/\sqrt{\varepsilon_r}$ \qquad (16.5)

As can be seen from these equations the characteristic impedance (Z_o) and the wavelength (λ) both are functions of the geometry (w, h) of the microstrip line. This variation is shown in Figures 16.2 and 16.3.

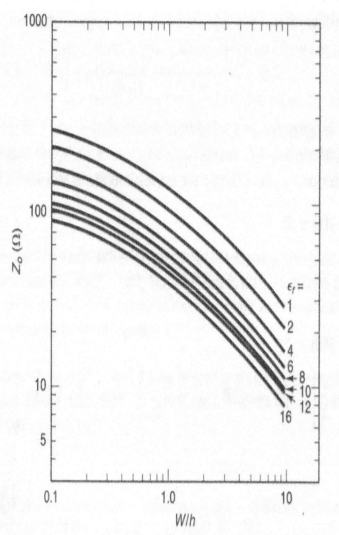

Figure 16.2 Plots of Z_o vs. W/h with ε_r as a parameter.

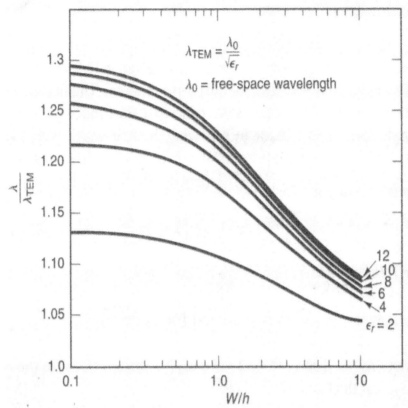

Figure 16.3 Plots of Normalized wavelengths vs. W/h with ε_r as a parameter.

16.4 EMPIRICAL FORMULAS

The essential empirical formulas for a microstrip line can be categorized as follows (assuming zero or negligible thickness of the strip of metal on top of the dielectric, i.e., t/h<0.005):

16.4.1 ε_{ff} Formula

The effective dielectric constant (ε_{ff}) is given by [assuming that the dimensions of the microstrip line (W, h) are known]:

For W/h ≤ 1:

$$\varepsilon_{ff} = \frac{\varepsilon_r + 1}{2} + \frac{\varepsilon_r - 1}{2}\left[\left(1 + 12\frac{h}{W}\right)^{-1/2} + 0.04\left(1 - \frac{W}{h}\right)^2\right], \quad (16.6)$$

For W/h ≥ 1:

$$\varepsilon_{ff} = \frac{\varepsilon_r + 1}{2} + \frac{\varepsilon_r - 1}{2}\left(1 + 12\frac{h}{W}\right)^{-1/2} \quad (16.7)$$

The effective dielectric constant (ε_{ff}) can be thought of as the dielectric constant of a homogeneous medium that would fill the entire space, replacing air and dielectric regions.

16.4.2 Z_0 FORMULA

The Characteristic impedance is given by [assuming that the dimensions of the microstrip line (W, h) are given or known]:

For W/h ≤ 1:

$$Z_0 = \frac{60}{\sqrt{\varepsilon_{ff}}}\ln\left(\frac{8h}{W} + \frac{W}{4h}\right) \quad (16.8)$$

For W/h ≥ 1:

$$Z_0 = \frac{120\pi}{\sqrt{\varepsilon_{ff}}\left[W/h + 1.393 + 0.667\ln(W/h + 1.444)\right]} \quad (16.9)$$

16.4.3   W/h Formula

Assuming (ε_{ff}) and Z_0 are given, then the microstrip dimensions (W/h) can be found as follows (a design problem):

For W/h ≤ 2:

$$\frac{W}{h} = \frac{8e^A}{e^{2A} - 2} \quad (16.10)$$

For W/h ≥ 2:

$$\frac{W}{h} = \frac{2}{\pi}\left[B - 1 - \ln(2B - 1) + \frac{\varepsilon_r - 1}{2\varepsilon_r}\left\{\ln(B - 1) + 0.39 - \frac{0.61}{\varepsilon_r}\right\}\right]$$

(16.11)

Where

$$A = \frac{Z_0}{60}\sqrt{\frac{\varepsilon_r + 1}{2}} + \frac{\varepsilon_r - 1}{\varepsilon_r + 1}\left(0.23 + \frac{0.11}{\varepsilon_r}\right)$$

(16.12)

and

$$B = \frac{377\pi}{2Z_0\sqrt{\varepsilon_r}}$$

(16.13)

16.4.4 λ Formula

The wavelength in the microstrip line (λ) is given by:
For W/h < 0.6:

$$\lambda = \frac{\lambda_0}{\sqrt{\varepsilon_r}}\left[\frac{\varepsilon_r}{1 + 0.6(\varepsilon_r - 1)(W/h)^{0.0297}}\right]^{1/2}$$

(16.14)

For W/h ≥ 0.6:

$$\lambda = \frac{\lambda_0}{\sqrt{\varepsilon_r}}\left[\frac{\varepsilon_r}{1 + 0.63(\varepsilon_r - 1)(W/h)^{0.1255}}\right]^{1/2}$$

(16.15)

16.4.5 α Formulas (Attenuation Factors)

Another characteristic of the microstrip line is its attenuation when signals travel on it. There are two types of losses in a microstrip line:
◆ Dielectric substrate loss due to dielectric conductivity
◆ Conductor Ohmic loss due to skin effect

The loss factor (α) can be found by noting that the power carried along a transmission line in (+x direction) in a quasi-TEM mode can be written as:

$$P^+(x) = \frac{1}{2}\left[V^+(x)I^+(x)^*\right] = \frac{\left[V^+(x)\right]^2}{Z_O} \tag{16.16}$$

Where

$$V^+(x) = |V^+|e^{-\alpha x}\,e^{-j\beta x} \tag{16.17}$$

Thus we have:

$$P^+(x) = \frac{|V^+|^2}{2Z_O}e^{-2\alpha x}e^{-j2\beta x} = |P^+|e^{-j2\beta x} \tag{16.18}$$

Where

$$|P^+| = \frac{|V^+|^2}{2Z_O}e^{-2\alpha x}$$

and α is the total attenuation factor which is composed of two components:

$$\alpha = \alpha_d + \alpha_c \tag{16.19}$$

where

α_d = Dielectric loss factor, and

α_c = Conductor loss factor

These two loss factors are discussed next:

16.4.6 α_d Formula

Attenuation Due to Dielectric Loss

Attenuation due to dielectric loss identified by "dielectric loss factor (α_d)" using the quasi-TEM mode of propagation, is given by:

a. For Low-loss Dielectrics

$$\alpha_d = 27.3\frac{\tan\delta}{\lambda_0}\left(\frac{\varepsilon_r}{\varepsilon_r - 1}\right)\left(\frac{\varepsilon_{ff} - 1}{\sqrt{\varepsilon_{ff}}}\right) \quad \text{(dB/cm)} \tag{16.20}$$

Where ($\tan\delta$) is the loss tangent given by:

$$\tan\delta = \frac{\sigma}{\omega\varepsilon} \tag{16.21}$$

b. For high-loss Dielectrics

$$\alpha_d = 4.34\sigma \left(\frac{\mu_o}{\varepsilon_o}\right)^{1/2}\left(\frac{1}{\varepsilon_r - 1}\right)\left(\frac{\varepsilon_{ff} - 1}{\sqrt{\varepsilon_{ff}}}\right) \quad \text{(dB/cm)} \qquad (16.22)$$

Where σ is the conductivity of the dielectric and $\mu_o = 4\pi \times 10^{-7}$ (H/m) is the permittivity of the free space.

16.4.7 α_c Formula
Attenuation Due to Conductor Loss
Attenuation due to dielectric loss identified by "conductor loss factor (α_c)" using the quasi-TEM mode of propagation (for W/h $\to\infty$), is given approximately by:

W/h $\to\infty$,

$$\alpha_c = \frac{R_S}{Z_0 W} \quad \text{(Np/m)} \qquad (16.23)$$

Where

$$R_S = \sqrt{\frac{\pi f \mu_o}{\sigma}} \qquad (16.24)$$

is the surface resistivity of the conductor. Usually conductor loss is more dominant than the dielectric loss in most microstrip lines, i.e.,

$$\alpha_c >> \alpha_d; \Rightarrow \alpha = \alpha_c + \alpha_d \approx \alpha_c$$

However, there are some cases (such as in silicon substrates) where the dielectric loss factor (α_d) is of the same order or larger than the conductor loss Factor (α_c).

EXAMPLE 16.1
A 50 Ω microstrip transmission line needs to be designed using a sheet of Epsilam-10® ($\varepsilon_r = 10$) with h=1.02 mm. Determine W, λ and ε_{ff} by:
a. An exact method
b. An approximate method

Solution:

a. Exact method

We will design a microstrip line with W/h≤2:

$$\frac{W}{h} = \frac{8e^A}{e^{2A} - 2}$$

Where

$$A = \frac{Z_0}{60}\sqrt{\frac{\varepsilon_r + 1}{2}} + \frac{\varepsilon_r - 1}{\varepsilon_r + 1}\left(0.23 + \frac{0.11}{\varepsilon_r}\right) = \frac{50}{60}\sqrt{\frac{10+1}{2}} + \frac{10-1}{10+1}\left(0.23 + \frac{0.11}{10}\right)$$

$$\Rightarrow A = 2.152$$

Thus (W/h) is obtained to be:

$$\frac{W}{h} = 0.96$$

and

W=1.02x0.96=0.98 mm

Since W/h>0.6, we find λ and ε_{ff} as follows:

$$\lambda = \frac{\lambda_0}{\sqrt{\varepsilon_r}}\left[\frac{\varepsilon_r}{1 + 0.63(\varepsilon_r - 1)(W/h)^{0.1255}}\right]^{1/2} = \frac{\lambda_0}{\sqrt{10}}\left[\frac{\varepsilon_r}{1 + 0.63(10-1)(0.96)^{0.1255}}\right]^{1/2}$$

$$\Rightarrow \lambda = 0.39\lambda_0$$

and

$$\lambda = 0.39\lambda_0 = \lambda_0/\sqrt{\varepsilon_{ff}}$$

$$\Rightarrow \varepsilon_{ff} = (1/0.39)^2 = 6.6$$

b. Approximate method

Using Figure 16.2, we obtain W/h for Z_0=50 Ω to be:

Z_0=50 $\Rightarrow$ W/h≈1 $\Rightarrow$ W=h=1.02 mm

From Figure 16.3 for W/h=1, we obtain:

λ/λ_{TEM}=1.23

From (16.5) we have;

$\lambda_{TEM} = \lambda_0/\sqrt{\varepsilon_r} = \lambda_0/\sqrt{10} = 0.316\lambda_0$

Thus λ is found to be:

$\lambda=1.23x0.316\lambda_o=0.39\lambda_o$
$\lambda=\lambda_o/\sqrt{\varepsilon_{ff}}$ $\Rightarrow \varepsilon_{ff}=(\lambda_o/\lambda)^2$
$\varepsilon_{ff}=(1/0.39)^2=6.6$

EXAMPLE 16.2

Design a 50 Ω transmission line that provides 90° phase shift at 2.5 GHz. Assume h=1.27 mm and $\varepsilon_r=2.2$.

Solution:
To find "W", we assume that W/h≥2 and will verify this assumption later. Thus we have:

$$B = \frac{377\pi}{2Z_0\sqrt{\varepsilon_r}}$$

B=7.985,
And

$$\frac{W}{h} = \frac{2}{\pi}\left[B-1-\ln(2B-1)+\frac{\varepsilon_r-1}{2\varepsilon_r}\left\{\ln(B-1)+0.39-\frac{0.61}{\varepsilon_r}\right\}\right]$$

Yielding:
W/h=3.08 $\Rightarrow$ W=3.08x1.27 =3.91 mm

The value of W/h=3.08 is obviously greater than 2, which justifies our earlier assumption.

So far we have found the width of the line, now we need to know the length of the line. Using the given phase shift of 90° yields:
$\phi=\beta\ell=\omega\ell/V_p=2\pi f\ell/(c/\sqrt{\varepsilon_{ff}})=2\pi f\ell\sqrt{\varepsilon_{ff}}/c=90°=\pi/2$
$\Rightarrow \ell=c/(4f\sqrt{\varepsilon_{ff}})$

From the above equation we can see that in order to find ℓ, we need to find ε_{ff}. Using microstrip Equations, we obtain:
For W/h ≥ 1:

$$\varepsilon_{ff} = \frac{\varepsilon_r+1}{2}+\frac{\varepsilon_r-1}{2}\left(1+12\frac{h}{W}\right)^{-1/2}$$

$\varepsilon_{ff}=1.87$

Thus the length of the transmission line is given by:
$\ell = 3 \times 10^8 / (4 \times 2.5 \times 10^9 \times \sqrt{1.87}) = 0.0219$ m $= 2.19$ cm

---

Chapter 16- Symbol List

A symbol will not be repeated again, once it has been identified and defined in an earlier chapter, with its definition remaining unchanged.

C_0 - Capacitance per unit length

EM – Electro-Magnetic

k – Arbitrary constant

TEM – Transverse Electro-Magnetic

TL – Transmission Line

v – Velocity of motion

V_P - Phase velocity

V^+ - Incident voltage

V^- - Reflected voltage

Z_0 – Characteristic Impedance

Z_{OC} - Open circuit impedance

Z_{SC} - Short circuit impedance

$Z_{\lambda/4}$ - Impedance at the location $\lambda/4$.

β - Phase constant

Γ - Reflection coefficient

Γ_L - Reflection coefficient at the load

$\Gamma(x)$ - Reflection coefficient at location x

ε – Dielectric permittivity

ε_{ff} – Effective relative dielectric constant

ε_o – Permittivity of vacuum (8.85×10^{-12} F/m)

ε_r – Dielectric constant of a material

γ - Propagation constant

λ_o - Wavelength in free space

ω - Angular frequency ($\omega = \beta v$)

CHAPTER -16 PROBLEMS

16.1) A microstrip line has width of 1 mm over a dielectric (ε_r=6.25) which has a thickness of 1 cm. Determine ε_{ff}, β, and Z_o at f= 8 GHz.

16.2) Design a $\lambda/4$ microstrip line (50 Ω) at f= 10 GHz, using a dielectric (ε_r=16) with a thickness of 0.5 mm. Draw the final diagram for the layout with accurate scale for dimensions.

16.3) Design a single stub matching circuit (see Figure P16.3) that transforms a load (Z_L=100+j100 Ω) to a 50 Ω feed transmission line operating at f=10 GHz, with Z_{O1}=100 Ω and Z_{O2}=200 Ω. Now using the values of "d" and "ℓ" as obtained above, build the circuit shown in Figure P16.3 utilizing microstrip line technology, with a dielectric material (ε_r=10) which has a thickness of 2 mm. Draw the final diagram for the layout with accurate scale for dimensions.

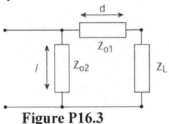

Figure P16.3

16.4) **16.4)** Design the matching network shown in Figure P16.4 to match the load, Z_L=80+j80 Ω to a 50 Ω transmission line operating at f=20 GHz. Now using the values of "Z_{o1}" and "ℓ" from the design, build the circuit utilizing microstrip line technology, with a dielectric material which has a thickness of 1 mm and ε_r=16. Draw the final diagram for the layout with accurate scale for dimensions.

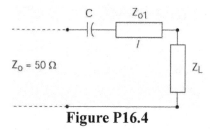

Figure P16.4

16.5) **16.5)** A lossless transmission line (Z_O=50 Ω) is to be matched to a load, Z_L=5.5-j10.5, by means of a short circuited stub (Z_{O1}=75 Ω) as shown in Figure P16.5. Determine the position and length of the stub. Build the circuit utilizing microstrip line technology, with a dielectric material which has a thickness of 5 mm and ε_r=8. Draw the final diagram for the layout with accurate scale for dimensions.

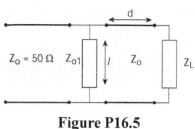

Figure P16.5

16.6) Determine the size reduction that is obtained for the longitudinal and transverse dimensions of problem 16.2 when the dielectric is replaced with a substrate having ε_r=2.

16.7) Design a $7\lambda/8$ microstrip line (100 Ω) at f= 50 GHz, using a dielectric (ε_r=10) with a thickness of 0.5 cm. What is the phase and time delay for a signal entering at one end and emerging at the other? Draw the final diagram for the layout with accurate scale for dimensions.

CHAPTER 17

Transients in Lossless Lines

17.1 INTRODUCTION

As noted in earlier chapters, use of phasors is helpful in solving many practical cases which involve either one sine wave or a summation of many sinusoidal waves obtained as a result of Fourier Analysis of a complex periodic wave. Each sine wave can be analyzed by our analysis techniques amply covered in earlier chapters.

When a lossless transmission line (TL) is operated in switching or pulsed applications, the voltage is suddenly changed in extremely short periods of time, either suddenly up or down. These sudden changes in voltage are called transients and are either man-made (such as sudden changes in loading, occurrence of shorts in a line causing large currents which leads to electromagnetic interference or EMI, etc.), or made by nature (such as lightning strokes, Sun's electrical storms, etc.).

Transients on transmission lines in the form of pulses become important as they travel down the line and reflect back from the load. Such a pulsed condition of operation is often encountered in modern digital computers, internally as well as externally, in many of the connecting lines. The analysis of transients has become increasingly more and more important as the speed of computers are increased on a relentless basis by the manufacturers of such and other digital devices (such as cell phones, satellite TV, etc.)

17.2 GRAPHICAL ANALYSIS

In the analysis of such a condition of operation, we generally have to recourse to the time domain analysis and leave behind the phasor domain, which is extremely useful for sinusoidal waves at steady state.

In the special case of a lossless line, a simple graphical technique could be employed with tremendous benefit. This is a book keeping technique which helps us visualize the incident and reflection of signals at either end of the transmission line.

17.3 A SPECIAL CASE: TRANSIENT DC CASE

If we restrict our analysis strictly to transient DC cases, we will simplify our work greatly. In this special case we will assume that a DC voltage is suddenly applied to a lossless line with a characteristic impedance Z_0 as shown in Figure 17.1.

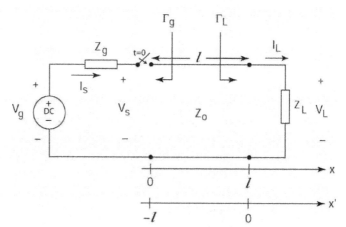

Figure 17.1: TL transient circuit diagram

In this special case, all impedances become simple resistances and we need to replace Z_g with R_g and Z_L with R_L in all of the subsequent equations. However, to be consistent and maintain uniformity, we will retain Z_o as the characteristic impedance of the transmission line.

From this Figure, we see that when the switch is closed at t=0, a DC voltage pulse is applied to the transmission line at the source end, which causes a current to flow in the line. The voltage and current pulses travel on the line at the speed of speed of phase velocity given by:

$V_P = 1/\sqrt{L/C}$

If the length of the line (ℓ) is known, then the voltage (or current) pulse will arrive at the load after a delay time (t_D) given by:

$T_D = \ell / V_P$

If the load is not matched to the line, the reflected wave will travel back to the source after a delay time of t_D. Now if the source is not matched at the load end, then there will be another voltage wave reflected back to the load and this whole process will repeat many times until the wave is reduced in magnitude to zero.

17.3.1 The Bounce Diagram

The bounce diagram is a "Graphical Analysis" technique, which greatly simplifies the analysis of transients on a line and provides a tremendous amount of clarity to the way transients affect any given load. In other words, the bounce diagram provides a pictorial tool showing clearly how waves reflect and combine at each end of the line.

To draw a bounce diagram for the incident and the reflection of voltage and current waves at each end of the TL, we need to prepare the stage properly. Therefore, before we start the diagram, we need to calculate and have ready for use the results of the following parameters:

a. $Z_o = \sqrt{L/C}$,   (A real positive number for lossless lines)

b. $\Gamma_g = \dfrac{R_g - Z_o}{R_g + Z_o}$ (Reflection coefficient at source end)

c. $\Gamma_L = \dfrac{R_L - Z_0}{R_L + Z_0}$ (Reflection coefficient at load end)

d. $V_P = 1/\sqrt{LC} = \omega/\beta = c/\sqrt{(\mu_r \varepsilon_r)}$ (Phase velocity or the speed of travel of waves)

Note: For air-filled TLs, $V_P = c = 1/\sqrt{(\mu_0 \varepsilon_0)} = 3 \times 10^8$ m/s

e. $T_D = \ell/V_P$ (Time of travel of waves from source to load)

f. $V_1^+ = V_g Z_0/(R_g + Z_0)$ (Incident voltage wave pulse-magnitude at source end traveling toward the load)
The final value, which is the summation of infinite number of reflections is designated as the sending end voltage (V_S) at $t = \infty$.

g. For current bounce diagram we use:
$\Gamma_i = -\Gamma_v$

h. At $t = \infty$ when all of the transients have died out, we have a simple DC circuit with the transmission line shorted out, connecting source to load as shown below:

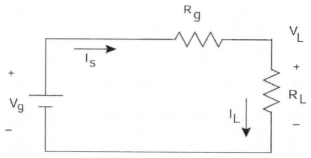

Figure 17.2 Final DC circuit at $t = \infty$

From this diagram we can see that:
$I_S(t = \infty) = V_g/(R_g + R_L)$
$V_L(t = \infty) = V_g R_L/(R_g + R_L)$
$I_L(t = \infty) = V_L/R_L = V_g/(R_g + R_L) = I_S(t = \infty)$

17.3.2 How To Draw The Bounce Diagram
In drawing the bounce diagram, we nee to heed the following points:

a. The horizontal axis represents position along the TL, while the vertical axis shows time.

b. The bounce diagram is a zigzag line clearly showing the progress of voltage or current waves as time elapses.

c. The reflection coefficient for the source (Γ_g) is shown on the left side, whereas the load reflection coefficient (Γ_L) is shown on the right side.

d. The first incident wave is V_1^+ or I_1^+ and starts at x=0 and t=0 and travels to the load.

e. The first reflected wave is $V_1^- = \Gamma_L V_1^+$ or $I_1^- = \Gamma_{Li} I_1^+$ and starts at x=ℓ and t=T_D and travels back to the source.

f. The amplitude of each new line segment is equal to the product of the preceding line segment and the reflection coefficient at that end.

g. Using the bounce diagram, the voltage or current plot as a function of time at any point (x = x_o) can be determined by drawing a dashed vertical line through point x_o and then adding the voltages or currents of all the zigzag segments intersected by the dashed line for different time values.

NOTE: *For current waves, the reflection coefficients are the negative values of the voltage reflection coefficients as shown below:*
$$\Gamma_i = \Gamma^-/\Gamma^+ = (-V^-/Zo)/(V^+/Zo) = -V^-/V^+ = -\Gamma_v$$
Therefore: $\Gamma_i = -\Gamma_v$

The following example will illuminate these concepts further.

Example 17.1
Assume an air-filled transmission line of length 1m with Z_o=50 Ω is connected to a 20 V DC source and an internal resistance of 150 Ω at one end, and to an open-circuit load at the other end as shown below:

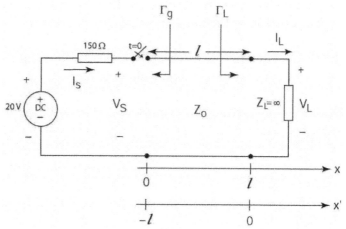

Figure 17.3 Plots of Z_o vs. W/h with ε_r as a parameter.

Part 1. Draw the bounce diagram for both voltage and current up to $4T_D$.
Part 2. Draw a table showing the equation and values of voltage and
        current waves at 0.5 TD time intervals
Part 3. Plot the voltage as a function of time at midpoint ($\ell/2$) on the TL.
Part 4. Plot the current as a function of time at source end.

Solution:
Following the steps delineated above we have:
a. $Z_o = 50\ \Omega$

b. $\Gamma_g = \dfrac{R_g - Z_o}{R_g + Z_o} = (150-100)/(150+100) = 1/2$

c. $\Gamma_L = \dfrac{R_L - Z_o}{R_L + Z_o} = (\infty-100)/(\infty+100) = 1$

d. For air-filled TLs, $V_P = c = 1/\sqrt{(\mu_o \varepsilon_o)} = 3 \times 10^8$ m/s

e. $T_D = \ell/c = 1/3 \times 10^8 = 3.3$ ns

f. $V_s = V_g Z_o/(R_g + Z_o) = 20 \times 50/(150+50) = 5$ V

g.   Knowing $\Gamma_i = -\Gamma_v$, we have:
     $(\Gamma_g)_i = -1/2$
     $(\Gamma_L)_i = -1$

h. $V_L(t=\infty)=V_gR_L/(R_g+R_L)=20$ V
     $I_L(t=\infty)=0$ A

Part 1. The voltage and current bounce diagrams, clearly showing successive reflections from both ends vs. time, are drawn in Figure 17.4 and 17.5.

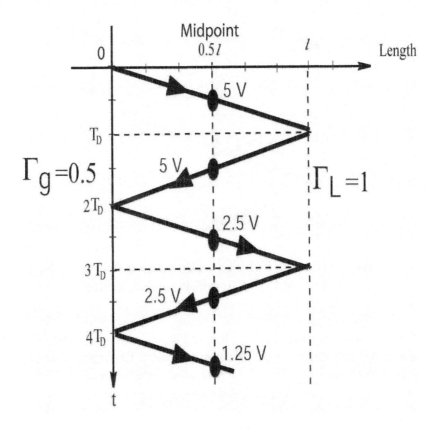

Figure 17.4 Voltage bounce diagram

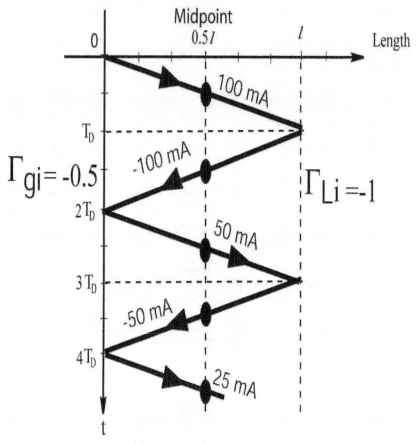

Figure 17.5 Current bounce diagram

Part 2. Now we draw a table showing the equation and values of voltage and current waves at 0.5TD time intervals. This table summarizes the equation for the cumulative incident and reflected voltage waves as time elapses and its value at the midpoint ($\ell/2$) on the TL.

The first voltage wave being launched on the TL is given by the voltage division rule:
$$V_1^+=V_gZ_o/(R_g+Z_o)=5 \text{ V}$$

t/T_D	Voltage Wave Eq. (Incident + Reflected)	Voltage Value at $\ell/2$	Γ_g or Γ_L
0	V_1^+	0 V	-
0.5	V_1^+	5 V	-
1.0	$V_1^+(1+\Gamma_L)$	5 V	1
1.5	$V_1^+(1+\Gamma_L)$	10	1
2.0	$V_1^+(1+\Gamma_L+\Gamma_g\Gamma_L)$	10 V	1/2
2.5	$V_1^+(1+\Gamma_L+\Gamma_g\Gamma_L)$	12.5 V	1/2
3.0	$V_1^+(1+\Gamma_L+\Gamma_g\Gamma_L+\Gamma_g\Gamma_L^2)$	12.5 V	1
3.5	$V_1^+(1+\Gamma_L+\Gamma_g\Gamma_L+\Gamma_g\Gamma_L^2)$	15 V	1
4.0	$V_1^+(1+\Gamma_L+\Gamma_g\Gamma_L+\Gamma_g\Gamma_L^2+\Gamma_g^2\Gamma_L^2)$	15 V	1/2
4.5	$V_1^+(1+\Gamma_L+\Gamma_g\Gamma_L+\Gamma_g\Gamma_L^2+\Gamma_g^2\Gamma_L^2)$	16.25 V	1/2

Table 17.1 Total voltage equation and values at midpoint on the TL

The final sending end voltage (at t=∞) is given by:
$$V_S= V_1^+(1+ \Gamma_L +\Gamma_g \Gamma_L+ \Gamma_g \Gamma_L^2 + \Gamma_g^2 \Gamma_L^2+....)= V_1^+(1+ \Gamma_L)(1 +\Gamma_g \Gamma_L+ \Gamma_g^2\Gamma_L^2 + \Gamma_g^3 \Gamma_L^3+....)$$

Let $\delta= \Gamma_g \Gamma_L$, so now we can write above as:
$$V_S= V_1^+ (1+ \Gamma_L)(1 + \delta + \delta^2 + \delta^3+....), \quad |\delta|<1$$

This geometric series converges to:
$$1 + \delta + \delta^2 + \delta^3+....=1/(1- \delta)$$

Thus V_S can be written as:
$$V_S= V_1^+ (1+ \Gamma_L)/(1- \Gamma_g \Gamma_L)= V_g R_L/(R_g+R_L)$$
This is the same equation obtained earlier.

For the current waves, we use the same concept as discussed above for the voltage waves, but we need to use the following values:
$$I_1^+= V_1^+/ Z_0 =V_g/(R_g+Z_0)=0.1 \text{ A} =100 \text{ mA}$$
$$(\Gamma_g)_i =- \Gamma_g =-1/2$$
$$(\Gamma_L)_i = -\Gamma_L =-1$$

The following table summarizes the incident and reflected current wave equations at $0.5T_D$ intervals and its values at the midpoint ($\ell/2$) on the TL as time elapses:

t/T_D	Current Wave Eq. (Incident + Reflected)	Current Value at $\ell/2$ (mA)	$(\Gamma_g)_i$ or $(\Gamma_L)_i$
0	I_1^+	0	-
0.5	I_1^+	100	-
1.0	$I_1^+(1+\Gamma_{Li})$	100	-1
1.5	$I_1^+(1+\Gamma_{Li})$	0.0	-1
2.0	$I_1^+(1+\Gamma_{Li}+\Gamma_{gi}\,\Gamma_{Li})$	0.0	-1/2
2.5	$I_1^+(1+\Gamma_{Li}+\Gamma_{gi}\,\Gamma_{Li})$	50	-1/2
3.0	$I_1^+(1+\Gamma_{Li}+\Gamma_{gi}\,\Gamma_{Li}+\Gamma_{gi}\,\Gamma_{Li}^2)$	50	-1
3.5	$I_1^+(1+\Gamma_{Li}+\Gamma_{gi}\,\Gamma_{Li}+\Gamma_{gi}\,\Gamma_{Li}^2)$	0	-1
4.0	$I_1^+(1+\Gamma_{Li}+\Gamma_{gi}\,\Gamma_{Li}+\Gamma_{gi}\,\Gamma_{Li}^2+\Gamma_{gi}^2\,\Gamma_{Li}^2)$	0	-1/2
4.5	$I_1^+(1+\Gamma_{Li}+\Gamma_{gi}\,\Gamma_{Li}+\Gamma_{gi}\,\Gamma_{Li}^2+\Gamma_{gi}^2\,\Gamma_{Li}^2)$	25	-1/2

Table 17.2 Total current equation and values at midpoint on the TL.

The final sending end current (at t=∞) is given by:
$$I_S= I_1^+(1+\Gamma_{Li}+\Gamma_{gi}\,\Gamma_{Li}+\Gamma_{gi}^2\,\Gamma_{Li}^2+....)= I_1^+(1+\Gamma_{Li})(1+\Gamma_{gi}\,\Gamma_{Li}+\Gamma_{gi}^2\,\Gamma_{Li}^2+\Gamma_{gi}^3\,\Gamma_{Li}^3+....)$$

Let $\delta' = \Gamma_{gi}\,\Gamma_{Li}$, so now we can write above as:
$$I_S= I_1^+ (1+\Gamma_L)(1 + \delta' + \delta'^2 + \delta'^3 +....), \quad |\delta'|<1$$

This geometric series converges to:
$$1 + \delta' + \delta'^2 + \delta'^3+....=1/(1-\delta')$$

Thus V_S can be written as:
$$I_S= I_1^+ (1+\Gamma_{Li})/(1-\Gamma_{gi}\,\Gamma_{Li})= V_g/(R_g+R_L)$$
This is the same equation obtained earlier.

Part 3: Using the bounce diagrams above, we can draw the voltage plot by adding all zigzag line segment values at $x_o=0.5\ell$. The result is plotted in Figure 17.6.

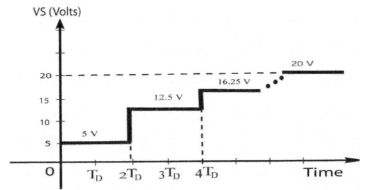

Figure 17.6   Voltage at midpoint as a function of time.

Part 4: Using the bounce diagrams above, we can draw the voltage plot by adding all zigzag line segment values at $x_o=0$. The result is plotted Figure 17.7.

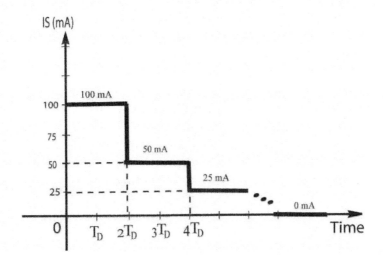

Figure 17.7   Current at source end as a function of time.

Exercise 17.1
Find the voltage at source end for example 17.1.

17.4 Voltage-Pulse Propagation
Digital signals, consisting of a series of high frequency pulses that propagate on transmission lines, are commonly encountered in modern computers and all digital chips, circuits and equipment. The signals in digital equipment due to their pulsed nature, can not be analyzed using the ZY smith chart techniques or standard transmission line methodology discussed in earlier chapters.

However, if we consider a single rectangular voltage pulse of period T, duration τ and amplitude V_o, it can be decomposed into two DC voltage step function waves, with one delayed by the pulse duration, where both are propagating on the TL .

Therefore, the previous transient analysis used to analyze a single step function has a direct application here and we can devise a procedure to obtain the output response when the input is a rectangular pulse. The procedure to obtain the final output response can be summarized as follows:

1. $V_1(t)$--DC wave #1: is a DC wave with an amplitude $+V_o$ propagating at t=0 (i.e., a step function of amplitude $+V_o$) ,

2. $V_2(t)$--DC wave #2: is a DC wave with opposite amplitude of $-V_o$, which is delayed by τ seconds, that is to say, it starts propagating at $t=\tau$ (i.e., a step function of amplitude $-V_o$ starting at t= τ).

In summary,
$$V(t)=V_1(t)+V_2(t), \tag{17.1}$$
Where
$$V_1(t)=V_o\, u(t), \tag{17.2}$$
$$V_2(t)= -V_o\, u(t-\tau), \tag{17.3}$$

and u(t) is a unit step function given by:
u(t)=1 for t>0,   (17.4a)
u(t)=0 for t<0.   (17.4b)

NOTE: *Adding the DC waves #1 and #2 gives the original pulse on the line.*

3. The bounce diagrams for each of the two DC waves are now drawn accurately in the same plot. The two bounce diagrams are identical, and are drawn parallel to each other due to the fact that one is being displaced by τ but with an opposite voltage value.

4. The total response of the TL to the pulse is obtained by using the superposition theorem since the TL is a linear system. The response of the two waves at any point on the line is obtained by adding the two bounce diagrams to obtain the final desired response.

Therefore we can see that the decomposition of a pulse in terms of two DC voltage waves allows us to analyze the transient behavior of any pulse of any duration by using the superposition of two DC waves delayed by the pulse duration.

Example 17.2
Assume an air-filled transmission line of length 1m with $Z_o=50$ Ω is excited by a pulse generator with an internal resistance of Rs=150 Ω, sending a 20 V pulse of duration $T_D/2$ that starts at t=0. The TL is connected to an open-circuit load at the other end as shown below. Find the waveform of the voltage response at the source end.

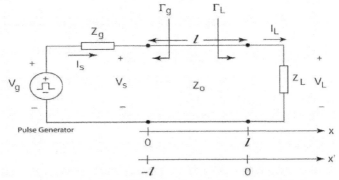

Figure 17.8   TL circuit for Example 17.2.

Solution:

Following the steps delineated earlier, we have:

a. $Z_o = 50 \ \Omega$

b. $\Gamma_g = \dfrac{R_g - Z_O}{R_g + Z_O} = (150-100)/(150+100)=1/2$

c. $\Gamma_L = \dfrac{R_L - Z_O}{R_L + Z_O} = (\infty-100)/(\infty+100)= 1$

d. For air-filled TLs, $V_P = c = 1/\sqrt{(\mu_o \varepsilon_o)} = 3 \times 10^8$ m/s

e. $T_D = \ell / c = 1/3 \times 10^8 = 3.3$ ns

f. $V_s = V_g Z_o/(R_g+Z_o)=20 \times 50/(150+50)=5$ V Pulse

The generator pulse is shown below:

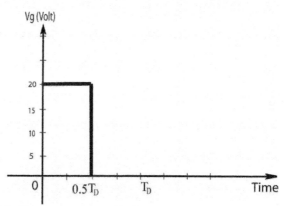

Figure 17.9 The generator Pulse.

g. $V_1(t)$-DC wave #1: is a DC wave with an amplitude +5 V propagating at t=0 (heavy line on the bounce diagram.)

h. $V_2(t)$-DC wave #2: is a DC wave with an opposite amplitude (-5V), which is delayed by $\tau = T_D/2$ seconds, that is to say, it starts propagating at t= $T_D/2$ (thin line on the bounce diagram.)

Therefore the sending pulse can be written as:
V(t)= 5 u(t) -5 u(t- T$_D$/2),

i. The bounce diagrams for each of the two DC waves are now drawn accurately in the same plot. The two bounce diagrams are identical, and are drawn parallel to each other due to the fact that one is being displaced by T$_D$/2 but with an opposite voltage value.

Following the results from Example 17.1, we draw the bounce diagram as shown below:

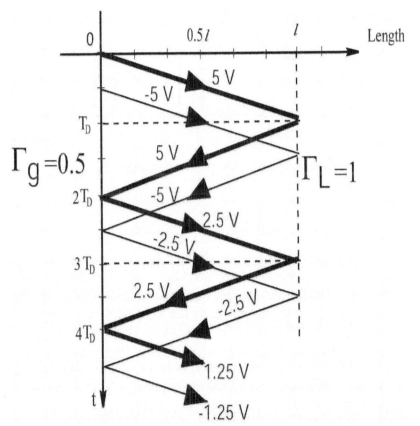

Figure 17.10 The two bounce diagrams combined. The thicker line is the first step function and the lighter line is the second step function.

j. The total response of the TL to the pulse is obtained by using the superposition theorem . The response of the two waves at the source end is obtained by adding the two bounce diagrams as they approach and reflect from the source end. The result is shown below:

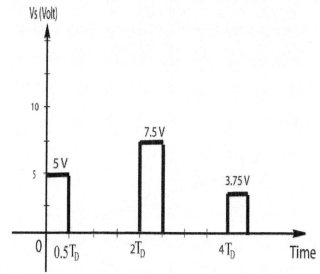

Figure 17.11 Voltage waveform at source end.

CHAPTER -17 PROBLEMS

17.1) A 50 Ω transmission line with a length of 60 m and a phase velocity of 2×10^8 m/s is terminated in a short load. The line is connected at t=0 to a 30 V DC source having an internal resistance of 25 Ω. Plot the sending-end voltage and current up to the time when the voltage drops below 0.15 V.

17.2) A 90 Ω line with a length of 130 m and ε_r=2.8 is connected at t=0 to a 75 V DC source with an internal resistance of 100 Ω. It is terminated in an open-circuit load. Plot the voltage and current waves up to $5T_D$ at the sending end of the line. What are the final values at the load?

17.3) A pulse generator with an internal resistance of 150 Ω produces a 10 V pulse with a duration of 20 μs at a frequency of 250 Hz. It is connected to a 50 Ω lossless TL which has T_D=200 μs and terminated in a 100 Ω load. Plot the voltage and current waves at the sending end from t=0 to 1.5 ms.

17.4) A 225 V DC source with an internal resistance of 150 Ω is connected to a 50 Ω load via a 75 Ω lossless TL. a) Plot the voltage waves as a function of time at the sending and receiving end up to $5T_D$, b) Draw the bounce diagram, and c) Calculate the final values of voltage and current at the load.

17.5) A 100 Ω transmission line is terminated in a 300 Ω load. The line is connected at t=0 to a 150 V DC source having an internal resistance of 50 Ω.
a) Plot the sending-end and receiving-end voltages and currents up to $4T_D$.
b) What are the final values for the voltages and currents at both ends of the line.

17.6) A 75 Ω line is connected at t=0 to a 225 V DC source with an internal resistance of 50 Ω. It is terminated in a 200 Ω load.
a) Plot the voltage waves up to $6T_D$ at both ends of the line.
b) Plot the current and voltage midway on the transmission line up to $6T_D$ and determine their final values.

17.7) A 225 V DC pulse generator with an internal resistance of 150 Ω sends a pulse with a duration of $T_D/4$ into a 50 Ω load via a 75 Ω lossless TL. a) Draw the combined bounce diagram, and b) Plot the voltage waveform as a function of time at the sending end, midpoint and receiving end up to $6T_D$.

PART IV

APPENDICES

APPENDIX A

Physical Constants

Quantity	Symbol	Value
Angstrom unit	A^o	$1\ A° = 10^{-4}\ \mu m = 10^{-10}\ m$
Avogadro constant	N_{AVO}	$6.02204 \times 10^{23}\ mol^{-1}$
Boltzmann constant	k	$1.38066 \times 10^{-23}\ J/K$
Charge of electron	q_e	$1.60218 \times 10^{-19}\ C$
Electron charge/mass ratio	q_e/m_e	$1.75880 \times 10^{11}\ C/kg$
Electron rest mass	m_e	$9.1095 \times 10^{-31}\ kg$
Electron volt	eV	$1\ eV = 1.60218 \times 10^{-19}\ J$
Intrinsic impedance (vacuum)	η_0	$120\pi = 377\ \Omega$
Neutron rest mass	m_n	$1.67495 \times 10^{-27}\ kg$
Permeability (vacuum)	$\mu_o\ (=1/\varepsilon_o c^2)$	$4\pi \times 10^{-7} = 1.25663 \times 10^{-6}\ H/m$
Permittivity (vacuum)	$\varepsilon_0\ (=1/\mu_o c^2)$	$8.85418 \times 10^{-12}\ F/m$
Planck constant	h	$6.62617 \times 10^{-34}\ J\text{-}s$
Proton rest mass	M_p	$1.67264 \times 10^{-27}\ kg$
Speed of light (vacuum)	c	$2.99792 \times 10^8\ m/s$
Thermal voltage (at $293°$ K)	$V_T = kT/q$	$0.0252\ V \approx 25\ mV$

APPENDIX B

International System of Units (SI)

QUANTITY	UNIT	SYMBOL	DIMENSION	TYPE
CAPACITANCE	FARAD	F	C/V	Derived unit
CHARGE	COULOMB	C	A-s	Derived unit
CONDUCTANCE	SIEMENS	S	A/V	Derived unit
CURRENT	AMPERE	A	Basic dimension	Base unit
ENERGY	JOULE	J	N-m	Derived unit
FORCE	NEWTON	N	$Kg\text{-}m/s^2$	Derived unit
FREQUENCY	HERTZ	Hz	1/s	Derived unit
INDUCTANCE	HENRY	H	Wb/A	Derived unit
LENGTH	METER	m	Basic dimension	Base unit
MAGNETIC FLUX	WEBER	Wb	V-s	Derived unit
MAGNETIC INDUCTION	TESLA	T	Wb/m^2	Derived unit
MASS	KILOGRAM	kg	Basic dimension	Base unit
POTENTIAL	VOLT	V	J/C	Derived unit
POWER	WATT	W	J/s	Derived unit
PRESSURE	PASCAL	Pa	N/m^2	Derived unit
RESISTANCE	OHM	Ω	V/A	Derived unit
TEMPERATURE	KELVIN	K	Basic dimension	Base unit
TIME	SECOND	s	Basic dimension	Base unit

APPENDIX C

Unit Prefixes

MULTIPLE	PREFIX	SYMBOL
10^{18}	exa-	E
10^{15}	peta-	P
10^{12}	tera-	T
10^{9}	giga-	G
10^{6}	mega-	M
10^{3}	kilo-	k
10^{2}	hecta-	h
10	deka	da
10^{-1}	deci-	d
10^{-2}	centi-	c
10^{-3}	milli-	m
10^{-6}	micro-	μ
10^{-9}	nano-	n
10^{-12}	pico-	p
10^{-15}	femto-	f
10^{-18}	atto-	a

APPENDIX D

Greek Alphabets

LETTER	LOWERCASE	UPPERCASE
ALPHA	α	A
BETA	β	B
GAMMA	γ	Γ
DELTA	δ	Δ
EPSILON	ε	E
ZETA	ζ	Z
ETA	η	H
THETA	θ	Θ
IOTA	ι	I
KAPPA	κ	K
LAMBDA	λ	Λ
MU	μ	M
NU	ν	N
XI	ξ	Ξ
OMICRON	ο	O
PI	π	Π
RHO	ρ	P
SIGMA	σ	Σ
TAU	τ	T
UPSILON	υ	Y
PHI	φ	Φ
CHI	χ	X
PSI	ψ	Ψ
OMEGA	ω	Ω

APPENDIX E

Fragmented Energy Forms

I. POTENTIAL ENERGY

1) **STATIC CHARGE (Q)**

2) **STATIC MAGNETIC POLE (M)**

3) **STATIC FORCE (ELECTRIC)**

$$\overline{F} = Q\overline{E} \qquad (E.1)$$

4) **STATIC FIELDS**

    a) **Electric Field $(\overline{E}, \overline{D})$**

$$\overline{D}(x,y,z) = \varepsilon\overline{E}(x,y,z) \qquad (E.2)$$

    b) **Magnetic Field $(\overline{H}, \overline{B})$**

$$\overline{B}(x,y,z) = \mu\overline{H}(x,y,z) \qquad (E.3)$$

5) **WORK**

$$W = q\int_{0}^{\ell} \overline{E} \cdot \overline{d\ell} \qquad (E.4)$$

Where $\overline{E}$ is the electric field vector defined as the electrical force exerted on a unit of charge and $\overline{d\ell}$ is an infinitesimal displacement vector. Differentiating (E.4) with respect to "q" gives the differential form:

$$\frac{dW}{dq} = \int_0^\ell \overline{E} \cdot \overline{d\ell} \qquad (E.5)$$

Equation (E.5) in essence gives the equation for the work performed per unit charge between two points, which basically is equivalent to the concept of voltage.

If the particle moves in the same direction as the applied force, then equation for work simplifies into:

$W=qE\ell,$ (E.6)

which simply states that work accomplished is the applied force (qE) multiplied by the distance (ℓ).

NOTE: *By close examination of the definition of "work", we can observe that it is the result of energy in action and represents "spent energy".*

6) VOLTAGE (ELECTRICAL POTENTIAL DIFFERENCE)

The work performed in moving a charge (q) from A to B is given by:

$$W_{BA} = \int_A^B (-q\overline{E}) \cdot \overline{d\ell} \qquad (E.7)$$

The voltage (or potential difference) is defined in terms of the work performed and is mathematically expressed as:

$$V_{BA} = V_B - V_A = W_{BA}/q = -\int_A^B \overline{E.d\ell} \qquad (E.8a)$$

Or in differential form:

$$V = \frac{dW}{dq} \qquad (E.8b)$$

NOTE: *Theoretically speaking, the reference point (or ground) at which the potential function (V) is assumed to be zero is at an infinite distance away from the point of measurement (i.e. at infinity); however, in practice* *and in actual circuit analysis the ground can be assumed to be any designated point in the circuit, purely by prior agreement.*

II. KINETIC ENERGY

7) **MOMENTUM**

Linear: $\bar{p} = m\bar{v}$ (E.9)

Angular: $\bar{L} = \bar{r} \times \bar{p}$ (E.10)

Where $\bar{r}$ and $\bar{v}$ are the lever arm and the velocity of a particle with mass m, respectively.

NOTE: *Mechanical Force* ($\bar{F}$) *on a body is a vector (having a magnitude and a direction) equal to the time rate of change of linear momentum* ($\bar{p} = m\bar{v}$), *i.e.,*

$$\bar{F} = \frac{d(\bar{p})}{dt} \qquad\qquad (E.11)$$

Where m is the mass and $(\bar{v})$ is the velocity of the object.

8) **TIME VARYING OR MOVING ELECTRIC CHARGE, Q(X,Y,Z,T), LEADING TO CURRENT (I) GIVEN BY:**

I=dQ(x,y,z,t)/dt

9) **DYNAMIC FORCES**

a) Electric Force:

$\bar{F}_e(x,y,z,t) = Q\bar{E}(x,y,z,t)$ (E.12)

b) Magnetic Force:

$\bar{F}_m(x,y,z,t) = Q\bar{V} \times \bar{B}(x,y,z,t)$ (E.13)

10) **DYNAMIC FIELDS**

a) **Electric Field $(\bar{E}, \bar{D})$**

$$\overline{D}(x,y,z,t) = \varepsilon\overline{E}(x,y,z,t) \qquad (E.14)$$

b) Magnetic Field $(\overline{H}, \overline{B})$

$$\overline{B}(x,y,z,t) = \mu\overline{H}(x,y,z,t) \qquad (E.15)$$

11) POWER

$$P = \frac{dW}{dt} \qquad (E.16)$$

Or, in integral form:

$$W = \int_0^t P\,dt \qquad (E.17)$$

Using the chain rule, Equation (E.16) can also be written as:

$$P = \frac{dW}{dt} = \frac{dW}{dq} \times \frac{dq}{dt} = VI \qquad (E.18)$$

Thus the total work performed or total energy transferred (or spent) is:

$$W = \int_0^t VI\,dt \qquad (E.19)$$

12) ELECTRONIC WAVES
   a) The General Form:
      A wave traveling in +x direction:
      $U^+(x,y,z,t) = f^+(x - vt) = g^+(\omega t - \beta x)$ (E.20)

      A wave traveling in -x direction:
      $U^-(x,y,z,t) = f^-(x + vt) = g^-(\omega t + \beta x)$ (E.21)
   b) Sinusoidal Waves:
      I. *Plane wave in ±x direction*
         Time Domain:
         $u(x,y,z,t) = U_o\cos(\omega t \pm \beta x)$ (E.22a)
         Phasor Domain:
         $U(x,y,z) = U_o e^{-(\pm j\beta x)}$ (E.22b)

APPENDIX F

Materials Constants

&

Frequency Bands

Conductivity σ (S/m)

Material	σ
Aluminum	3.82×10^7
Bakelite	10^{-9}
Brass	1.50×10^7
Bronze	1.00×10^7
Clay	10^{-4}
Copper	5.80×10^7
Diamond	10^{-13}
Ferrite	10^{-2}
Glass	10^{-12}
Gold	4.10×10^7
Ground (wet)	10^{-2}-10^{-3}
Iron	1.03×10^7
Marble	10^{-8}
Mica	10^{-14}
Nichrome	0.10×10^7
Nickel	1.45×10^7
Polystrene	10^{-16}
Porcelain	10^{-13}
Quartz	10^{-17}
Rubber (hard)	10^{-15}
Silicon	1.20×10^3
Silver	6.17×10^7
Soil (sandy)	10^{-5}
Solder	0.70×10^7
Steel (stainless)	0.11×10^7
Tungsten	1.82×10^7

Material	σ
Water (distilled)	2×10^{-4}
Water (fresh)	10^{-3}
Water (sea)	3-5
Zinc	1.67×10^{7}

Relative Permittivity (ε_r)
(Also called Dielectric Constant)

Material	ε_r
Air	1
Alcohol	25
Bakelite	4.8
Gallium Arsenide(GaAs)	
Glass	4-7
Ground (dry)	2-5
Ice	4.2
Indium Phosphide (InP)	14
Mica (ruby)	5.4
Nylon	4
Paper	2-4
Plexiglass	2.6-3.5
Polyethylene	2.25
Polystrene	2.55-6
Porcelain	6
Quartz (fused)	3.8
Rubber	2.5-4
Salt (NaCl)	5.9
Sand (dry)	4
Silica (fused)	3.8
Silicon	11.7
Snow	3.3
Soil (dry)	2.8
Styrofoam	1.03
Teflon	2.1
Water (Distilled)	80
Water (fresh)	80
Water (Sea)	20
Wood (dry)	1.5-4

Relative Permeability (μ_r)

Dielectric	μ_r
Aluminum	1.00000065
Beryllium	1.00000079
Bismuth	0.99999860
Cast Iron	60
Cobalt	60
Ferrite	1,000
Iron (Pure)	4,000
Iron (transformer)	3,000
Machine Steel	300
Mu-metal	20,000
Nickel	50
Parafin	0.99999942
Silicon Iron	4,000
Silver	0.99999981
Supermalloy	100,000
Wood	0.99999950

Semiconductor substrate material Constants

Property	Si	Si on Sapphire	GaAs	InP
Semi-Insulating	No	Yes	Yes	Yes
Resistivity	10^3-10^5	$>10^{14}$	10^7-10^9	10^7
Dielectric constant (ε_r)	11.7	11.6	12.9	14
Mobility (cm^2/V-s)†	700	700	4300	3000
Saturation velocity (cm/s)	9×10^6	9×10^6	1.3×10^7	1.9×10^7
Radiation Hardness	Poor	Poor	Very good	Good
Density (g/cm^3)	2.3	3.9	5.3	4.8
Thermal Conductivity (W/cm-°C)	1.5	0.46	0.46	0.68
Operating Temperature (°C)	250	250	350	300

†Doping level=10^{17} cm^{-3}

Commercial Radio Frequency Band

NAME OF BAND	ABBREVIATION	FREQUENCY RANGE
VERY LOW FREQ.	VLF	3-30 kHz
LOW FREQ.	LF	30-300 kHz
MEDIUM FREQ.	MF	300 kHz-3 MHz
HIGH FREQ.	HF	3-30 MHz
VERY HIGH FREQ.	VHF	30-300 MHz
ULTRA-HIGH FREQ.	UHF	0.3-3 GHz
SUPER-HIGH FREQ.	SHF	3-30 GHz
EXTRA-HIGH FREQ.	EHF	30-300 GHz

IEEE and commercial Microwave band designations

BAND DESIGNATION	FREQUENCY RANGE (GHz)
L Band	1.0-2.0
S band	2.0-4.0
C band	4.0-8.0
X band	8.0-12.0
Ku band	12.0-18.0
K band	18.0-26.5
Ka band (mmw)	26.5-40.0
Q band (mmw)	33.0-50.0
U band (mmw)	40.0-60.0
V band (mmw)	50.0-75.0
E band (mmw)	60.0-90.0
W band (mmw)	75.0-110.0
F band (mmw)	90.0-140.0
D band (mmw)	110.0-170.0
G band (mmw)	140.0-220.0

APPENDIX G

MATHEMATICAL IDENTITIES

A) BINOMIAL FORMULAS

$(x \pm y)^2 = x^2 \pm 2xy + y^2$
$(x \pm y)^3 = x^3 \pm 3x^2y + 3xy^2 \pm y^3$
$(x \pm y)^4 = x^4 \pm 4x^3y + 6x^2y^2 \pm 4xy^3 + y^4$

Or, in general:

$$(x+y)^n = x^n + nx^{n-1} + \frac{n(n-1)}{2!}x^{n-2}y^2 + \frac{n(n-1)(n-2)}{3!}x^{n-3}y^3 + \dots + y^n$$

Where factorial n (n!) is defined by:
n!=1.2.3.......n
Note: Zero factorial is defined by: 0!=1

B) SPECIAL PRODUCTS

$x^2 - y^2 = (x-y)(x+y)$
$x^3 - y^3 = (x-y)(x^2 + xy + y^2)$
$x^3 + y^3 = (x+y)(x^2 - xy + y^2)$
$x^4 - y^4 = (x^2 - y^2)(x^2 + y^2) = (x-y)(x+y)(x^2 + y^2)$

C) TRIGONOMETRIC FUNCTION RELATIONS

$$\sin(-x) = -\sin x$$

$$\cos(-x) = \cos x$$

$$\tan x = \frac{\sin x}{\cos x}$$

$$\cot x = \frac{\cos x}{\sin x}$$

$$\sec x = \frac{1}{\cos x}$$

$$\csc x = \frac{1}{\sin x}$$

$$\sin^2 x + \cos^2 x = 1$$

$$\sin 2x = 2\sin x \cos x$$

$$\cos 2x = \cos^2 x - \sin^2 x = 1 - 2\sin^2 x = 2\cos^2 x - 1$$

$$\sin 3x = 3\sin x - 4\sin^3 x$$

$$\cos 3x = -3\cos x + 4\cos^3 x$$

$$\sin^2 x = \frac{1 - \cos 2x}{2}$$

$$\cos^2 x = \frac{1 + \cos 2x}{2}$$

$$\sin^3 x = \frac{3\sin x - \sin 3x}{4}$$

$$\cos^3 x = \frac{3\cos x + \cos 3x}{4}$$

$$\sin x \pm \sin y = 2\sin(\frac{x \pm y}{2})\cos(\frac{x \mp y}{2})$$

$$\cos x + \cos y = 2\cos(\frac{x + y}{2})\cos(\frac{x - y}{2})$$

$$\cos x - \cos y = -2\sin(\frac{x + y}{2})\cos(\frac{x - y}{2})$$

$$\sin x \sin y = \frac{1}{2}\left[\cos(x-y) - \cos(x+y)\right]$$

$$\cos x \cos y = \frac{1}{2}\left[\cos(x-y) + \cos(x+y)\right]$$

$$\sin x \cos y = \frac{1}{2}\left[\sin(x-y) + \sin(x+y)\right]$$

D) HYPERBOLIC FUNCTION RELATIONS

$$\sinh x = \frac{e^x - e^{-x}}{2}$$

$$\cosh x = \frac{e^x + e^{-x}}{2}$$

$$\tanh x = \frac{\sinh x}{\cosh x} = \frac{e^x - e^{-x}}{e^x + e^{-x}}$$

$$\coth x = \frac{1}{\tanh x}$$

$$\sec hx = \frac{1}{\cosh x}$$

$$\cosh x = \frac{1}{\sinh x}$$

$$\cosh^2 x - \sinh^2 x = 1$$

$$\sinh(-x) = -\sinh x$$

$$\cosh(-x) = \cosh x$$

$$\tanh(-x) = -\tanh x$$

$$\sinh(x \pm y) = \sinh x \cosh y \pm \cosh x \sinh y$$

$$\cosh(x \pm y) = \cosh x \cosh y \pm \sinh x \sinh y$$

$$\tanh(x \pm y) = \frac{\tanh x \pm \tanh y}{1 \pm \tanh x \tanh y}$$

$\sinh 2x = 2\sinh x\cosh x$

$\cosh 2x = \cosh^2 x + \sinh^2 x = 2\cosh^2 x - 1 = 1 + 2\sinh^2 x$

$\tanh 2x = \dfrac{2\tanh x}{1 + \tanh^2 x}$

$\sinh^2 x = \dfrac{1}{2}\left[\cosh 2x - 1\right]$

$\cosh^2 x = \dfrac{1}{2}\left[\cosh 2x + 1\right]$

$\sinh x \pm \sinh y = 2\sinh\dfrac{(x \pm y)}{2}\cosh\dfrac{(x \mp y)}{2}$

$\cosh x + \cosh y = 2\cosh\dfrac{(x + y)}{2}\cosh\dfrac{(x - y)}{2}$

$\cosh x - \cosh y = 2\sinh\dfrac{(x + y)}{2}\sinh\dfrac{(x - y)}{2}$

$\sinh x\sinh y = \dfrac{1}{2}\left[\cosh(x + y) - \cosh(x - y)\right]$

$\cosh x\cosh y = \dfrac{1}{2}\left[\cosh(x + y) + \cosh(x - y)\right]$

$\sinh x\cosh y = \dfrac{1}{2}\left[\sinh(x + y) + \sinh(x - y)\right]$

E) LOGARITHMIC RELATIONS

$\log_a xy = \log_a x + \log_a y$

$\log_a \dfrac{x}{y} = \log_a x - \log_a y$

$\log_a x^y = y\log_a x$

$\log_a x = \dfrac{\log_b x}{\log_b a}$

$\log_a a = 1$

F) COMPLEX NUMBERS

$x + jy = re^{j\theta}$ (conversion from rectangular to polar form)

and

$re^{j\theta} = r(\cos\theta + \sin\theta)$ (Euler's Identity)

Where,
$j = \sqrt{-1}$,

$r = \sqrt{x^2 + y^2}$

$\theta = \tan^{-1}(\dfrac{y}{x})$

$(re^{j\theta})^n = r^n e^{jn\theta}$

$(r_1 e^{j\theta_1})(r_2 e^{j\theta_2}) = r_1 r_2 e^{j(\theta_1 + \theta_2)}$

G) RELATIONSHIP BETWEEN EXPONENTIAL, TRIGONOMETRIC AND HYPERBOLIC FUNCTIONS

$e^{\pm j\pi} = -1$

$e^{\pm j\pi/2} = \pm j$

$e^{\pm j(x+2k\pi)} = e^{\pm jx}$

$e^{\pm j[x+(2k+1)\pi]} = -e^{\pm jx}$

$e^{\pm jx} = \cos x \pm j\sin x$ (Euler's identity)

$\sin x = \dfrac{e^{jx} - e^{-jx}}{2j}$

$\cos x = \dfrac{e^{jx} + e^{-jx}}{2}$

$\tan x = -j(\dfrac{e^{jx} - e^{-jx}}{e^{jx} + e^{-jx}})$

$$\sin(jx) = j\sinh x$$

$$\cos(jx) = \cosh x$$

$$\tan(jx) = j\tanh x$$

$$\sinh(jx) = j\sin x$$

$$\cosh(jx) = \cos x$$

$$\tanh(jx) = j\tan x$$

Where $j = \sqrt{-1}$ and k is an integer.

H) DERIVATIVES

$$\frac{d}{dx}(u^n) = nu^{n-1}\frac{du}{dx}$$

$$\frac{d}{dx}(uv) = u\frac{dv}{dx} + v\frac{du}{dx}$$

$$\frac{d}{dx}(\frac{u}{v}) = \frac{v(du/dx) - u(dv/dx)}{v^2}$$

$$\frac{d}{dx}\sin u = \cos u\frac{du}{dx}$$

$$\frac{d}{dx}\cos u = -\sin u\frac{du}{dx}$$

$$\frac{d}{dx}\tan u = \sec^2 u\frac{du}{dx}$$

$$\frac{d}{dx}\cot u = \csc^2 u\frac{du}{dx}$$

$$\frac{d}{dx}\log_a u = \frac{\log_a e}{u}\frac{du}{dx}$$

$$\frac{d}{dx}\log_e u = \frac{1}{u}\frac{du}{dx}$$

$$\frac{d}{dx}a^u = a^u\log_e a\frac{du}{dx}$$

$$\frac{d}{dx}e^u = e^u\frac{du}{dx}$$

$$\frac{d}{dx}\sinh u = \cosh u \frac{du}{dx}$$

$$\frac{d}{dx}\cosh u = \sinh u \frac{du}{dx}$$

$$\frac{d}{dx}\tanh u = \operatorname{sech}^2 u \frac{du}{dx}$$

$$\frac{d}{dx}\coth u = -\operatorname{csch}^2 u \frac{du}{dx}$$

I) INTEGRALS

$$\int u^n du = \frac{u^{n+1}}{n+1} + C$$

$$\int u\,dv = uv - \int v\,du$$

$$\int \frac{du}{u} = \log_e |u| + C$$

$$\int a^u du = \frac{a^u}{\log_e u} + C$$

$$\int e^u du = e^u + C$$

$$\int \log_e x = x \log_e x - x + C$$

$$\int \sin u\,du = -\cos u + C$$

$$\int \cos u\,du = \sin u + C$$

$$\int \tan u\,du = -\log_e \cos u + C$$

$$\int \cot u\,du = \log_e \sin u + C$$

$$\int \sinh u\,du = \cosh u + C$$

$$\int \cosh u\,du = \sinh u + C$$

$$\int \tanh u \, du = \log_e \cosh u + C$$

$$\int \coth u \, du = \log_e \sinh u + C$$

$$\int \sin^2 u \, du = \frac{u - \sin u \cos u}{2} + C$$

$$\int \cos^2 u \, du = \frac{u + \sin u \cos u}{2} + C$$

J) TAYLOR SERIES EXPANSION

$$f(x)\big|_{x=a} = f(a) + f'(a)(x-a) + \frac{f''(a)(x-a)^2}{2!} + \cdots + \frac{f^{(n-1)}(a)(x-a)^{n-1}}{(n-1)!} + \cdots$$

$$e^x \big|_{x=0} = 1 + x + \frac{x^2}{2!} + \frac{x^3}{3!} + \cdots$$

$$\sin x \big|_{x=0} = x - x^3/3! + x^5/5! - x^7/7! + \ldots$$

$$\cos x \big|_{x=0} = 1 - x^2/2! + x^4/4! - x^6/6! + \ldots$$

$$\ln(1+x)\big|_{x=0} = x - x^2/2! + x^3/3! - x^4/4! + \ldots$$

K) EQUATION OF A CIRCLE

$$(x-a)^2 + (y-b)^2 = R^2$$

where (a,b) is the center of the circle having a radius R.

APPENDIX H

CD ROM Download

A. INSTRUCTIONS

1. To Download the CD ROM, please type in the following link exactly:

http://www.csun.edu/~matt/electronic-waves.zip

2. Once a pop up window shows up, click on "open" to unzip the file. Make sure you have the "WinZip" software to unzip the files properly.

3. After unzipping the files, create a folder called "E-book" in the C: drive.

4. Save all of the files in this folder.

5. To start the software, double click on the Microsoft® file called **"StartMenu"** file.

NOTE: *There is a stand-alone pdf file called "Smith ZY_chart.pdf" included in the downloaded bundle of files, which can be printed out and used for solving problems that require a ZY Smith Chart.*

B. MAIN FEATURES

A CD containing software in the form of an electronic book (E-book), which contains all numerical examples from the text, is bound into the back of each textbook. The solutions are programmed using

Visual Basic software, which is built into the "Microsoft Excel®" application software. The main features of this CD are as follows:

1. It is a powerful interactive tool for learning the textbook content and also for solving the numerical problems.
2. The software includes 90 solved problems based on the numerical examples in the book.
3. The big advantage of the interactive software tool is its use of live math. Every number and formula is interactive. The reader can change the starting parameters of a problem and watch as the final results change before his or her eyes. This feature allows the reader to experiment with every number, formula, etc.
4. Each solved problem becomes a worksheet that the reader can modify to solve dozens of related problems.
5. The electronic book takes advantage of the powerful Microsoft Excel® environment to perform many tedious and complicated RF and microwave design calculations (usually using complex numbers), allowing the student to focus on the essential concepts.
6. This is an excellent tool for students, engineers, and educators, to:
  a.   Understand the fundamentals and practical concepts of RF and Microwaves and,
  b.   Encourage applications and new RF/Microwave circuit designs using the concepts presented in the book.

C. HOW TO START THE PROGRAM

The following steps need to be carried out before the software is ready to use:

1. Either one of the following two methods may be used to utilize the contents of the CD-ROM:
  a.   Read all the files directly from the CD-ROM or,
  b.   Create a folder called "E-book" in the C: Drive. Copy the entire content of the CD-ROM into the folder entitled "E-book."
2. Open Microsoft Excel 2000 software (or Excel 97 with SR-1 or SR-2 revision) and open the "E-book" folder.
3. You may begin the program by double clicking on the "StartMenu" file.

NOTE: *You may double click on the* "Start Menu" *file directly as a shortcut without opening the Excel software.*

4. Once the "StartMenu" file opens up, click on "Analysis Hub" and then open up the "about the CD" file at the top left corner by clicking on it.

5. Carefully read all the information in the "about the CD" file and close it by either

    a. holding the ALT + TAB keys and choosing EXCEL or,

    b. clicking "return to Start Menu" ARROW to return to the E-book Start Menu.

6. Turn on both *Analysis Toolpack* and *Analysis Toolpack— VBA* as discussed below.

7. Proceed to the desired example by clicking on it and selecting "Enable Macros."

D. HOW TO USE THE E-BOOK SOFTWARE

Before proceeding to the worked-out examples, we need to select from the toolbar menu "Tools," "Add-ins," and, from the dialog box, select both "Analysis Tool-pack" and "Analysis Toolpack—VBA " in order to set up the software properly.

When a particular example is selected and clicked for interactive use, the user will encounter a dialogue box where "Enable Macros" must be selected. When the example is opened, the user will observe that each numerical example consists of several sections, which can be briefly summarized as:

1. Problem statement: Word for word text taken from the book that describes the nature of the problem.

2. Input data: This section provides all the manipulatable data, which the reader may have at his or her own disposal to vary interactively and experiment with, in order to examine different scenarios and obtain answers to "what if" questions. *Inside the input data box, the user may change the values of the parameters only, and not any of the units. The user should type the new value in the appropriate box and press enter/return to observe the desired change.*

This is the only place where the user is allowed to make any changes to the software.

3.   Output data: This section contains a step-by-step solution of the problem as well as easy explanations provided for quick assimilation of the results. Most of the complicated calculations are done in complex numbers using the Visual Basic programming technique, which is part of the Microsoft Excel® software.

4.   Problem format and color codes: All problems are formatted and color-coded in the same manner throughout the software. This is done for the user's easy recognition and reference, and is delineated as follows:

Example xx.xx	Cyan
Problem text	Tan
Solution:	Navy Blue

Input data (interactive part)

Heading	Red
Content	Turquoise/Brown

Output data

Heading	Sky Blue
Content	Yellow
Interactive Answers	Green
Caution	Red
Note/Conclusion	Pink
Reference	Violet

E. SOFTWARE KNOWLEDGE REQUIRED

A rudimentary knowledge of Microsoft Excel® is required to operate the software successfully. The user does *not* need to know Visual Basic programming techniques to work with the examples' solutions interactively.

F. MINIMUM SOFTWARE/HARDWARE REQUIREMENTS

The user needs to have the following:

1.   Hardware requirements: A personal computer (PC) with a

Pentium chip, preferably.

2.   **Software requirements:** Windows 95/98/XP/NT operating system and Microsoft Excel 2000/2002 (or Excel 97 with: SR-1 or SR-2 revisions).

NOTE 1: *To obtain the Service Release 1 or 2 (SR-1 or SR-2), the user should download the required software from the following Website: http://www.microsoft. com/*

Go to the search link and find the SR-1 or SR-2 revision, which is suitable to the version of Microsoft Office that you own. Download and install the SR-1 or SR-2 upgrade to repair all known bugs in Microsoft Excel 97. Without this correction, Excel 97 gives incomplete values for the worked-out examples in the textbook CD.

NOTE 2: *If you own Microsoft Excel 2000/2002, please ignore "Note 1." Install the textbook CD directly without any changes to the Microsoft Excel software using the procedure outlined in the previous section. If you experience any problems, you need to download and install the SR-1A revision for Microsoft Excel 2000/2002 from the site mentioned previously.*

G. TROUBLESHOOTING PROBLEMS

If the following problems occur, you may correct them as follows:

1.   If "###### " appears in place of a numerical answer, it means that the cell is too small and you have to resize that cell in order to display the final numerical result correctly. To resize the cell, go to the Excel toolbar menu and select **Format, Column,** and **Autofit Selection.**

2.   If "#VALUE!" appears, it means that any of the following conditions may have occurred:

a.   Divide by zero.

b.   Negative number under a square root.

c.   The number is out of range.

d.   Excel 97 software is not used with SR-1 or SR-2 revision.

e.   The *Analysis Toolpack* and *Analysis Toolpack— VBA* are not turned on.*

* You need to select from the toolbar menu "Tools," "Add-ins," and from the dialog box select *Analysis Toolpack* and *Analysis Toolpack—VBA* in order to set up the software properly.

NOTE: *There is a stand-alone pdf file called "Smith ZY_chart.pdf" included in the downloaded bundle of files, which can be printed out and used for solving problems that require a ZY Smith Chart.*

APPENDIX I

CD ROM Download
Analysis & Design Examples

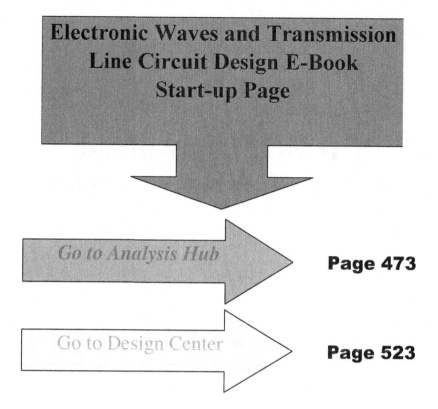

E-Book
Analysis Hub

Analysis Hub

Chapter 3 Examples

EXAMPLE 3.1

Determine the total sinusoidal function, X(t), when it is given by:

$X(t)=20 \cos(10t-30°) + 40 \cos(10t+60°)$

SOLUTION:

$X(t)=X_1(t) + X_2(t)$

Where:

$X_1(t)=A_1 \cos(\omega t + \theta_1)$

$X_2(t)=A_2 \cos(\omega t + \theta_2)$

INPUT DATA	
Variable	Value
A_1	20
A_2	40
θ_1	-30
θ_2	60
ω	10

OUTPUT DATA
$X_1(t)= 20.0$ *   cos[10t + (-30°)]
$X_2(t)= 40.0$ *   cos[10t + (60°)]
$A=A_1[\cos(\theta_1) + j\sin(\theta_1)] + A_2[\cos(\theta_2) + j\sin(\theta_2)]$
A= 37.3 +   j24.6
= 44.7   ∠   33.4°
Once the sum phasor (A) is known, the corresponding sum sinusoid in the time domain [X(t)] can easily be found by the inverse function. The total sinusoidal function is:
$X(t)=$ 44.7   *   cos[10t +(33.4°)]

EXAMPLE 3.2

Given the following circuit (as shown opposite):
a) Find the voltage across the load (Z_L) using Norton's theorem.
b) Find the Thevenin's equivalent.

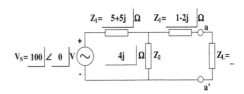

SOLUTION:		
INPUT DATA		

Element	Real	Imaginary
V_S	100	0
Z_1	5	5
Z_2	0	4
Z_3	1	2
Z_L	100	0

Enter in a new value for either the Real value (second column) or the Imaginary value (third column) to observe how the Output Data varies as a result of the change in the circuit element.

OUTPUT DATA		

Element	Value	Unit
V_S	100	V
Z_1	5+5j	Ω
Z_2	4j	Ω
Z_3	1-2j	Ω
Z_L	100	Ω

a) To find the load voltage and the Norton's equivalent, we do the following steps:

Step #1) Disconnect the load and find $Y_T=1/Z_T$ by shorting the voltage source.
Thus Z_T is given by:

$$Z_T = Z_3 + Z_1 \| Z_2$$

Z_T= 1.75 +   j0.64   Ω

Step #2) We now find I_{SC} by shorting the terminal a-a' as shown opposite:

$$I = V_S/(Z_1 + Z_2 \| Z_3)$$

I= 11.1 +   -j3.51 A

$$I_{SC} = [(Z_2/(Z_2 + Z_3))]I$$

I_{SC}= 20.5 +   j3.24 A

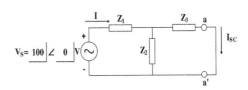

Step #3) The Norton equivalent is as shown opposite. The current through the load is found by using current division rule:

$$I_L = I_{SC}(Z_T/(Z_T + Z_L))$$

I_L= 0.33 +   j0.18 A
= 0.38   ∠ 29° A

$V_L = Z_L I_L$
V_L= 38.18   ∠   29° V

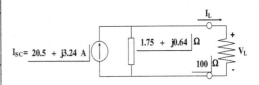

b.) Thevenin's Equivalent

$$V_{OC} = Z_T I_{SC}$$

V_{OC}= 33.96 + j18.87 V
= 38.9   ∠   29° V

The Thevenin's Equivalent circuit is shown opposite.

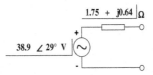

EXAMPLE 3.3

Given the circuit shown opposite, find its corresponding dual.

SOLUTION:

INPUT DATA		
Element	Value	Unit
V_s	20	V
R_s	10	Ω

OUTPUT DATA
We know that the dual quantities are:
Voltage $\Leftrightarrow$ Current
Series $\Leftrightarrow$ Parallel
Thus the voltage source is transformed into a current source (I_p) connected in parallel with a resistor R_p as shown opposite.
In order to have equivalent performance, the output voltage (V_o) must be equal to V_s and the input impedance equal to R_s. Thus we have:
$R_s=R_p$
$R_p= 10 \qquad \Omega$
Using Ohm's law, we obtain:
$V_o=I_pR_p \Rightarrow I_p=V_o/R_p$
$I_p= 2.0000$ A

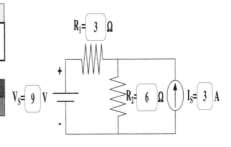

EXAMPLE 3.4

Find the current (I) in the 6 Ω resistor as shown opposite.

SOLUTION:

INPUT DATA		
Element	Value	Unit
V_S	9	V
I_S	3	A
R_1	3	Ω
R_2	6	Ω

OUTPUT DATA
Step 1) Set the current source to zero as shown opposite
$I_1 = V/(R_1 + R_2)$
$I_1 = 1.0000$ A

Step 2) Set the voltage source to zero:
$I_2 = I_S R_1/(R_1 + R_2)$
$I_2 = 1.0000$ A

Step 3) Thus the total current (I) is given by:
$I = I_1 + I_2$
$I = 2.0000$ A

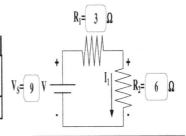

Circuit for step 1 of solution

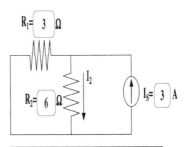

Circuit for step 2 of solution

EXAMPLE 3.5

A broadband amplifier has an input impedance of R_{in}=100 kΩ at low frequencies. Calculate the total input impedance at a higher frequency of f =1 MHz. The feedback capacitor value is C=1 pF and the overall gain is measured to be: K= -100 at f =100 MHz (see opposite figure).

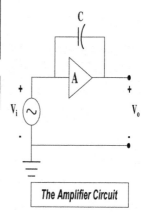

The Amplifier Circuit

SOLUTION:

INPUT DATA

Element	Value	Units
R_{in}	100	kΩ
C	1	pF
f	1	MHz
K	-100	

OUTPUT DATA

The Miller's equivalent circuit is shown opposite where:

C_i= (1-K)C

C_i= 101 pF

C_o= (1-1/K)C

C_o= 1.01 pF

Feedback capacitor appears at the input with a reactance of X_{Ci}=-1/2πfC_i given by:

X_{Ci}= -1.5758   kΩ

The total input impedance is the parallel combination of jX_{Ci} and R_{in}

$(Z_{in})_{new}$=R_{in}*$(jX_{ci})/(R_{in}+jX_{ci})$

$(Z_{in})_{new}$= 0.0248   -j1.5754   kΩ

This substantial reduction in the input impedance is equivalent to "shorting out the input," which leads to tremendous deterioration of the high frequency performance of the amplifier.

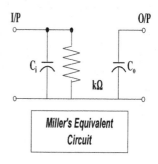

Miller's Equivalent Circuit

EXAMPLE 3.6

Convert the following into dBm or dBW:

SOLUTION:

INPUT DATA

a) To convert mW to dBm

Variable	Value	Unit
P_1	10.0	mW

b) To convert W to dBW

Variable	Value	Unit
P_2	20.0	W

OUTPUT DATA

a) $N(dBm) = 10 \log(P_1/1 \text{ mW})$

$P_1(dBm) = 10$ dBm

b) $N(dBW) = 10 \log(P_2/1 \text{ W})$

$P_2(dBW) = 13.0103$ dBW

Therefore the dBm and dBW units measure "Above or below" one milliwatt and one Watt, respectively.

EXAMPLE 3.7

If a voltage at the input of a circuit attenuates from 1 volt to 0.5 when it reaches the output, what is the voltage ratio in dB and Nepers?

SOLUTION:

INPUT

Variable	Value
V_o/V_i	0.5

◄ ►

Caution: To enter data you may:
a) Use the arrow keys on the adjacent box to enter desired numbers. Or,
b) Enter numbers manually, which disables the arrow keys. To use the arrow keys again, you need to reopen the file.

OUTPUT

$N(dB)=20\log(V_o/V_i)$		$N(Np)=\ln(V_i/V_o)$
$N(dB)$		$N(Np)$
-6.0206 dB	Or	0.6931 Np

Chapter 7 Examples

EXAMPLE 7.3

The microwave power at one point (P_1) on a transmission line is measured to be 10 mW. At a distance of d=50 cm away, another power measurement (P_2) indicates a power of 7 mW. Determine the attenuation constant of the transmission line.

SOLUTION:

INPUT DATA

Element	Value	Unit		
P_1	10	mW	Choose P_1 and P_2 such that P_1 value is always greater than P_2 value, i.e., $P_1 > P_2$	
P_2	7	mW		
d	0.5	m		

OUTPUT DATA

$\Lambda = [-(P_2 - P_1)/d]/2P_1$

$\Lambda = 0.3$	Np/m

EXAMPLE 7.4

What is the VSWR for a matched transmission line (Z_o=50 Ω)?

SOLUTION:

INPUT DATA		
Element	Value	Unit
Z_o	50	Ω
Z_L	50	Ω

OUTPUT DATA
$\Gamma_L=(Z_L-Z_o)/(Z_L+Z_o)$
$\Gamma_L= 0$
VSWR=$(1+|\Gamma_L|)/(1-|\Gamma_L|)$
VSWR= 1

EXAMPLE 7.5

What is the VSWR for:

a) An open load ($Z_L=\infty$),

b) A short load ($Z_L=0$)? Assume $Z_o=50\ \Omega$.

SOLUTION:

INPUT DATA

Element	Value	Unit
Z_o	50	Ω
Z_L	100	Ω

OUTPUT DATA

When $Z_L=0$ or ∞, we have two special cases, which need to be discussed separately. Therefore these two cases are treated first and then the most general case is presented at the end.

a) Special Case I: open-circuit load

$Z_L=\infty \Rightarrow \Gamma_L=\lim_{ZL\to\infty}(Z_L-Z_o)/(Z_L+Z_o)$

$\qquad \Gamma_L=1$

$VSWR=(1+|\Gamma_L|)/(1-|\Gamma_L|)=\infty$

b) Special Case II: short-circuit load

$Z_L=0 \Rightarrow \Gamma_L=(Z_L-Z_o)/(Z_L+Z_o)$

$\qquad \Gamma_L=-1$

$\Rightarrow |\Gamma_L|=1$

$VSWR=(1+|\Gamma_L|)/(1-|\Gamma_L|)=\infty$

c) General case:

$\qquad Z_L=100$

$\Gamma_L=(Z_L-Z_o)/(Z_L+Z_o)$

$\qquad \Gamma_L=0.333333$

$VSWR=(1+|\Gamma_L|)/(1-|\Gamma_L|)$

$\quad VSWR=2$

Conclusion: From Special Cases I & II, we can see that:

$1\le VSWR\le\infty$.

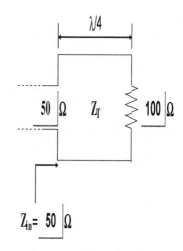

EXAMPLE 7.9

What is Z_T of a quarter-wave transformer to transform a load of 100 Ω to a 50 Ω line as shown opposite?

SOLUTION:

INPUT DATA

Element	Value	Unit
Z_{in}	50	Ω
Z_L	100	Ω

OUTPUT DATA

Using $Z_T = (Z_L Z_{in})^{1/2}$, we obtain:

$Z_T = 70.7$ Ω

EXAMPLE 7.10

Consider a 50 Ω lossless transmission line of length ℓ=1 m, connected to a generator operating at f=1 GHz, having V_g=10 V and Z_g=50 Ω at one end and to a load Z_L=100 Ω at the other (see opposite figure). Determine:

a) The voltage and current at any point on the transmission line.

b) The voltage at the generator (V_i) and load (V_L) ends.

c) The reflection coefficient and VSWR at any point on the line.

d) The average power delivered to the load.

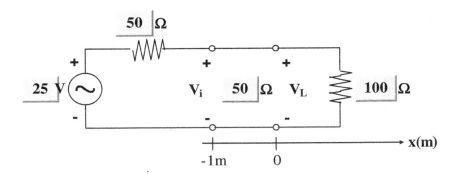

SOLUTION:

$c = 3*10^8$ m/s

	INPUT DATA	
Element	Value	Unit
Z_O	50	Ω
Z_L	100	Ω
V_g	25	V
f	1.00000	GHz

OUTPUT DATA
a) $\Gamma_g = (Z_g - Z_O)/(Z_g + Z_O)$
$\quad Z_g = Z_O = 50 \qquad \Omega$
$\qquad \Gamma_g = 0.000$
$\beta = \omega/c$
$\qquad \beta = 20.944 \qquad$ rad/m
$\Gamma_L = (Z_L - Z_O)/(Z_L + Z_O)$
$\qquad \Gamma_L = 0.333$
$V(x) = (V_g/2)e^{-jb(x+l)}(1 + \Gamma_L e^{j2bx})$
$\quad V(x) = \underline{12.5}\left\|e^{-j\,\underline{20.944}}\right\|^{(x+1)}\left(1 + \underline{0.333}\left\|e^{j\,\underline{20.944}}\right\|^x\right)$
$I(x) = (V_g/2Z_O)e^{-jb(x+l)}(1 - \Gamma_L e^{j2bx})$
$\quad I(x) = \underline{0.25}\left\|e^{-j\,\underline{20.944}}\right\|^{(x+1)}\left(1 - \underline{0.333}\left\|e^{j\,\underline{41.887}}\right\|^x\right)$

b) At the generator end (x=-1 m), we have:

$$V_i = V(-1) = \boxed{12.5} \left[1 + \boxed{0.333} \, e^{-j\,\boxed{41.88}} \right]$$

$$\Rightarrow V_i = \underline{10.4167} \quad -j3.61 \text{ V}$$

At the load end, we have:

x=0

$$V_L = V(0) = \boxed{12.5} \, e^{-j\,\underline{20.944}} \left[1 + \underline{0.333} \right]$$

$$V_L = V(0) = \boxed{16.667} \, e^{-j\,\underline{20.944}}$$

c) The reflection coefficient and VSWR are as follows:

$$\Gamma(x) = \Gamma_L e^{j2\beta x} = \boxed{0.333} \, e^{j\,\boxed{41.887}\,x}$$

$$VSWR = \frac{1 + |\Gamma_L|}{1 - |\Gamma_L|}$$

VSWR= 2

d) The average power delivered to the load is (assume Z_L is real):

$\alpha = 0$

$$P_L = P(x) = \frac{1}{2} \text{Re}\left[V_L(x) I_L^*(x) \right] = \frac{|V_L|^2}{2Z_L}$$

$P_L = 1.3889 \text{ W}$

Note: If the load was completely matched to the line the power delivered to the load would have been:

$Z_L = Z_g = Z_O$

$Z_L = 50 \quad \Omega$

$|V_i| = |V_L| = V_g/2 = 13 \text{ V}$

$$(P_{av})_{max} = \frac{|V_L|^2}{2Z_L}$$

$P_{av}(x)_{max} = 1.5625 \text{ W}$

Since there is no reflected power, $P_{av}(x)_{max}$ is also the incdient power (P_i), which is higher than the (P_{av}) calculated earlier under unmatched condition. The difference in the two powers is due to the reflected power back to the source:

$$P_r = |\Gamma_L|^2 P_i = 0.1736 \text{ W}$$

The value of P_r can also be found by:

$P_r = P_i - P_L$

$P_r = 0.1736 \text{ W}$

EXAMPLE 7.11

A 50 Ω microstip transmission line needs to be designed using a sheet of Epsilam-10® ($\varepsilon_r=10$) with h=1.02 mm. Determine W, λ, and ε_{ff} by:

a) An exact method.

b) An approximate method.

SOLUTION:

INPUT DATA

Element	Value	Unit
Z_o	50	Ω
h	1.02	mm
ε_r	10	
λ/λ_{tem}	1.23	From graph

OUTPUT DATA

a) Exact method--we will design a microstrip line with W/h$\leq$2.

$$\frac{W}{h} = \frac{8e^A}{e^{2A}-2}$$

Where

$$A = \frac{Z_0}{60}\sqrt{\frac{\varepsilon_r+1}{2}} + \frac{\varepsilon_r-1}{\varepsilon_r+1}\left(0.23+\frac{0.11}{\varepsilon_r}\right)$$

A= 2.152

Thus (W/h) is obtained to be:
W/h= 0.96

and

W=h*(W/h)

W= 0.98

Since W/h>0.6, we use the following equation to find λ and then use the result to find ε_{ff}:

$$\lambda = \frac{\lambda_0}{\sqrt{\varepsilon_r}}\left[\frac{\varepsilon_r}{1+0.63(\varepsilon_r-1)(W/h)^{0.1255}}\right]^{1/2}$$

λ= 0.39 λ_o

and

$\lambda=\lambda_o/\sqrt{\varepsilon_{ff}} \Rightarrow \varepsilon_{ff}=(\lambda_o/\lambda)^2$

ε_{ff}= 6.6

b) Approximate method

Using the plot of Zo vs. W/h as given in text , we obtain W/h:

$Z_o=$ **50** Ω:

W/h$\approx$1 $\Rightarrow$ W=h   From graph

From "normalized wavelength vs. W/h" graph for W/h=1, we obtain:

λ/λ_{tem}= 1.23   (From graph)

Furthermore, we know:

$\lambda_{tem}=\lambda_o/\sqrt{\varepsilon_r}$

$\Rightarrow \lambda_{tem}$= 0.316   *$\lambda_o$

Thus λ is found to be:

λ= 1.23   *   0.316   *λ_o

$\Rightarrow \lambda$= 0.39   *λ_o

We also know that $\lambda=\lambda_o/\sqrt{\varepsilon_{ff}}$. Thus, ε_{ff} is found to be:

$\varepsilon_{ff}=(\lambda_o/\lambda)^2$

ε_{ff}= 6.6

EXAMPLE 7.12

Design a 50 Ω transmission line that provides 90° phase shift at 2.5 GHz. Assume h=1.27 mm and ε_r=2.2.

SOLUTION:

INPUT DATA

Element	Value	Unit
Zo	50	Ω
f	2.5	GHz
h	1.27	mm
ε_r	2.2	
ϕ	90°	

OUTPUT DATA

To find "W," we assume that W/h≥2 and will verify this assumption later. Thus we have:

$$\frac{W}{h}=\frac{2}{\pi}\left[B-1-\ln(2B-1)+\frac{\varepsilon_r-1}{2\varepsilon_r}\left\{\ln(B-1)+0.39-\frac{0.61}{\varepsilon_r}\right\}\right]$$

$B=(377\pi)/(2Z_o\sqrt{\varepsilon_r})$

B= 7.985

And

W/h= 3.08

W=h*W/h

W= 3.91   mm

Note: If the obtained value of W/h≥2, our assumption is justified. Otherwise, we need to go back and satisfy our original assumption.

So far we have found the width of the line, now we need to know the length of the line. The phase shift gives:

$\phi=\beta*\ell=\omega*\ell/V_p=2\pi f*\ell/(c/\sqrt{\varepsilon_{ff}})$

We need to find ε_{ff} first in order to find "ℓ":

$$\varepsilon_{ff}=\frac{\varepsilon_r+1}{2}+\frac{\varepsilon_r-1}{2}\left(1+12\frac{h}{W}\right)^{-1/2}$$

ε_{ff}= 1.87

Thus the length of the transmission line is given by:

$\ell=c*\phi/2\pi*f*\sqrt{\varepsilon_{ff}}$

ℓ= 0.02193   m

ℓ= 2.193   cm

Chapter 10 Examples

EXAMPLE 10.1

Find the input impedance of a transmission line (Z_O=50 Ω) that has a length of $\lambda/8$ and is connected to a load impedance of Z_L=50+j50 Ω?

SOLUTION:

INPUT DATA

Parameter	Real	Imag	Unit
Z_O	50		Ω
Z_L	50	50	Ω
ℓ	0.125		λ

OUTPUT DATA

Element	Value	Unit
Z_L	50+50j	Ω

$$Z_{IN}(-\ell) = Z_0 \frac{Z_L + jZ_0 \tan \beta\ell}{Z_0 + jZ_L \tan \beta\ell}$$

Z_{IN}= 100.00   -j50.00   Ω

EXAMPLE 10.2

What is the impedance (Z_D) of a device having $\Gamma_D = 2.23\angle 26.5°$?
Assume $Z_0 = 50\ \Omega$.

SOLUTION:

INPUT DATA		

Parameter	Real	Unit
Z_O	50	Ω

Parameter	Mag.	Angle
Γ_D	2.23	26.5°

OUTPUT DATA
1) Plot $1/\Gamma_D^*$ on the Smith chart and read off Z_D' as:

$1/\Gamma_D^*= 0.448$	$\angle$	26.5°	
$Z_D' = 100.25$	+	j50.22	Ω

Since $|\Gamma_D| > 1$ thus the device impedance (Z_D) has a negative resistance, i.e.

$Z_D = -100.25$	+	j50.22	Ω

EXAMPLE 10.3

Find the admittance value for an impedance value of $Z=50+j50\ \Omega$, in a 50 Ω system.

SOLUTION:

INPUT DATA			
Parameter	Mag.	Angle	Unit
Z_O	50		Ω
Z	50	50	Ω

OUTPUT DATA		
Element	Value	Unit
Z	50+50j	Ω
$Z_N=Z/Z_O=$ 1.00	+j1.00	
$Y_N=1/Z_N$		
$Y_N=$ 0.5	-j0.50	
$Y=Y_O*Y_N$		
$Y_O=1/Z_O=$ 0.02	S	
$Y=$ 0.01	-j0.0100 S	

EXAMPLE 10.4

A microwave signal is travelling on a transmission line which has $Z_O= 50 \ \Omega$ and a load value of $Z_L=100 \ \Omega$. Find the values of Z_{max} and Z_{min} and their location on the transmission line.

SOLUTION:

INPUT DATA

Parameter	Value	Unit
Z_O	50	Ω
Z_L	100	Ω

Caution: Choose values such that the following condition is satisfied:
$Z_L \geq Z_O$

OUTPUT DATA

$\Gamma_L=(Z_L-Z_O)/(Z_L+Z_O)$
$\Gamma_L= 0.333$
$\text{VSWR} = \dfrac{1+|\Gamma_L|}{1-|\Gamma_L|}$
$\text{VSWR}= 2$
$Z_L>Z_O$ Because Z_L is real, therefore Z_{max} occurs at the load:
$Z_{max}=Z_L=$ 100 Ω
Z_{min} occurs $\lambda/4$ away, thus we have:
$Z_{min}=Z_O^2/Z_{max}= 25$ Ω

Note: Z_{max} and Z_{min} could have also been obtained by the following technique:

$Z_{max}=Z_O*\text{VSWR}$
$Z_{max}= 100$ Ω
$Z_{min}=Z_O/\text{VSWR}$
$Z_{min}= 25$ Ω

EXAMPLE 10.5

A microwave signal at a frequency of f=1 GHz, is travelling on a transmission line having Z_O=50 Ω, and terminated in a load of Z_L=20 Ω. Find the values of Z_{max} and Z_{min} and their location on the transmission line.

SOLUTION:

$c=3*10^8$ m/s

INPUT DATA			
Parameter	Mag.	Unit	**Caution:** Choose values such that the following condition is satisfied: $Z_L \leq Z_O$
Z_O	50	Ω	
Z_L	20	Ω	
f	1	GHz	

OUTPUT DATA
$\Gamma_L=(Z_L-Z_O)/(Z_L+Z_O)$
Γ_L= -0.429
$VSWR = \dfrac{1+|\Gamma_L|}{1-|\Gamma_L|}$
VSWR= 2.5
$Z_L<Z_O$ Because Z_L is real, therefore Z_{min} occurs at the load:
$Z_{min}=Z_L=$ 20   Ω
Z_{max} occurs λ/4 away, thus we have:
$Z_{max}=Z_O^2/Z_{min}=$ 125   Ω
λ=c/f
λ= 0.3   m   =30   cm
Thus ℓ_{max}=λ/4= 7.5   cm
Note: Z_{max} and Z_{min} could have also been obtained by the following technique:
$Z_{max}=Z_O*VSWR$
Z_{max}= 125   Ω
$Z_{min}=Z_O/VSWR$
Z_{min}= 20   Ω

EXAMPLE 10.6

Determine the standing wave pattern on a transmission line (Z_O=50 Ω) terminated in Z_L=100+j100 Ω with an incident voltage of V^+=1∠0° as shown opposite.

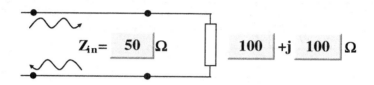

SOLUTION:

INPUT DATA

Parameter	Real	Imag	Unit
Z_O	50		Ω
Z_L	100	100	Ω
V^+	1	$0°$	V

OUTPUT DATA

Element	Value	Unit
Z_1	100+100j	Ω

$\Gamma_L = (Z_L - Z_O)/(Z_L + Z_O)$

$\Gamma_L = 0.620 \quad \angle \ 29.74°$

$$VSWR = \frac{1 + |\Gamma_L|}{1 - |\Gamma_L|}$$

VSWR= 4.27

$Z_{max} = Z_O * VSWR$

Z_{max}= 213.28 Ω

$2\beta\ell_{max} = \theta_\Gamma * (\pi/180) \Rightarrow \ell_{max} = (\theta_\Gamma/720) * \lambda$

ℓ_{max}= 0.0413 λ

$V_{max} = |V^+|(2*VSWR)/(1+VSWR)$

V_{max}= 1.620   V

$I_{min} = V_{max}/Z_{max}$

I_{min}= 7.60   mA

$Z_{min} = Z_O/VSWR$

Z_{min}= 11.72 Ω

$\ell_{min} = \ell_{max} + \lambda/4$

ℓ_{min}= 0.2913 λ

$V_{min} = 2/(1+VSWR)$

V_{min}= 0.380   V

$I_{max} = V_{min}/Z_{min}$

I_{max}= 32.40   mA

Note: An alternate would be to calculate V_{max} and V_{min} using VSWR and then finding Imax and Imin as follows

V_{max}= 1.620	V	
V_{min}= 0.380	V	
$I_{max}=V_{max}/Z_O$		
I_{max}= 32.40	mA	
$I_{min}=V_{min}/Z_O$		
I_{min}= 7.60	mA	

EXAMPLE 10.7

Consider a transmission line (Z_O=50 Ω) terminated in a load Z_L=15+j10 as shown opposite. Calculate the input impedance of the line where the shunt open stub is located a distance of d=0.044λ from the load and has a length of ℓ=0.147λ.

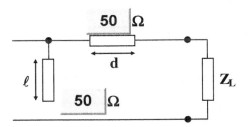

SOLUTION:

INPUT DATA

Parameter	Real	Imag	Unit
Z_O	50		Ω
Z_L	15	10	Ω
d	0.044		λ
ℓ	0.147		λ

OUTPUT DATA

Element	Value	Unit
Z_L	15+10j	Ω

Because we are dealing with a shunt stub, we need to calculate admittance values as follows:

$Z_{OC}=-jZ_O*\cot\beta\ell \Rightarrow Y_{OC}=+jY_O*\tan\beta\ell$

$Y_O=1/Z_O=$ 0.02   S

   $Y_{OC}=$ j0.0265   S

$$Z_{IN}(-d) = Z_0 \frac{Z_L + jZ_0 \tan\beta d}{Z_0 + jZ_L \tan\beta d}$$

   $Z_{IN}'=$ 18.07   j24.01 Ω

$Y_{IN}'=1/Z_{IN}'$

   $Y_{IN}'=$ 0.0200098   -j0.03   S

$Y_{IN}=Y_{IN}'+Y_{OC}$

   $Y_{IN}=$ 0.0200098   -j0.00013 S

$Z_{IN}=1/Y_{IN}$

   $Z_{IN}=$ 49.97   j0.31 Ω

EXAMPLE 10.8

Consider a transmission line (Z_O=50 Ω) with Z_L=100 Ω as shown opposite. Calculate the input impedance of the line where the shorted series stub is located a distance of d=λ/4 from the load and has a length ℓ=λ/8.

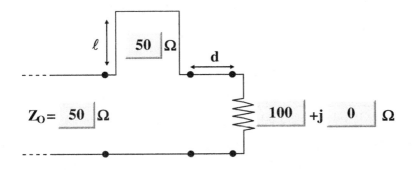

SOLUTION:

INPUT DATA

Parameter	Real	Imag	Unit
Z_O	50		Ω
Z_L	100	0	Ω
d	0.25		λ
ℓ	0.125		λ

OUTPUT DATA

Because we are dealing with a series stub, we need to work in impedances. We calculate impedance values as follows:

$Z_{SC}=jZ_O*\tan\beta\ell$ (short stub)

$Z_{SC}= j50.00$ Ω

$$Z_{IN}{}'(-d) = Z_0\frac{Z_L+jZ_0\tan\beta d}{Z_0+jZ_L\tan\beta d}$$

$Z_{IN}'= 25.00$ $+(j0.00)$ Ω

$Z_{IN}=Z_{IN}'+Z_{SC}$

$Z_{IN}= 25$ $+(j50.00)$ Ω

EXAMPLE 10.9

Calculate the total input admittance of a combination of a load $Z_L=50+j50$ Ω with a shunt inductor of L=8 nH at $f_O=1$ GHz as shown opposite. Assume a 50 Ω system.

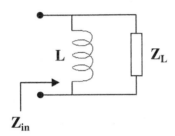

SOLUTION:

INPUT DATA

Parameter	Mag.	Angle	Unit
Z_O	50		Ω
Z_L	50	50	Ω
L	8		nH
f_O	1		GHz

OUTPUT DATA

Element	Value	Unit
Z_1	50+50j	Ω

Because we are dealing with a shunt element, we need to calculate admittance values as follows:

$jB_p=-j/(\omega_O*L)$

$jB_p=$ -j0.0199	S	

$Y_L=1/Z_L$

$Y_L=$ 0.01	+(-j0.01)	S	

$Y_{in}=Y_L+jB_p$

$Y_{in}=$ 0.01	+(-j0.0299)	S	

$Z_{in}=1/Y_{in}$

$Z_{in}=$ 10.064	+(j30.08)	Ω	

EXAMPLE 10.10

Find the input impedance at f=100 MHz for the circuit as shown opposite.

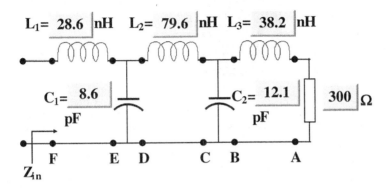

SOLUTION:

INPUT DATA

Parameter	Real	Imag	Unit
Z_L	300	0	Ω
C_1	8.6		pF
C_2	12.1		pF
L_1	28.6		nH
L_2	79.6		nH
L_3	38.2		nH
f	100		MHz

OUTPUT DATA

First, we calculate all impedance of the series elements and admittance of the shunt elements:

$$(jX_1) = j\omega L_1 = j17.97 \qquad \Omega$$

$$(jB_1) = j\omega C_1 = j0.00540 \qquad S$$

$$(jX_2) = j\omega L_2 = j50.01 \qquad \Omega$$

$$(jB_2) = j\omega C_2 = j0.00760 \qquad S$$

$$(jX_3) = j\omega L_3 = j24.00 \qquad \Omega$$

Next, we calculate the impedance at each point on the circuit as follows:		
$Z_A = Z_L$		
$Z_A = 300$	Ω	
$Z_B = Z_A + jX_3$		
$Z_B = 300$	$+(j24.00)$	Ω
$Y_B = 1/Z_B$		
$Y_B = 0.00331$	$+(-j0.00026)$	S
$Y_C = Y_B + jB_2$		
$Y_C = 0.00331$	$+(j0.00734)$	S
$Z_C = 1/Y_C$		
$Z_C = 51.10$	$+(-j113.22)$	Ω
$Z_D = Z_C + jX_2$		
$Z_D = 51.10$	$+(-j63.20)$	Ω
$Y_D = 1/Z_D$		
$Y_D = 0.00774$	$+(j0.00957)$	S
$Y_E = Y_D + jB_1$		
$Y_E = 0.00774$	$+(j0.01497)$	S
$Z_E = 1/Y_E$		
$Z_E = 27.24$	$+(-j52.72)$	Ω
$Z_F = Z_E + jX_1$		
$Z_F = 27.24$	$+(-j34.75)$	Ω

EXAMPLE 10.12

Plot the frequency response of the input impedance of a shorted transmission line as shown opposite.

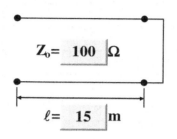

$$Z_0 = \boxed{100} \ \Omega$$

$$\ell = \boxed{15} \ m$$

SOLUTION:

INPUT DATA

Parameter	Mag.	Unit
Z_0	100	Ω
ℓ	15	m
n	0	

OUTPUT DATA

A shorted stub has the following input impedance value

$Z_{SC} = jZ_0 * \tan\beta\ell$

$\beta\ell = 2\pi\ell/\lambda$

$\lambda = 300/f_O(MHz)$ (meters)

$\Rightarrow \beta\ell = (2\pi f_O \ell/300)$

At resonance, $Z_{IN} = \pm\infty \Rightarrow \tan\beta\ell = \pm\infty$

Thus the resonant frequency (f_O) is given by:

$\beta\ell = (2n+1)\pi/2$

$f_O = 75*(2n+1)/\ell$ MHz

$f_O = 5$	MHz

EXAMPLE 10.13

In the circuit shown opposite, determine the input impedance at f=10 GHz.

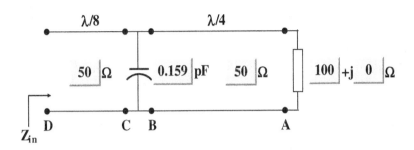

SOLUTION:

INPUT DATA			
Parameter	Real	Imag	Unit
Z_O	50		Ω
Z_L	100	0	Ω
C	0.159		pF
ℓ_1	0.25		λ
ℓ_2	0.125		λ
f	10		GHz

OUTPUT DATA
a) $Z_A = Z_L$
$Z_A = 100 \quad + \; j0$
b) The next element is a series transmission line, therefore we work in impedances: $Z_B(-\ell_1) = Z_0 \dfrac{Z_L + jZ_0 \tan \beta\ell_1}{Z_0 + jZ_L \tan \beta\ell_1}$
$Z_B = 25.00 \quad +(\; j0.00) \quad \Omega$
Since the next element is a shunt capacitor, we need to work in admittances: $Y_B = 1/Z_B$
$Y_B = 0.04000 \; +(\; j0.00000) \; S$
$Y_{CAP} = j\omega C$
$Y_{CAP} = j0.00999 \quad S$
$Y_C = Y_B + Y_{CAP}$
$Y_C = 0.04000 \; +(\; j0.00999) \; \Omega$

c) The next element is a series transmission line with Z_C as load, therefore we need to work in impedances:

$Z_C = 1/Y_C$

$Z_C = 23.53$	$+(-j5.88)$ Ω

$$Z_D(-\ell_2) = Z_0 \frac{Z_c + jZ_0 \tan \beta\ell_2}{Z_0 + jZ_c \tan \beta\ell_2}$$

$Z_{in} = Z_D = 32.01$	$+(j26.00)$ Ω

Chapter 11 Examples

Case I Example

EXAMPLE 11.2
Given the circuit shown in the textbook, design a lumped element matching network at 1 GHz that would transform $Z_L=10+j10\ \Omega$ into a 50 Ω transmission line.

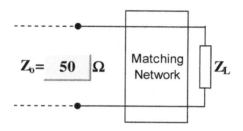

SOLUTION:			
INPUT DATA			
Parameter	Real	Imag	Unit
Z_O	50		Ω
Z_L	10	10	Ω
f	1		GHz

OUTPUT DATA		
Element	Value	Unit
Z_L	10+10j	Ω

Assume:
$x=X/Z_O$,
$b=B/Y_O$.

Caution: The user should be aware where the load is located, i.e., whether it is inside the (1+jx) circle or outside of it, which brings about the following two cases. Thus it's imperative to know which case it is so that the proper solution is used. Furthermore, when case I is used, case II is useless and vice versa.

Case I: Z_L is outside (1+jx) circle ($R_L < Z_O$)
There are two solutions for the series and shunt elements as follows:
A) Series elements
Assume $Z_L = R_L + X_L$
$X_S = -X_L \pm \sqrt{[R_L(Z_O - R_L)]}$

1) $jX_{S1} = j10$ Ω
2) $jX_{S2} = -j30$ Ω

B) Shunt elements
$B = (1 - R_L/Z_O)/(X_L + X_S)$
The corresponding shunt elements are given by:

1) $jB_{P1} = j0.04$
2) $jB_{P2} = -j0.04$

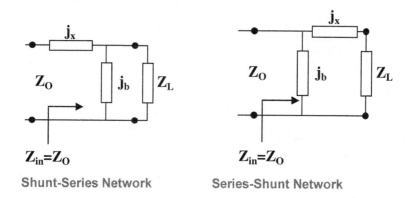

Shunt-Series Network   **Series-Shunt Network**

Case II Example

EXAMPLE 11.2

Given the circuit shown in the textbook, design a lumped element matching network at 1 GHz that would transform $Z_L=10+j10\ \Omega$ into a 50 Ω transmission line.

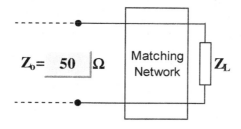

OUTPUT DATA		
Element	Value	Unit
Z_L	100+10j	Ω

Assume:

$x = X/Z_O$,

$b = B/Y_O$.

Caution: The user should be aware where the load is located, i.e., whether it is inside the (1+jx) circle or outside of it, which brings about the following two cases. Thus it's imperative to know which case it is so that the proper solution is used. Furthermore, when case I is used, case II is useless and vice versa.

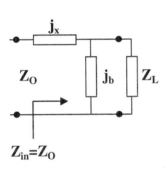

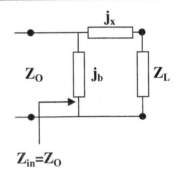

Shunt-Series Network   **Series-Shunt Network**

Case II: Z_L is inside (1+jx) circle ($R_L > Z_O$)

When the load is inside the (1+jx) circle we need to use the following formulas for the series and shunt elements.

A) Shunt elements

$B_P = [X_L \pm \sqrt{(R_L/Z_O)}][\sqrt{(R_L^2 + X_L^2 - Z_O R_L)}]/(R_L^2 + X_L^2)$

1) $jB_{P1} = j0.01099$	Ω
2) $jB_{P2} = -j0.00901$	Ω

The corresponding series elements are given by:

$X_S = 1/B_P + X_L Z_O/R_L - Z_O/B_P R_L$

1) $jX_{S1} = j50.49752$

2) $jX_{S2} = -j50.49752$

EXAMPLE 11.3

Design a matching network using a single shunt open stub as a tuning element to match a load impedance $Z_L=15+j10\ \Omega$ to a $50\ \Omega$ transmission line.

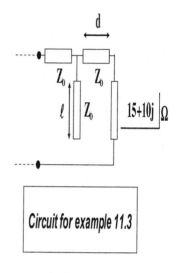

Circuit for example 11.3

SOLUTION:

INPUT DATA

Parameter	Real	Imag	Unit
Z_O	50		Ω
Z_L	15	10	Ω

OUTPUT DATA

Element	Value	Unit
Z_L	15+10j	Ω

We need to derive formulas for the location of the stub (d) and length of the stub (ℓ) as follows:

1) Calculation of "d" (when $R_L \neq Z_O$)

$$\tan\beta d = \{X_L \pm \sqrt{(R_L[(Z_O-R_L)^2+X_L^2]/Z_O)}\}/(R_L-Z_O)$$

a) $\tan\beta d_1 = -0.855354$

$\qquad d_1 = 0.387383\ \ \lambda$

b) $\tan\beta d_2 = 0.283926$

$\qquad d_2 = 0.044029\ \ \lambda$

2) Since we are dealing with shunt stubs, we need to work in admittances. At the location (d) on the T.L., the input admittance value (Y) is given by:

$Y=G+jB$

$t=\tan\beta d$

$G=[R_L(1+t^2)]/D$

$B=R_L^2*t-(Z_0-X_L*t)(X_L+Z_0*t)/(D*Z_0)$

Where

$D=R_L^2+(X_L+Z_0t)^2$

There are two solutions to the given problem:

a) $G_1=0.02$ S

   $B_1=0.02658$ S

b) $G_2=0.02$ S

   $B_2=-0.02658$ S

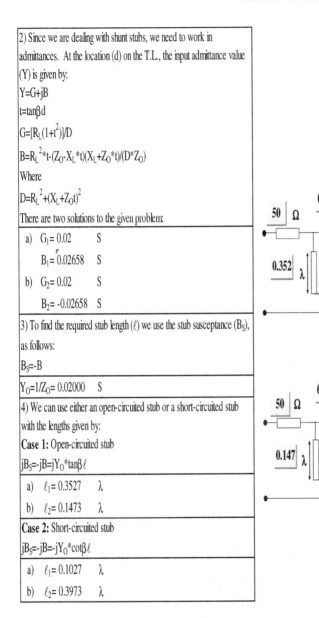

3) To find the required stub length (ℓ) we use the stub susceptance (B_S), as follows:

$B_S=-B$

$Y_0=1/Z_0=0.02000$ S

4) We can use either an open-circuited stub or a short-circuited stub with the lengths given by:

Case 1: Open-circuited stub

$jB_S=-jB=jY_0*\tan\beta\ell$

a) $\ell_1=0.3527$ λ

b) $\ell_2=0.1473$ λ

Case 2: Short-circuited stub

$jB_S=-jB=-jY_0*\cot\beta\ell$

a) $\ell_1=0.1027$ λ

b) $\ell_2=0.3973$ λ

Reference: D. M. Pozar, "Microwave Engineering", 2nd edition, pp.258-262 Wiley & Sons, 1998.

EXAMPLE 11.4

Using a single series open stub, design a matching network that will transform a load impedance $Z_L=100+j80$ Ω to a 50 Ω feed transmission line as shown below.

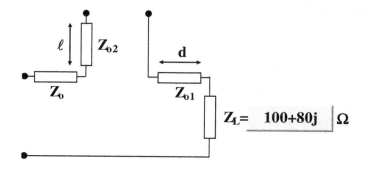

SOLUTION:

INPUT DATA

Parameter	Real	Imag	Unit
Z_O	50		Ω
Z_L	100	80	Ω

OUTPUT DATA

Element	Value	Unit
Z_L	100+80j	Ω

Y_L= 0.00610   -j0.00488

Y_O=1/Z_O= 0.02000   S

We need to derive formulas for the location of the stub (d) and length of the stub (ℓ) as follows:

1) Calculation of "d" (when $G_L \neq Y_O$)

$\tan\beta d = \{B_L \pm \sqrt{(G_L[(Y_O-G_L)^2+B_L^2]/Y_O)}\}/(G_L-Y_O)$

a) $\tan\beta d_1$= -0.2343

d_1= 0.4634 λ

b) $\tan\beta d_2$= 0.9360

d_2= 0.1197 λ

2) Since we are dealing with series stubs, we need to work in impedances. At the location (d) on the T.L., the input impedance value (Y) is given by:

$Z=R+jX$

$t=\tan\beta d$

$G=[G_L(1+t^2)]/D$

$X=G_L^2*t-(Y_O-B_L*t)(B_L+Y_O*t)/(D*Y_O)$

$D=G_L^2+(B_L+Y_Ot)^2$

There are two solutions to the given problem:

a) $R_1 = 50$ Ω

$X_1 = 66.71$ Ω

b) $R_2 = 50$ Ω

$X_2 = -66.71$ Ω

3) To find the required stub length (ℓ) we use the stub reactance (X_S), to cancel out the line reactance (X), as follows:

$X_S = -X$

4) We can use either an open-circuited stub or a short-circuited stub with the lengths given by:

Case 1: Open-circuited stub

$jX_S = -jX = -jZ_0 * \cot\beta\ell$

a) $\ell_1 = 0.1024$ λ

b) $\ell_2 = 0.3976$ λ

Case 2: Short-circuited stub

$jX_S = -jX = jZ_0 * \tan\beta\ell$

a) $\ell_1 = 0.3524$ λ

b) $\ell_2 = 0.1476$ λ

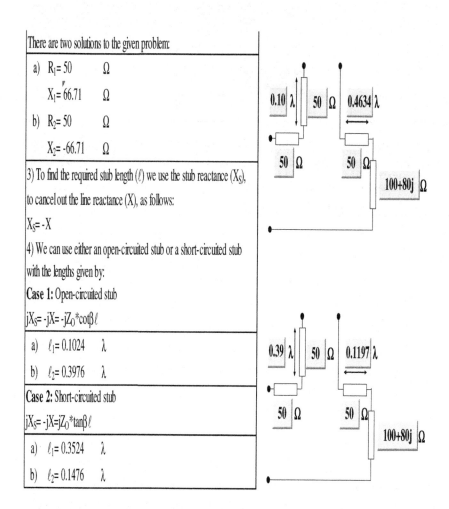

Reference: D. M. Pozar, "Microwave Engineering", 2nd edition, pp.259-262 Wiley & Sons, 1998.

EXAMPLE 11.5

Design a matching network using a quarter-wave transformer that would transform a 50 Ω load to $\Gamma_{in}=0.68\angle97°$ as shown opposite.

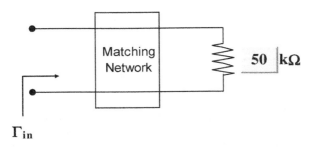

Γ_{in}

SOLUTION:

INPUT DATA

Parameter	Real	Unit
Z_O	50	Ω
Z_L	50	Ω

Parameter	Mag.	Angle
Γ_{in}	0.68	97°

OUTPUT DATA

$Z_{in}= 16.51$	$+j41.45$	Ω

$Y_{in}=1/Z_{in}=G_{in}+jB_{in}$

$Y_{in}= 0.00829 \quad -j0.02082 \quad$ S

Because we will be using shunt stubs we need to work in admittances, thus we use Y_{in} ($=G_{in}+jB_{in}$) to solve the problem.

a) We use a quarter-wave transformer (Z_{O1}) to transform the load (Z_L) to R_{in} ($=1/G_{in}$):

$$Z_L * R_{in}=Z_{O1}^2 \Rightarrow Z_{O1}=\sqrt{(Z_L * R_{in})}=\sqrt{(Z_L/G_{in})}$$

$Z_{O1}= 77.65 \quad \Omega$

b) The reactive part (jB_{in}) can now be synthesized by using an open-circuited shunt stub of length $\ell=3\lambda/8$ and a characteristic impedance (Z_{02}) given by:

$Z_{02}=|1/B_{in}|$

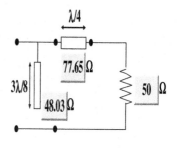

$Z_{02}= 48.03$ Ω

Note: Open-circuited stub

$Y_{OC}=jB_{in}=jY_{02}\tan\beta\,\ell$

$Y_{02}=B_{in}/\tan\beta\,\ell \Rightarrow Z_{02}=(\tan\beta\,\ell)/B_{in}$

If $B_{in}<0$ then we need $\ell=3\lambda/8$,

$\Rightarrow \tan\beta\,\ell=\tan\beta\,(3\lambda/8)=-1$

If $B_{in}>0$ then we need $\ell=\lambda/8$,

$\Rightarrow \tan\beta\,\ell=\tan\beta\,(\lambda/8)=1$

Reference: D. M. Pozar, "Microwave Engineering", 2nd edition, pp.262-266 Wiley & Sons, 1998.

Design Center

RF/MW Calculations

Matching Network Design

RF/MW Calculations

Decibel (db) Unit Calculations

Transmission Line Calculations

Matching Circuit Designs

Lumped Element Designs

Distributed Single Stub Designs

Single Stub Matching Network Designs

Series Stub Matching

Parallel Stub Matching

Generalized Stub Matching

Different Impedance Stub Matching

Parallel Stub Matching Network Designs

Unbalanced Parallel Stub Matching

Balanced Parallel Stub Matching

Design Center
RF/MW Calculations

Decibel (dB) Unit Calculations

INPUT DATA	
Power	mW
P1	100
P2	50

SOLUTION:			
Power	dBm	dBW	dBuW
P1	20	-10	50
P2	17.0	-13.0	47.0

Power Ratio	Ratio	Ratio (dB)	Ratio in Neper
P1/P2	2	3.0	0.35

Note:

$$Np = \ln(\frac{V1}{V2}) = \ln(\frac{\sqrt{P1}}{\sqrt{P2}})$$

where

$$V1 = k * \sqrt{P1}$$
$$V2 = k * \sqrt{P2}$$

Transmission Line Calculations

Lossless Transmission Line

INPUT DATA			
Parameter	Value	Unit	
f (GHz)	3	GHz	
ε_r	4	F/m	
d	0.32	λ	
l	0.32	λ	
Zo	50	Ohm	
Parameter	Real	Imag	Unit
Z_L	50	90	Ohm
Zg	50	90	Ohm

SOLUTION:			
OUTPUT DATA			
Parameter	Real	Angle	Unit
λ_o	10.000		cm
λ	5.000		cm
β	1.257		rad/cm
Vp	1.50E+10		cm/sec
Γ_L	0.67	48.01	
Γg	0.67	48.01	
VSWR	5.042		
Parameter	Real	Imag	Unit
Zin(-d)	9.9	1.0	Ohm
Zin(-l)	9.9	1.0	Ohm
$\Gamma_{in(-d)}$	-0.67	0.017	
$\Gamma_{in(-l)}$	-0.67	0.017	

Quasi-TEM Transmission Line (micro

INPUT DATA		
Parameter	Value	Unit
f	3	Ghz
w	1	mm
h	1	cm
εr	1.1	

SOLUTION:		
OUTPUT DATA		
Parameter	Value	Unit
εff	1.06	
λo	10.000	cm
λ_{TEM}	9.53	cm
λ	9.695	cm
Vp	2.8E+10	cm/sec
fo	3.77	GHz

Matching Network Design

Lumped Element Designs

Parameter	Real	Imag	Unit
		INPUT DATA	
Z_O	50		Ω
Z_L	75	45	Ω
f	1		GHz

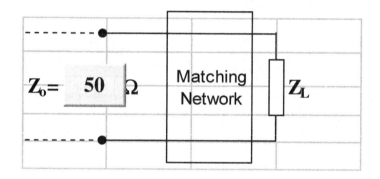

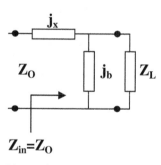

Shunt-Series Network

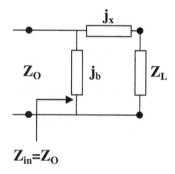

Series-Shunt Network

OUTPUT DATA		
Element	Value	Unit
Z_L	75+45j	Ω

Assume: $x=X/Zo$, $b=B/Yo$ and $Z_L=R_L+X_L$

Caution: Case I

Go to Case I calculations, the load is inside of circle (1+jx)

Case I: Z_L **is inside (1+jx) circle ($R_L > Z_O$)**

When the load is inside the (1+jx) circle we need to use the following formulas for the series and shunt elements.

A) Shunt elements

$B_P=[X_L \pm \sqrt{(R_L/Z_O)}][\sqrt{(R_L^2+X_L^2-Z_OR_L)}]/(R_L^2+X_L^2)$

1) $jB_{P1}=$ j0.02	Ω ==>	Cshunt =	2.53	pF
2) $jB_{P2}=$ -j0.00412	Ω ==>	**Lshunt =**	**38.67**	**nH**

The corresponding series elements are given by:

$X_S=1/B_P+X_LZ_O/R_L-Z_O/B_PR_L$

1) $jX_{S1}=$ j50.9902	Ω ==>	Lseries =	8.12	nH
2) $jX_{S2}=$ -j50.9902	Ω ==>	**Cseries =**	**3.12**	**pF**

INPUT DATA			
Parameter	Real	Imag	Unit
Z_O	50		Ω
Z_L	10	10	Ω
f	1		GHz

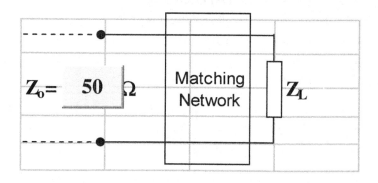

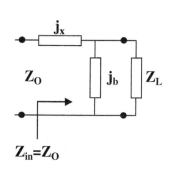

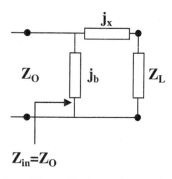

Shunt-Series Network   **Series-Shunt Network**

OUTPUT DATA		
Element	Value	Unit
Z_L	10+10j	Ω
Assume: x=X/Zo, b=B/Yo and $Z_L=R_L+X_L$		
Caution: Case II		
Go to Case II or III, the load is outside circle (1+jx)		

Case II	Z_L is outside $(1+jx)$ circle $(R_L<Z_O)$			
There are two solutions for the series and shunt elements as follows:				
A) Series elements				
Assume $Z_L=R_L+X_L$				
$X_S=-X_L\pm\sqrt{[R_L(Z_O-R_L)]}$				
1) $jX_{S1}= j10$	Ω ==>	Lseries =	1.59	nH
2) $jX_{S2}=$ -j30	Ω ==>	**Cseries =**	**5.31**	**pF**
B) Shunt elements				
$B=(1-R_L/Z_O)/(X_L+X_S)$				
The corresponding shunt elements are given by:				
1) $jB_{P1}= j0.04$	Ω ==>	Cshunt =	6.37	pF
2) $jB_{P2}=$ -j0.04	Ω ==>	**Lshunt =**	**3.98**	**nH**

Distributed Single Stub Designs

Series Stub Matching

INPUT DATA			
Parameter	Real	Imag	Unit
Z_O	50		Ω
Z_L	100	80	Ω

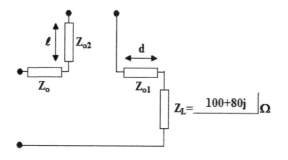

OUTPUT DATA		

Element	Value	Unit
Z_L	100+80j	Ω

Element	Real	Imaginary	Unit
$Y_L=$	0.00610	-0.00488	S
$Y_0=1/Z_0=$	0.020	0	S

1) Calcule "d" to bring the impedance to the unity resistance circle

$\tan\beta d = \{B_L \pm \sqrt{(G_L[(Y_0-G_L)^2+B_L^2]/Y_0)}\}/(G_L-Y_0)$

a) $\tan\beta d_1 = -0.2343$ or	b) $\tan\beta d_2 = 0.9360$
$d_1 = 0.4634$ $\quad\lambda$	$d_2 = 0.1197$ $\quad\lambda$

2) Since we are dealing with series stubs, we need to work in impedances. At the location (d) on the T.L., the input impedance value (Y) is given by:

$Z=R+jX$

$t=\tan\beta d$

$G=[G_L(1+t^2)]/D$

$X=G_L^2 *t-(Y_0-B_L*t)(B_L+Y_0*t)/(D*Y_0)$

$D=G_L^2+(B_L+Y_0 t)^2$

There are two solutions to the given problem:

a) $R_1 = 50$ $\qquad\Omega$	b) $R_2 = 50$ $\qquad\Omega$
$X_1 = 66.71$ $\qquad\Omega$	$X_2 = -66.71$ $\qquad\Omega$

3) To find the required stub length (ℓ) we use the stub reactance (X_S), to cancel out the line reactance (X), as follows:

$X_S = -X$

4) We can use either an open-circuited stub or a short-circuited stub with the lengths given by:

Case 1: Open-circuited stub

$jX_S = -jX = -jZ_o * \cot\beta\ell$

a)	$\ell_1 = 0.1024$	λ
b)	$\ell_2 = 0.3976$	λ

Case 2: Short-circuited stub

$jX_S = -jX = jZ_o * \tan\beta\ell$

a)	$\ell_1 = 0.3524$	λ
b)	$\ell_2 = 0.1476$	λ

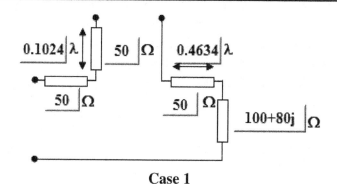

Case 1

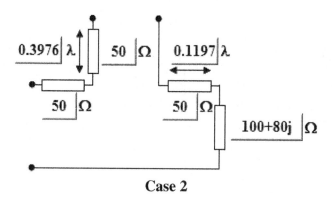

Case 2

Parallel Stub Matching

Unbalanced Parallel Stub Matching

INPUT DATA			
Parameter	Real	Imag	Unit
Z_O	50		Ω
Z_L	15	10	Ω

Element	Value	Unit
Z_L	15+10j	Ω

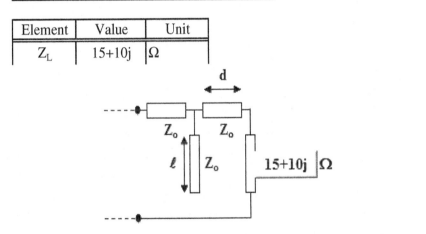

We need to derive formulas for the location of the stub (d) and length of the stub (ℓ) as follows:

1) Calculation of "d" (when $R_L \neq Z_O$)

$$\tan\beta d = \{X_L \pm \sqrt{(R_L[(Z_O - R_L)^2 + X_L^2]/Z_O)}\}/(R_L - Z_O)$$

a) $\tan\beta d_1 = -0.855354$	b) $\tan\beta d_2 = 0.28392577$
$d_1 = 0.3873829$ λ	$d_2 = 0.04402947$ λ

2) Since we are dealing with shunt stubs, we need to work in admittances. At the location (d) on the T.L., the input admittance value (Y) is given by:

$Y = G + jB$

$t = \tan\beta d$

$G = [R_L(1 + t^2)]/D$

$B = R_L^2 * t - (Z_O - X_L * t)(X_L + Z_O * t)/(D * Z_O)$

Where

$D = R_L^2 + (X_L + Z_O t)^2$

There are two solutions to the given problem:

a) G1 = 0.02 S	b) G2 = 0.02 S
B1 = 0.02658 S	B2 = -0.02658 S

3) To find the required stub length (ℓ) we use the stub susceptance (B_S), as follows:

$B_S = -B$

$Y_O = 1/Z_O = 0.02000$ S

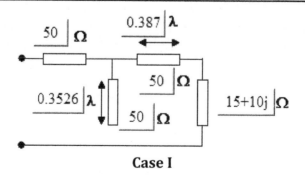

Case I

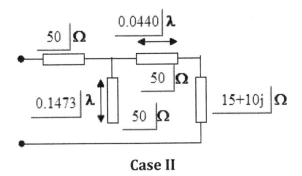

Case II

4) We can use either an open-circuited stub or a short-circuited stub with the lengths given by: **Case 1:** Open-circuited stub $jB_S=-jB=jY_O*\tan\beta\ell$	
a) $\ell_1=$ 0.352656 λ	
b) $\ell_2=$ 0.147344 λ	
Case 2: Short-circuited stub $jB_S=-jB=-jY_O*\cot\beta\ell$	
a) $\ell_1=$ 0.102656 λ	
b) $\ell_2=$ 0.397344 λ	

Balanced Parallel Stub Matching

INPUT DATA			
Parameter	Real	Imag	Unit
Z_O	50		Ω
Z_L	15	10	Ω

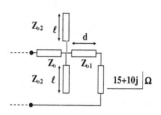

OUTPUT DATA		
Element	Value	Unit
Z_L	15+10j	Ω
Z_{02}	100	Ω

Calculate the lengths of the series and parallel stubs as in the Unbalanced stub matching network. Simply split the parallel stub into two stubs with equal length but double the characterisitic impedance.

First, use a series TL to convert the impedance to lie on unity conductance circle.

$$\tan\beta d=\{X_L\pm\sqrt{(R_L[(Z_O-R_L)^2+X_L^2]/Z_O)}\}/(R_L-Z_O)$$

a) $\tan\beta d_1$ = -0.855354	or	b) $\tan\beta d_2$= 0.2839258
d_1= 0.387 λ		d_2= 0.044 λ

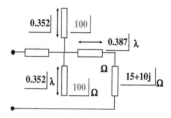

2) Since we are dealing with shunt stubs, we need to work in admittances. At the location (d) on the T.L., the input admittance value (Y) is given by:

$Y=G+jB$

$t=\tan\beta d$

$G=[R_L(1+t^2)]/D$

$B=R_L^2*t-(Z_O-X_L*t)(X_L+Z_O*t)/(D*Z_O)$

Where

$D=R_L^2+(X_L+Z_Ot)^2$

There are two solutions to the given problem:

- a) G_1= 0.02   S
- B_1= 0.02658   S
- b) G_2= 0.02   S
- B_2= -0.02658 S

3) To find the required stub length (ℓ) we use the stub susceptance (B_S), as follows:

B_S=-B

$Y_O=1/Z_O$= 0.02000   S

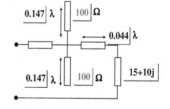

4) We can use either an open-circuited stub or a short-circuited stub with the lengths given by:

Case 1: Open-circuited stub

$jB_S=-jB=jY_O*\tan\beta\ell$

- a) ℓ_1= 0.3527 λ
- b) ℓ_2= 0.1473 λ

Case 2: Short-circuited stub

$jB_S=-jB=-jY_O*\cot\beta\ell$

- a) ℓ_1= 0.1027 λ
- b) ℓ_2= 0.3973 λ

Generalized Stub Matching (Case III)

Parameter	Real	Imag	Unit
INPUT DATA			
Z_O	50		Ω
Z_1	25	50	Ω
Z_2	20	50	Ω
f	1		GHz

To find the matching circuit that matches Z1 to Z2 in the figure below

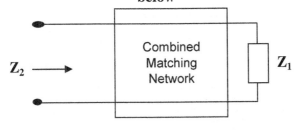

First match Z1 to Zo per the figure below

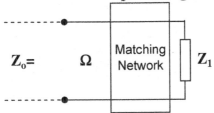

Element	Value	Unit
Z_1	25+50j	Ω
Assume:	x=X/Zo, b=B/Yo and $Z_L=R_L+X_L$	

Caution: Case III		Zload is outside (1+jx) and (1+jb) circles		
		Case III		

Case III:	Z_L is outside of (1+jx) and (1+jb) circles			
There are **four solutions** (C-L, L-C, C-C and L-L combimations).				
1) $jB_{P1}=$	j0.026	S ==>	Cshunt =	-6.17	pF
1) $jX_{S1}=$	j61.237	Ω ==>	Lseries =	9.75	nH
2) $jB_{P2}=$	j0.00620	S ==>	Cshunt =	-25.66	pF
2) $jX_{S2}=$	-j61.24	Ω ==>	Cseries =	2.60	pF
3) $jX_{S1}=$	-j25.00	Ω ==>	Cseries =	-3.98	pF
3) $jB_{P1}=$	j0.02	S ==>	Cshunt =	3.18	pF
4) $jX_{S2}=$	-j75.00	Ω ==>	Cseries =	-11.94	pF
4) $jB_{P2}=$	-j0.02	S ==>	Lshunt =	7.96	nH

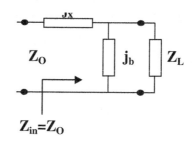

Shunt-Series Network

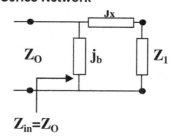

Series-Shunt Network

Now that we have matched Z_1 to Z_o, we need to match Z_2 to Z_o in the circuit below

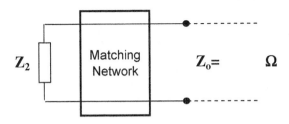

INPUT DATA			
Parameter	Real	Imag	Unit
Z_2	20	50	Ω

Caution: Case III		Zload is outside (1+jx) and (1+jb) circles			
		Case III			
1) Cseries:	2.31	pF ==>	1) Lshunt	5.95	nH
2) Lseries	10.97	nH ==>	2) Lshunt:	20.58	nH
3) Lshunt:	6.50	pF ==>	3) Lseries	4.06	nH
4) Cshunt	3.90	pF ==>	4) Lseries	11.86	nH

The final solution is the combination of the two circuits found above, as shown below:

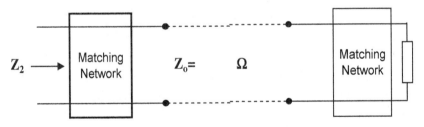

Different Impedance Stub Matching

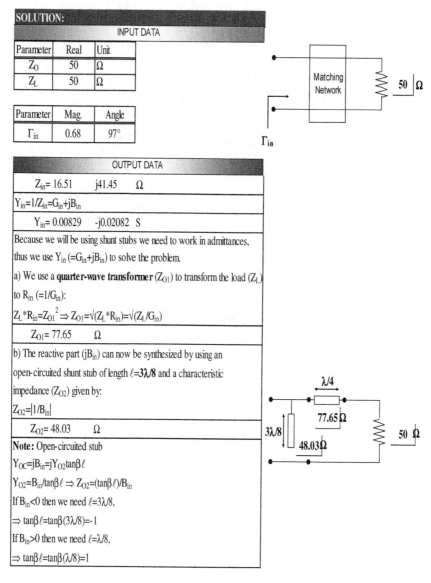

Reference: D. M. Pozar, "Microwave Engineering", 2nd edition,
pp.262-266 Wiley & Sons, 1998.

APPENDIX J

Power Calculations

Sinusoidal Steady State

In Chapter 2, power was generally defined as;

$$P(t)=v(t)i(t) \tag{J.0}$$

We shall now use this equation to define several specific power terms for signals in the sinusoidal steady state for a general circuit as shown in Figure below.

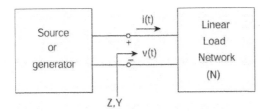

Let us define,

$$v(t)=V_m\cos(\omega t+\varphi_v)$$

$$i(t)=I_m\cos(\omega t+\varphi_i)$$

Where $\omega=2\pi f=2\pi/T$ is the frequency of operation, with f and T being the frequency and period of the sinusoid, respectively.

Instantaneous Power, p(t)

Instantaneous Power, p(t), is defined as:

p(t)=v(t)i(t)

$$=I_m V_m \cos(\omega t+\varphi_v)\,\cos(\omega t+\varphi_i)$$

$$=\frac{1}{2}\,[I_m V_m \cos(\varphi_v - \varphi_i)] + \frac{1}{2}\,[I_m V_m \cos(2\omega t+\varphi_v+\varphi_i)] \qquad (J.1)$$

Average Power, P_{av}

Average power is defined as:

$$P_{av} = \frac{1}{T}\int_0^T p(t)dt = \frac{1}{T}\int_0^T v(t)i(t)dt, \quad n=1,2,3,.... \qquad (J.2)$$

We know that the integral of any sinusoid over any number of its period is zero, i.e.,

$$\int_0^{nT} \cos(\omega t + \phi) = 0$$

Thus Equation (J.2) gives:

$$P_{av}= \frac{1}{2}\,[I_m V_m \cos(\varphi_v - \varphi_i)] \qquad (J.3)$$

Figure below shows the relationship of the P_{av} and p(t) to v(t) and i(t).

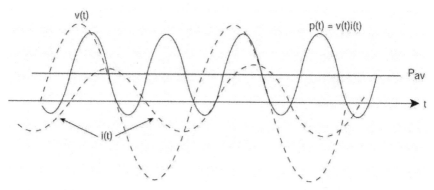

NOTE 1: *For a linear resistor, $\varphi_v = \varphi_i = 0$, thus (J.2) can be written as:*

$$P_{av}= \frac{1}{2} [I_mV_m]= \frac{1}{2} [RI_m^2]= \frac{1}{2} [V_m^2/R] \qquad (J.4a)$$

NOTE 2: *For a DC signal ($\omega=0$) since $\varphi_v =\varphi_i=0$ and $V_m=V_{DC}$ and $I_m=I_{DC}$, then the average power delivered to a resistive load (R) is simply given by:*

$$P_{av}=V_{DC}I_{DC}=RI_{DC}^2=V_{DC}^2/R \qquad (J.4b)$$

Complex Power, P

Complex power can now be defined as:

$$P=\frac{1}{2} [VI^*] \qquad (J.5)$$

Where V and I are phasors for v(t) and i(t), respectively, and are defined as:

$$V= V_m e^{j\varphi_v}$$

$$I= I_m e^{j\varphi_i}$$

Thus Equation (J.5) can be written as:

$$P= \frac{1}{2} [I_mV_m e^{j(\varphi_v -\varphi_i)}]$$

$$= \frac{1}{2} \{I_mV_m[\cos(\varphi_v- \varphi_i) + j \sin(\varphi_v- \varphi_i)]\} \qquad (J.6)$$

Average Power

$$P_{av}=Re(P)= \frac{1}{2} Re(VI^*) \qquad (J.7)$$

Letting $Z(j\omega)$ [or $Y(j\omega)$] to be the input impedance (or input admittance) of the load network, then we have:

$$Z(j\omega) = \frac{1}{Y(j\omega)} = \frac{V}{I} = \frac{V_m}{I_m} e^{j(\phi_v - \phi_i)} = Z_m e^{j\phi_z}$$

Where

$Z_m = V_m / I_m,$

$\varphi_z = \varphi_v - \varphi_i$

$$P_{av} = \frac{1}{2} (I_m V_m \cos\varphi_z)$$

$$= \frac{1}{2} [I_m^2 \, ReZ(j\omega)]$$

$$= \frac{1}{2} [V_m^2 \, ReY(j\omega)] \qquad (J.8)$$

Which indicates that the average power delivered to a load can be changed by merely changing the phase of the load without changing its magnitude.

Superposition of Average Powers

The instantaneous power, being a nonlinear function, does not follow the superposition theorem. However, it can easily be shown that superposition holds valid for average power (P_{av}) as follows:

$$(P_{av})_{total} = P_{av,\omega_1} + P_{av,\omega_2} + \dots + P_{av,\omega_n} \qquad (J.9)$$

The Effective or Root-Mean-Square (rms) Value

The concept of an "effective value" comes from a desire to have a periodic signal (voltage or current) deliver to a resistor load (R), the same average power (P_{av}) as an equivalent DC signal (voltage or current) would. Thus the effective value of a signal (V_{eff} or I_{eff}) is a measure of its effectiveness in delivering real power to a load resistor (R).

To find the effective value of a signal, we need to find an equivalent DC value (V_{eff} or I_{eff}) that will deliver the same average power (P_{av}) to a resistor load (R) as would be delivered by the periodic signal itself. Thus from (J.2) and (J.4b), we can write:

For a DC Signal

$$(P_{av})_{DC} = RI_{eff}^2,$$
(J.10)

For A Periodic Signal

$$P_{av} = \frac{1}{T}\int_0^T v(t)i(t)dt$$
(J.11)

substituting for $v(t)=Ri(t)$ and equating Equation (J.10) with (J.11), we have:

$$P_{av} = \frac{1}{T}\int_0^T Ri(t)^2 dt = RI_{eff}^2$$
(J.12)

Or,

$$I_{eff} = \left[\frac{1}{T}\int_0^T i(t)^2 dt\right]^{1/2}$$
(J.13)

From (J.13) we see that I_{eff} is the square root of the mean of the squared (or root-mean-square) value of the current. Thus the effective current (I_{eff}) is commonly referred to as the "**root-mean-square**" current (I_{rms}), i.e.,

$I_{eff} = I_{rms}$

Similarly, V_{eff} is found as follows:

$$P_{av} = \frac{1}{T}\int_0^T \frac{v(t)^2}{R}dt = \frac{V_{eff}^2}{R}$$
(J.14)

$$V_{eff} = \left[\frac{1}{T} \int_0^T v(t)^2 dt \right]^{1/2} \tag{J.15}$$

NOTE: *Since $V_{eff} = RI_{eff}$ and,*

$$P_{av} = RI_{eff}^2 = V_{eff}^2 / R$$

Thus we can write:

$$P_{av} = I_{eff}V_{eff} = I_{rms}V_{rms} \tag{J.16}$$

In other words the "1/2" factor caused by the averaging process disappears and we calculate the average power as if we were dealing with DC signals.

Special Case- Sinusoidal Signals

When the periodic signal is sinusoidal [e.g. $i(t) = I_m \cos\omega t$], I_{rms} (or I_{eff}) can be calculated as follows:

$$i(t) = I_m \cos\omega t$$

$$I_{rms} = \left[\frac{1}{T} \int_0^T I_m^2 \cos^2 \omega t dt \right]^{1/2} = \left[\frac{I_m^2}{T} \int_0^T \frac{(1 + \cos 2\omega t)}{2} dt \right]^{1/2} = \left[\frac{I_m^2}{T} x \frac{T}{2} \right]^{1/2}$$

Or,

$$I_{rms} = I_{eff} = \frac{I_m}{\sqrt{2}} \tag{J.17a}$$

For $i(t) = I_m \sin\omega t$ we get identical result as follows:

$$I_{rms} = \left[\frac{1}{T} \int_0^T I_m^2 \sin^2 \omega t dt \right]^{1/2} = \left[\frac{I_m^2}{T} \int_0^T \frac{(1 - \cos 2\omega t)}{2} dt \right]^{1/2} = \left[\frac{I_m^2}{T} x \frac{T}{2} \right]^{1/2}$$

Or,

$$I_{rms} = I_{eff} = \frac{I_m}{\sqrt{2}} \qquad \text{(J.17b)}$$

Note 1:

$$\cos^2 \omega t = \frac{1 + \cos 2\omega t}{2}$$

$$\sin^2 \omega t = \frac{1 - \cos 2\omega t}{2}$$

For $\omega = 2\pi f$ and $T = 1/f$, we have:

$$\int_0^T \cos 2\omega t = 0 .$$

Similarly, for sinusoidal voltage:

$$v(t) = V_m \cos \omega t,$$

Or

$$v(t) = V_m \sin \omega t$$

the effective (or rms) value is given by

$$V_{rms} = V_{eff} = \frac{V_m}{\sqrt{2}} \qquad \text{(J.18)}$$

Note 2: *Similar to average powers, superposition also holds valid for the rms values of several sinusoids as follows:*

$$\left(P_{rms}\right)_{total} = P_{rms,\omega_1} + P_{rms,\omega_2} + \ldots\ldots + P_{rms,\omega_n} \qquad \text{(J.19)}$$

Note 3: *For a nonresistive load (Z), from (J.3) the average power delivered can now be written in terms of I_{rms} and V_{rms} as:*

$$Z = R + jX = |Z|e^{j\phi_z}$$

$$P_{av} = \frac{I_m V_m}{2} \cos(\phi_v - \phi_i)$$

Or,

$$P_{av} = I_{rms} V_{rms} \cos(\varphi_z) \tag{J.20}$$

Glossary of Technical Terms

The following glossary supplements the presented materials in the text, but does not replace the use of an unabridged technical dictionary, which is a must for mastery of sciences.

Absolute
a) That which is without reference to anything else and thus not comparative or dependent upon external conditions for its existence (opposed to relative), **b)** That which is free from any limitations or restrictions and is thus unconditionally true at all times.

Absolute Temperature Scale
A scale with which temperatures are measured relative to absolute zero (the temperature of –273.15 °C or –459.67 °F or 0 K). The absolute temperature scale leads to the absolute temperatures, which are: a) The temperature in Celsius degrees, relative to –273.15 °C (giving rise to the Kelvin scale), and b) The temperature in Fahrenheit degrees, relative to –459.67 °F (giving rise to the Rankine scale). At absolute zero temperature, molecular motion theoretically vanishes and a body would have no heat energy. The absolute zero temperature is approachable but never attainable. *See also* **Temperature**.

Active Device
An electronic component such as a transistor that can be used to produce amplification (or gain) in a circuit.

Admittance
The measure of ease of AC current flow in a circuit, the reciprocal of impedance expressed in Siemens (symbol Y or y).

Ampere (A)

The unit of electric current defined as the flow of one Coulomb of charge per second. Alternately, it can also be defined as the constant current that would produce a force of 2×10^{-7} Newton per meter of length in two straight parallel conductors of infinite length, and of negligible cross section, placed one meter apart in a vacuum.

Ampere's Law

Current (either conduction or displacement) flowing in a wire or in space generates a magnetic flux that encircles the wire in a clockwise direction when the current is moving away from the observer. The direction of the magnetic field follows the right hand rule (This law may also be referred to as the law of magnetic field generation).

Differential form: $\mathrm{Curl}\overline{H} = \overline{J} + \dfrac{\partial \overline{D}}{\partial t}$,

Integral form : $\oint_C \overline{H} \cdot \overline{d\ell} = I + \int_s \dfrac{\partial \overline{D}}{\partial t} \cdot \overline{dS}$

Amplitude

The extent to which an alternating current or pulsating current or voltage swings from zero or a mean value.

Analog

Pertaining to the general class of devices or circuits in which the output varies as a continuous function of the input.

Anode

The positive electrode of a device (such as a diode, etc.) toward which the electrons move during current flow.

Application Mass

All of the related masses that are connected and/or obtained as a result of the application of a science. This includes all physical devices, machines, experimental setups, and other physical materials that are directly or indirectly derived from and are a result of the application. In this book when we say application mass, we really mean "technical application mass." See also Generalized application mass, Technical application mass and personalized application mass.

Attenuation

The decrease in amplitude of a signal during its transmission from one point to another.

Attenuation Constant
The real component of the propagation constant.

Attenuator
A resistive network that provides reduction of the amplitude of an electrical signal without introducing appreciable phase or frequency distortion.

Average Power
The power averaged over one cycle.

Axiom
A self-evident truth accepted without proof.

B

Bias
The steady and constant current or voltage applied to an electrical device to establish an operating point for proper operation of the device.

Bidirectional
Responsive in both directions.

Bilateral
Having a voltage-current characteristic curve that is symmetrical with respect to the origin. If a positive voltage produces a positive current magnitude, then an equal negative voltage produces a negative current of the same magnitude.

Brewster Angle
The angle of incidence of light reflected from a dielectric surface at which the reflection coefficient becomes zero when the light's electrical field vector lies in the plane of incidence (parallel polarization). In other words, if a parallel polarized wave is incident at a dielectric surface at the Brewster angle, all of the wave will be transmitted through and there will be no reflection. Generally speaking, the concept of Brewster angle applies to any electronic wave of any frequency, not just light waves [$\theta_B = \tan^{-1}(\varepsilon_2/\varepsilon_1)^{1/2}$].

C

Capacitance
The property that permits the storage of electrically separated charges when a potential difference exists between two conductors. The capacitance of a capacitor is defined as the ratio between the electric charge of one electrode, and the difference in potential between the electrodes.

Capacitor
A device consisting essentially of two conducting surfaces separated by an insulating material (or a dielectric) such as air, paper, mica, etc., that can store electric charge.

Cathode
The portion or element of a two-terminal device that is the primary source of electrons during operation.

Cavity (Also Called a Cavity Resonator)
A metallic enclosure inside which resonant fields at microwave frequencies are excited in such a way that it becomes a source of electromagnetic oscillations frequencies.

Cell
A single and basic unit for producing electricity by electrochemical or biochemical action. For example, a battery consists of a series of connected cells.

Celsius (°C)
$1/100^{th}$ of the temperature difference between the freezing point of water (0°C) and the boiling point of water (100°C) on the Celsius temperature scale given by:

$$T(°C) = T(K) - 273.15 = \frac{5}{9} \{T(°F) - 32\}.$$

Characteristic Impedance
The driving-point impedance of a transmission line if it were of infinite length. This can also be defined as the ratio of the voltage to current at every point along a transmission line on which there are no standing waves. It is given in general by:

$$Z_0 = \sqrt{(R + j\omega L)/(G + j\omega C)}$$

Charge

A basic property of elementary particles of matter (electrons, protons, etc.) that is capable of creating a force field in its vicinity. The built-in force field is a result of stored electric energy.

Chip

A single substrate upon which all the active and passive circuit elements are fabricated using one or all of the semiconductor techniques of diffusion, passivation, masking, photoresist, epitaxial growth, etc.

Circuit

The interconnection of a number of devices in one or more closed paths to perform a desired electrical or electronic function.

Classical Mechanics (Also Called Classical Physics, Non-Quantized Physics or Continuum Physics)

Is the branch of physics based on concepts established before quantum physics, and includes materials in conformity with Newton's mechanics and Maxwell's electromagnetic theory.

Coaxial Transmission Line (Also Called Coaxial Cable)

A concentric transmission line in which one conductor completely surrounds the other, the two being separated by a continuous solid dielectric or by dielectric spacers. Such a line has no external field and is not susceptible to external fields.

Coulomb (C)

The unit of electric charge defined as the charge transported across a surface in one second by an electric current of one ampere. An electron has a charge of 1.602×10^{-19} Coulomb.

Coulomb's Laws

The laws that state that the force (F) of attraction or repulsion between two electric charges (or magnetic poles) is directly proportional to the product of the magnitude of charges, Q (or magnetic pole strengths, M), and is inversely proportional to the square of distance (d) between them; that is,

Electric: $F = \dfrac{Q_1 Q_2}{4\pi\varepsilon d^2}$,

Magnetic: $F = \dfrac{M_1 M_2}{4\pi\mu d^2}$

The force between unlike charges, Q_1 and Q_2 (or poles, M_1 and M_2) is an *attraction*, and between like charges (or poles) is a *repulsion*.

Communication Principle (Also Called Universal Communication Principle)

A fundamental concept in life and livingness that is intertwined throughout the entire field of sciences that states for communication to take place between two or more entities, three elements must be present: a source point, a receipt point, and an imposed space or distance between the two.

Complex Power

Power calculated based on the reactance of a component.

Component

A packaged functional unit consisting of one or more circuits made up of devices, which in turn may be part of an operating system or subsystem.

Conductivity

The ratio of the current density (J) to the electric field (E) in a material. It represents the ability to conduct or transmit electricity.

Conductor

a) A material that conducts electricity with ease, such as metals, electrolytes, and ionized gases; b) An individual metal wire in a cable, insulated or un-insulated.

Curl Operation

Curl is an operation on a vector field, which creates another vector whose magnitude measures the maximum net circulation per unit area of the vector field at any given point and has a direction perpendicular to the area, as the area size tends toward zero. The cause of the curl of a vector field is a vortex source. For example electric current (conduction or displacement) is the vortex source for magnetic field.

Current

Net transfer of electrical charges across a surface per unit time, usually represented by (I) and measured in Ampere (A). Current density (J) is current per unit area.

D

DC (Also Called Direct Current)
A current which always flows in one direction (e.g., a current delivered by a battery).

Decibel (dB)
The logarithmic ratio of two powers or intensities or the logarithmic ratio of a power to a reference power, multiplied by 10. It is one-tenth of an international unit known as *Bel*: $N(dB)=10\log_{10}(P_2/P_1)$.

Device
A single discrete conventional electronic part such as a resistor, a transistor, etc.

Diamagnetics
are materials (such as glass, wood, lead, sulfur and others), which avoid magnetic lines of force.

Dichotomy
Two things or concepts that are sharply or distinguishably opposite to each other.

Die (Also Called Chip)
A single substrate on which all the active and passive elements of an electronic circuit have been fabricated. This is one portion taken from a wafer bearing many chips, but it is not ready for use until it is packaged and provided with terminals for connection to the outside world.

Dielectric
A material that is a non-conductor of electricity. It is characterized by a parameter called *dielectric constant* or *relative permittivity* (ε_r).

Dielectric Constant
The property of a dielectric defined as the ratio of the capacitance of a capacitor (filled with the given dielectric) to the capacitance filled with air as the dielectric, but otherwise identical in geometry.

Diffraction
Is the redistribution of intensity of waves in space, which results from the presence of an object (such as a grating, consisting of narrow slits or grooves) in the path of the beam of light waves. This shall split up the beam into many rays, causing interference and thus

producing patterns of dark and light bands downstream (i.e., regions with variations of wave amplitude and phase).

Digital

Circuitry in which data-carrying signals are restricted to either of two voltage levels.

Discovery

The gaining of knowledge about something previously unknown.

Discrete Device

An individual electrical component such as a resistor, capacitor, or transistor as opposed to an integrated circuit that consists of several discrete components.

Distributed Element

An element whose property is spread out over an electrically significant length or area of a circuit instead of being concentrated at one location or within a specific component.

Divergence

a) The emanation of many flows from a single point, or reversely, the convergence of many flows to one point; b) (of a vector field, F) The net outflux per unit volume at any given point in a vector field, as the volume size shrinks to zero (symbolized by divF). The cause of the divergence of a vector field is called a flow source. For example, positive electric charge is the flow source for the electric field and creates a net outflux of electric field per unit volume at any given point.

Dual

Two concepts, energy forms or physical things that are of comparable magnitudes but of opposite nature, thus becoming counterpart of each other.

Duality Theorem

States that when a theorem is true, it will remain true if each quantity and operation is replaced by its dual quantity and operation. In circuit theory, the dual quantities are "voltage and current" and "impedance and admittance." The dual operations are "series and parallel" and "meshes and nodes."

E

Electric Charge (or Charge)
(Microscopic) A basic property of elementary particles of matter (e.g., electron, protons, etc.) that is capable of creating a force field in its vicinity. This built-in force field is a result of stored electric energy. **(Macroscopic)** The charge of an object is the algebraic sum of the charges of its constituents (such as electrons, protons, etc.), and may be zero, a positive or a negative number.

Electric Current (or Current)
The net transfer of electric charges (Q) across a surface per unit time.

Electric Field
The region about a charged body capable of exerting force. The intensity of the electric field at any point is defined to be the force that would be exerted on a unit positive charge at that point.

Electric Field Intensity
The electric force on a stationary positive unit charge at a point in an electric field (also called *electric field strength*, *electric field vector*, and *electric vector*).

Electrical Noise (or Noise)
Any unwanted electrical disturbance or spurious signal. These unwanted signals are random in nature, and are generated either internally in the electronic components or externally through impinging electromagnetic radiation.

Electricity
Is a form of energy, which can be subdivided into two major categories: a) Electrostatics, and b) Electrokinetics.

Electrodynamics
Is a scientific field of study dealing with the various phenomena of electricity in motion, including the interactions between current-carrying wires as well as the forces on current wires in an independent magnetic field.

Electrokinetics
Is that broad and general field of study dealing with electric charges in motion. It studies moving electric charges (such as electrons) in

electric circuits and electrified particles (such as ions, etc.) in electric fields.

Electrolysis

The action whereby a current passing through a conductive solution (called an *electrolyte*) produces a chemical change in the solution and the electrodes.

Electrolyte

A substance that ionizes when dissolved in a solution. Electrolytes conduct electricity, and in batteries they are instrumental in producing electricity by chemical action.

Electrolytic Cell

In general, a cell containing an electrolyte and at least two electrodes. Examples include voltaic cells, electrolytic capacitors, and electrolytic resistors.

Electromagnetic (EM) Wave

A radiant energy flow produced by oscillation of an electric charge as the source of radiation. In free space and away from the source, EM rays of waves consist of vibrating electric and magnetic fields that move at the speed of light (in vacuum), and are at right angles to each other and to the direction of motion. EM waves propagate with no actual transport of matter, and grow weaker in amplitude as they travel farther in space. EM waves include radio, microwaves, infrared, visible/ultraviolet light waves, X-ray, gamma rays, and cosmic rays.

Electromagnetics

The branch of physics that deals with the theory and application of electromagnetism.

Electromagnetism

a) Magnetism resulting from kinetic electricity; b) Electromagnetics.

Electron

A stable elementary particle of matter, which carries a negative electric charge of one electronic unit equal to $q = -1.602 \times 10^{-19}$ C and has a mass of about 9.11×10^{-31} kg and a spin of ½.

Electronics

The study, control, and application of the conduction of electricity through different media (e.g., semiconductors, conductors, gases, vacuum, etc.).

Electroplating

Depositing one metal on the surface of another by electrolytic action.

Electrostatics

The branch of physics concerned with static charges and charged objects at rest.

Elementary Particle

A particle, which can not be described as a compound of other particles and is thus one of the fundamental constituents of all matter (e.g. electron, proton, etc.).

Energy

The capacity or ability of a body to perform work. Energy of a body is either potential motion (called *potential energy*) or due to its actual motion (called *kinetic energy*).

F

Fahrenheit (°F)

$1/180^{th}$ of the temperature difference between the freezing point of water ($32°F$) and the boiling point of water ($212°F$) on the Fahrenheit temperature scale.

$$T(°F) = T(°R) - 459.67 = \frac{9}{5} T(°C) + 32$$

Where °R and °C are symbols for degrees Rankin and Celsius, respectively.

Farad (F)

The unit of capacitance in the MKSA system of units equal to the capacitance of a capacitor that has a charge of one Coulomb when a potential difference of one volt is applied.

Faraday's Law (also called the law of electromagnetic induction)

When a magnetic field cuts a conductor, or when a conductor cuts a magnetic field, an electrical current will flow through the conductor if a closed path is provided over which the current can circulate; i.e.,

Differential form: $\mathrm{Curl}\overline{E} = \dfrac{-\partial \overline{B}}{\partial t}$,

Integral form: $\oint_C \overline{E} \cdot \overline{d\ell} = -\int_S \frac{\partial \overline{B}}{\partial t} \cdot \overline{dS} = -\frac{d\Phi}{dt}$

Ferrimagnetics

Ferrimagnetics are materials with the relative permeability (μ_r) much greater than that of vacuum having $\mu_r=1$. Ferrimagnetic materials are materials made of iron oxides (chemical formula: XFe_2O_3, where X is a metal ion), where their internal magnetic moments are not all aligned in one direction, that is to say some are aligned antiparallel, but with smaller magnitudes, so that the net magnetic field output is still much higher than a paramagnetic material. Examples of ferrimagnetics include materials such as manganese-zinc ferrite, barium ferrite, and a whole class of materials, having a high electrical resistance, called ferrites. Ferrimagnetic materials exhibit hysteresis, which is a type of material behavior characterized by an inability to retrace exactly the input-output curve when the magnetizing force is reversed. This nonlinear behavior is caused by the fact that the material will retain some of the magnetic effects internally (called the remnant magnetism) even when the external magnetizing force is completely removed.

Ferromagnetics

ferromagnetics are materials with the relative permeability (μ_r) much greater than that of vacuum ($\mu_r=1$), the amount depending on the magnetizing force. Ferromagnetic materials are a group of materials whose internal magnetic moments align in a common direction such as iron, nickel, cobalt, and their alloys. Ferromagnetic materials exhibit hysteresis, which is a type of material behavior characterized by an inability to retrace exactly the input-output curve when the magnetizing force is reversed. This nonlinear behavior is caused by the fact that the material will retain some of the magnetic effects internally (called the remnant magnetism) even when the external magnetizing force is completely removed.

Field

An entity that acts as an intermediary agent in interactions between particles, is distributed over a region of space, and whose properties are a function of space and time, in general.

Field Theory

The concept that, within a space in the vicinity of a particle, there exists a field containing energy and momentum, and that this field interacts with neighboring particles and their fields.

Flow

The passage of particles (e.g., electrons, etc.) between two points. Example: electrons moving from one terminal of a battery to the other terminal through a conductor. The direction of flows are from higher to lower potential energy levels.

Force

That form of energy that puts an unmoving object into motion, or alters the motion of a moving object (i.e., its speed, direction or both). Furthermore, it is the agency that accomplishes work.

Frequency

The number of complete cycles in one second of a repeating quantity, such as an alternating current, voltage, electromagnetic waves, etc.

G

Gain

The ratio that identifies the increase in signal or amplification that occurs when the signal passes through a circuit.

Gauss

The unit of magnetic induction (also called *magnetic flux density*) in the cgs system of units equal to one line per square centimeter, which is the magnetic flux density of one Maxwell per square centimeter, or 10^{-4} Tesla.

Gauss's Law (electric)

The summation of the normal component of the electrical displacement vector over any closed surface is equal to the electric charges within the surface, which means that the source of the electric flux lines is the electric charge; i.e.,

Differential form: $Div \overline{D} = \rho$

Integral form: $\oint_S \overline{D} \cdot \overline{dS} = \int_V \rho dv = Q$

Gauss's Law (magnetic)

The summation of the normal component of the magnetic flux density vector over any closed surface is equal to zero, which in essence means that the magnetic flux lines have no source or magnetic charge; i.e.,

Differential form: $\text{Div}\overline{B} = 0$,

Integral form: $\oint_s \overline{B} \cdot \overline{dS} = 0$

Generalized Application Mass (G.A.M.)

In general, is any created space, which contains created energies and created matter of any form, shape or size existing as a function of time. In simple terms, generalized application mass is any matter and energy, condensed and packaged into an object form, which exists in a time-stream (from its inception to now). The generalized concept of application mass includes the entire mechanical space containing all energies and matter such as electrons, atoms, molecules and all the existing gigantic masses of planets, stars, galaxies, which are not the direct byproduct of Man's sciences.

Generalized Ohm's Law

When dealing with linear circuits under the influence of time harmonic signals, Ohm's law can be restated under the steady-state condition in the phasor domain as V=ZI, where Z is a complex number called impedance and V and I are voltage and current phasors, respectively.

Gilbert (Gi)

The unit of magnetomotive force in the cgs system of units, equal to the magnetomotive force of a closed loop of one turn in which there is a current of $10/4\pi$ amperes. One Gilbert equals $10/4\pi$ Ampere-turn.

Gradient (of a scalar function)

Gradient (of a scalar function) is a vector, which lies in the direction of maximum rate of increase of the function at any given point and therefore is normal to the constant-value surfaces. Mathematically, it is a vector obtained from a real function f(x,y,z), whose components are the partial derivatives of f(x,y,z), e.g., in Cartesian coordinate system we can write: gradf=($\partial f/\partial x$, $\partial f/\partial y$, $\partial f/\partial z$).

Ground
(a) A metallic connection with the earth to establish zero potential (used for protection against short circuit); (b) The voltage reference point in a circuit. There may or may not be an actual connection to earth but it is understood that a point in the circuit said to be at ground potential could be connected to earth without disturbing the operation of the circuit in any way.

H

Henry (H)
The unit of self and mutual inductance in the MKSA system of units equal to the inductance of a closed loop that gives rise to a magnetic flux of one Weber for each ampere of current that flows through.

Hertz (Hz)
The unit of frequency equal to the number of cycles of a periodic function that occur in one second.

Hole
A vacant electron energy state near the top of the valence band in a semiconductor material. It behaves as a positively charged particle having a certain mass and mobility. It is the dual of electron, unlike a proton which is the dichotomy of an electron.

Hypothesis
An unproven theory or proposition tentatively accepted to explain certain facts or to provide a basis for further investigation.

I

Impedance
The total opposition that a circuit presents to an AC signal, and is a complex number equal to the ratio of the voltage phasor (V) to the current phasor (I).

Incident Wave
A wave that encounters a discontinuity in a medium, or encounters a medium having a different propagation characteristics.

Inductance (L)
The inertial property of an element (caused by an induced reverse voltage), which opposes the flow of current when a voltage is applied; it opposes a change in current that has been established.

Inductor
A conductor used to introduce inductance into an electric circuit, normally configured as a coil to maximize the inductance value.

Input
The current, voltage, power, or other driving force applied to a circuit or device.

Insulator
A material in which the outer electrons are tightly bound to the atom and are not free to move. Thus, there is negligible current through the material when a voltage is applied.

Integrated Circuit (IC)
An electrical network composed of two or more circuit elements on a single semiconductor substrate.

Isolation
Electrical separation between two points.

J

Joule (J)
The unit of energy or work in the MKSA system of units, which is equal to the work performed as the point of application of a force of one Newton moves the object through a distance of one meter in the direction of the force.

Junction
A joining of two different semiconductors or of semiconductor and metal.

Junction Capacitance
The capacitance associated with a junction such as the capacitance of a region of transition between p- and n-type semiconductor materials.

K

Kelvin (K)
The unit of measurement of temperature in the absolute scale (based on Celsius temperature scale), in which the absolute zero is at − 273.15 °C. It is precisely equal to a value of 1/273.15 of the absolute temperature of the triple point of water, being a particular pressure and temperature point, 273.15 K, at which three different phases of water (i.e., vapor, liquid, and ice) can coexist at equilibrium. *See also* **temperature**.

Kinetic
(*Adjective*) Pertaining to motion or change. (*Noun*) Something which is moving or changing constantly such as a piece of matter.

Kinetic Energy (K.E.)
The energy of a particle in motion. The motion of the particle is caused by a force on the particle.

Kirchhoff's Current Law (KCL)
The law of conservation of charge that states that the total current flowing to a given point in a circuit is equal to the total current flowing away from that point.

Kirchhoff's Voltage Law (KVL)
An electrical version of the law of conservation of energy that states that the algebraic sum of the voltage drops in any closed path in a circuit is equal to the algebraic sum of the electromotive forces in that path.

Knowledge
Is a body of facts, principles, data, and conclusions (aligned or unaligned) on a subject, accumulated through years of research and investigation, that provides answers and solutions in that subject.

L

Law
An exact formulation of the operating principle in nature observed to occur with unvarying uniformity under the same conditions.

Law of Conservation of Energy (Excluding All Metaphysical Sources of Energy)
This fundamental law simply states that any form of energy in the physical universe can neither be created nor destroyed, but only converted into another form of energy (also known as the principle of conservation of energy).

Leyden Jar
The first electric capacitor (or condenser) capable of storing charge; it consists of a glass jar with a coat of tin foil outside and inside and a metallic rod passing through the lid and connecting with the inner tin lining. It is named after the city of Leyden (also written as Leiden) in Holland, where it was invented.

Light Waves
Electromagnetic waves in the visible frequency range, which ranges from 400 nm to 770 nm in wavelength.

Linear Network
A network in which the parameters of resistance, inductance, and capacitance of the lumped elements are constant with respect to current or voltage, and in which the voltage or current sources are independent of or directly proportional to other voltages and currents or their derivatives, in the network.

Load
The impedance to which energy is being supplied.

Lossless
A theoretically perfect component that has no loss and hence, transmits all of the energy fed to it.

Lumped Element
A self-contained and localized element that offers one particular electrical property throughout the frequency range of interest.

M

Magnet
A piece of ferromagnetic or ferromagnetic material whose internal domains are sufficiently aligned so that it produces a considerable net magnetic field outside of itself and can experience a net torque when placed in an external magnetic field.

Magnetic Field

The space surrounding a magnetic pole, a current-carrying conductor, or a magnetized body that is permeated by magnetic energy and is capable of exerting a magnetic force. This space can be characterized by magnetic lines of force.

Magnetic Field Intensity (H)

The force that a magnetic field would exert on a unit magnetic pole placed at a point of interest, which expresses the free space strength of the magnetic field at that point (also called *magnetic field strength, magnetic intensity, magnetic field, magnetic force,* and *magnetizing force*).

Magnetostatics

The study of magnetic fields that are neither moving nor changing direction.

Man

Homo sapiens (literally, the knowing or intelligent man); mankind.

Mathematics

Mathematics are short-hand methods of stating, analyzing, or resolving real or abstract problems and expressing their solutions by symbolizing data, decisions, conclusions, and assumptions.

Matter

Matter particles are a condensation of energy particles into a very small volume.

Maxwell (Mx)

The unit for magnetic flux in the cgs system of units, equal to 10^{-8} Weber.

Maxwell's Equations

A series of four advanced classical equations developed by James Clerk Maxwell between 1864 and 1873, which describe the behavior of electromagnetic fields and waves in all practical situations. They relate the vector quantities for electric and magnetic fields as well as electric charges existing (at any point or in a volume), and set forth stringent requirements that the fields must satisfy. These celebrated equations are given as follows:

	Differential form	Integral form

1) Ampere's Law: $\mathrm{Curl}\overline{H} = \overline{J} + \dfrac{\partial \overline{D}}{\partial t}$, $\quad \oint_c \overline{H} \cdot \overline{d\ell} = I + \int_s \dfrac{\partial \overline{D}}{\partial t} \cdot \overline{dS}$

2) Faraday's Law: $\text{Curl}\overline{E} = \dfrac{-\partial \overline{B}}{\partial t}$, $\qquad \oint_C \overline{E} \cdot \overline{d\ell} = -\int_S \dfrac{\partial \overline{B}}{\partial t} \cdot \overline{dS} = -\dfrac{d\Phi}{dt}$

3) Gauss's Law (electric): $\text{Div}\overline{D} = \rho$, $\qquad \oint_S \overline{D} \cdot \overline{dS} = \int_V \rho dv = Q$

4) Gauss's Law (magnetic): $\text{Div}\overline{B} = 0$, $\qquad \oint_S \overline{B} \cdot \overline{dS} = 0$

From these equations, Maxwell predicted the existence of electromagnetic waves whose later discovery made radio possible. He showed that where a varying electric field exists, it is accompanied by a varying magnetic field induced at right angles, and vice versa, and the two form an electromagnetic field pair that could propagate as a transverse wave. He calculated that in a vacuum, the speed of the wave was given by $1/\sqrt{(\varepsilon_0 \mu_0)}$, where ε_0 and μ_0 are the permittivity and permeability of vacuum. The calculated value for this speed was in remarkable agreement with the measured speed of light, and Maxwell concluded that light is propagated as electromagnetic waves.

Mechanics
The totality of the three categories of application mass: a) Generalized application Mass; b) Technical application mass, and c) Personalized application mass. See also classical mechanics and quantum mechanics.

Microelectronics
The body of electronics that is associated with or applied to the realization of electronic systems from extremely small electronic parts.

Microstrip Line
A microwave transmission line that is composed of a single conductor supported above a ground plane by a dielectric.

Microwave Integrated Circuit (MIC)
A circuit that consists of an assembly of different circuit functions that are connected by Microstrip transmission lines. These different circuits all incorporate planar semiconductor devices, passive lumped elements, and distributed elements.

Microwaves
Waves in the frequency range of 1 GHz to 300 GHz.

Millimeter Wave

Electromagnetic radiation in the frequency range of 30 to 300 GHz, corresponding to wavelength ranging from 10 mm to 1 mm.

Model

A physical (e.g., a small working replica), abstract (e.g., a procedure) or a mathematical representation (e.g., a formula) of a process, a device, a circuit, or a system and is employed to facilitate their analysis.

Monolithic Integrated Circuit

An integrated circuit that is formed in a single block or wafer of semiconductor materials. The term is derived from Greek, "monolithos", which means "made of one stone."

Monolithic Circuits

Are integrated circuits entirely on a single chip of semiconductor.

Monolithic Microwave Integrated Circuit (MMIC)

A microwave circuit obtained through a multilevel process approach comprising of all active and passive circuit elements as well as interconnecting transmission lines, which are formed into the bulk or onto the surface of a semi-insulating semiconductor substrate by some deposition scheme such as epitaxy, ion implantation, sputtering, evaporation, diffusion, etc.

Monumental Discovery

Any of the six major un-ravelings or breakthroughs of knowledge about a significant phenomenon in the field of electricity, which shifted the subject in a substantial way and expanded all of the hitherto knowledge amply.

N

Natural Laws

A body of workable principles considered as derived solely from reason and study of nature.

Neper (Np)

A unit of attenuation used for expressing the ratio of two currents , voltages, or fields by taking the natural logarithm (logarithm to base e) of this ratio. If voltage V_1 is attenuated to V_2 so that $V_2/V_1 = e^{-N}$, then N is attenuation in Nepers (always a positive number) and is defined by: N (Np)=$\log_e(V_1/V_2)$=$\ln(V_1/V_2)$, where $V_1 > V_2$.

Neutron

One of uncharged stable elementary particles of an atom having the same mass as a proton. A free neutron decomposes into a proton, an electron, and a neutrino. A neutrino is a neutral uncharged particle but is an unstable particle since it has a mass that approaches zero very rapidly (a half-life of about 13 minutes).

Network

A collection of electric devices and elements (such as resistors, capacitors, etc.) connected together to form several interrelated circuits.

Newton (N)

The unit of force in MKSA system of units equal to the force that imparts an acceleration of one m/s^2 to a mass of one kilogram.

Noise

Random unwanted electrical signals that cause unwanted and false output signals in a circuit.

Nomenclature

The set of names used in a specific activity or branch of learning; terminology.

Nonlinear

Having an output that does not rise and fall in direct proportion to the input.

Nucleus

The core of an atom composed of protons and neutrons, having a positive charge equal to the charge of the number of protons that it contains. The nucleus contains most of the mass of the atom, pretty much like the sun containing most of the mass of the solar system.

O

Occam's (or Ockham's) Razor Doctrine

A principle that assumptions introduced to explain a thing must not be multiplied beyond necessity. In simple terms, it is a principle stating that the simplest explanation of a phenomenon, which relates all of the facts, is the most valid one. Thus by using the Occam's razor doctrine a complicated problem can be solved through the use of simple explanations, much like a razor cutting away all undue complexities (after William of Occam, an English philosopher, 1300-1349, who made a great effort to simplify scholasticism).

Oersted (Oe)
The unit of magnetic field in the cgs system of units equal to the field strength at the center of a plane circular coil of one turn and 1-cm radius when there is a current of $10/2\pi$ ampere in the coil.

Ohm (Ω)
The unit of resistance in the MKSA system of units equal to the resistance between two points on a conductor through which a current of one ampere flows as a result of a potential difference of one volt applied between the two points.

Ohm's Law
The potential difference V across the resistor terminals is directly proportional to the electrical current flowing through the resistor. The proportionality constant is called resistance (R); i.e., V=RI. Ohm's Law can also be interpreted as the conversion of potential energy (V) into kinetic energy (I), which is a simple statement expressing the principle of conservation of energy.

Original Postulates
A series of exact postulate (space, energy, change) that have gone into the construction of the physical universe. See primary postulates.

Oscillator
An electronic device that generates alternating-current power at a frequency determined by constants in its circuits.

Output
The current, voltage, power, or driving force delivered by a circuit or device.

P

Paramagnetics
are materials (such as aluminum, beryllium, etc.), which accept magnetism.

Particle
Any tiny piece of matter, so small as to be considered theoretically without magnitude (i.e., zero size), though having mass, inertia and the force of attraction. Knowing zero size is an absolute and thus impossible in the physical universe, practical particles range in diameter from a fraction of angstrom (as with electrons, atoms and molecules) to a few millimeters (as with large rain drops).

Passive
A component that may control but does not create or amplify electrical energy.

Perfect Conductor
Is a conductor having infinite conductivity or zero resistivity.

Personalized Application Mass (P.A.M.)
Is the category of application mass, which has been created and is based solely upon the viewpoint's own postulates and considerations. Examples of this category include such things as one's own customized possessions, any piece of artwork or music, one's own body characteristics (such as hairdo, clothing, shape, etc.), a book's layout or cover design, so on and so forth. see also **application mass, Technical application mass, and Generalized application mass.**

Phase
The angular relationship of a wave to some time reference or other wave.

Phase Constant
The imaginary component of the propagation constant for a traveling wave at a given frequency.

Phasor
A result of a mathematical transformation of a sinusoidal waveform (voltage, current, or EM wave) from the time domain into the complex number domain (or frequency domain) whereby the magnitude and phase angle information of the sinusoid is retained.

Physical Universe (Also Called Material Universe; The Universe)
Is a universe based upon three postulates, called original postulates (space, energy and change) and has four main components (matter, energy, space and time).

Plane Wave
A wave whose wave fronts are plane surfaces and normal to the direction of propagation.

Plating
See electroplating.

PN Junction
An abrupt transition between p-type and n-type semiconductor regions within a crystal lattice. Such a junction possesses specific electrical properties such as the ability to conduct in only one direction, and is used as the basis for semiconductor devices, such as diodes, transistors, etc.

Port
Access point to a system or circuit.

Postulate
a) (NOUN) is an assumption or assertion set forth and assumed to be true unconditionally and for all times without requiring proof; especially as a basis for reasoning or future scientific development;
b) (VERB) To put forth or assume a datum as true or exist without proof.

Potential Difference (or Voltage)
The electrical pressure or force between any two points caused by accumulation of charges at one point relative to another, which has the capability of creating a current between the two points.

Potential Energy (P.E.)
Any form of stored energy that has the capability of performing work when released. This energy is due to the position of particles relative to each other.

Power
The rate at which work is performed; i.e., the rate at which energy is being either generated or absorbed.

Primary Postulates
A series of four postulates derived from original postulates. These postulates are responsible for the four basic components of the physical universe: matter, energy, created space, and mechanical time. See original postulates.

Principle
A rule or law illustrating a natural phenomenon, operation of a machine, the working of a system, etc.

Processing
The act of converting material from one form into another more desired form, such as in integrated circuit fabrication where one starts with a wafer and through many steps ends up with a functional circuit on a chip.

Propagation
The travel of electromagnetic waves through a medium.

Propagation Constant
A number showing the effect (such as losses, wave velocity, etc.) a transmission line has on a wave as it propagates along the line. It is a complex term having a real term called the *attenuation factor* and an imaginary term called the *phase constant*.

Proton
An elementary particle, which is one of the three basic subatomic particles, with a positive charge equivalent to the charge of an electron (q= +1.602x10^{-19} C) and has a mass of about 1.67x10^{-27} kg with a spin of ½. Proton together with neutron is the building block of all atomic nuclei.

Pulse
A variation of a quantity, which is characterized by a rise to a certain level (amplitude), a finite duration, and a decay back to the normal level.

Pyramid of Knowledge
Workable knowledge forms a pyramid, where from a handful of common denominators efficiently expressed by a series of basic postulates, axioms and natural laws, which form the foundation of a science, an almost innumerable number of devices, circuits and systems can be thought up and developed. The plethora of the mass of devices, circuits and systems generated is known as the "application mass", which practically approaches infinity in sheer number.

Q

Quantum Mechanics (Also Called Quantum Physics or Quantum Theory)

Is the study of atomic structure which states that an atom or molecule does not radiate or absorb energy continuously. Rather, it does so in a *series of steps, each step being the emission or absorption of an amount of energy packet (E) called a quantum.* Quantum physics is the modern theory of matter, electromagnetic radiation and their interaction with each other. It differs from classical physics in that it generalizes and supersedes it, mainly in the realm of atomic and subatomic phenomena.

Quark

A hypothetical basic particle having a fraction of charge of an electron (such as 1/3 or 2/3) from which many of the elementary particles (such as electrons, protons, neutrons, mesons, etc.) may be built up theoretically. No experimental evidence for the actual existence of free quarks has been found.

R

Radio Frequency (RF)

Any wave in the frequency range of a few kHz to 300 MHz, at which coherent electromagnetic radiation of energy is possible.

Rankine (°R)

The unit of measurement of temperature in the absolute scale (based on Fahrenheit temperature scale), in which the absolute zero is at -459.67 °F. *See also* **temperature**.

Reactance

Is a parameter that is the measure of the opposition to the flow of alternating current (Symbolized by X).

Reactive Element

Is an element, which impedes the flow of current in a wire. An inductor or a capacitor are reactive elements. A purely reactive element does not dissipate energy as does a resistor, but stores it in the associated electric and/or magnetic fields.

Rectifier
Is a device having an asymmetrical conduction characteristic such that current can flow in only one direction through the device.

Reflected Waves
The waves reflected from a discontinuity back into the original medium, in which they are traveling.

Reflection Coefficient
The ratio of the reflected wave phasor to the incident wave phasor.

Resistance
A property of a resistive material that determines the amount of current flow when a voltage is applied across it. The resistor value is dependent upon geometrical dimensions, material, and temperature.

Resistor
A lumped bilateral and linear element that impedes the flow of current, i(t), through it when a potential difference, V (t), is imposed between its two terminals. The resistor's value is found by: R=V(t)/i(t).

Resonant Frequency
The frequency at which a given system or circuit will respond with maximum amplitude when driven by an external sinusoidal force.

Right-Hand Rule
For a current-carrying wire, the rule that if the fingers of the right hand are placed around the wire so that the thumb points in the direction of the current flow, the finger curling around the wire will be pointing in the direction of the magnetic field produced by the wire.

S

Science
A branch of study concerned with establishing, systematizing, and aligning laws, facts, principles, and methods that are derived from hypothesis, observation, study and experiments.

Semiconductor
A material having a resistance between that of conductors and insulators, and usually having a negative temperature coefficient of resistance.

Signal
An electrical quantity (such as a current or voltage) that can be used to convey information for communication, control, etc.

Silicon (Si)
A semiconductor material element in column IV of the periodic table used as in device fabrication.

Sinusoidal
Varying in proportion to the sine or cosine of an angle or time function. For example, the ordinary AC signal is a sinusoidal.

Small Signal
A low-amplitude signal that covers such a small part of the operating characteristic curve of a device that operation is nearly always linear.

Solid-State Device
Any element that can control current without moving parts, heated filaments, or vacuum gaps. All semiconductors are solid-state devices, although not all solid-state devices (such as transformers, ferrite circulators, etc.) are semiconductors.

Space (Also Called Created Space)
The continuous three-dimensional expanse extending in all directions, within which all things under consideration exist.

Standing Wave
A standing, apparent motionless-ness, of particles causing an apparent no out-flow, no in-flow. A standing wave is caused by two energy flows, impinging against one another, with comparable magnitudes to cause a suspension of energy particles in space, enduring with a duration longer than the duration of the flows themselves.

Standing Wave Ratio (SWR)
The ratio of current or voltage on a transmission line that results from two waves having the same frequency and traveling in opposite directions meeting and creating a standing wave.

Static
(**Adjective**) Pertaining to no-motion or no-change. (**Noun**) Something which is without motion or change such as truth (an abstract concept). In physics, one may consider a very distant star (a physical universe object) a static on a short term basis, but it is not totally correct because the distant star is moving over a long period

of time, thus is not truly a static but only an approximation, or a physical analogue of a true static.

Subjective Time
Is the consideration of time in one's mind, which can be a nonlinear or linear quantity depending on one's viewpoint.

Substrate
A single body of material on or in which one or more electronic circuit elements or integrated circuits are fabricated.

Superposition Theorem
This theorem states that in a linear network, the voltage or current in any element resulting from several sources acting together is the sum of the voltages or currents resulting from each source acting alone, while all other independent sources are set to zero; i.e.,
$$f(v_1+v_2+\ldots\ldots\ldots\ldots+v_n)=f(v_1)+f(v_2)+\ldots\ldots\ldots\ldots+f(v_n)$$

Supplemental Discovery
Any of the eight subordinate discoveries (along with their magnetic duals), which fill in the gaps left behind by the six monumental discoveries of electricity.

Switch
A mechanical or electrical device that completes or breaks the path of the current or sends it over a different path.

Switching
Is the making, breaking, or changing of connections in an electronic or electric circuit.

Symbiont
An organism living in a state of association and interdependence with another kind of organism, especially where such association is of mutual advantage, such as a pet. Such a state of mutual interdependence is called "symbiosis."

T

Technical Application Mass (T.A.M.)
Is the category of man-made application mass that is produced directly as a result of application of a science using its scientific postulates, axioms, laws and other technical data. Examples include such things as a television set, a computer, an automobile, a power

generator, a telephone system, a rocket, etc. See also **Application mass, Personalized application mass, and Generalized application mass.**

Technology
The application of a science for practical ends.

Temperature
The degree of hotness or coldness measured with respect to an arbitrary zero or an absolute zero, and expressed on a degree scale. Examples of arbitrary-zero degree scales are Celsius scale (°C) and Fahrenheit scale (°F); and examples of absolute-zero degree scales are Kelvin degree scale (based on Celsius degree scale) and Rankine degree scale (based on Fahrenheit degree scale).

Tesla (T)
The unit of magnetic field in the MKSA system of units equal to one Weber per square meter.

TEM (Transverse Electro-Magnetic) Wave
Waves having the electric and magnetic fields perpendicular to each other and to the direction of propagation. These waves have no field components in the direction of propagation.

Theorem
A proposition that is not self-evident but can be proven from accepted premises and therefore, is established as a principle.

Theory
An explanation based on observation and reasoning, which explains the operation and mechanics of a certain phenomenon. It is a generalization reached by inference from observed particulars and implies a larger body of tested evidence and thus a greater degree of probability. It uses a hypothesis as a basis or guide for its observation and further development.

Thermal Noise (Johnson Noise or Nyquist Noise)
The most basic type of noise that is caused by thermal vibration of bound charges and thermal agitation of electrons in a conductive material. This is common to all passive or active devices.

Time (Also Called Mechanical Time or Objective Time)
That characteristic of the physical universe at a given location that orders the sequence of events on a microscopic or macroscopic level. It proceeds from the interaction of matter and energy and is merely an "index of change," used to keep track of a particle's location. The fundamental unit of time measurement is supplied by

the earth's rotation on its axis while orbiting around the sun. It can also alternately be defined as the co-motion and co-action of moving particles relative to one another in space. See also subjective time.

Torque
A force that tends to produce rotation or twisting.

Transformer
An electrical device that, by electromagnetic induction, transforms electric energy from one (or more) circuit(s) to one (or more) other circuit(s) at the same frequency, but usually at a different voltage and current value.

Transmission Line (T.L.)
Any system of conductors suitable for conducting electric or electromagnetic energy efficiently between two or more terminals.

Transmitted wave
That portion of an incident wave that is not reflected at the interface, but actually travels from one medium to another.

Two-port network
A network that has only two access ports, one for input or excitation, and one for output or response.

U

Unidirectional
Flowing in only one direction (e.g., direct current).

Unilateral
Flowing or acting in one direction only causing a non-reciprocal characteristic.

Universal Communication Principle (Also Called Communication Principle)
A fundamental concept in life and livingness that is intertwined throughout the entire field of sciences that states for communication to take place between two or more entities, three elements must be present: a source point, a receipt point, and an imposed space or distance between the two.

Universe (Derived From Latin Meaning "Turned Into One", "A Whole)
Is the totality or the set of all things that exist in an area under consideration, at any one time. In simple terms, it is an area consisting of things (such as ideas, masses, symbols, etc.) that can be classified under one heading and be regarded as one whole thing.

Viewpoint
Is a point on a mental plane from which one creates (called postulating viewpoint) or observes (called observing viewpoint) an idea, an intended subject or a physical object.

Volt (V)
The unit of potential difference (or electromotive force) in the MKSA system of units equal to the potential difference between two points for which one Coulomb of charge will do one joule of work in going from one point to the other.

Voltage
Voltage or potential difference between two points is defined to be the amount of work done against an electric field in order to move a unit charge from one point to the other.

Voltage Source
The device or generator connected to the input of a network or circuit.

Voltage Standing Wave Ratio (VSWR)
The ratio of maximum voltage to the minimum voltage on a transmission. The standing wave on a line results from two voltage (or current) waves having the same frequency, and traveling in opposite directions.

Wafer
A thin semiconductor slice of silicon or germanium on which matrices of microcircuits or individual semiconductors can be

formed using manufacturing processes. After processing, the wafer is separated into chips (or *die*) containing individual circuits.

Watt (W)

The unit of power in MKSA system of units defined as the work of one joule done in one second.

Wave

A disturbance that propagates from one point in a medium to other points without giving the medium as a whole any permanent displacement.

Wave Propagation

The travel of waves (e.g., electromagnetic waves) through a medium.

Waveguide

A transmission line comprised of a hollow conducting tube within which electromagnetic waves are propagated.

Wavelength

The physical distance between two points having the same phase in two consecutive cycles of a periodic wave along a line in the direction of propagation.

Weber (Wb)

The unit of magnetic flux in the MKSA system of units equal to the magnetic flux, which linking a circuit of one turn, produces an electromotive force of one volt when the flux is reduced to zero at a uniform rate in one second.

Work

The advancement of the point of application of a force on a particle.

Index

Technical References

1. Anderson, R. W. *S-Parameter Techniques for Faster, More Accurate Network Design.* Hewlett-Packard Application Note 95–1, 1967.
2. Bahl, I. and P. Bhartia. *Microwave Solid State Circuit Design.* New York: Wiley Interscience, 1988.
3. Gonzalez, G. *Microwave Transistor Amplifiers, Analysis and Design,* 2nd ed. Upper Saddle River: Prentice Hall, 1997.
4. Carson, R. S. *High-Frequency Amplifiers.* New York: Wiley Interscience, 1975.
5. Chang, K. *Microwave Solid-State Circuits and Applications.* New York: John Wiley & Sons, 1994.
6. Froehner, W. H. Quick Amplifier Design with Scattering Parameters, *Electronics,* October 1967.
7. Gardiol, F *Microstrip Circuits,* New York: John Wiley & Sons, 1994.
8. Liao, S. Y. *Microwave Circuit Analysis and Amplifier Design.* Upper Saddle River: Prentice Hall, 1987.
9. Pozar, D. M. *Microwave Engineering,* 2nd ed. New York: John Wiley & Sons, 1998.
10. Radmanesh, M. M. *Advanced RF & Microwave Circuit Design,* AuthorHouse, 2009.
11. Radmanesh, M. M., and J. M. Cadwallader. Millimeter-Wave Noise Sources at V-Band (50 to 75 GHz), *Microwave Journal,* Vol. 36, No. 2, pp. 128–134, Sept. 1993.
12. Radmanesh, M. M. and J. M. Cadwallader. Solid State Noise Sources at mm-Waves: Theory and Experiment. *Microwave Journal,* Vol. 34, No. 10, pp. 125–133, Oct. 1991.
13. Radmanesh, M. M. *The Gateway to Understanding: Electrons to Waves and Beyond,* AuthorHouse, 2005.
14. Radmanesh, M. M. *Cracking the Code of Our Physical Universe,* AuthorHouse, 2006.
15. White, J., *High Frequency Techniques,* New York: John Wiley & Sons, 2004.

About the Author

Matthew M. Radmanesh received his BSEE degree from Pahlavi University in electrical engineering in 1978, his MSEE and Ph.D. degrees from the University of Michigan, Ann Arbor, in Microwave Electronics and Electro-Optics in 1980 and 1984, respectively.

He has worked in academia for Kettering University (formerly GMI Engineering & Management) and in industry for Hughes Aircraft Co., Maury Microwave Corp. and Boeing Aircraft Co. He is currently a faculty member in the electrical and computer engineering department at California State University, Northridge, CA.

Dr. Radmanesh is a senior member of IEEE, Eta Kappa Nu Honor society and a past president (three years) of the SFV Chapter of the IEEE Microwave Theory and Technique (MTT) society. His many years of experience in both microwave industry and academia have led to over 40 technical papers in national and international journals and several design handbooks in microwave engineering and in solid state devices and integrated circuit engineering.

His current research interests include design of RF and Microwave devices and circuits, millimeter-wave circuit applications, photonic engineering as well as engineering education. He received the distinguished lecturer award at the 1994 IEEE international Microwave Symposium and was awarded twice by IEEE LA council for his contributions to the MTT society (1994, 1995). He also received two awards for commitment and dedication to education from IEEE in 2002 and 2003.

Dr. Radmanesh won the MPD divisional award while at Hughes Aircraft Co. for his pioneering work in the development and design of solid state millimeter wave noise sources in Ka- and V-band, and a similar award for his outstanding contributions to the HERF project from Boeing Aircraft Co. He holds two patents for his pioneering work and novel designs of two millimeter-wave noise sources.

Dr. Radmanesh several authored popular books including *"Advanced RF & Microwave Circuit Design,"* in 2009, *"RF & Microwave Design Essentials,"* in 2007, *"The Ultimate Keys to Success in Business & Science,"* in 2008, *"Cracking the Code of Our Physical Universe,"* in 2006, and another *"The Gateway to Understanding: Electrons to Waves and Beyond,"* accompanied by a comprehensive WORKBOOK in 2005, all published by AuthorHouse; as well as another textbook entitled *"Radio Frequency and Microwave Electronics Illustrated"* published by Prentice Hall in 2001, with its Chinese edition (ISBN 7-5053-7628-4) published in 2002, and the Korean language translation (ISBN 89-7283-264-2) in 2005. His hobbies include chess, philosophy, soccer and tennis.

Dr. Radmanesh intends to bring about a higher level of understanding in the scientific community and the society at large, about the basic principles of life and livingness of which the knowledge about sciences and engineering is but a subset.

Other Books By The Author

Cracking The Code of Our Physical Universe Waves and Beyond, AuthorHouse, 2006.

The Gateway to Understanding: Electrons to Waves and Beyond, AuthorHouse, 2005.

The Gateway to Understanding: Electrons to Waves and Beyond WORKBOOK, Author House, 2005.

RF & Microwave Design Essentials AuthorHouse, 2007.

Advanced RF & Microwave Circuit Design, AuthorHouse, 2009.

The Ultimate Keys to Success in Business & Science, AuthorHouse, 2008.

For more information or to order any of the books, please visit:
www.KRCbooks.com

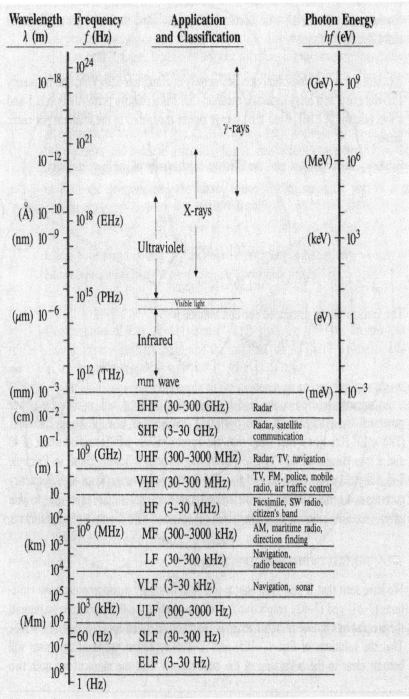

Spectrum of electromagnetic waves.

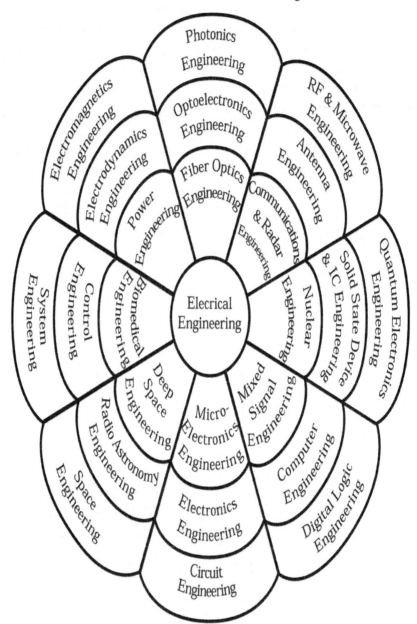

The field of electrical engineering and its many subdivisions.

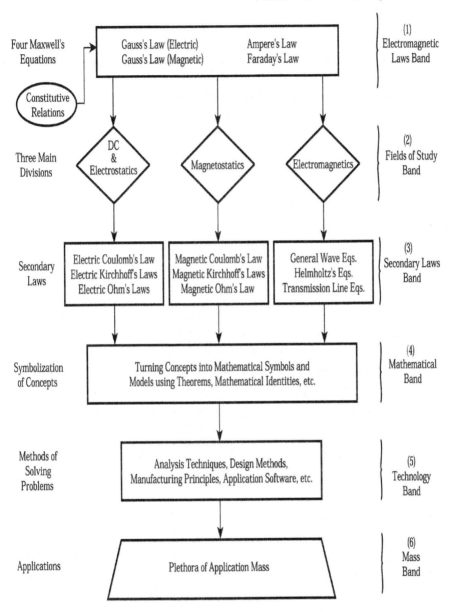

NOTE: Electromagnetics includes, Electrokinetics,
Elecrodynamics, and Electronic Waves.

A summary of the main laws and divisions of electricity.

Cartesian (or Rectangular) Coordinate System

1. The Del Operator, as a vector operator, is given by:
$$\nabla = (\partial/\partial x, \partial/\partial y, \partial/\partial z)$$

2. Divergence Operator (Dot Product):
$$\nabla \cdot E = (\partial/\partial x, \partial/\partial y, \partial/\partial z) \cdot (E_x, E_y, E_z)$$
$$= (\partial E_x/\partial x + \partial E_y/\partial y + \partial E_z/\partial z)$$

3. Gradient Operator:
$$\nabla V = (\partial/\partial x, \partial/\partial y, \partial/\partial z) V$$
$$= (\partial V/\partial x, \partial V/\partial y, \partial V/\partial z)$$

4. Curl Operator (A Conceptual Cross Product):
$$\nabla x E = (\partial E_z/\partial y - \partial E_y/\partial z, \ \partial E_x/\partial z - \partial E_z/\partial x, \ \partial E_y/\partial x - \partial E_x/\partial y)$$

5. The Laplacian Operator, as a scalar operator, is given by:
$$\nabla^2 V = \partial^2 V/\partial x^2 + \partial^2 V/\partial y^2 + \partial^2 V/\partial z^2$$

Useful Vector Identities

(Assume A, B, C, E and H are vector functions;
V, V_1, and V_2 are scalar functions)

$$\mathbf{A} . (\mathbf{B} x \mathbf{C}) = \mathbf{B} . (\mathbf{C} x \mathbf{A}) = \mathbf{C} . (\mathbf{A} x \mathbf{B})$$

$$\mathbf{A} \; x \; (\mathbf{B} x \mathbf{C}) = \mathbf{B}(\mathbf{A} . \mathbf{C}) - \mathbf{C}(\mathbf{A} . \mathbf{B})$$

$$\nabla . (V\mathbf{E}) = \mathbf{E} . \nabla V + V \nabla . \mathbf{E}$$

$$\nabla . (\mathbf{E} x \mathbf{H}) = \mathbf{H} . \nabla x \mathbf{E} - \mathbf{E} . \nabla x \mathbf{H}$$

$$\nabla (V_1 V_2) = V_1 \nabla V_2 + V_2 \nabla V_1$$

$$\nabla \; x \; (V\mathbf{E}) = \nabla V \; x \; \mathbf{E} + V \nabla x \mathbf{E}$$

$$\nabla . (\nabla x \mathbf{E}) = 0$$

$$\nabla \; x \; (\nabla V) = 0$$

$$\nabla \; x \; (\nabla x \mathbf{E}) = \nabla(\nabla . \mathbf{E}) - \nabla^2 \mathbf{E}$$

Derivation of the Wave Equation

In source-free ($\rho=0$), nonconducting ($\sigma=0$) media characterized by ε and μ, Maxwell's equations reduce to:

$$\nabla \times \overline{E} = -\mu \frac{\partial \overline{H}}{\partial t}$$

$$\nabla \times \overline{H} = \varepsilon \frac{\partial \overline{E}}{\partial t}$$

$$\nabla \cdot \overline{E} = 0$$

$$\nabla \cdot \overline{H} = 0$$

For sine waves and using phasors, $\overline{E}(t) = \overline{E}e^{j\omega t}, \overline{H}(t) = \overline{H}e^{j\omega t}$:

$$\nabla \times \overline{E} = -j\omega\mu \overline{H}$$

$$\nabla \times \overline{H} = j\omega\varepsilon \overline{E}$$

$$\nabla \cdot \overline{E} = 0$$

$$\nabla \cdot \overline{H} = 0$$

Taking the curl of the first two equations and noting that:

$$\nabla \times (\nabla \times \overline{E}) = \nabla(\nabla \cdot \overline{E}) - \nabla^2 \overline{E} = -\nabla^2 \overline{E}$$
$$\nabla \times (\nabla \times \overline{H}) = \nabla(\nabla \cdot \overline{H}) - \nabla^2 \overline{H} = -\nabla^2 \overline{H}$$

The wave equation for sine waves (Helmholtz's equation) for lossless media is obtained as:

$$\nabla^2 \overline{E} + k^2 \overline{E} = 0,$$
$$\nabla^2 \overline{H} + k^2 \overline{H} = 0$$

Where

$$k = \omega\sqrt{\mu\varepsilon} = \omega/v_P = 2\pi/\lambda,$$
$$V_P = 1/\sqrt{\mu\varepsilon} = c/\sqrt{\mu_r\varepsilon_r},$$
$$c = 1/\sqrt{\mu_o\varepsilon_o} = 3 \times 10^8 \text{ m/s}$$